TEXT, IMAGE, AND OTHERNESS
IN CHILDREN'S BIBLES

Society of Biblical Literature

Semeia Studies

Gerald O. West, General Editor

Number 56

TEXT, IMAGE, AND OTHERNESS IN CHILDREN'S BIBLES
What Is in the Picture?

TEXT, IMAGE, AND OTHERNESS
IN CHILDREN'S BIBLES

WHAT IS IN THE PICTURE?

Edited by

Caroline Vander Stichele

and

Hugh S. Pyper

Society of Biblical Literature
Atlanta

TEXT, IMAGE, AND OTHERNESS IN CHILDREN'S BIBLES
What Is in the Picture?

Copyright © 2012 by the Society of Biblical Literature

Library of Congress Cataloging-in-Publication Data

Text, image, and otherness in children's Bibles : what is in the picture? / edited by Caroline Vander Stichele and Hugh S. Pyper.
         p. cm. — (Society of Biblical Literature. Semeia studies ; no. 56)
    Includes bibliographical references and index.
    ISBN 978-1-58983-661-7 (paper binding : alk. paper) — ISBN 978-1-58983-662-4 (electronic format)
    1. Bible—Criticism, Narrative. 2. Strangers in the Bible. 3. Bible—Language, style. 4. Bible—Criticism, interpretation, etc. 5. Imagery (Psychology) in children. 6. Imagination—Religious aspects. I. Vander Stichele, Caroline. II. Pyper, Hugh S.
    BS521.7.T49 2012b
    220.9'505—dc23   2012006600

Printed on acid-free, recycled paper conforming to
ANSI/NISO Z39.48-1992 (R1997) and ISO 9706:1994
standards for paper permanence.

For Athalya Brenner

CONTENTS

Acknowledgements

First of all, we would like to thank Athalya Brenner, who got us started on this project in the summer of 2007 at the International SBL Meeting in Vienna, Austria. Athalya has been Caroline's colleague at the University of Amsterdam and a source of inspiration for many years. One of the courses Athalya developed at the Department of Religious Studies was entitled "Afterlives of the Bible." Not only did Caroline take over this course from her with pleasure, but three students taking this course did an excellent job serving as editorial assistants to this volume, namely, Azaria Boots, Joke Dekker, and Graziëlla de Guytenaere. Colleagues who have set up and contributed to the SBL Section on Children in Biblical World have also been invaluable as this book was being prepared, especially in hosting two sessions and serving as a forum for contributors to this volume at the 2009 Annual Meeting in Atlanta. We are particularly grateful for the assistance that we received from the SBL staff, especially Leigh Andersen, Bob Buller, and Kathie Klein, who did a wonderful job in guiding this volume through its final stages, and from Rosemarie Kossov for her work on the indices of this volume.

Hugh Pyper would like to thank colleagues, both staff and students, in the Department of Biblical Studies at Sheffield for allowing him the luxury of research leave at a particularly busy time in the department's life and for supporting him in exploring some unlikely byways of the Bible's afterlife. A particular debt is owed to conversations over many years with Professor Cheryl Exum. A debt of another kind is owed to his father, John Pyper, who died as this book was being prepared. His love and knowledge of the classics of English children's literature was shared generously with his sons and formed the foundation of all the subsequent reading and study that has fed into this volume.

Caroline Vander Stichele also wants to thank her family, friends, and colleagues for their moral support during the completion of this project. A special thanks goes to her housemates, Jan Jans and the cat community that shares their house, including Lilith and her sons, Achilles and Adonis, Kali, Isis, Oedipuss, and Krishna, who all grace her life with their presence, as well as Shiva, who sadly passed away as she was working on this book. Most of all, however, she wants to express gratitude and love to her parents, who introduced her to the Bible and its fascinating stories as a child.

Abbreviations

AB	Anchor Bible
ABD	*Anchor Bible Dictionary*. Edited by David Noel Freedman. 6 vols. New York: Doubleday, 1992.
ANTC	Abingdon New Testament Commentaries
ASBR	Amsterdam Studies in the Bible and Religion
BI	Biblical Interpretation Series
BibInt	*Biblical Interpretation*
BMW	The Bible in the Modern World
BT	*The Bible Translator*
CBET	Contributions to Biblical Exegesis and Theology
CBQ	*Catholic Biblical Quarterly*
CEV	Contemporary English Version
CurBS	*Currents in Research: Biblical Studies*
FCB	Feminist Companion to the Bible
FOTL	Forms of the Old Testament Literature
GCT	Gender, Culture, Theory
HBM	Hebrew Bible Monographs
HTR	*Harvard Theological Review*
IBC	Interpretation: A Bible Commentary for Teaching and Preaching
JANESCU	*Journal of the Ancient Near Eastern Society of Columbia University*
JB	Jerusalem Bible
JR	*Journal of Religion*
JSem	*Journal of Semitics*
JSNT	*Journal for the Study of the New Testament*
JSOT	*Journal for the Study of the Old Testament*
JSOTSup	Journal for the Study of the Old Testament Supplement Series
KJV	King James Version

LHBOTS	Library of Hebrew Bible/Old Testament Studies
NIB	*The New Interpreter's Bible.* Edited by Leander E. Keck et al. 12 vols. Nashville: Abingdon, 1994–2004.
NICNT	New International Commentary on the New Testament
NIV	New International Version
NJB	New Jerusalem Bible
NJV	New Jewish Version
NRSV	New Revised Standard Version
NLT	New Living Translation
NTS	*New Testament Studies*
OTL	Old Testament Library
PSB	*Princeton Seminary Bulletin*
RSV	Revised Standard Version
SBLEJL	Society of Biblical Literature Early Judaism and Its Literature
SemeiaSt	Semeia Studies
SJT	*Scottish Journal of Theology*
SSN	Studia Semitica Neerlandica
VT	*Vetus Testamentum*
WBC	Word Biblical Commentary
ZNW	*Zeitschrift für neutestamentliche Wissenschaft und die Kunde der älteren Kirche*

Introduction

Caroline Vander Stichele and Hugh S. Pyper

Children's Bibles are not only widely distributed; they are also often the first contact people have with the Bible, and as such they can shape their perception of its stories and characters at an early age. The pictures in such Bibles also play an important role in how certain characters and events are remembered later in life. Think, for instance, of Adam and Eve or Noah's ark, but also more disturbing events such as the Akedah. Such images not only illustrate the events narrated in the biblical text, sometimes they even have a story of their own to tell. The balance between text and image is not always the same either, but can shift in one or other direction, sometimes giving precedence to the text, sometimes to the image. The relationship and even tension between text and image is the main topic of this book, and it is discussed from different angles in the essays. The material under discussion not only includes children's Bibles in the more traditional sense, but also more recent phenomena such as manga Bibles and animated films for children.

This volume connects with research on the history of children's Bibles, such as Ruth Bottigheimer's *The Bible for Children* (1996), but in many respects offers new perspectives, which are intentionally diverse in both method and scope. The connection between the contributions is their shared focus on the representation of others in predominantly Hebrew Bible stories. As a whole this volume intends to give concrete examples of approaches to particular stories rather than making any claim to comprehensiveness as such. It also engages an array of different approaches and theoretical lenses through which to view the relationship between text and image in children's Bibles. This volume focuses on the interaction between text and image in Bibles for children up to age twelve. The theme discussed in the contributions to this volume is the way various others are represented in illustrations to Bible stories as retold or repackaged for this age group of readers. The others in question may be women, foreigners, enemies, children, disabled people, poor people, "bad" people. This topic is dealt with from a variety of angles and/or ideology-critical approaches, including gender studies and postcolonial studies. Questions discussed in the contributions to this volume are: What stories are included and illustrated in children's Bibles? What interpretative choices are made in the process? How are characters represented in both text and image? What childhood reading is assumed in the text? What ideological implications are there in these choices and assumptions?

Although some work has already been done on the relationship between biblical texts and images in art, popular culture, and film from a more ideology-critical perspective, no such effort has as yet been made in the case of children's Bibles. As a whole this area is still a relatively unexplored and even neglected field of research within biblical studies that definitely needs more attention. The suggestion to put together a volume of Semeia Studies on this important topic came from Athalya Brenner. This book is also dedicated to her. It is a token of our appreciation for the many efforts she has made to push and transgress established boundaries in the academy, especially in the field of biblical studies. She has often been at the forefront of innovative approaches, including feminist and gendered, contextual and autobiographical readings of the Bible, as is made clear by both her own writings and her editorial work.

To dedicate a volume of Semeia Studies to Athalya is all the more appropriate because she herself served on the editorial board of its predecessor *Semeia* and in that capacity coedited volume 86 (*Food and Drink in the Biblical World*; 2001) and served as editorial board editor of volume 87 (*The Social World of the Hebrew Bible: Twenty-Five Years of Social Sciences in the Academy*; 2001).

Brenner's interest in children's Bibles is not only long-standing; it also serves a political agenda. At the end of her article on Bible films for children, she recommends exposing children to a multiplicity of images rather than showing them the same material again and again. Not only are children very well able to deal with such representational diversity, but we should also "aspire to the appreciation of such diversity if we wish for the Bible to remain alive and kicking; and if we wish for future adults to read it for cultural heritage and pleasure, beyond religious doctrine or scholarly nitpicking" (Brenner: 33). Beyond this more practical concern, Brenner also strongly advocated the recognition of children's Bibles as a serious topic of scholarly investigation by submitting research projects to the Netherlands Organisation for Scientific Research (NWO) about Bibles for children. That these projects were not funded may signal that in this respect there is still a long way to go.

With the present volume we hope to put this issue on the scholarly map. We also hope this book will have wide appeal, from scholars with specific research interests in the area of children's Bibles and/or illustrated Bibles to those situated more generally within biblical studies, to seminary and doctoral students as well as pastors or religious professionals working with children. This volume also aims at fostering a dialogue for exploring points of contact among diverse approaches to the material in question. We hope that it will also be a significant volume for those interested in exploring similar issues in other illustrated Bibles and that more scholars will be encouraged to take children's Bibles seriously as objects of scholarly research.

The contents of this volume could be arranged in many ways, but three basic questions recur in the contributions: How is the child reader taught to identify the other? What models are offered of ways to engage with the other? And how is the issue of the other as potential enemy dealt with? In a time when children are being actively taught to be aware of "stranger danger," these issues are particularly fraught ones. When that wariness of the stranger meets biblical stories set in an Eastern Mediterranean context, the problems are compounded. How these stories relate to the people and places that appear daily on the news and in adult conversation becomes a complicating issue. How do the Israelites and Philistines of the children's Bibles map onto the Israelis and Palestinians of the present day? Stereotypes are unavoidable as children are taught to make distinctions between "us" and "them" and the "good" and the "bad." How conscious are the illustrators of children's Bibles of the stereotypes they are adopting, and do they reinforce or critique them? How far are they reproducing and therefore implicitly endorsing stereotypes that belong to the ideological framework of the biblical writers, and how far are they drawing on identifiable stereotypes from the modern world and introducing them anachronistically into the biblical stories? Is there a mutual reinforcement between ancient and modern views of the other or does one offer a critique of the other? It might well be objected that young children cannot be expected to deal with subtleties and need a clear black and white view of the world. This may be the case, but attitudes acquired in childhood may persist unquestioned in later years, especially if they are vested with some kind of biblical authority.

A clear instance of this stereotyping, moreover, is in the role of children themselves in the Bible and in its retellings. Children are categorically distinct from adults in modern cultures, but can that distinction be carried back into the ancient world? The Bible does contain references to children, but, along with women and servants, they are often invisible in stories where their presence can be inferred. How is the modern child reader to find him- or herself in the biblical text? How do biblical illustrators help the child both to identify with the story and to retain a critical and historical distance?

In the first section, "Identifying the Strange Other," the issues of identification are dealt with in a number of contexts. Laurel Koepf looks at the example of the unnamed servant girl in the story of Naaman in 2 Kings in order to question the assumptions that lead most commentators and children's Bible readers to overlook her existence and her point of view. Jaqueline du Toit examines retellings of the biblical stories of creation by exponents of creationism. She makes the point that this can be done only by taking a highly selective attitude to the biblical canon. The claim that this reading is *the* biblical account is thus contradictory. In setting itself against the wider society that is described as the unbiblical other, paradoxically this stance has to exclude aspects of the Bible itself. The story of Daniel in the lion's den is the subject of Hugh Pyper's contribution, which explores the way in which orientalizing stereotypes are used to signal the villains and heroes of the story in order to reinforce a moralistic reading of the story. On the other hand, illustrators, sometimes against the grain of a moralizing reading of the text, know that the lion, and the fascination with escaping what could devour one, is what children find in the story. The way in which children are subtly schooled in the politics of communal identity is demonstrated by Jeremy Punt in his survey of Afrikaans children's Bibles and the changing use of black characters in their illustrations. Issues of gender rather than race are Susanne Scholz's concern as she examines biblical films and DVDs directed at children and questions the absence of engagement with feminist scholarship in the depiction of biblical women. All of these contributions reveal how writers and illustrators of children's Bibles consciously and unconsciously draw on and reinforce the identity politics of the social groups within which they work, lending them the authority of the Bible.

The contributions in the second section, "Learning How to Deal with the Other," go further in looking at how some awkward aspects of the biblical texts have been dealt with by the illustrators of the children's Bibles.

Cynthia Rogers and Diana Nolan Fewell look at the story of David and Jonathan and how children's Bibles deal with the sexual undertones some contemporary critics find in their relationship. They argue that the story can be used with children of different ages to explore the complexity of friendship and the scope of relationships between people of the same sex, but only if the richness of the character of Jonathan is given full scope. A similar problem is identified in Melody Briggs's study of the way in which the rebellious boy Jesus in Luke's Gospel is reduced to the model obedient Western child in too many retellings for children, instead of being presented in all his complexity for children to encounter imaginatively. Such assimilation of biblical narratives and characters to the pedagogical interests of the culture that produces children's versions of the text is also starkly present in Archie Lee's study of the *Taiping Trimetrical Classic*, an astonishing reworking of biblical stories in a Chinese context that is programmatically designed to indoctrinate the children of the followers of Hong Xiuquan into becoming faithful members of his Heavenly Kingdom movement. In Mark Roncace's study of the way in which the multiple creation accounts and the divergent stories of Jesus's birth are harmonized and simplified in children's Bibles, we see a less striking but equally potent way in which the Bible is made to support one story, rather than allowing children to have a sense of the continuing conversations over creation and the nature of Jesus that the Bible contains. In all these cases, the Bible is rewritten to reinforce conscious and unconscious assumptions that are then given the legitimacy of being "biblical." Other accounts and other characters are more or less quietly written out of the text, giving a deceptive familiarity and acceptability to difficult and disruptive narratives.

In the third section, "Destroying the Other," rather than this quiet erasure of otherness, the explicit violence to which the other is subjected in many biblical stories is brought to the fore. Should children be sheltered from this violence, at the risk of distorting the biblical text, or should they be exposed to it, at the risk either of making such violence acceptable or of traumatizing the child reader? Emma England looks at the way in which illustrators have glossed over this issue in the flood story, either by ignoring the violence or making it lighthearted, with some interesting and harrowing exceptions. Again, she argues not for a particular reading of the text but that adult readers should be prepared to answer and raise questions with the child rather than simply endorsing the "acceptable" version of the story. Another incident of mass violence that may implicitly involve the death of many children and explicitly involves one child character is Samson's destruction of the Philistine temple in the book of Judges. David Gunn traces the history of interpretations of this story and the way in which commentators and illustrators seek to defend Samson's actions while shying away from the full endorsement of the biblical implication that all Philistines, women and children included, deserve to die. The shifting ideas of what are acceptable theological and moral justifications for Samson's actions provide another reminder that the moral code of the readers is being imposed on the text while at the same time the rhetoric is that this moral code is biblically grounded. One counter to this is the *Brick Testament*, which uses a children's toy (Lego) to produce comic but graphic illustrations of the sex and violence of biblical stories. It forms an important part of Rubén Dupertuis's reflection on the understandable but misleading bowdlerization in the illustrations to most children's Bibles. Finally, Caroline Vander Stichele explains the treatment of Delilah in a number of animated films designed for children. She examines how cultural assumptions about the foreign woman both in the biblical text itself and in the response of the filmmakers are prevalent, but makes the point that later more culturally conscious adaptations that play down Delilah's exoticism may actually emphasize the role of her gender in her moral failure.

A common theme in these contributions is the risk that, in adapting the Bible for children, moral and cultural assumptions become the driver at the expense of the complexity and diversity that characterize the biblical canon. The biblical narratives are themselves narrowed in focus and reduced to a simple moral message, often one that is not borne out by the biblical text itself. The simple messages depend on stereotypes and reinforce the stereotypes they endorse. In order to instill in children what is claimed to be a biblical set of categories to distinguish us and them, good and bad, the biblical text and the range of its possible readings is also separated into what is suitable or unsuitable for children on the basis of a culturally determined sense of what children can cope with. All the authors of these essays point to this. The implications they would draw from this are not so uniform. How far children should or can be exposed to the Bible and how far they should be taught to accept or reject the ideology of any biblical text remains controversial, but all can agree that it is helpful to be as honest as we can about what is actually going on as we attempt to present these complex texts to children.

Works Cited

Bottigheimer, Ruth. 1996. *The Bible for Children: From the Age of Gutenberg to the Present*. New Haven: Yale University Press.

Brenner, Athalya. 2006. "Recreating the Biblical Creation for Western Children: Provisional Reflections on Some Case Studies." Pages 11–34 in *Creation and Creativity: From Genesis to Genetics and Back*. Edited by Caroline Vander Stichele and Alastair G. Hunter. BMW 9/ASBR 1. Sheffield: Sheffield Phoenix.

PART 1
IDENTIFYING THE STRANGE OTHER

INSIDE OUT: THE OTHERED CHILD
IN THE BIBLE FOR CHILDREN

Laurel Koepf

Biblical scholarship has increasingly brought attention to the roles and presentations of various others in biblical narratives. Scholars have rightly problematized the assumed normativity of the Israelite male within the text. More recently, some have begun to look more closely at children in the text, thus bringing the assumed normativity of the adult into question as well (Berquist 2009, Bunge 2008, Fewell 2003, Parker 2009). Although such a critique has great potential effect on the way contemporary readers interpret and write about the Bible, it does not change the primary text as we have received it. We may retranslate and reinterpret the Bible through any number of lenses but the source text itself remains standard.

Bibles for children, however, stand in contrast to biblical translation's history of resolute reliance on the original text. Authors and illustrators reedit, retell, reinterpret, and reimagine the Bible with each new publication of a Bible for children. In doing so, they make choices about how and whether to portray characters and groups, including the many others present in or notably absent from the Bible in story and in image. Some authors, for example, now make a point of including narratives that focus on female characters. Increasingly, illustrated Bibles for children include images of primary characters with a variety of facial features, skin tones, and hair textures, giving attention to multiple ancient ethnicities and moving people of color out of the background. The authors of today's Bibles for children have the opportunity to respond to the problems within the primary text that ideologically conscious biblical scholars have critiqued. Authors of children's Bibles can consciously affirm, reject, or ignore a variety of others. A close reading of the texts and illustrations in Bibles for children reveals the decisions that the adult creators of these texts have made as to how to present multiple others, significantly including children themselves. As children, they are other to the author and to the assumedly normative adult male Israelite. They are small in size and do not have power within official political and familial structures. They are therefore vulnerable and often ignored. Thorough analysis of the inclusion and presentation of the othered child in the biblical text is therefore vital to the full examination of the other in the Bible, especially Bibles for children.

To that end, I will begin by examining childhood in the ancient world as contrasted with modern Western childhood and the common accompanying adult assumptions about children and childhood. Having done so, I will explore the ethical and practical complexities and repercussions of the adult creation of Bibles for children in light of these constructions of childhood. Finally, I will examine 2 Kgs 5:1–15 as a sample text and compare its retelling in three popular illustrated Bible story collections marketed for a child audience. This analysis will pay particular attention to the child as potential other, both inside the text as a character and outside the text as a reader receiving messages about his or her self as communicated by a powerful cultural text.

Biblical Children

When considering biblical children, it is necessary to look beyond anachronistic assumptions around children and childhood so as to examine the boundaries that would have defined childhood as a social category in ancient Israel. The archeological record is one source that can provide clues to how a culture defined differences in maturity and life stage. Rituals around the end of life are especially revealing. Hence, mortuary evidence at archeological sites proves to be particularly useful in discerning how ancient Israelites delineated infancy, childhood, and adulthood.

David Ilan's work on Middle Bronze Age burials at Tel Dan points to three primary burial types (and one exception) corresponding with these three life stages. He describes this typology in ascending age order: "Four basic burial types have been recognized in the Middle Bronze Age layers at Tel Dan, (1) jar burials, (2) built cist tombs, (3) built chamber tombs and (4) a single shaft burial" (1995, 120–22). The jar burials at Tel Dan contain solitary remains of persons up to age two or three inside a buried jar with assorted burial goods. Built cist tombs hold the remains of persons from age two to age twelve or thirteen, usually buried singly with their burial goods. Multiple persons over the age of twelve or thirteen are interred with their burial goods in the built chamber tombs and the single shaft burial.

Although not found at all sites in the Levant, this approximate age delineation at burial is significant in that it matches the approximate ages of significant rites of passage attested in the Bible as well as in ethnographic evidence; weaning often took place at age two or three (Gruber 1989, 66),[1] and human bodies usually begin to reach reproductive maturity at twelve or thirteen. Since these are both biological processes, they cannot be counted upon to take place on schedule, thus accounting for the slight age variation in the transitional points to be found in the archeological record. The points at which burial practices shift at Tel Dan coincide with life-stage transitions rather than strict age transitions. This evidence suggests that childhood was understood to last from weaning to the onset of reproductive maturity, approximately from age two or three to twelve or thirteen, in ancient Israel and its environs. Therefore, this will be my working definition of childhood in ancient Israel as depicted in the Hebrew Bible.

Unlike Western children today, children in ancient Israel spent a great deal of their time working. Carol Meyers concludes: "By and large, children in the ancient Near East worked once from a very young age" (1997, 27). Beyond what we would call chores or even apprenticeship, these children would have performed tasks that were essential to the survival of their families. Just as ethnographic studies have identified traditionally gendered tasks in subsistence agricultural cultures, similar studies paying greater attention to children have also discovered traditionally "aged" tasks that are no less important to the family than "men's" or "women's" work (Nag et al. 1978). Labor and its accompanying agency would have been a large part of children's lives in the biblical world. As David Rudd observes: "In societies where children work alongside adults, they are often seen in more egalitarian terms. In contrast, the more 'useless' children become, as in America towards the end of the nineteenth century, the more emotionally priceless seems their value" (1999, 18). The differences between adult beliefs about children and childhood in the ancient world and today are highly significant for interpretation.

---

1. Weaning at this time is also attested in 2 Macc 7:27, in which a mother says to her son: "I carried you nine months in my womb, and I nursed you for three years."

In the modern Western world, child labor is forbidden, keeping children decidedly separate from adults in the cultural imagination as well as in the lived reality. Although often assumed to be normative, this kind of division between childhood and adult life is both culturally specific and relatively recent, having developed in response to Victorian constructions of childhood. Philippe Ariès's assumption that Victorian notions of childhood innocence and separateness were the sole definition of childhood led him to conclude that little or no conception of childhood existed prior to that period. This assumption has now been broadly discounted (Hendrick 1992, 1). Yet constructions of childhood similar to these Victorian ideals have led modern Western culture to create institutions that cause children and adults to live separately during working hours and have hence led adults to associate children with leisure, seeing them as completely isolated from the adult world of labor and economic concerns. This separation makes children all the more other to the adult authors and illustrators of Bibles for children today than to the biblical writers of the ancient world.

BIBLES FOR CHILDREN?

The very creation of a Bible for children is ethically complex. "Children's literature" as a genre is also a relatively recent construction. Scholars of children's literature have problematized the genre's delineation, distinguished by the audience for whom it is created (by another category of persons), rather than its by content and purpose (Jones 2006; Rose 1984; Rudd 1999). Bibles for children are similarly defined and therefore face similar problems as children's literature in general. Problematically, titling a Bible "for children" implicitly states that the Bible is not for children without the editing, retelling, and illustrating that adults perform to render it appropriate for children's use. Yet the implicit communication that the Bible was created for a solely adult audience assumes anachronistically an age-segregated societal and literary genre division. Therefore, whatever the adult creators' intentions, the act of publishing a Bible for children excludes children from a central cultural text and from participating more fully in its interpretation.

Admittedly, real barriers exist to children's Bible reading. The original text of the Hebrew Bible is written in Hebrew and Aramaic, which very few nonnative speakers of any age read fluently. Most people require a vernacular translation, and all translation is a form of interpretation. In this way, both children and adults who do not read Hebrew fluently face similar barriers to interpretation. Yet children's reading levels should be taken into account as well. A Bible translation that is far beyond one's reading level is othering to the reader in its own way. The more literal vernacular translations in English read at approximately a seventh-grade level as measured by the Fry readability formula (Fry 1977), render them inaccessible to many children. Alternatively, the CEV was purposely translated with "limited and non-technical vocabulary that nine year olds can easily read and that five year olds can understand" (Hodgson 1992, 118), but a great deal more interpretation went into this "functional equivalence" translation than goes into those that stay closer to the Hebrew.

Still, most Bibles for children are not translations that have been attentive to children's reading level, but are rather paraphrases or story collections with illustrations. The versions of the text that children receive have been interpreted for them in both word and image[2] because their adult authors and illustrators assume that the Bible translations adults read are too long, difficult, and dull for children. This assumption constructs the child as inferior other, incapable of understanding and interpreting the text. As Lissa Paul notes: "The ideological assumption is that primitives and children are too naïve (or stupid) to look after themselves, so need protecting" (2005, 124). Such "protection" is often enacted in the creation of Bibles for children. The authors, editors, and illustrators of Bibles for children protect their intended audience from the struggle that results from morally complex and seemingly contradictory texts and topics.

However the protection of the implied child reader breaks down because the raceless, genderless, protectable implied child reader is indeed fictional (Jones 2006, 294). Real children are individuals who live in a variety of contexts. They experience difficult and unavoidable struggles that are emotionally threatening to the adults who cannot protect them. When the adult creators of Bibles for children remove difficulties from the text, they protect their own alleged omnipotence and underestimate children's ability to process complexity, denying children a potential mirror of their most trying experiences and emotions.

---

2. Alternatively, children's participation in the illustration of Madeleine L'Engle's *Ladder of Angels: Scenes from the Bible Illustrated by Children of the World* (1979) evidences a divergent interpretation of "children's Bible." Although it was not explicitly designated or marketed for children, children were agents in its creation. Their artwork offers visual interpretations of the texts that L'Engle retells on facing pages.

The practice of creating Bibles for children that underestimate children's abilities teaches children to underestimate themselves. In noting the parallels between adult perceptions of childhood and Western orientalist perceptions of the Orient, Perry Nodelman observes that such perceptions are self-fulfilling:

> If we assume children have short attention spans and therefore never let them try to read long books, they do not in fact read long books. They will seem to us to be incapable of reading long books and we will see those that do manage to transcend our influence and read long books as atypical, paradoxically freaks in being more like us than our other. It may well be for this reason that a depressingly large number of children do seem to fit into Piagetian categorizations of childlike behavior, and that an equally large number of children do seem to like the kinds of books that adult experts claim to be the kind of books children like. (1992, 32)

It follows that if adults assume that the Bible is too long, difficult, and dull for children and communicate this to them by paraphrasing a few bland Bible stories for children, children will not read the Bible. Rather, they will believe that it is too long, difficult, and dull and that reading it is beyond their capability and interest.

The belief that the Bible is difficult and boring often carries into adulthood. In cultures and traditions in which the use of Bibles for children is prominent, a common result is that that many adults' biblical literacy is based primarily if not solely in their initial impressions from children's Bibles (Buzzetti 2000, 410). In this way, the contents and perspectives to be found in Bibles for children inform how children and adults alike perceive the Bible and its message. Authorial decisions to leave out graphic and unpleasant details or to present each narrative as a clear-cut moral lesson so as to protect children play a vital role in creating and affirming widespread assumptions that the Bible is a moral, straightforward, and didactic text. In this way, authorial protection of children has major repercussions for the contemporary development and perception of Judaism and Christianity, as well as for secular (yet highly religiously influenced) Western culture.

Oversimplified constructions of the Bible and its contents such as those found in many Bibles for children have suggested that there can be a single moral to each story and hence a singular biblical perspective on a multitude of topics. Yet the collected texts of the Hebrew Bible offer a much more nuanced point of view. Such nuance does not lend itself well to the moral didacticism with which simplified Bible story collections teach children and adults to approach the text. Rather, the imperfect protagonists in biblical narratives live difficult lives, and the Bible's more instructive genres take complex situational distinctions into account. Both defy the search for happy endings, easy answers, and straightforward values that pervades much of Western religious and secular culture.

Both the Bible and children are othered by way of idealization in modern Western culture. Each is constructed as innocent, kept at a distance by removing its full complexity. In both cases, this assumption is far from true. Anyone who has observed a child's interaction with his or her siblings can attest that her or his personality is more layered than constructions of childhood innocence would suggest. The idealization of children and their lives in children's literature expresses nostalgia for childhood, not the reality of childhood itself (Nodelman 2008, 220). This nostalgic idealization of a mythic childhood is particularly prominent in Bibles for children, in which the assumedly innocent child is protected from morally complex passages in the Bible and the assumed moral and structural simplicity of the Bible is protected from children's capacity to perceive its true complexity.

Like children, the Bible is far more multifaceted than assumptions of innocence would suggest. It includes many narratives that are neither pleasant nor moralistic, some of which are ignored because of their graphic nature while others have been tamed by overuse. The story of the Levite's concubine, gang-raped and then cut into twelve pieces and sent to the tribes of Israel in Judg 19, is rarely included in sermons, not to mention Bibles for children. Images of Noah and his ark, however, can be found in children's books, toys, and textiles to name just a few. As noted by Danna Nolan Fewell (2003, 29–30), this proliferation of cleaned-up biblical imagery in contemporary children's material culture ignores the way that these images are reflections of the story of a divinely decreed mass drowning of all the people and animals in the world excepting two of each animal species and eight humans, all adult. Every child in the flood narrative dies, but most people do not notice this. The flood's victims, like the Levite's concubine, frequently go unmentioned or unimaged in modern Bibles for children,[3] leading those adults who grew up reading censored Bibles to

---

3. For an excellent and more detailed analysis of the multiple ways in which

ignore these victims as well and thus preserving the adult belief in idealized otherness of both the child and the Bible.

Both censorship and sentimentalization are common in the translation of literature for children. Scholars examining the translation of children's books have observed far greater liberties in translation for children than in that for adults. Whereas translation theory for adults focuses on fidelity to the text, translators for children often change or omit aspects of the text that they find inappropriate for children and add moralisms that were not originally a part of the source material (Shavit 2006, 26). To that end, many of the potential delights of literature for children have been scrubbed from children's books when transferred from one culture to another, as they have been from the Bible when translated for children. These include wordplay, mockery of adults, violence, and bodily functions. These same elements, found frequently throughout the Hebrew Bible, are often absent in Bibles for children. More frequently, readers will find a superimposed moral lesson, showing a distinction between the goals of Bible translation for adults and for children similar to that between the translation of other literature for adult or child audiences.

Beyond the implicit othering of children by segregating their Bible reading options from those of adults, the choices authors and illustrators make regarding the inclusion and presentation of child characters communicate their assumptions about children and childhood. These portrayals of children in the Bible are hence presented as normative, even ideal conceptions of self for the assumed child audiences of each of these Bibles for children. As Nodelman notes, such images in children's literature "teach children how to be childlike" (2008, 203). The idealized place that the Bible holds in Western culture reemphasizes the didacticism of such images in Bibles for children.

In adult-written and adult-illustrated Bible story collections, points of departure from the biblical narrative are particularly telling. Authors choose whether to include certain narratives prominently or peripherally featuring child characters, as well as how to portray the children they decide to include. Their texts and especially their illustrations can specify age and appearance in ways that the Bible does not. Authors also choose whether to present children as significant or insignificant, as pas-

---

authors and illustrators have chosen to present the flood narrative for a child audience, see Emma England's contribution to this volume.

sive objects or as active agents. Each of these choices communicates the appropriate roles of children in the hyperidealized world of the Bible for children.

ONE SUCH CHILD

One telling example of a child character found in some Bibles for children is the nameless Israelite slave girl in 2 Kgs 5:1–15. Female, young, enslaved, and living in a foreign land, she is multiply disempowered. Furthermore, the biblical text does not name her; she is one of the many anonymous child characters concentrated in 2 Kings (Parker 2009). Adele Reinhartz calls anonymous female characters in 1–2 Kings "the narrative antonyms of the major players—named male kings and prophets" (1994, 45). She observes that their anonymity detracts from them as characters, focusing the reader's attention on their roles in the narrative and the moments in which they break from these roles. This anonymous child fills the role of the slave but breaks from this role by speaking. In doing so, her agency initiates the narrative action and leads to the healing of a very powerful man. The child is not heard from again after this initial speech, but the contrast in imagery between this child and her powerful master becomes thematic throughout the text, offering a variety of interpretive options for the authors and illustrators of Bibles for children.

Esther Menn notes the significance of the contrast between great and small throughout 2 Kgs 5:1–15 (2008a, 2008b). The text first introduces the powerful Naaman as a "great man" (*ish gadol*), which can also be translated "big." In stark contrast, his wife's slave is introduced without name as a "small girl," a *na'arah qetannah*. The Hebrew opposites make this contrast clear. In specifying that the girl is small, this designation also layers the meaning of *na'arah* as both an age and a class designation. In Hebrew, as in many languages, words for boy and girl can also designate status as a servant or slave. The specification that she is a small girl specifies that the nameless slave is indeed also a child.

The contrast between big and small continues into the narrative even after the child is seemingly forgotten. Naaman objects to being asked to wash in the Jordan because he, as a big/great man, expected to be given a big welcome and a big task to do. He even objects to the Jordan, suggesting that he has bigger, better rivers at home. In the end, when he finally does wash in the Jordan, his leprous flesh is restored "like that of a little boy [*na'ar qaton*]." Robert Cohn notes the inclusio created here: "The young

maiden initiates the action which results in the figurative transformation of Naaman into a young boy" (1983, 177). Paired with this childlike
transformation, the contrast between big and little symbolically continues
the nameless girl's presence in the text. Through the pervasive juxtaposition of the great Naaman (*na'aman hagadol*) and the small girl (*hana'arah
haqetannah*), 2 Kgs 5:1–15 communicates a radical valuing of small deeds
and small people. Big and small is a visually compelling theme that invites
illustration. It is also a contrast that children live out and of which they
are therefore very much aware, making this text potentially fruitful for
presentation in a Bible for children.

Readers can learn much from comparing how this narrative is treated
in three Bibles for children, published in different decades of the second
half of the twentieth century. Golden Press's *The Children's Bible* (1965),
Karyn Henley's *The Beginner's Bible* (1989), and Ralph Milton's *The Family
Story Bible* (1996) each include this narrative, told with very different
words and images. Each was published recently enough to have responded
to the advent of ideological criticism. They represent a range of priori-
ties in the creation of a Bible for children, as portrayed in their selections,
paraphrases, illustrations, and introductory material.

Golden Bible

Published in 1965, Golden Press's *The Children's Bible* marked a major shift
in the history of Bibles for children. Although individual authors and illustrators had previously published collections of Bible stories or excerpts
with woodcuts or other artistic renditions of the narrative, the Golden
Bible was created by an ecumenical effort, with a Catholic, a Protestant,
and a Jewish representative on its editorial board. Other than the three
members of the board, the text does not list its author or illustrator. The
text as a whole reflects some of the language of the KJV but does not follow
any translation directly. Pages are text heavy, with illustrations scattered
among paraphrases of approximately the same length as translations of
the same narratives.

As cited by Bottigheimer, the Golden Bible's illustrations have been
roundly criticized in recent years for a lack of cultural diversity and appro-
priateness (1996, 212–13). Although clothing is somewhat culturally
reflective in the illustrations and some variation of skin tone is attested,
facial features are universally European in the Golden Bible. Women are
portrayed as slim and men as muscular. Children are notably absent from

assemblies unless explicitly mentioned by the text and certain potential child characters such as Samuel and Miriam are portrayed in late adolescence. Notably, the sacrifice of Isaac is missing, but that of Jephthah's daughter remains, with the victim portrayed as a young woman.

Second Kgs 5:1–15 takes up one page of the 510-page Golden Bible and is given the title "Elisha Heals a Leper." This title removes the focus not only from the slave girl but also from her master, Naaman. Her part in the story is given a few lines:

> The Syrians had gone out by companies and had brought back as a captive out of the land of Israel a little girl. She was a maidservant to Naaman's wife. She said to her mistress: "I would to God my lord were with the prophet who is in Samaria, for he would cure him of his leprosy." When the king of Syria heard what the girl had spoken, he said: "Go now, go, and I will send a letter to the king of Israel." (282)

Although the text reflects the girl's agency in launching the action of the narrative, she is quickly dropped entirely. She is not present in the illustration, which shows Naaman washing in a very deep, clean Jordan River as his adult male servants look on.

In the Golden Bible, children are presented as peripheral. The images throughout the text in particular assume that children are not a part of the community unless they are brought in for an explicit purpose. In 2 Kgs 5:1–15, the child who begins the story is insignificant, and even the significance of her insignificance, as emphasized in the Hebrew, is lost. Although the text preserves the mention of her and concludes that Naaman's "flesh was once again like the flesh of a little child," the illustration neglects the implication of this imagery by only portraying an event that does not include the child and by portraying the Jordan River as big, deep, and clean.

BEGINNER'S BIBLE

The Beginner's Bible, by Karyn Henley and illustrated by Dennas Davis, was published in 1989. It became very popular, with Zondervan launching a line of single Bible storybooks, videos, and DVDs under that title, as well as a second edition illustrated by Kelly Pulley. Both editions, as well as the other media under the same title are commonly used with very young children and early readers. The following is based on the Henley edition. The text gives very simplified, cheerful versions of a large number of biblical narratives. Its range of stories is notable, as are its bright, cartoonish illustrations.

The Beginner's Bible reflects a trend in the illustration of Bibles for children along with other children's literature toward showing a broader range of skin tones, but Davis includes a surprising number of blondes for its Middle Eastern context and has a habit of portraying nose size and shape as specific to age and gender (small and round for women and children, larger and angular for men). Bottigheimer notes the increased cultural awareness that begins emerging in this period as directly related to trade and immigration as contrasted with colonization: "Active proselytization of Africans and Asians into the nineteenth century had left Bible imagery unchanged, but economic and urban experiences of the 1970s and 1980s took visible form on the pages of children's Bibles" (1996, 214). Where Western exposure to a variety of peoples in a colonial context made little impression on biblical illustrators, interactions closer to home and in the global marketplace appear to have had greater effect.

The Beginner's Bible includes the narrative from 2 Kgs 5:1–15 under the title "Naaman," placing the focus on him and making him a more sympathetic character. Henley's paraphrase begins with a concise contrast between Naaman and the slave girl, here protectively toned down to "servant": "Naaman was the leader of a great army. His wife had a little servant girl from Israel" (Henley and Davis 1989, 233). The text then goes on to assume emotions of sadness and worry for Naaman before continuing with the child's action: "One day the servant girl said to Naaman's wife, 'I wish Naaman would go see Elisha. Elisha would help him get well'" (234). As in the biblical text, the girl does not reappear. However, The Beginner's Bible does not include the statement that Naaman's flesh was like a little boy; it merely concludes that he was "well."

Davis illustrates the story with a series of five images in primary colors. Naaman, whose clothes transition from red to white throughout the narrative, is shown with sad eyebrows and a tear in the first image. His leprosy is not made apparent. Naaman's wife and the "servant girl" are featured in the second picture. The wife is blonde and fair, wears jewelry, and (unlike the other characters imaged in this narrative) has eyelashes. The "servant girl" is smiling. She is darker skinned than the other woman and has very long black hair. Notably, she is not presented as a child but as a young woman. Although slightly shorter and slimmer than Naaman's wife, she is drawn with perceptible breasts. Although the author removed the word "slave," she preserved the word "little" in her text. Yet the illustrator's image contradicts this, making it visually clear that this "servant girl" was not a child. The unpleasantness in the life of this child has been completely removed from the narrative by its retelling and illustration. This suggests a need on the part of both author and illustrator to protect the child reader from the idea of enslaved children. The girl is completely absent from the final three images, which show Naaman in a golden chariot, then scowling as he thinks about the Jordan River, then happily splashing waist deep in it.

The cleaned-up text and cheerful images of *The Beginner's Bible* suggest that nothing bad can happen to children, especially in the Bible. They are not taken away from their families and their homes and made slaves. Even servants must have adult bodies, anachronistically reflecting modern Western mores requiring that children do not work. Disturbingly, it appears that the young woman who has replaced the child in 2 Kgs 5:1–15 is portrayed as a "servant" by way of significantly darker coloring than that of her mistress. The illustration implicitly suggests that nothing bad can happen to *white* children, and that this message is far more important than that of the original narrative, which suggests that being small and unimportant is sometimes better than being big and powerful.

FAMILY STORY BIBLE

Ralph Milton's *The Family Story Bible*, illustrated by Margaret Kyle and published in the United States in 1996, is striking in its honesty. It begins with an introduction entitled "How the Bible Came to Be" that explains the Bible's ancient oral roots, that "nobody knows if all the things really happened just the way they were told. Maybe some parts of the stories changed little by little as people told the story over and over" (Milton and Kyle 1996, 9). Milton goes on to disclose that he has changed the stories in his book and why, encouraging readers to seek out the differences and tell the story themselves in their own way:

> Sometimes, I put things into the stories that I imagined. Sometimes I put things in that I think might have happened or probably happened. That's why I tell things in my stories that are not in the Bible. . . . See if you can find out what parts of my story are different from the way the stories are in the Bible. Then you could tell the story in your own words. (9)

Notably, Milton's title names the book as a "family," not a "children's" Bible, thus avoiding the othering connotations of a separate Bible for children.

He also includes an introduction for adults, warning them against using a "stained glass voice," looking for a tidy moral and other pitfalls common to adults who think they know what the Bible is and how it should be read. Although including two introductions separates children from adults, such a practice also recognizes different generational experiences of the Bible and resultant different needs.

The body of Milton's text continues in its honesty. It avoids euphemisms, favoring "was a slave," "have sex with," and "feed the baby milk from her breasts" over phrases that obscure uncomfortable meanings and bodily functions, and does not take the other option of simply leaving out stories and sentences that would force that choice. His frankness allows him to include many more stories about women and girls than other Bibles for children do. In particular, his openness about bodily functions eliminates any need to censor the many stories about women that focus on child bearing. Honesty gives Milton freedom to flesh out stories based on brief mentions of named and anonymous women. The flexibility of Kyle's watercolor illustrations fits well with Milton's text and reflects the ethnic diversity that the Bible itself suggests without artificial insertions.

Milton titles his retelling of 2 Kgs 5:1–15 "Miriam Smiles." Miriam is the name he has given to the little slave girl, around whom his narrative centers. In selecting this name, he does not make any explicit attempt to connect her to the Miriam of the exodus, whose childhood he also imagines in Moses's birth narrative. A reader might deduce that the name was commonly used. Milton also names the other anonymous woman in the narrative. For Naaman's wife, he has chosen the name "Ghazal," which is an ancient Persian poetic form associated with women and sorrow.

Milton tells the story from the slave girl's point of view, expressing her homesickness and her loneliness, imagining the context in which she would have spoken the one line the Bible gives her. He even goes so far as to give her an age: "Miriam worked all the time, even though she was only ten years old. She never went to school. She never had time to play. Whatever Ghazal wanted, Miriam had to do" (Milton and Kyle 1996, 121). Milton places the narration of Naaman's action in Ghazal's mouth as she relates it to Miriam, who set it all in motion. In Milton's retelling, the contrast between big and small is regrettably lost, but he chooses to name and make room for female voices, including one belonging to a child.

Kyle provides two illustrations for Milton's three-page large print narrative. In the first, Miriam talks to Ghazal as she rubs her back. Miriam is clearly imaged as a child wearing a blue shift and headband. Her hair appears less cared for, standing in contrast to her sumptuous surroundings. On the facing page, an olive-complexioned and visibly leprous Naaman stands in the shallow Jordan River, with his servants and the dry Israelite landscape behind him. The juxtaposition between small and big as embodied by Miriam and Naaman is made visibly apparent in the pairing of these two images.

The Family Story Bible makes a point of speaking honestly with children and bringing them to the center. It gives Miriam a name, a story, and a complex emotional reality. It admits that her life is hard, as many children's lives are. Still, the difficulty of her life creates an opportunity for her to exercise agency. Milton changes 2 Kgs 5:1–15 for children, but he is honest about his intent to do so. Artificially putting a child at the center could certainly be seen as patronizing, but the inclusion of children in everyday life is authentic to the Bible's ancient Near Eastern context. The construction of childhood that Milton projects in his retelling is therefore not only empowering to children but appropriately so in that it is also contextually accurate.

A Slave Girl Speaks

The anonymous enslaved child of 2 Kgs 5:1–15 continues to speak out in this selection of adults' retellings of her story for a modern child audience. Reading and rereading her story suggests two especially telling questions that readers can ask of Bible story texts and illustrations created by adults for children: What has been removed from or added to the text? And what is the nature of the child's or children's role in the text? Each retelling and illustration has its own implicit or explicit goal, and readers of any age can read more closely if they are aware of such goals. These and other questions can help to clarify what they are and whether the authors' and illustrators' goals are potentially empowering or othering to children.

In light of the frequent censorship that takes place in the translation of literature for children and Bibles for children in particular, questioning what has been removed from the text and what has been added in both the retelling and the illustration is an excellent starting point. This was especially helpful in examples such as the removal of the slave girl's slave and child status in *The Beginner's Bible* and the fleshing out of the child's life as a slave in *The Family Story Bible*. Where the former reflects an attempt to remove unpleasantness from the narrative in seeking to protect the child reader, the latter imagines some of the difficult details, bringing the story's focus to the child and her experience.

Another important element is the child's role in the text, especially in that children are its implied audience. In 2 Kgs 5:1–15, the child character's agency launches the narrative, but careful exegesis shows that she also plays a thematic role. Although each retelling noted her character's action, none of them explored the full potential of the comparison between big and small that pervades the source text.[4] If a child or children are not mentioned in a narrative, it is important not to neglect the full implication of whether a child or children should or would have been present but are not mentioned. As seen in the flood narrative, asking after unmentioned children can be both important and fruitful.

OUTSIDERS IN

The othering of children in Bible translations, paraphrases, and story collections published explicitly for children presents an ethical dilemma. The authors and illustrators of such texts create them to be accessible and enjoyable for a child audience. They often state their intention to encourage children to read the Bible. Yet titling and marketing a Bible "for children" implies that the Bible is for adults and implicitly excludes children from participating in biblical reading and interpretation.

In any translation, paraphrase, or story collection, translators, authors, illustrators, and editors make interpretive choices about how to present children, some of which are empowering and others of which are marginalizing. However, I do not suggest that all potentially othering texts should be rejected or altered so as to be made more acceptable for children and their adult advocates. Mitzi Myers rightly critiques the indiscriminate rejection of texts as othering to children:

---

4. Scholarly commentaries have taken note of this theme to varying degrees. Cohn 1983, 174, 177; 2000 36, 38; Long 1991, 78–72; and Seow 1999, 193, 195 make note of the contrast between the girl and her master that opens and closes the passage. Cohn further observes the pervading wisdom of servants in comparison to great men throughout the passage (2000, 38). As noted above, Esther Menn more fully explores the significance of these contrasts where children are concerned (2008a, 2008b). Although Cogan and Tadmor (1988, 66–68) ignore the child's role entirely, choosing to focus instead on Gehazi's greed, Kim (2005, 60–61) and Sweeney (2007, 298) both highlight the contrast between the girl and Gehazi in their analyses of the broader narrative.

> However much we need revisionary, culturally situated accounts of literary childhood, thinking of representations of children only as unproblematic socialization narratives that "Other," smother, and colonize the child subject may prove as reductive as the commonplaces of idealizing Romantic regression or the currently modish voyeurism of the erotic gaze. (1999, 50)

As an alternative to participation in such full-scale rejection, the creators of vernacular Bibles could be attentive to the marginalization of children through increased awareness of cultural constructions of childhood and the ways in which they are communicated. Since all vernacular Bibles involve interpretation, much can be accomplished through critical examination of the assumptions about children and childhood that inform such interpretation. Indeed, the texts examined above already begin to show the influence of this kind of critical examination where race and gender are concerned, as do translations marketed to adults using gender-inclusive language for God and humanity.

Some children may prefer Bible story collections, paraphrases, and functional-equivalence translations to more literal vernacular translations of the Hebrew Bible. Notably, some adults prefer these versions also; people of any age can appreciate artful retellings and illustrations of biblical narratives. In this way, such texts do not have to be othering to children. Rather, children are othered in the intentional censorship of these texts in their name when an oversimplified Bible is titled and marketed for children. For any vernacular Bible to be empowering to children, as to adults, it should speak honestly about the goals and processes that led its authors, translators, illustrators, and editors to make interpretive choices. When making such choices, whether in illustration, translation, or retelling, these professionals can accomplish a great deal toward the empowerment of children by being attentive and honest about their implicit communication about children, as with all others in the biblical text.

Works Cited

Ariès, Philippe. 1962. *Centuries of Childhood: A Social History of Family Life*. Translated by Robert Baldick. New York: Vintage.

Berquist, Jon L. 2009. "Childhood and Age in the Bible." *Pastoral Psychology* 58:521–30.

Bottigheimer, Ruth B. 1996. *The Bible for Children: From the Age of Gutenberg to the Present*. New Haven: Yale University Press.

Bunge, Marcia J., ed. 2008. *The Child in the Bible*. Grand Rapids: Eerd-mans.

Buzzetti, Carlo. 2000. "Young People's Bibles (YPB): Is It Possible to Make a Good Choice?" *BT* 51:410–17.

The Children's Bible: The Old Testament, the New Testament. 1965. New York: Golden Press.

Cogan, Mordechai, and Hayim Tadmor. 1988. *II Kings: A New Translation with Introduction and Commentary*. AB 11. New York: Doubleday.

Cohn, Robert L. 1983. "Form and Perspective in 2 Kings v." *VT* 33:171–84.

———. 2000. *2 Kings*. Berit Olam. Collegeville, Minn.: Liturgical Press.

Fewell, Danna Nolan. 2003. *The Children of Israel: Reading the Bible for the Sake of Our Children*. Nashville: Abingdon.

Fry, Edward B. 1977. *Elementary Reading Instruction*. New York: McGraw-Hill.

Gruber, Mayer I. 1989. "Breast-Feeding Practices in Biblical Israel and in Babylonian Mesopotamia." *JANESCU* 19:61–83.

Hendrick, Harry. 1992. "Children and Childhood." *ReFresh* 14:1–4.

Henley, Karyn, and Dennas Davis (ill.). 1989. *The Beginner's Bible: Timeless Children's Stories*. Sisters, Ore.: Questar.

Hodgson, Robert, Jr. 1992. "Translating 1 Maccabees for Children." *BT* 43:117–24.

Ilan, David. 1995. "Mortuary Practices at Tel Dan in the Middle Bronze Age: A Reflection of Canaanite Society and Ideology." Pages 117–37 in *Archaeology of Death in the Ancient Near East*. Edited by Stuart Camp-bell and Anthony Green. Oxford: Oxbow.

Jones, Katharine. 2006. "Getting Rid of Children's Literature." *The Lion and the Unicorn* 30:287–315.

Kim, Jean Kyuong. 2005. "Reading and Retelling Naaman's Story (2 Kings 5)." *JSOT* 30:49–61.

L'Engle, Madeleine. 1979. *Ladder of Angels: Scenes from the Bible Illustrated by Children of the World*. New York: Seabury.

Long, Burke O. 1991. *2 Kings*. FOTL 10. Grand Rapids: Eerdmans.

Menn, Esther M. 2008a. "Child Characters in Biblical Narratives." Pages 234–52 in *The Child in the Bible*. Edited by Marcia J. Bunge. Grand Rapids: Eerdmans.

———. 2008b. "A Little Child Shall Lead Them: The Role of the Little Isra-elite Servant Girl (2 Kings 5:1–19)." *Currents in Theology and Mission* 35:340–48.

Meyers, Carol. 1997. "The Family in Early Israel." Pages 1–47 in *Families in Ancient Israel*. Edited by Leo G. Perdue et al. Louisville: Westminster John Knox.

Milton, Ralph, and Margaret Kyle (ill.). 1996. *The Family Story Bible*. Louisville: Westminster John Knox.

Myers, Mitzi. 1999. "Reading Children and Homeopathic Romanticism: Paradigm Lost, Revisionary Gleam, or 'Plus ça change, plus c'est la meme chose.'" Pages 44–84 in *Literature and the Child: Romantic Continuation, Postmodern Contestations*. Edited by James Holt Mc Gavran. Iowa City: University of Iowa Press.

Nag, Moni, et al. 1978. "An Anthropological Approach to the Study of the Economic Value of Children in Java and Nepal." *Current Anthropology* 19:293–306.

Nodelman, Perry. 1992. "The Other: Orientalism, Colonialism, and Children's Literature." *Children's Literature Association Quarterly* 17:29–35.

———. 2005. "How to Read a Picture Book." Pages 128–39 in *Understanding Children's Literature*. Edited by Peter Hunt. New York: Routledge.

———. 2008. *The Hidden Adult: Defining Children's Literature*. Baltimore: Johns Hopkins University Press.

Parker, Julie Faith. 2009. "You Are a Bible Child: Exploring the Lives of Children and Mothers through the Elisha Cycle." Pages 59–69 in *Women in the Biblical World: A Survey of Old and New Testament Perspectives*. Edited by Elizabeth A. McCabe. Lanham, Md.: University Press of America.

Paul, Lissa. 2005. "Feminism Revisited." Pages 114–27 in *Understanding Children's Literature*. Edited by Peter Hunt. 2nd ed. New York: Routledge.

Reinhartz, Adele. 1994. "Anonymous Women and the Collapse of the Monarchy: A Study in Narrative Technique." Pages 43–65 in *A Feminist Companion to Samuel and Kings*. Edited by Athalya Brenner. FCB 5. Sheffield: Sheffield Academic Press.

Rose, Jacqueline. 1984. *The Case of Peter Pan; or, the Impossibility of Children's Fiction*. London: Macmillan.

Rudd, David. 1999. "Theorizing and Theories: How Does Children's Literature Exist?" Pages 15–29 in *Understanding Children's Literature*. Edited by Peter Hunt. 2nd ed. New York: Routledge.

Seow, Choon-Leong. 1999. "1 and 2 Kings." *NIB* 3:3–295.

Shavit, Zohar. 2006. "Translation of Children's Literature." Pages 25–40 in *The Translation of Children's Literature: A Reader*. Edited by Gillian Lathey. Topics in Translation 31. Clevedon, Eng.: Multilingual Matters.

Stolt, Birgit. 2006. "How Emil Becomes Michel: On the Translation of Children's Books." Pages 67–83 in *The Translation of Children's Literature: A Reader*. Edited by Gillian Lathey. Topics in Translation 31. Clevedon, Eng.: Multilingual Matters.

Sweeney, Marvin A. 2007. *I and II Kings: A Commentary*. OTL. Louisville: Westminster John Knox.

"All God's Children": Authority Figures, Places of Learning, and Society as the Other in Creationist Children's Bibles[*]

Jaqueline S. du Toit

Children's Bibles constitute the religious norms and moral values an adult community treasures and intends to impart to the next generation. These Bibles are vehicles for the transfer of what the adult religious collective considers to be long-standing, traditional, and universal and therefore essential to their belief system, their way of life, and also their identity. For lap readers[1] this is presented by means of Bible stories traditionally told and interpreted at bedtime by the parent(s) while the child follows the

* This article is dedicated in equal parts to Athalya Brenner for her indefatigable encouragement of the visual palate as crucial to the reading endeavor for children *and* adults and her courageous encouragement by example of critical discourse in a field hitherto neglected and discarded by the serious, adult, predominantly male voice of biblical scholarship; and to Ruth Bottigheimer, whose thorough, insightful, and clear presentation of the history of the development of children's Bibles have been my constant guide in studying the intricacies of translating the Bible for children. The research conducted for this article is part of a larger project entitled "Bible Interpretation in Children's Literature: The Transfer and Interpretation of Bible (Religious) Knowledge from Diverse Institutional and Parental Sources to Children: Visual and Literary Interplay." The project is funded by the South African National Research Foundation's (NRF) Thuthuka Program. Any opinion, findings, and conclusions or recommendations expressed in this material are those of the author. The NRF does not accept any liability in regard thereto.

1. On the quandary of defining "child" and "childhood," see Oittinen 2006, 41. I follow Oittinen in my focus on children seven years old and younger, still dependent or semidependent on the parent for the reading of the text. Hence the use of the term "lap reader" to emphasize the interdependent parent-child relationship required for the reading of children's Bibles at this age.

accompanying depictions of the narrative. These stories are impregnated with traditional values emphasized and embroidered upon by the most trusted adult authority and intermediary for the young child, the parent. They incorporate matters such as respect for parents and elders (including God, portrayed as the ultimate father figure); the recognition of and obedience to societal structures (school, church, state, etc.); guidelines for ethical behavior (obedience, telling the truth, respect for others, etc.); but also an introduction to the known world by means of religious constructs used to explain its creation and purpose, as well as the maintenance thereof for the preservation of the social good.

At first glance the title of this chapter therefore appears all wrong: contradictory to an othering of authority figures and institutions of authority, children's Bibles are playful, colorful, and often irreverent but dedicated vehicles par excellence for celebrating figures of authority along with an emphasis on obedience and adherence to rules presented in a religious guise (see, e.g., Larsen 1995, 46–52, 60–66; DeVries 2007, 60–65; Larsen 2009, 32–37).[2] Children's Bibles as purveyors of traditional societal norms and values tend to represent a conservative religious stance. Just as conservative Christian (and Jewish) collectives, these Bibles tend to hold the integrity of the nuclear family dear. This includes an emphasis on respect for authority as represented for the young child by her parents, and especially the father, as physical manifestation of God as the divine father figure (see, e.g., Exod 20:12 and Matt 6:9). The instilled respect for figures and institutions of authority is extended to include a tight hierarchy of older siblings, caregivers, religious functionaries, teachers and professors, political office bearers, and ultimately also societal structures such as church, school, and state in a nod to Matt 17:24–27, a matter especially emphasized by Calvinist Reformed theology. Children's Bibles as purveyors of these social mores may therefore be expected to instill respect for and adherence to authority rather than the opposite. As active agents in the process of establishing religious authority over the next generation, any undermining of authority would be

---

2. The project of which this article forms part is based on children's Bible resources readily available in commercial bookstores and online stores in South Africa. All children's Bibles quoted, unless otherwise indicated, are in either English or Afrikaans, two of the eleven official languages of South Africa. For a discussion of the disproportionate nature of representation of children's Bibles on the South African market, see Du Toit and Beard 2007.

an anathema to children's Bible authors, as this would prove subversive to the authority of children's Bibles and indeed the authors themselves.

My inclusion of Jewish children in the above general statements is deliberate especially given the globalization, commercialization, and inevitable homogenization of religious publications of this nature in recent years. The form and content of early-twenty-first-century children's Bibles in South Africa, for example, are largely determined by market forces set in motion by the demands of a predominantly North American, Protestant readership. Penny Schine Gold explains this in *Making the Bible Modern* (2004, 81) by pointing to the inextricable link between the influence of nineteenth- and twentieth-century American Protestant education on the development of American Jewish education and the characteristics of Jewish children's Bibles. In this respect two matters stand out. In both Christian and Jewish children's Bibles we find (1) that the "*development of Protestant institutions and methods of religious education* provided a ready model for Jewish imitation" and (2) that the "*emphasis in public schooling on character education* contributed to the highly moralized adaptations of biblical text into Bible story" (emphasis original).

Such approaches to childhood, education, and knowledge transfer reflect the othering in contemporary society's approach to children over the past two centuries insofar as it much resembles the manner in which early missionaries approached their potential converts or, as Karen Sánchez-Eppler (1996, 419) refers to it, the "identification of the child with the heathen." Alan Prout explains:

> Viewing children as natural primitives played into nineteenth and twentieth century concerns with Empire and race. The child became an instance of the "Other," a homologue for all such "primitives" and a demonstration of the gulf that divided the "civilized" from the "uncivilized." ... However, alongside its ideological kinship with such ideas the Child Study movement can also be seen as part of another key development of the nineteenth century: the construction of children as a concern of the Nation. ... Children became a target for investment and were seen as the "children of the nation." (2008, 25)

Adults (the nation) therefore participate to bring children (the other) into the fold by a process of identity formation through formal and informal education. This collective concern with the education of children, whether nationally or religiously (in the present context) defined, and the concomitant instillation of societal values by means of such an educational outlook is therefore only to be expected. In fact, education based on the Bible became the linchpin to both missionaries' and religious communities' attempts to inculcate the social mores of the tradition in the perceived other, the convert or child. As Norman Etherington explains of the missionary endeavor post-Reformation: "Especially for Protestants, the chief accomplishment of the Reformation had been to put the Bible in the hands of ordinary people. Because the ability to read and interpret Scripture was central to the faith, teaching converts to read the Bible was a top priority" (2005, 9).[3] That children's Bibles are instrumental in the child's progression from illiteracy to literacy may therefore be assumed along with the privileging of didactics over the entertainment value of the medium.[4]

The child audience, rather than the adult author, therefore poses as the other with religious education and children's Bibles as the agents of enculturation, as Riitta Oittinen explains also for children's books in general: "Children's books need to conform to adult tastes and likes and dislikes: to put it explicitly, the adults are the producers and the children the consumers of children's literature. … Even though translators need to translate for children, it is the adults who select the books that need to be translated; it is the adults who translate them and buy the translations for children. It is also the adults who usually read the books aloud" (2006, 36). In addition, for children's Bibles, it is the adult religious community that establishes the normative qualities of the tradition chosen for transfer in child-appropriate format.

Creationist children's Bibles prove to be a subversive exception to the above by engaging the child reader in an act of open questioning, if not defiance, of the validity of the knowledge base presented by secular education and science through teachers and educational institutions. This is done by means of distancing the religious child from secular society in a deliberate act of othering. This in itself is curious, especially because of this religious collective's affirmation of a return to traditional Bible-based truth. For conservative religious collectives across the world, biblical truth

---

3. I elaborate on the corollary between missionary Bibles and children's Bibles in Du Toit 2011.

4. Note the pervasive presence of children's Bibles adapted to teach children their numbers and ABCs. Gilbert Beers, e.g., explains the intimate link between didactics and entertainment in his "A Note to Parents": "Whether 'read-to-me' for young children or 'I-can-read' for older children, this book will delight your child. Bible learning will be an experience of joy" (2001, 13).

as a rule represents a return to an adherence to authority and an acknowledgment of hierarchical solidarity, situated first of all in the nuclear family but extended to all sources of authority within society.

In what follows I consider how the creationist children's Bibles other the traditional Christian emphasis on respect for authority figures by evaluating the ways in which the creationist author turns convention on its head. Rather than inculcating implicit adherence to the values of the dominant social hierarchies, in these Bibles the child reader is made complicit in the othering of the society in which she lives. This is done by offering the children's Bible, and the adult reader (presumably the parent) thereof, as substitute source of authority. Of particular importance are the attestations to truth in the presentation of "what really happened" and how these are used by the creationist author to compromise Christian, Protestant tradition by creating a hermeneutics of suspicion regarding the established foundations of societal authority and its knowledge base. This is done by radically amending the biblical canon in the guise of simplification for a child audience and by simultaneously questioning traditional sources of knowledge as well as institutions of learning (teachers, schools, museums, even public libraries, universities, and so forth). This approach facilitates the distancing of the child reader at the moment of identity formation from the larger secular community that by default becomes the implied other. Such othering of society is acute as it represents the very community to which the child and her parents would otherwise belong: the community where she lives, matures, and in which she will eventually function as citizen. The creationist children's Bible therefore achieves this othering of secular society while at the same time paradoxically emphasizing a return to traditional values and an idealized former good.

Despite the obvious seriousness of the implications of the above, the question may nevertheless be posed as to why creationist children's Bibles, predominantly published in a parochial Middle American social environment, should even matter to my own South African context or to that of the rest of the world? It matters because the globalization of the marketplace has homogenized the representation of the other the world over: with a click of a button it is now possible to disseminate by means of online bookstores similar media all over the world. The result has been a far less diversified, culturally and contextually sensitive presentation of children's Bibles as commercial demands for sales have come to overshadow cultural requirements of contextual specificity. This also leads to the systematic erosion of difference and the ultimate assumption of a homogenous readership made obvious by a gradual decline in the commissioning of "original" children's Bibles in favor of imported (primarily from the United States and the United Kingdom) Bibles. One can also add to it the "non-translation" of accompanying pictures in children's Bibles translated, for example, from an American or British model for the South African child (cf. Du Toit and Beard 2007).

Two parallel and sometimes conflicting positions on othering are therefore identified in the children's Bibles to be discussed. The first is the children's Bible itself as vehicle of conversion from a child state to an adult state by means of the instilment of social and religious values from a position of othering to sameness of the child reader by the adult writer. The second is how creationist children's Bibles make the child reader complicit in the othering of secular society and the common social knowledge base. For the discussion of these issues I make use of a selection of publications by one of the most vocal proponents of creationism in the United States and an avid author of children's Bibles and Bible storybooks, Ken A. Ham.[5]

CHILDREN'S BIBLES: A WORKING DEFINITION

"One wonders why publishers bother to translate Bible stories when every nation with a print tradition already has access to the canonical Bible as source," surmises Ruth Bottigheimer in *The Bible for Children* (1996, 51). The answer is simple: children's Bibles serve a function very different from what is assumed, namely, the accessibility granted by translation of the biblical text from one language into another, from one culture into another, and from an adult register into a child register. Rather, children's Bibles offer the opportunity for a religious community to canonize, repackage, and transfer their rendition of what they consider normative to the next generation in the guise of translation of the adult source text with its implied adherence to accuracy, faithfulness, and truth.

The claim that a children's Bible is a translation rather than an adaptation, no matter how loosely defined, is vitally important to the present context. It allows for the acceptable assumption of "sacralization" (Bottigheimer 1996, 43), invested in the adult source text, on behalf of

---

5. Ham is president and CEO of Answers in Genesis–USA and of the Creation Museum near Cincinnati in the United States, which opened in 2007 to great popular appeal. The emphasis on an alternative educational outlook is clear from the broad range of educational material in its on-premises bookstore and online.

the contextualized child-friendly derivative.[6] Children's Bibles can thus be defined as "books of Old Testament and New Testament stories for children to read at home, either alone or together with family members. They bear the stamp of parental authority along with intimations of divine wisdom and, unlike other children's literature, occupy a normative space immediately adjacent to divine authority itself" (Bottigheimer 1996, 4). The text *and pictures* of children's Bibles are therefore, despite claims of adherence to the original source text, contextually sensitive and highly selective commentaries on the original Hebrew and/or Greek adult source text. This is achieved while both text and picture assume the guise of translation and hence a claim to divine authority in which the source text is cloaked because of its divinely sanctioned canonicity for Judeo-Christian tradition.

THE ROLE OF PARENTS

For children's Bibles, the medium and manner of information transfer is as important as the message itself. Children's Bibles and children's stories in general are most often read at bedtime. This is a shared, intimate activity whereby the parent as closest and loving authority figure to the young child becomes the vehicle for the child's introduction into the text and the norms of the religious community. Penny Schine Gold elaborates on the typical setting when she reminisces about her own experiences: "Reading stories at bedtime was a cherished ritual throughout my child's early years. From *Goodnight, Moon* to *The Jolly Postman* and *Box Car Children*, stories provided the occasion for the quiet, intimate communication of love and truth: sitting on the bed, one of my arms around Jeremy and the other on the book, we ended together a busy, active day" (2004, ix).

Children's Bibles are therefore written for a dual audience: while the young, illiterate or semiliterate lap reader follows the accompanying pictorial presentations of the story being read, the parent interprets the text and pictures by means of voice, intonation, dramatization, expansion, and elaboration on the text as presented in order to contextualize the story within the immediate cognitive and religious framework of the child.

---

6. Pictures in children's Bibles by the same token tend to veer toward hyperrealistic presentation of the narrative in an attempt to mimic the same attestation to truthfulness and adherence to the source text as is claimed for the accompanying translation.

THE CREATIONIST IMAGE OF CHILD AND TEXT

Creationism, briefly, refers to a combination of beliefs in a young earth and universe, flood geology and the miraculous origination of all living things (Numbers 1999, 240). This leads to a hyperliteral interpretation of Gen 1–11 and an unquestioning acceptance of Genesis, not the New Testament, as fundamental to Christianity. In creationist children's Bibles this is coupled with the foregrounding of the Bible (regarded as an expansion of Gen 1–11) as a true and accurate reflection of history. This conception is linked to an insistence on word-for-word or literal translation, so that the truth of the original history may not be obscured. Anything inconsistent with such a worldview is immediately considered suspect, strange, or evil and therefore a representation of the other (cf. Schrag 2006). The Bible is "the only book of history that's totally reliable," says Ken Ham in *All God's Children: Why We Look Different* (2005, n.p.). In the same vein, Mike Matthews, director of content development of the Creation Museum in Petersburg, Kentucky, describes his own encounter with this tradition and the othering of secular institutions of higher learning as follows: "When I was a lowly freshman at the University of Chicago, [an old friend] introduced me to the radical idea that Gen 1–11 is real history. As a result of his sharing God's Word with me, I trusted Christ as my Savior in the dormitory of that *heathen center of learning*" (2007, 97, emphasis added).

Although biblical creationism in various guises has historically been part of the Protestant landscape (Numbers 1999), it is only in recent years that its account of origins became a contender to the account given of it by mainstream science, rather than just an alternative theological interpretative position (Numbers 1982; also Morris 2000). According to historian of science Ronald Numbers (quoting sociologist V. L. Bates), by the 1970s "creationists began stressing the scientific legitimacy of their enterprise because 'their theological legitimation of reality was no longer sufficient for maintaining their world and passing on their world view to their children'" (1982, 543).

The creationist presumption of an inerrant biblical text as the basis of all knowledge is crucial to this claim of creationism as an alternative "scientific approach." Ironically, the claim to teach kids "to trust the Bible from the very first verse," as the front cover of Ken Ham's *My Creation Bible* (2006) proclaims, is contradicted by a radical truncation of the canonized source text to include only the Gen 1–11 stories of creation, Noah's flood, and the tower of Babel, followed by the birth of Jesus and an extremely brief rendering of the New Testament.

This invasive and radical shortening—in firm contradiction to Judeo-Christian tradition's strict imperative to refrain from adding or removing anything from the canon—is integral to the rendering of what is considered essential in the transmission of the Bible's message to the children in this religious community.[7]

To connect Christian salvation to a historical (read: literal) interpretation of the creation and flood narratives might seem a rather extravagant leap, but it exemplifies a pervasive trend in biblical interpretation (Bray 1996, 539–83) aimed at establishing a worldview and a redemptive discourse for Middle America. This in turn is conveyed via an already existing tradition of translating children's Bibles and educational material as means of knowledge transfer for the subsequent generation and by means of favorable market forces to the rest of the world.

In creationist discourse all is related back to primeval history. Evolution or "evolutionism" thus becomes the center of evil, and all proponents thereof are considered the hand puppets of Satan, originating "at the primeval rebellion of Satan against God" (Morris 2000, 261). In his *The Long War against God*, Henry Morris, for example, states that "despite the prevalence of evolutionary philosophy age after age, the evidences of creation have always borne their witness, and there has always been a remnant witnessing to the ungodly world concerning the Creator and his great promises of redemption and salvation" (2000, 262).

The target audience for this discourse is children, and the forum for its dissemination is envisioned as a counter to secular institutions of learning such as schools, museums, and also universities. As *Answers* magazine, mouthpiece of a significant contingent of the biblical creationist movement, explains in an article titled "Teaching the Truth from an Early Age,"

---

7. Although Numbers (1982, 543) argues that the latter part of the twentieth century signaled a move away from the emphasis on the literal rendering of Genesis and toward a predominantly antievolution campaign, this is not borne out by the representative sampling of creationist children's Bibles considered for this study and culled from a representative website for the creationist movement "Answers in Genesis" (http://www.answersingenesis.org) as written for children in the age group two to eleven years old.

Whether your children attend school in a traditional classroom setting—such as a public or Christian school—or in a less formal homeschool setting, they need to understand the scientific aspects of our world from a biblical, creationist worldview. Without a creation-based Christian worldview, they soon begin to think that secular scientists have the "facts," while churches have "stories." ... Moms and dads of public school students must closely monitor and supplement what their children are being taught in class. Homeschooling parents should carefully choose primary curricula that present the biblical creation interpretation of the world while also explaining the basics of the evolutionary interpretation. It is essential that you get the right information into your children's minds early and often. (2007, 94)

THE RIGHT INFORMATION?

The primeval history of creation, flood narrative, and the tower of Babel[8] stands central to any creationist "translation" of the Bible for children. For example, Ken and Mally Ham indicate on the back cover of *A Is for Adam: The Gospel from Genesis* (1995): "Many adults today cannot adequately defend their Christian faith because they do not understand the book of Genesis—yet all major Christian doctrines, including salvation, have their foundation in this book of beginnings." The authors' intention is clearly stipulated in the text: the book should become foundational to every level of institutional authority. The reason for its publication is that adults—not children—are considered deficient in their understanding of the Christian faith, hence the required need for a "book of beginnings," to raise a new generation of future adults proficient in these matters.

This is achieved by making the child audience (and parental reader) complicit in the retelling of Gen 1–11, the story of beginnings. In this, creationist children's Bibles are by no means unique. All children's Bible authors make use of techniques to foster interactivity. They also use implied complicity in the outcome of narratives. For instance, pop-up stories whereby the child would be required to flip a pop-up lid on a depiction of a fish to reveal Jonah emerging from the belly of the fish thereby make the child responsible for the story movement (see, e.g., *My Favorite Bible*

---

8. Note the absence of Gen 9:18–27 (Noah's drunkenness), a clear example of a story that may foster disrespect or a questioning of the primary authority figure, the father. For how this story was treated by mainstream children's Bible authors, see Bottigheimer 1996, 103–15.

Storybook for Toddlers 2003). Other such techniques include embedding modern child characters with whom the child audience may then identify within a biblical rendition, implying the child's presence at the moment the story took place and thus strengthening a sense of the faithfulness or historicity of the narrative by making the modern child audience the "eye-witnesses" (thus, e.g., the recurring baby in pajamas in Holmes 2008).

The latter technique is used to full effect in Ken Ham's *Dinosaurs of Eden* (2001) by employing a "time machine"[9] (as metaphor for the Bible) that transports two Caucasian children, one male and one female, to the beginning of time (creation or Gen 1). Their movement in time is signaled by dress and depiction. The children are dressed in space outfits and are depicted in a white/blue hue to distinguish the observers from the characters in the story. The less than definite lines used for the depiction of the observers, along with the blue and white coloring that predominates, also imply the invisibility of the eyewitnesses to the characters in the story.[10] Parallel to the story set in the garden of Eden is a depiction of the boy and girl time travelers observing Adam and Eve peacefully eating fruit in the garden or feeding berries to a selection of dinosaurs.

Throughout the book the time traveler motif is used to place the modern child audience within the story as a way of bearing direct witness to the truth of this literal reading of the primeval history. This is explained on the back cover:

> This captivating adventure … projects you back to the Garden of Eden and to the real world inhabited by dinosaurs—and to the exciting days of Noah's flood and the Tower of Babel. You'll be there watching … traveling through the centuries … learning the true history of the earth, and along the way discovering the very meaning and purpose of life! (Ham 2001)

---

9. The time machine motif is not unique to creationist children's Bibles. See, e.g., Brenner's discussion of a similar motif in a (noncreationist) film version of the creation narrative (2006, 14–17). The opposite of this journey back in time by means of the time machine is a chronological sequencing of narrative enabled by, e.g., tabs allowing the child to effect the continuation of the timeline by flipping from one page to the next by means of the illustrated tabs, thus making the child instrumental in the progression of history and narrative (see Dennis 2006).

10. Eyewitness reporting is crucial to Ham's approach. He has become known for posing the question "were you there?" whenever confronted by scientists explaining the long timespan of evolution.

"No Innocent Act": Secular Education as the Other

Riitta Oittinen makes the observation in her discussion of translation for children that children's literature is often approached by critics in a manner that focuses on the reader (the child audience) rather than on the text or the author's intent: "From this we might draw the conclusion that children's literature tends to be adapted to a particular image of childhood. … Child image is a very complex issue: on the one hand, it is something unique … on the other hand, it is something collectivized in all society. Anything we create for children reflects our views on being a child. It shows our respect or disrespect for childhood as an important stage of life, the basis for an adult future" (2006, 41).

Translating a children's Bible in any mold, creationist or otherwise, is therefore "no innocent act," as Oittinen (2006) emphasizes. In fact, the creationist children's Bible author deliberately selects elements from the biblical text under the guise of education for the child audience in order to render a closely demarcated and unassailable religious truth. This is achieved by cloaking the text in the guise of historicity for purposes of education when the real objective is far closer aligned to religious persuasion (or biblicity). The creationist children's Bible does not merely endeavor to educate the child in the creationist mold. It overtly others figures, scientific constructs, and institutions of secular authority by questioning the validity of their educational output and by ridiculing the status quo. The child audience is thus persuaded to adopt an alternative way of thinking that, in turn, ironically expects blind obedience and adherence from the same child previously persuaded to relentlessly question the alternative: evolution and everything and everyone associated therewith by the creationist author, such as, for example, same-sex marriage:

> With monkeys and apes, Adam still was alone,
> So God put him to sleep and took a rib bone.
> He made the first woman, Adam's wife was she.
> A man and a woman, that's what marriage should be. (Ham 2006, n.p.)

In his 2002 treatise on creation evangelism, Ken Ham furthermore establishes an overt link between disrespect for traditional authority figures and the "worrisome trend" (15) of the negation of the authority of the Bible in the secular school curriculum:

> Here's the problem. During their school hours, students are being taught more and more that evolution is a fact and science has proved the Bible wrong. They don't believe that God created everything. The textbooks tell them that the universe and life arose by chance, random processes. The students know that evolution and its teachings about "ape-men" contradict the Bible's teaching about Adam and Eve. Increasingly, some teachers are beginning to be vocal about attacking the Bible. (Ham 2002, 17)

The teaching of evolution is therefore, according to Ham, privileged by secular education to the detriment of biblical authority in schools. More so, the teaching of evolution is presented as an attack on the literal interpretation of the biblical narrative. As the Bible is considered the mouthpiece of God, the ultimate authority figure, then the presence of evolution in the school curriculum and the teaching thereof is interpreted as an act of defiance against divine authority. Because the perpetrators of such anarchy are institutions of secular learning, they become the other whereby the creationist identity is defined and an alternative authority legitimized. This allows the creationist author to call into question all representations of established authority in the secular world thereby allowing children and their parents (should they prove open to a creationist perspective) the prerogative to determine a strict dichotomy and establish right from wrong, truth from lie, science from fiction, even should this contradict socially established, institutionalized agreement on these matters.[11] This in turn allows for the overt undermining of authority in a medium (children's Bibles) that has to date held this very aspect sacred.

An excellent example of this strategy is found in Ken and Mally Ham's *D Is for Dinosaur* (1991, 8–9; see fig. 2.1 below) and it is the pictorial depiction that is particularly telling (a matter of no small import as this is the only part of the text read by the lap reader without assistance from the adult mediator). Here a depiction is offered of a gray-haired teacher (gray hair by convention emphasizes age, wisdom, and authority), standing in front of a blackboard on which he has written "25 <u>Million</u> Years Ago." A student in the foreground with his back to the reader is raising his hand with a speech bubble that reads: "Were you there?" The student is questioning the

---

11. Displays in the Creation Museum are dominated by the pairing that distinguishes "Human Reason" from "God's Word" as an evident substitute for evolution versus creationism or lie versus truth.

teacher's authority on matters of science in the absence of a direct presence at the moment the event is proposed to have happened. In the foreground of the picture a book is open in front of the student. It simply reads: "Job" (referring to the latter part of the book of Job [38–42] in which this searching question is asked by God of the biblical character, Job). The teacher is ridiculed in the depiction with a question mark in a bubble next to him and sweat pouring from his forehead indicating evident anguish and an inability to respond. His old-fashioned dress code (bowtie) underscores the othering and promotes an image of "old-fashioned ideas" (evolution) associated with the teacher. By default the creationist views purported by the book and transferred to the child reader, is presented as new, innovative, and therefore also with greater truth value. On the opposite page the alphabet letters V W X Y Z are followed by the promising rider: "We'll learn the truth about history."

In *The Answers Book for Kids* Ken Ham counters a similar question from a seven-year-old, Annabel H., on the authority of the Bible (and the creationist version of a literal, six-day creation) based on the presence of God at creation. Ham's response is posed in the same dichotomous fashion

Fig. 2.1. Creationism's challenge to secular learning: "Were you there?" (Ham 1991, 9).

thus undermining secular authority by establishing God (or the creation-ist interpretation of God and Bible) as the alternative to the secular other by implying that truth is the sole prerogative of God and the Bible:

> Question: How did the authors of the Bible know what all God did during the creation, since there was no one to see what He did, how do we know what really happened?
>
> Answer: ... There are people who believe in evolution who think that billions of years ago (when no one was there to see) the universe came into existence by a big bang. Then billions of years ago (when no one was there to see) the earth came into existence. Then billions of years ago (when no one was there to see) life formed on earth. Then millions of years ago (still no one there to see!) animals began changing into other animals. Then two million years ago (yep, still no one there!) an animal like an ape began to change into a human being. That's their story ... but there wasn't anyone around to see it. Well, guess what? In the Bible we are told God has given His word to men to write down so we can know how everything came to be. The Bible, which is God's Word, though penned by man, tells us that God WAS there and He has given us an eyewitness account of exactly how the universe and everything in it was created. The Bible tells us thousands of times that it is the Word of God. My questions to you is [sic], "Do you trust God, who knows everything, who has always been there, who never changes, and who doesn't tell a lie OR a human being who doesn't know everything, changes his mind, changes his story, and wasn't always there?" Well, I believe God and that makes real sense! (Ham and Malott 2009a, 34–35)

Conclusion

What, then, is the purpose of such extraordinarily radical truncation of the canon, especially as such children's Bibles are simultaneously pro-moted as divinely inspired textual authorities within the Judeo-Christian tradition? What are the implications of this move on the margins of the tradition for mainstream Christianity and the tradition's image of child-hood? Historically the canon was routinely adapted by tradition in the guise of simplification with little condemnation from or ill effect to the legitimacy of either the canon or the continuation of the tradition because of the contextual imperative paramount in children's Bibles: "Content fol-lowed context" (Bottigheimer 1996, 71; see also Du Toit 2008).

On the surface, the missionary children's Bibles generated by "creation evangelism" (cf. Ham 2002) share with other children's Bibles their persuasive properties and instilled respect for a higher authority.[12] However, different from the adaptive history of children's Bibles in general, creationist children's Bibles with their radical and irreversible truncation of a canon within a canon (Gen 1–11) and no tolerance for variety in the interpretation of truth have permanently changed the meaning and authority of the Bible for creationists. This allows little room for adapting content according to any future generation's change of context or circumstances. It is therefore possible to claim that a closing of this abbreviated canon has taken place with the acceptance of the principle that Gen 1–11 is representative of the entire Christian Bible, including all manner of salvation. This polemical stance inherent to creationist children's Bibles has therefore permanently deprived the consumers of these Bibles of access to the possibility of a responsive contextual elasticity over a generational timeline. For children's Bibles in general, this elasticity has allowed successive generations of children's Bibles in mainstream Christian tradition to remain contextually relevant and responsive to the changing context of their child audience and religious collectives.

As the creationist tradition also tolerates little choice in the nature and variety of the offering, with ultimate authority settled in the few (essentially similar in message and scope) creationist children's Bibles available per age group, the authors have established an intentionally consistent and uniform approach to religious education. It allows for little adaptation or growth within the tradition and leads to a rigid acceptance of a single truth.[13] And although this may serve the aspiration of the religious tradition toward firm standardization, it leaves the genre of children's Bibles unable to attend to its historical maxim of context governing content (Bottigheimer 1996, 71).

As the variety of children's Bibles diminishes with the commercial drive for sameness, the diversity of story depiction and interpretation are impoverished accordingly. The result is that any fixed truncation of canon and overt othering of the secular by a subset of children's Bibles become all

---

12. For overt creationist missionary vehicles written for children, see, e.g., Ham 2005 and 2009b.

13. Schine Gold (2004, 141) observes a similar movement of "evening out" regarding problematic or patently complicated character traits of human characters, but also of God, in children's Bibles in general.

the more pronounced in their influence on the genre as a whole. This, in turn, poses a detrimental effect on future generations of children's Bibles and the reception of that which religious collectives hold sacred.

Athalya Brenner calls for a continuous establishment of difference rather than sameness in this genre when she recalls:

> The children in my son's class, all of 25 years ago, aged seven, enjoyed coping with 10 different images of Noah's ark. Suspension of disbelief worked even in the case of a multiplicity of images. Their own life vocabulary concerning the bible, thus acquired, allowed for representational diversity immediately. And we should aspire to the appreciation of such diversity if we wish for the bible to remain alive and kicking; and if we wish for future adults to read it for cultural heritage and pleasure, beyond religious doctrine or scholarly nitpicking. (2006, 33)

It is within this context that the othering of society as evidenced in creationist children's Bibles is most worrisome. In order for children's Bibles to continue as effective vehicles of knowledge transfer of the religious tradition, the responsive nature of the inclusion and exclusion of canonical content is to be guarded as the ultimate indicators of religious tradition's healthy exchange of ideas with adult society. Any attempt at othering to delegitimize the figures and institutions of authority attempted through overidentification with a heavily truncated canon, is a concern. As Brenner indicated, diversity is important and choice is vital to children's identity formation within religious tradition and for the future of the Bible as lived experience to children and adults.

Works Cited

Barr, James. 1977. *Fundamentalism*. Philadelphia: Westminster.

Beers, V. Gilbert. 2001. *The One Year Bible for Children*. Oxford: Candle.

Die Belangrikste Storie ooit Vertel. 2000. Translated by Rosalie van Aswegen. Vereeniging: Christelike Uitgewersmaatskappy.

Bottigheimer, Ruth B. 1996. *The Bible for Children: From the Age of Gutenberg to the Present*. New Haven: Yale University Press.

Bray, Gilbert. 1996. *Biblical Interpretation: Past and Present*. Downers Grove, Ill.: InterVarsity Press.

Brenner, Athalya. 2006. "Recreating the Biblical Creation for Western Children: Provisional Reflections on Some Case Studies." Pages 11–34 in *Creation and Creativity: From Genesis to Genetics and Back*. Edited by Caroline Vander Stichele and Alastair G. Hunter. BMW 9. Sheffield: Sheffield Phoenix.

Dennis, Nicholas. 2006. *Leap through Time: The First Humans.* New York: Backpack Books.

DeVries, Catherine, and Kelly Pulley (ill.). 2007. *The Beginner's Bible. Book Devotions: My Time with God.* Grand Rapids: Zonderkidz.

Du Toit, Jaqueline S. 2008. "'Content Follows Context': Translating the Bible for Children." Pages 33–44 in *Whose Story? Translating the Verbal and the Visual in Literature for Young Readers.* Edited by Riitta Oittinen and Maria Gonzalez Davies. Newcastle: Cambridge Scholars.

———. 2011. "Translated and Improved: Retelling the Bible to Children." Pages 383–96 in *Retelling the Bible: Literary, Historical, and Social Contexts.* Edited by Lucie Doležalová and Tamás Visi. Bern: Peter Lang.

Du Toit, Jaqueline S., and Beard, Luna. 2007. "The Publication of Children's Bibles in Indigenous South African Languages: An Investigation into the Current State of Affairs." *JSem* 16:297–311.

Etherington, Norman. 2005. "Introduction." Pages 1–18 in *Missions and Empire.* Edited by Norman Etherington. Oxford History of the British Empire Companion Series. Oxford: Oxford University Press.

Ham, Ken. 1987. *The Lie: Evolution. Genesis—The Key to Defending Your Faith.* Green Forest: Master Books.

———. 2002. *Why Won't They Listen? The Power of Creation Evangelism.* Green Forest: Master Books.

———. 2005. *All God's Children: Why We Look Different.* Green Forest: Master Books.

Ham, Ken, and Cindy Malott. 2009a. *The Answers Book for Kids*, vol. 3: *22 Questions from Kids on God and the Bible.* Green Forest: Master Books.

———. 2009b. *The Answers Book for Kids*, vol. 4: *22 Questions from Kids on Sin, Salvation, and the Christian Life.* Green Forest: Master Books.

Ham, Ken, and Earl and Bonnie Snellenberger (ill.). 2001. *Dinosaurs of Eden: A Biblical Journey through Time.* Green Forest: Master Books.

Ham, Ken, and Jonathan Taylor (ill.). 2006. *My Creation Bible.* Green Forest: Master Books.

Ham, Ken, Mally Ham, and Dan Lietha (ill.). 1995. *A Is for Adam: The Gospel from Genesis.* Green Forest: Master Books.

Ham, Ken, Mally Ham, and Ron Hight (ill.). 1991. *D Is for Dinosaur: A Rhyme Book and More.* Green Forest: Master Books.

Holmes, Andy, and Tim O'Connor (ill.). 2008. *My Pajama Bybel: 30 Bybelstories vir Slaaptyd.* Vereeniging: Christian Art Kids.

Indaba Ebalulekile Kunazo Zonke Ezake Zaxoxwa. 1999. Translated by Manie van den Heever. Vereeniging: Christelike Uitgewersmaatskappy.

Kinane e e Gaisang Tsothle: The Most Important Story Ever Told. 2002. Translated by Johannes Kelber. Vereeniging: Christelike Uitgewersmaatskappy.

Larsen, Carolyn, and Caron Turk (ill.). 2009. *Bedtime Blessings for Girls.* Vereeniging: Christian Art Kids.

Larsen, Carolyn, and Rick Incrocci (ill.). 1995. *My Slaaptyd-Bybel: 365 Dagstukkies vir Kinders.* Translated by Rosalie van Aswegen. Adapted by Solly Ozrovech. Vereeniging: Christelike Uitgewersmaatskappy.

Matthews, Mike. 2007. "Meeting Scientists behind Closed Doors: A Museum Scriptwriter Shares His Inside Story." *Answers* 2:96–97.

Morris, Henry. 2000. *The Long War against God: The History and Impact of The Creation/Evolution Conflict.* Green Forest: Master Books.

The Most Important Story Ever Told. 2000. Vereeniging: Christelike Uitgewersmaatskappy.

My Favorite Bible Storybook for Toddlers. 2003. Vereeniging: Christian Art Publishers.

Numbers, Ronald L. 1982. "Creationism in 20th-Century America." *Science* 218:538–44.

———. 1999. "Creating Creationism: Meanings and Uses since the Age of Agassiz." Pages 234–43 in *Evangelicals and Science in Historical Perspective.* Edited by D. N. Livingstone, D. G. Hart, and M. A. Noll. Oxford: Oxford University Press.

Oittinen, Riitta. 2006. "No Innocent Act: On the Ethics of Translating for Children." Pages 35–45 in *Children's Literature in Translation: Challenges and Strategies.* Edited by Jan Van Coillie and Walter P. Verschueren. Manchester: St. Jerome.

Prout, Alan. 2008. "Culture—Nature and the Construction of Childhood." Pages 21–35 in *The International Handbook of Children, Media, and Culture.* Edited by Kirsten Drotner and Sonia Livingstone. Los Angeles: Sage.

Sánchez-Eppler, Karen. 1996. "Raising Empires like Children: Race, Nation, and Religious Education." *American Literary History* 8:399–425.

Schine Gold, Penny. 2004. *Making the Bible Modern: Children's Bibles and Jewish Education in Twentieth-Century America.* Ithaca: Cornell University Press.

Schrag, Calvin O. 2006. "Otherness and the Problem of Evil: How Does That Which Is Other Become Evil?" *International Journal for Philosophy of Religion* 60:149–56.

Shavit, Zohar. 2006. "Translation of Children's Literature." Pages 25–40 in *The Translation of Children's Literature: A Reader*. Edited by Gillian Lathey. Clevedon: Multilingual Matters.

"Teaching the Truth from an Early Age." 2007. *Answers* 2:94.

Looking into the Lions' Den:
Otherness, Ideology, and Illustration
in Children's Versions of Daniel 6

Hugh S. Pyper

In her introduction to the Dover edition of Gustave Doré's Bible illustrations, that staple amusement of those nineteenth-century children who were forbidden frivolous books on Sunday, Millicent Rose discusses the scenes that she judges are particularly "for the children." She points to those including "the Biblical animals: Daniel's lions, the dogs who ate Jezebel, the she bears who punished the small boys who made fun of Elisha, all were brought to life in convincing form" (1974, ix). "For the children": a list of scenes where people, including children, are devoured by animals.[1] Rose seems oblivious to the ghoulish implications of selecting just these stories, but my argument in this essay will be that she has unconsciously hit upon a key element that sheds an interesting light on the question of the ideology of otherness in children's Bibles and their illustrations.

It is undeniable that she is far from alone in seeing the story of Daniel and the lions as one that is somehow particularly appropriate for children. By my reckoning, there are some fifty adaptations of this story in Dan 6 currently available on Amazon as illustrated books for children or picturebooks. That does not take into account at least as many versions of the story to be found in complete children's Bibles and other collections, where Dan 6 is one of the standard components. Yet why this is so bears further examination.

---

1. A fascinating treatment of the interpretation history of the story of Elisha and the bears that deals explicitly with the attitudes to children that this history reveals is to be found in Ziolkowski 2001.

It is not as if this is a story that obviously involves children. Children make only one fleeting appearance in this chapter of Daniel; indeed, that is the only time they are mentioned in the entire book.[2] Daniel 6:24 tells us that, after Daniel's rescue, King Darius has his accusers "with their children and their wives" thrown into the lions' den: "and before they reached the bottom of the den, the lions overpowered them and broke all their bones to pieces." That is how children appear in this story: torn apart by lions as innocent accomplices in their fathers' crimes, apparently with the approval of the king, the narrator, and God.

I have yet to find a version of Daniel for children that includes this detail.[3] Indeed, many versions omit the demise of the plotters against Daniel altogether, ending the story with the happy reconciliation of Daniel with the king. Others, for interesting reasons, make a feature of the plotters' death. No illustrations are known to me, however, where children and women appear in this final scene, let alone being included in the grisly feast. If children's literature is, as some have defined it, "literature with something left out," rather counterintuitively what is left out on this occasion are the children. This makes it all the more intriguing to ask what is going on, consciously and unconsciously, in the composition of children's versions of Daniel and what makes it so popular. At the least, the suggestion that the appeal to children has to be made by suppressing the mention of children raises a question.

---

2. I owe thanks to my former doctoral student Matt Hazell for this insight. Undeniably, the situation is complicated by the choice of the KJV translators, following their predecessors, to use "children" as the translation of *yeladim* in Dan 1:3, 4, 5, 6, 13, 17. The Vulgate translates the word as *pueri* (boys), and this is picked up by the JB, for instance. The association between Daniel and children is thus made explicit in the Western, and subsequently the English-speaking, traditions in a way that is not the case in the Hebrew. Most contemporary translations use a less age-specific expression such as "youths" or "young men" throughout Dan 1, in keeping with the semantic range of the Hebrew term. No translation, however, refers to Daniel in Dan 6 as a child.

3. In the course of this research, I examined in detail twenty currently available illustrated versions of the story of Daniel in the lions' den, but have scanned many more illustrations from a range of historical periods. None include the children of the advisors. Almost all, however, figure lions prominently on the cover.

"Dare to Be a Daniel"

Why then is Dan 6 so popular in adaptations for children? One reason is made explicit in the chorus of a popular hymn written in 1873 by Philip Bliss for his Sunday school class at the First Congregationalist Church, Chicago:

> Dare to be a Daniel!
> Dare to stand alone!
> Dare to have a purpose firm!
> Dare to make it known.[4]

There is an assumption that the young singers of this lusty chorus not only know Daniel's story, but should take him as a role model in the courageous assertion of an individual commitment to moral values in the face of the threats of the wider community. The ideal is for the child to identify with Daniel in a way that seems to ignore the gap in time, culture, experience, and expectations between the text and the child as reader. This aim is starkly set out in the "Faith Parenting Guide" helpfully provided at the end of *Daniel in the Dangerous Den*, a retelling of Dan 6 by the quaintly named duo Bek and Barb, which unequivocally states: "Life Issue: I want my child to follow God instead of man" and suggests finding pictures of "firefighters, police officers, nurses and disabled people" as a spur to this (2006, 26).

Yet this list of contemporary role models points to a key problem for any adaptors of Daniel who share this pedagogical approach. The aim is for the child to identify with a character in an ancient story, in an unfamiliar culture with unfamiliar aims and goals. Daniel is an adult, one of the three governors of Darius's empire, set within the world of the court in Babylon under the Medes. He is a Jewish visionary who speaks of angels, faces death under a code of law in a pit of wild beasts, and is the victim of a court intrigue; hardly a figure that the contemporary child is likely to encounter.

The book of Daniel and this story are replete with otherness. There is the otherness of the ancient Babylonian setting and of the Median court and its customs. This is compounded by the otherness of the animal world of the lions and the otherness of the angel. Perhaps most significantly is

---

4. For both the words and music, and a brief biography of Philip Bliss, see http://www.cyberhymnal.org/htm/d/a/daretobe.htm.

the otherness of Daniel as an adult and as a Jew. The latter may be more of an issue for the Christian appropriation of the story, but even for Jewish readers, an otherness exists: Daniel is not a twenty-first-century Jew of any persuasion.

Such problems are made if anything more acute for the illustrator of this story. Indeed, the very act of illustrating the biblical text is itself problematic, given the prohibitions on visual representation in the biblical text itself and the lack of visual evidence for ancient Jewish culture. How is an illustrator to convey both the otherness of the situation while maintaining the reader's identification with the characters, especially if the aim of the book is the kind of moral education that seems to be envisaged?

This problem of identification is compounded by any commercially successful book for children having to take account of at least two audiences: the child readers and the adults who read the book along with the child and who, more significantly, are very likely to have bought it in the first place. A book will be a commercial success only when both audiences are satisfied. What adult purchasers and readers respond to and what they think the child needs and wants matters quite as much as, if not more than, the preferences of the child.

All children's literature thus exemplifies a particularly clear form of what Bakhtin (1984, 185) calls "double-voicedness," in that the text and illustrations that serve as a transaction between child reader and author always also carry a dialogue between the adult producer of the book and the adult consumer, whether purchaser or reader. Both text and pictures are double voiced, at least. Indeed, when biblical stories are involved, there is almost always a third voice: either that of the religious authorities who may endorse the book and who may have published or commissioned it, or the voice of the publisher or author who has opted *not* to seek the endorsement of any such authority and is thus by default making their own ideological statement about the authority and role of the text.[5]

This is made unusually explicit in the editorial afterword addressed to parents in Louise Ulmer's *Daniel and the Roaring Lions*. This postscript is not ascribed to the author but to the editor as the voice of the approved interpretation of the text. In addition, a further layer of communication is also explicitly invoked, that of the angelic and divine and of the reader:

---

5. For an interesting discussion of many of these issues of the way that children are shaped by text and pictures in children's books, see Stephens 1992.

Dear Parents

Children delight in the trickery and bold action in this story. Let them enjoy the story at that level, but help them to also understand that God sends His angels to protect them in all situations. Discuss times when God's angels have obviously been on duty—a close call in the car, an accident while playing, a time when someone has been ill. Pray with your child, thanking God for His care and for sending His angels to surround you. (Ulmer 2009, 12)

The postscript continues in a tone that clearly implies that the adult reader is expected to be a model of Christian living, with an explicit (if problematic) theology of providence and belief in guardian angels and always on the lookout for an opportunity for mission. One suspects most parents who share the faith of the editor would find this an embarrassing reminder of their shortcomings with a didactic intent for the parent, let alone the child. Those who do not would find it off-putting.

The text and illustrations of such a retelling of a biblical tale, then, may be very simple at one level, but operate in a complex matrix of communication of which the child reader is only one component and where the author and illustrator are under complex constraints from competing ideological positions. There is not only an ideological component to such texts as contemporary pedagogical material. The author is not creating but adapting a biblical text that carries its own authority and ideology and to which the author must be responsible.

Yet, as the example above shows, for a child reader it is not sufficient to appeal to authority. Indeed, the existence of such retellings comes about because presenting the authoritative biblical text to children does not have the desired outcome. Paradoxically, it is the authority of the text that permits and requires the adaptation of it. In the light of all this, it may seem that the illustration of the story of Daniel and the lions as if it transparently conveys a simple moral lesson is almost impossible. Yet, as remarked before, such books exist in large numbers and continue to sell. My contention is that this is despite rather than because of the moral value that it may have and that the secret of this story's popularity is rather different.

In Charlotte Brontë's novel *Villette*, first published in 1853, there is an intriguing allusion to a child's reaction to the story of Daniel and the lions that may get us further. The narrator is describing the Sunday evening activities of the little girl Paulina:

> To the hymn would succeed some reading—perhaps a chapter in the
> Bible; correction was seldom required here, for the child could read
> any simple narrative chapter very well; and, when the subject was such
> as she could understand and take an interest in, her expression and
> emphasis were something remarkable. Joseph cast into the pit; the call-
> ing of Samuel; Daniel in the lion's den;—these were favourite passages:
> of the first especially she seemed perfectly to feel the pathos. (Brontë
> 1853, 25)

The stories are engaging this child at a level of emotional identification
very different from didactic moralism.[6] In what follows, I want to review
some of the ways in which illustrators have attempted to facilitate this
identification and to overcome the obstacles of the otherness of the book.
Furthermore, I want to suggest that the book of Daniel itself is at least one,
not insignificant, source of some of the strategies to deal with otherness
that have been adopted in the development of illustrated children's Bibles.
Moreover, it is at least one source of the impulse that suggested and permitted the development of this anomalous genre.

Daniel and Illustrating the Other

Daniel is a book that deals not just with the otherness of cultures but
also with the issue of communication between those who experience each
other as other. Throughout the book, there are scenes of reading where
the literal text is rewritten in the interest of interpretation as Daniel, or
his angelic instructors in later chapters, explain the cryptic meaning of
texts. Daniel's great feat of reading the writing on the wall in Dan 5, for
instance, is not so much a reading as a rewriting of the inscription. The
leap from the literal "mene, mene, tekel upharsin" (5:25) inscribed by the
mysterious hand to Daniel's "you have been weighed in the balance and
found wanting" (5:27) is far more than mere transcription or translation.
In order to get the message across to those who cannot either read or

---

6. In light of the argument of the rest of the essay, it may be significant that some
kind of wild ravening beast has a role in the story of Joseph in the pit as well. His
brothers plot to cover his death by a story that he has been eaten by an animal in Gen
37:20. Interestingly, they never actually allege this to Jacob. In 37:33 they merely hand
him the bloodstained and torn garment, and this is the conclusion Jacob reaches on
his own. Both Joseph and Daniel, in different ways, are the unexpectedly untouched
survivors of a supposed carnivorous attack.

understand it, Daniel rephrases and paraphrases the text. In turn, Daniel has to have Jeremiah's text rephrased for him and indeed increasingly fails to understand what he is told by the angels in the later chapters, even with their explanations.

Yet Daniel is not simply about reading letters and language, although nothing could be clearer than that this is a key element of the book, given the explicit reference to the programmatic education of Daniel and his companions in the "language and letters of the Chaldeans" in Dan 1:4. It is also a book full of visual images and the difficulty and necessity of interpreting them. In the story of Belshazzar, for instance, everyone but Daniel is reduced to functional illiteracy and cannot decipher the writing. What can be seen, however, is the image of the heavenly handwriting, and the narrator then gives a graphic visual description of the king's response as his face darkens, his limbs loosen, and his knees knock together. Belshazzar is displayed in his response to a striking visual stimulus, the meaning of which he cannot grasp. Scenes such as this have been grist to the mill for painters. The book is replete with dreams and visions that are described and then have to be interpreted. It is what people, Daniel included, *see* in these dreams and in visions—extraordinary monsters, mysterious trees, unidentifiable figures—that has to be described and explained, quite as much as what they hear or read.

This somewhat surprising importance of the visual image in the book is also part of its hybrid situation between Jewish and Babylonian culture. The fierce iconoclasm of the biblical culture is here met with the lavish iconic traditions of Babylon and the cultures that inhabited it. The great statue that Nebuchadnezzar sees in his dream in Dan 2:31–35, for instance, is both alien to the Jewish tradition but necessary for the allegorical point to be made, and we see the influence of this iconic tradition in the later chapters when the mysterious Ancient of Days appears and is described in ways that pick up Babylonian imagery.

In the way that so often happens in texts where one community's identity is being defended against a more powerful alternative, the effort to describe the threatening other—and the visual culture of Babylon is presented throughout the Bible as a potential threat to Israel's aniconic monotheism—means that the language and ideology of the other has to be incorporated into the language of the community that is resistant to it. Not only are Persian, Greek, and Aramaic words, not to mention Aramaic itself, incorporated into the text of Daniel, but in order to decry idolatry, idols and their worship have to be described.

This emphasis on the visual spills out into the rest of the book as well. Although the book of Daniel shares the general reticence of biblical literature over the description of characters and scene-setting, it nevertheless has a strong interest in what they look like and how this affects those who see them. Granted that none of the major characters is described in detail, their appearance certainly matters in determining their fate. We know that Daniel and his friends were chosen for their special role in the first place because they were "without blemish" and "handsome" (1:4) and that Daniel in particular then finds favor "in the sight of" the chief eunuch (1:9). The eunuch, in turn, is worried about Daniel's decision to fast because of the effect that this may have on the way he looks and, in turn, the impression that a less than perfect appearance may make on the king. In the end, it is the superior appearance of the four Judahites that vindicates their dietary peculiarities and confirms their status in the court.

In Dan 6 itself, what is seen and not seen is an important element of the narrative strategy. On hearing that the king's decree has been signed, Daniel goes to his house to pray. The narrator adds the detail that "he had windows in his upper chamber open towards Jerusalem" (6:10). This detail of the open windows, besides being one of only three mentions of the city of Jerusalem in the book, foregrounds the visual.[7] An open window works in two directions. If he can see out, the window presents the possibility that Daniel's accusers can see in and see him praying. That our attention is clearly drawn to his physical posture in prayer supports this: "he got down upon his knees three times a day and prayed" (6:10). Although the text never explicitly says that his enemies saw him through the window, as readers we watch him, perhaps through the window, and may surmise that his enemies do so too.

The counterpart of this emphasis on the visible, however, is that what is not seen also comes to play a significant role. The key episode of this chapter, Daniel's encounter with the lions, takes place in the dark. It is explicitly stated that the king gives up his attempt to rescue Daniel only

---

7. We know, of course, that Jerusalem is not visible from Daniel's window, but that simply adds another potential layer of poignancy to the text as we imagine Daniel forlornly gazing into the distance toward the home he cannot see, but that he knows lies beyond the horizon. The invisibility of the city merely adds to the longing and may, indeed, intensify his gaze as, for instance, in the common trope of the lover gazing out to sea in the hope of spotting a returning sail.

once the sun has set. It is dark by the time that Daniel is cast into the den. This is then sealed with a stone, blocking any possibility of light being shed on what happens. All during that night, however, the king's eyes remain open, although there is nothing to see. Sleep, we are told, "fled from him" (6:18), so we readers watch him gazing into the darkness.

At sunrise, when the king comes to discover Daniel's fate, he calls out to him from a distance in order to ascertain whether he is alive. This strongly suggests that he cannot see what has happened to Daniel, and the logic of the situation would suggest that this is impossible. The text is clear that the king has not even reached the den, let alone unsealed and moved the stone, when he calls out. The recognition scene is aural rather than visual. A return to the visual is implied, however, after Daniel is rescued and "no kind of hurt" (6:23) is found on him.

In the biblical text, we have only Daniel's report of his encounter with the lions, with no description of what happens apart from the mysterious intervention of the angel. There is literally nothing to see in the text, both because there is no account of the crucial moment and because it is set in an impenetrable darkness; the night is compounded by the pit sealed with a stone. All the king knows is that, incredibly, Daniel has survived and, by his own account, because of angelic intervention.

This cryptic visual dimension is crucial to the book's communicative strategy. The reporting of what a character sees, whether in reality or in dreams, leaves the readers with the same problem of interpretation that the character or his hearers have. We see what they see, or what they say they see, but have no more idea of what the significance of it is than they do. We are drawn into a re-creative act of visualization. The words conjure a picture, but what does the picture mean? A picture may paint a thousand words, but the question is *which* thousand words? Time and again, Daniel reveals the gap between seeing and understanding: "When I, Daniel, had seen the vision, I sought to understand it," he says quite plainly in 8:15. What is seen needs interpretation or, in other words, needs to be read.

THE RECOGNIZABLE OTHER

One of the key elements in the education of any child is the ability to categorize and to assign individual people or objects to the correct culturally and linguistically recognized categories. The process of language learning inevitably entails this, and the possession of language allows the categories to be refined. For instance, a child needs to learn that a Chihuahua and a Great Dane both fall into the category "dog" even though the Chihuahua may be closer in size and color to a cat. Size and color are obvious but in this case misleading criteria for categorization.

The same holds true with categories of people. The liberal message of the shared humanity of all people is itself a learned method of categorization just as much as any approach that seeks to teach children to discriminate between human beings on racial or cultural grounds. A child educated in a liberal environment has to learn which differences are considered essential and which are merely accidental and to look past obvious differences in color, language, and facial features to see the common humanity.[8]

At the same time, the child learns to negotiate the difference between the human and the animal worlds, again being taught what features are significant. Almost inevitably, however, the child interiorizes the categories she learns as natural categories, and indeed the ability to assign objects to the correct linguistic class without a prolonged process of assessment is vital if a child is to function in a given society. Indeed, in many circumstances the adult educator is in the business of affirming the naturalness of the classifications that are offered. This both confirms and conceals the ideological basis of any educational process.

This process applies to visual as well as linguistic categories. Children learn quickly what the conventional representation of a duck rather than a hen, or a rabbit rather than a rat, may be. Picturebooks are a key tool in learning this kind of visual vocabulary. The skill of recognizing a character and following its progress through a pictorial narrative where it may be depicted from different angles, at different sizes, and in different colors is a sophisticated one. It depends on the child being able to sort out the significant features that give continuity to the character from the accidental ones that reflect the changes due to the plot circumstances in which the character finds himself or herself. Yet there are clearly ideological assumptions behind the choices that the illustrator makes in order to mediate the need to register and educate on difference and the clues

---

8. Considerable literature is now available on the way in which illustrated children's books are read by children and the skills that this requires and instills. Two works I have found particularly useful are Lewis 2001 and Nikolajeva and Scott 2006. Also illuminating in the way that it offers empirical research on children's own responses to picturebooks is Arizpe and Styles 2003.

that are offered to identification in the complex set of communications outlined above. It is illuminating to look at some of the strategies that illustrators have adopted in dealing with specific aspects of the otherness of the book of Daniel.

The Otherness of Daniel

All the illustrations I have examined set Daniel historically in terms of the costumes of the characters and the physical environment. Typically, the characters wear tunics or robes. They are set apart as recognizably biblical characters. What does vary, however, is how far the historical verisimilitude is taken. We have already mentioned that Daniel represents a meeting of the aniconic biblical traditions and the visual culture of Babylon. For illustrators, Babylon is a treasure trove of archeological information, and since the late nineteenth century, monuments such as the Ishtar Gate and great ziggurats and the portraits of kings and even of more common life have penetrated into the popular consciousness. Hence, in many versions of the Daniel story, the gates and walls of the city are at least recognizable, and the king and his courtiers have the long curled beards and hairstyle that are popularly attributed to the Babylonians, although some of the iconography is more clearly Assyrian than Babylonian. We might inquire, however, for which of the complex constituency of readers of such books this is intended. Do child readers worry about the presence of the Ishtar Gate, or is it not rather either the adult purchaser, or the editorial oversight, who appreciates and responds to this level of accuracy?

In addition, verisimilitude is not truth, but can be easily mistaken for a claim to truth. Setting Daniel in a historically verifiable Babylonian context makes it easier to slip into or confirm an assumption that the historical Babylon was home to a historical Daniel. It is notable, for instance, that some children's Bibles for older children adopt a style of illustration that draws the book into the world of the historical encyclopedia, with labeled vignettes of historical and architectural sites and artifacts, evoking a subtle claim of historicity.

Yet, there are problems with this. For younger children, especially, Babylonian costume does not trigger the recognition of the roles of the characters. A vital character in Dan 6 is the king, and everyone knows that a king is identifiable by a crown, made of gold and with a number of points. This is not part of the royal regalia of Babylon. Does the illustrator go with the historically accurate but unrecognizable insignia or does he evoke another visual language, that most clearly associated with fairy stories with their courtly settings? That, of course, has its own implications for claims of verisimilitude by putting it into another generic orbit.

A particular problem in the book of Daniel, however, is the depiction of Daniel himself. As discussed above, Daniel is the character often held up as a model for imitation by the child, but it is clear that at this stage he is no child himself. Nothing in the text, however, specifies his age, and again we find a range of solutions in the illustrations. Again for younger children, we may find that Daniel's role in government is played down so that he can be depicted as a young protégé of the king. At the other extreme, Daniel is depicted as a grandfatherly figure, often with a comic edge, allowing a different kind of unthreatening possibility of identification. There are versions where Daniel is a middle-aged man, and others where he is more of an action hero, but these are rarer, partly because either as a young or old man Daniel is a more vulnerable prey for the lions.

The aspect of Daniel that is most striking by its absence in almost all the versions I have consulted, however, is his Jewishness. It is not entirely easy, however, to work out how an illustrator could do this without being accused of stereotyping. In any case, what elements would be used to identify him? Most of the distinctive visual symbols of contemporary Judaism would be anachronistic in Babylon. Even depictions of this story in explicitly Jewish versions do not clearly mark Daniel in this way. In books with a Christian prominence, references to Judaism and the Jewishness of Daniel and his friends are almost entirely missing in the texts as well as the illustrations. Christian children are asked to identify with a Daniel who prays devoutly in a way that is entirely assimilable into Christian practice and spirituality. At most, there may be a reference to Daniel's orientation toward Jerusalem as he prays, but this aspect of Daniel's otherness for non-Jewish readers is almost always simply glossed over.

More interesting is how the advisers of the king who betray Daniel are portrayed. One might naïvely think that children have little idea of such conspiracy, yet the jealous gossip and bullying of the playground make these figures all too familiar.[9] Almost without exception, the advisers are

---

9. The familiarity of this scenario is evoked in the title of Mary Manz Simons's *Daniel and the Tattletales* (1993), one of the very few versions not to have either the lions or the pit in the title. The cover illustration, however, has the usual lions well displayed.

depicted as dark-haired and bearded, perhaps reflecting the illustrator's assumptions about their ethnic background and appearance. Again, it would be easy, and at times quite accurate, to accuse the illustrators of stereotyping these Middle Eastern characters with their flowing robes, prominent noses, dark eyes and flowing hair and beards, and venial characters.

The king, however, is another matter. He should be the villain, but is actually on Daniel's side. Illustrators thus have the task of making him a sympathetic enemy. This is often accomplished by giving him comic attributes. Not unusually, he is smaller and/or fatter than his advisers, and it is not unusual for the king to be less obviously "Middle Eastern" in looks, thus reinforcing the stereotypes in a negative way. On the other hand, illustrators might defend themselves by asking quite legitimately how they are supposed to convey the nature of the characters to children without invoking stereotypes. The circularity of this issue comes to the fore again.

CHILDHOOD AND POSTCOLONIAL THEORY

In order to learn the visual language, children have to be introduced to recognizable stereotypes, yet by that very token stereotypes are reinforced and reapplied. In the case of biblical stories with their Eastern setting, it is hard not to invoke in such discussions the figure of Edward Said and to consider the way in which such depictions rely on and perpetuate the stereotypes of orientalism.

One writer who does make the connection between postcolonialism, and in particular orientalism, in Said's terms, and children's literature is Perry Nodelman.[10] Children's literature is an attempt to colonize the child, he argues, in the child's own interests, a sentiment to be found in some colonial statements. However, in this case, the child is being educated to be a colonizer in his or her own right. That could, at one level, be a reading of what happens to Daniel and his companions in Dan 1. Daniel, after all, rises to the highest office in the kingdom and there is no suggestion that

---

10. Nodelman's *The Hidden Adult: Defining Children's Literature* (2008) is the fruit of a long career devoted to exploring the distinctiveness of children's literature as a literary form, and in particular to the way in which adult agendas and experience are hidden in seemingly innocent texts. Although he does not explicitly engage with biblical retellings, by their very nature these demonstrate this phenomenon in a particularly prominent way.

he uses his position to subvert the colonial ambitions of his royal masters. His skills are used to preserve the king and his kingdom.

However, Nodelman underestimates the ambivalent relationship to the colonial authority that is also a clear parallel between writers for children and postcolonial writers. The children's writer does not necessarily represent the didactic voice of a colonial authority. The adult writing for children once was a child, just as the African novelist writing of village life once was a villager, even if the very education that has enabled him or her to write of that life has inevitably estranged him from it. Granted that, as Jacqueline Rose insists, all children's literature is about an imagined child, written by adults; all novelists who purport to give a voice to and celebrate a preliterate or certainly non-novel-reading local identity are caught in the same dilemma.[11]

There is an added complexity in this, of course, in that the adult writer for children is giving the child the tools that will bring him or her into the world of adult literacy and articulateness. The innocence that is being celebrated is being at least potentially subverted by the tools of literacy. However wholesome the book that a child learns to read from, she or he is gaining practice in using the tools with which to read unwholesome books as well.

On the other hand, we can get too nostalgic about such things. The writer who celebrates the loss of village solidarity does not often relinquish the material and cultural gains of his education and indeed may well be pressing for the relief of political and economic oppression for those she or he remembers. Equally, it is not as if children remain children in the absence of children's literature; they grow and mature innately, and children's literature can hardly be seen as the sole cause of that. The fantasy of Peter Pan is just that: a fantasy, impossible in practice and, on examination, not an enviable state of being.

It is intriguing that, just as Daniel is perpetually being adapted for children, it is increasingly being read through the lens of postcolonial theory. Is there some feature, or cluster of features, in both children's literature and postcolonial literature that ties together their appeal to the child and their ability to speak across cultures and age groups despite their manifest cultural specificity?

---

11. Rose's *The Case of Peter Pan* (1984) is a classic study that explores the implications of the obvious but often disregarded fact that children's literature is written by adults and that the child depicted in them is an adult construct.

The clue to what is going on, I think, is a consequence of the link between education, literacy, authority, and identity. The empire understands itself as a teacher, educating barbaric populations; teachers can then be seen as instruments of a social or generational imperialism toward children. Phillips writes:

> In its classic formulation the moment of imperialism is also the moment of education. Imperialism—a system of economic, political and cultural force that disavows borders in order to extract desirable resources and exploit an alien people—has never strayed far from a field of pedagogical imperatives, or what might be called an ideology of instruction. (Phillips 1993, 26)[12]

If education is the key to the imperial moment, however, it should be no surprise if stories of resistance to imperialism are stories of resistance to education or, more accurately, to the assumed superiority that gives one party the right to educate the other and to determine what education means.

Education and the resistance to the imposition of the cultural norms of adulthood are also the stock-in-trade of children's books. The more solemnly the text imparts the moral lessons that the adult world hopes to inculcate, the less attractive it may seem to the child. So too in Daniel, Dan 1 is not the chapter of choice for children's adaptations, but Dan 6 and Daniel's encounter with the lions. Almost all the children's versions of this story open up the pit and reveal the interaction between Daniel and the beasts, literally shedding light on a narrative passage that remains obscure and thus having to play fast and loose with the biblical idea of the pit. Somehow, in the face of the didactic readings, the lions reassert themselves visibly in the illustrations as a kind of eruption of the subtext or the repressed elements of the story that are withheld from the child reader in such moralistic adaptations.

The Lion's-Eye View

That the animals Daniel faces are lions is highly significant. Quite apart from their iconic connection with Babylon, lions abound in the rest of the

---

12. Phillips is polemicizing against Allan Bloom's *Closing of the American Mind*, which he sees as reinstating the colonial view of education.

Bible but in the peculiarly inconsistent ways characteristic of the cultural reception of the lion throughout the ages.[13] Popular surveys regularly find lions placed high both in the list of most feared animals and in the list of favorites of children. They are both loved and dreaded; as such, they become the living embodiment of ambivalence. They perform this function in the biblical texts as well. After all, Daniel may be rescued from lions, but other prophetic figures are among those who fall victim to lions sent as divine punishment (e.g., the man of god in 1 Kgs 13, the disobedient prophet in 20:36). Lions are figures for the heroes of Israel: in his blessings, Jacob likens Judah to a lion, and Moses likens both Gad and Dan to lions. Israel itself is a lion that attacks the nations (Mic 5:8) but also roars against Yahweh (Jer 12:8). The lion represents both the nation and its enemies, both its zeal for Yahweh and its rebelliousness.

Most importantly, however, Yahweh himself is compared to a lion, with the same ambivalence of protection and threat. He roars from Zion before attacking the nations in Amos's vision, but more often he roars against Israel as covenant breakers. In direct opposition to his metaphorical role as a shepherd, he becomes the predator who attacks his own flock, either the nation (Hos 4:16) or specific individuals: Job (Job 10:16), Hezekiah (Isa 28:13), or the writer of Lamentations (Lam 3:10).

In the light of this crucial but ambivalent role that lions play in the Bible and in wider cultural symbolism, it is instructive to turn to an interesting subgroup of Daniel retellings that are particularly revealing in regard to this subterranean stratum in the story. Those are tellings that take the lion's point of view. Read in this way, the story of Daniel is a rather frustrating one. Tim Dowley's *Lion Misses Breakfast* (2004) takes this approach for very young readers and ends with a disgruntled young lion, who has missed his breakfast, watching Daniel climb out of the pit. This leaves the reader rather unsatisfied as the main character, the lion, is himself left frustrated at the end of the story.

More to the point is the rather wonderful *Dinner in the Lions' Den* by Bob Hartman and Tim Raglin (2006). Featuring a frankly elderly and disheveled Daniel, the bulk of this story occurs in the pit, which is remarkably well lit, and concerns the various ploys of the angel to distract the

---

13. For a brief but rich exploration of the cultural symbolism of the lion through the centuries, see Jackson 2010. The definitive work on the lion in the Bible is Strawn 2005, which gives an encyclopedic reading of references to the lion, literal and metaphorical, in the Old Testament and other ancient Near Eastern literature.

lions by playing with them and offering them displacement activities every time they ask, "What time is it now, Mr Angel?" The story this time ends not with Daniel's rescue but with the dismayed-looking advisers being lowered into the den (minus wives and children, of course). Father Lion addresses the angel who has distracted the lions by rubbing their bellies as he prepares to depart to heaven with the formulaic question that has recurred during the narrative: "'What time is it now, Mr Angel?' The angel looked at Daniel's enemies, grinned a wide cat grin and said, 'What time is it now? IT'S DINNER TIME!'" (2006, 24). The illustrations for this version play up the way that the lion as predator and the lion as playful kitten writ large meld into one another but equally make no bones about the fate of the advisors. It is clear that they deserve no less.

EDIBLE BUT NOT EATEN

Hartman and Raglin's retelling is remarkable in the way it reveals how the appeal of this chapter can be related to a recurrent element in children's literature, brilliantly analyzed by Marina Warner in her book *No Go the Bogeyman*.[14] Warner points out how stories of wolves, bears, and lions gain a hold over the childish audience by playing on the fascination and fear of the notion of being devoured, being good enough to eat, of becoming meat rather than flesh.

Her argument relates to that of psychoanalyst Dorothy Bloch in her study of the child's fear of infanticide entitled "*So the Witch Won't Eat Me*" (1979). Bloch argues that the sense of vulnerability is pervasive in childhood. Children live in fear of the possibility that their parents might kill them. The underlying premise that leads the child to this conclusion is actually quite understandable. Anything or anyone that has the strength to defend me also has the power to hurt or kill me and so needs to be treated carefully. Childhood fantasies are a way of displacing the fear of being killed away from the parents and from other adults around the child onto less immediately threatening figures. Bloch sees such fantasies as defensive.

----

14. Warner 2000 is a dazzling exploration of the themes of this essay and part of an oeuvre that is essential reading in exploring the psychology and cultural impact of children's literature. Particularly relevant is chap. 6: "Now … We Can Begin to Feed" (136–60). For a further discussion of the points in this paragraph, see the chapter "The Bible as Wolf: Tracking a Carrollian Metaphor" in Pyper 2005.

Bloch's approach and that of Warner shed interesting light on each other. If they are correct, the depth of the child's interest in the story of someone who was on the lion's menu and yet was not eaten is due to its relevance for their own negotiation of their otherness and the relation between the child and the adult world. Animals as symbols are an important means of negotiating such relationships. Anthropological studies of totemism reveal that the adoption of a totemic animal is a widespread strategy for individuals and groups to express the characteristics, but also the ambivalences, of their identity. So too with children. It is not accidental that the pets of choice for much of the human race are predatory animals, miniaturized and often infantilized versions of much more fearsome creatures. Both dogs and cats retain the potential to do harm and can flash formidable teeth, but in many breeds this potential is diluted by their size and by selective breeding to make their features more childlike, with flattened faces, larger eyes and rounder heads. Nor is it accidental that anthropomorphized animals, again often clearly infantilized in their depiction, are such a feature of children's literature. By transposing the anxieties of human interaction on to the more manageable and yet legitimate otherness of the animal, a kind of distance can be set up that makes negotiating the anxieties of human relationships easier.

The ambivalent position of the lion, which is both the most formidable of predators and yet at other times can resemble the child's beloved pet cat writ large, makes it particularly suitable to play this role of the other that could be friend or enemy, protector or attacker. The story of Daniel acknowledges the reality of the danger this duality represents, but also shows that it can be survived.

From this point of view, another important figure in the appeal of this chapter is the king. Clearly fond of Daniel and distressed by his fate, the king, who represents power and potential protection, finds himself trapped by his own promise and unable to offer Daniel the protection he needs. As such, he embodies the important lesson that protection is limited. Even a loving parent cannot always avert every threat and may in certain circumstances be obliged to expose the child to danger. Any child who has had to say farewell to a parent at the school gate, knowing that the day ahead brings encounters with teachers and fellow pupils that may be dangerous and unpleasant, knows that well-intentioned love can only go as far as the school gates. After that, you are on your own.

Yet this realization is not simply a spur to fear. Angela Carter recalled the way in which her maternal grandmother told her the story of Little

Red Riding Hood: "At the conclusion, when the wolf jumps on Little Red Riding Hood and gobbles her up, my grandmother used to pretend to eat me, which made me squeak and gibber with excited pleasure" (quoted in Tatar 1999, 9). There is pleasure as well as fear in this knowledge, as Hélène Cixous explains in her essay "Love of the Wolf" (1998, 84–99). Being good enough to eat is to know the affirmation and danger of being desirable. If we know we are edible, we know we have worth, that we are desired. It is a sad thing, we might summarize this idea, when no one thinks us even good enough to eat. What Cixous calls the "hallelujah moment" comes when someone who could—and would—eat us refrains from eating us.

To be immune to the danger of being devoured is to be undesired. There are, of course, sexual resonances to this, but we can be misled by a Freudian rush to sexual interpretation and overlook the reality of the ambivalence at the more surface level. As Freud himself made clear, the oldest opposition is "I should like to eat that, or I should like to spit it out." Cixous shows us the power of the third moment "because I find that so desirable to eat, I will refrain from eating it." Never mind the moral uprightness of Daniel; what he represents is the possibility of being threatened with being devoured and yet safe.

Conclusion

The story of Daniel and the lions' den is one place where this profound aspect of the power of biblical narrative comes explicitly to the surface. It is this, I submit, that leads to its power to generate retellings, and it is an insight that becomes particularly clear when this story is read in conjunction with other stories for children and in the light of the critical examination of such stories. It is also an aspect that may be concealed in the text of children's adaptations, but that is much more difficult to conceal in the illustrations where the presence of the lion and its combination of threat and companionship can be demonstrated.

It is also important to set this in terms of the wider function of the lion in the biblical world and in cultural history. As the epitome of the dangerous protector, the lion is taken up as a metaphor for Yahweh himself, in both aspects. Yahweh thus can take the story role of the beast that may devour, but may miraculously refrain. The Yahweh of biblical narrative could consume his faithful readers, as he does his enemies. That he does not do so, these stories tell them, is not because they are unpalatable to him. On the contrary, the reality is that they are good enough to eat and yet spared. Daring to be a Daniel is daring to confront the danger and promise of the story of Yahweh the lion who chooses to miss breakfast.

The popularity of illustrated versions of this chapter of the book of Daniel for children then is not because of its moral message. Through the medium of Daniel's encounters with the jealous advisers and the well-meaning king who in the end abandons him to his fate, and above all in his encounter with the lions who could eat him, but do not, children can work through their own sense of otherness in the adult world and in their family. Being edible means both being endangered *and* desired, a potential prey *and* a potential treasure to the lovable, loving, and dangerous world of adulthood. In the end, it is the child's sense of otherness that generates her simultaneous longing for and dread of assimilation into adulthood that is at stake.

In this sense, Millicent Rose in her evaluation of Doré spoke better than she knew. In Doré's illustrations and those of the many other illustrators of this story for children, we have the record of someone who has looked into the pit to see what happened to Daniel and has drawn the results for children to look at in turn. The illustrated books that show us Daniel and the lions are indeed just the thing "for the children." In them, beneath all the moral messages of faithfulness and the power of prayer, children can find an expression of their fear both of being eaten and of being rejected by their devouring and loving protectors and the reassurance that those who can eat you can choose not to.

Works Cited

Arizpe, Evelyn, and Morag Styles. 2003. *Children Reading Pictures: Interpreting Visual Texts*. London: Routledge.

Bakhtin, Mikhail. 1984. *Problems of Dostoyevsky's Poetics*. Translated and edited by Caryl Emerson. Minneapolis: University of Minnesota Press.

Bek and Barb. 2006. *Daniel in the Dangerous Den*. Colorado Springs: Cook Communications Ministries.

Bloch, Dorothy. 1979. *"So the Witch Won't Eat Me": Fantasy and the Child's Fear of Infanticide*. London: Burnett.

Bloom, Allan. 1987. *The Closing of the American Mind*. New York: Simon & Schuster.

Brontë, Charlotte [writing as Currer Bell]. 1853. *Villette*. New York: Harper.

Cixous, Hélène. 1998. *Stigmata: Escaping Texts*. London: Routledge.

Dowley, Tim, and Steve Smallman (ill.). 2004. *Lion Misses Breakfast.* Candle Books. London: Hudson.

Hartman, Bob, and Tim Raglin (ill.). 2006. *Dinner in the Lions' Den.* Oxford: Lion.

Jackson, Deirdre. 2010. *Lion.* London: Reaktion.

Lewis, David. 2001. *Reading Contemporary Picturebooks: Picturing Texts.* London: Routledge.

Nikolajeva, Maria, and Carole Scott. 2006. *How Picturebooks Work.* London: Routledge.

Nodelman, Perry. 2008. *The Hidden Adult: Defining Children's Literature.* Baltimore: Johns Hopkins University Press.

Phillips, Jerry. 1993. "Educating the Savages: Melville, Bloom, and the Rhetoric of Imperialist Instruction." Pages 25–44 in *Recasting the World: Writing after Colonialism.* Edited by Jonathan White. Parallax: Revisions of Culture and Society. Baltimore: Johns Hopkins University Press.

Pyper, Hugh S. 2005. *An Unsuitable Book: The Bible as Scandalous Text.* Sheffield: Sheffield Phoenix.

Rose, Jaqueline. 1984. *The Case of Peter Pan, or, The Impossibility of Children's Fiction.* London: Macmillan.

Rose, Millicent. 1974. "Introduction." Pages v–ix in G. Doré, *The Doré Bible Illustrations.* New York: Dover.

Simons, Mary Manz. 1993. *Daniel and the Tattletales.* St Louis: Concordia.

Stephens, John. 1992. *Language and Ideology in Children's Fiction.* Harlow: Longman.

Strawn, Brent A. 2005. *What Is Stronger Than a Lion? Leonine Image and Metaphor in the Hebrew Bible and the Ancient Near East.* Fribourg: Academic Press.

Tatar, Maria. 1999. *The Classic Fairy Tales.* New York: Norton.

Ulmer, Louise. 2009. *Daniel and the Roaring Lions: Daniel 6:1–28 for Children.* St Louis: Concordia.

Warner, Marina. 2000. *No Go the Bogeyman: Scaring, Lulling, and Making Mock.* London: Vintage.

Ziolkowski, Eric. 2001. *Evil Children in Religion, Literature, and Art.* Basingstoke: Palgrave.

The Other in South African Children's Bibles: Politics and (Biblical) Systems of Othering

Jeremy Punt

The connection between children and the (Christian) Bible has in the past often been privileged at various levels in popular perception. On the one hand, children and positive attributes associated with them were used metaphorically (if somewhat predictably) to express the nature of the Bible: simple, unassuming, and even conscious of their dependency on others. On the other hand, a popular notion found in milieus as diverse as church announcement bulletins and bookshop flyers is that, more than any other format of the Christian gospel, children's Bibles are unadulterated, pure, and free from any bias; and ironically with the suggestion that, if anything, children's Bibles are rather naïve since they are so unprejudiced.

A Disillusioned Naïveté

Ironically, since of late there has been increasing acknowledgement that children's Bibles, rather than offering a simple, naïve presentation of contentious material especially when it involves matters related to sexual encounters or a compromising portrayal of God, show traces of careful and deliberate choices that were made regarding the inclusion of material as well its content and presentation (Bottigheimer 1996). One good example is how the sixteenth- and seventeenth-century portrayal of the character of God in children's Bibles changes from "a violently wrathful being," with "righteous anger" and a "fearsome temperament," so as to incorporate a gentleness together with "participatory wisdom and benevolence" into God's character in the eighteenth century. In the nineteenth century, the "wise, paternal, kindly governor of the universe" slowly changed into the most recent stage of God as "a fond and loving overseer of humanity":

the wrathful God was changed into a God of mercy (Bottigheimer 1996, 59–69).[1] In fact, among diverse and disparate religious groups, similar patterns can be identified according to which Bible stories for children were transformed over time, starting out by staying close to the scriptural text, but with troubling texts subsequently revised until an amended story, sometimes extensively so, eventually emerged.

Such resourceful compositional modifications and adaptations took place for a variety of reasons, not all of which were operative simultaneously or equally strongly in different contexts, and which include: confessional considerations, authorial gender, nationality, upheavals such as wars, pedagogy, social dynamics, cultural lag, and before 1850 social class in particular. In one sense children's Bibles are not attempts to provide theological, psychological, or even pedagogical explanations of ancient texts proving difficult to understand, but are "children's books written by sixteenth- to twentieth-century authors for sixteenth- to twentieth-century children." In another sense, though, "for authors, buyers, and readers in nearly every age children's Bibles have seemed to be texts faithful to the Bible itself. But their authors' common effort to use the Bible to shape a meaningful present has produced Bible stories that mingle sacred text with secular values" (Bottigheimer 1996, 74, 218). Keeping this fabric of children's Bibles in mind is of vital importance when their relationship with (and also presence and possible influence in) a particular sociopolitical context is considered.

What follows is a brief investigation of some aspects of Afrikaans children's Bibles during the Apartheid years (roughly the second half of the twentieth century) in South Africa.[2] The inquiry takes two general notions about children's Bibles as its point of departure. First, given that children's

---

1. Such amendments, Bottigheimer argues, were already true even of the two progenitors of children's Bibles, namely, Peter Comestor's *Historia Scholastica* (1996, 22–23) and Martin Luther's *Passional* (33); illustrated Bibles were around even earlier, such as the Dutch *Armenbijbel* and *de Spiegel*, which dates back to the 1440s (Barnard 2007, 31). Roux's position (1984, 7–8) that children's Bibles made their appearance in the nineteenth century needs some adjustment.

2. Apartheid became official state policy when the Nationalist Party came to power in 1948; notwithstanding certain minor changes and modifications during the years, Apartheid effectively and forcefully remained in place until April 1994 when the African National Congress (ANC) assumed power in a democratic dispensation that included all people in South Africa—at least to the extent that all South Africans received the vote.

Bibles pursue recognition for their (claims to be) *clear and textually correct presentation* of the biblical narratives (Bottigheimer 1996, 54–57), this essay will take a closer look at the presentation of others in South African children's Bibles. Second, from the perspective that children's Bibles are *powerfully persuasive handbooks* intent on drawing out social reaction (Bottigheimer 1996, 51), their persuasive power mustered during a troubling time in South Africa's history through their portrayal of otherness in Afrikaans children's Bibles, will particularly be in focus. With regard to both of these notions, considerable attention will be paid to the historical context in which Afrikaans children's Bibles in South Africa originated and, particularly, to their function within the South African context.

South Africa: Nationalism and Children's Bibles[3]

The first authentic South African children's Bible dates back to 1853 and was published in Dutch as *De Kinder-Bijbel* (The children's Bible) under the authorship of *een leraar der Gereformeerde Kerk in Zuid-Afrika* ("a minister of the Reformed church in South Africa"). A popular publication, with reprints totaling already fifteen by the end of the century, the author was widely speculated to have been the Reverend John Murray, minister in the rural Burgersdorp (1849–58) and later professor at the Theological Seminary in Stellenbosch. According to the concerns expressed in the preface, *De Kinder-Bijbel* did not intend to replace the Bible, but rather to serve as a children-directed *handleiding* ("manual") for parents to supplement catechism and Sunday school, through retelling the Bible in simple language, to make it easy to understand for children as young as four or five. And given the rural situation with its appalling opportunities for education in which many Afrikaners found themselves during the nineteenth and even early twentieth century (especially in the aftermath of the Anglo-Boer War) (Giliomee 2004, 170–73), a children's Bible served a further potentially valuable purpose among relatively uneducated adults.

---

3. Relatively few sustained studies on Afrikaans children's Bibles are available; however, see Barnard's 2007 study on children's Bibles and Afrikaner nationalism; Deist's plea (1986, 70–82) for responsible exegesis rather than an unsustainable claim to self-evident meaning in children's Bibles; Roux's pedagogical evaluation (1984, 1989, 1994—essentially the same material) of the shortcomings of Afrikaans children's Bibles, privileging the Bible generally as "closed canon" and using a literal reading of the Bible as benchmark for the text of children's Bibles.

Half a century later, the first children's Bible in Afrikaans made its appearance in South Africa in 1907[4] as *Afrikaansche Kinderbijbel—Bijbelse geschiedenis voor de jeugd met gekleurden platen* (Afrikaans children's Bible—biblical history for the youth with colored illustrations), by Andrew McGregor, a former minister of the Dutch Reformed Church (Roux 1994, 3–4). Two important considerations related to our inquiry are therefore already evident. First, even before the first Afrikaans translation of the Bible appeared in 1933, children's Bibles were already making their presence felt in South Africa—raising the question about the influence of the children's Bibles on the Bible-reading public of the time.[5] Second, with language considered to be such an important element within national identity, the reciprocal relationship between children's Bibles and Afrikaner nationalism is evidently part of the broader picture.[6]

AFRIKANER NATIONALISM

It is only toward the end of the eighteenth century that the term "Afrikaner" was claimed and used; up to this point, colonists at the Cape of Good Hope referred to themselves as *burgers* ("burghers, citizens"), Christians, or even Dutchmen. With an ever-widening gap between white and

---

4. Afrikaans developed from Dutch, simplified in its use by (initially mostly) slaves, servants, and maids around Cape Town, and further developed through Malayan-Portuguese phrases in particular (Giliomee 2004, 42, 175–80); diverse in region, dialect, and social class today, initially it was associated with poorness and "colouredness" (Barnard 2007, 16). The 1873 Afrikaans retelling of a biblical narrative, *Die Geskiedenis van Josef voor Afrikaanse kinders en Huisvrouwens* (The history of Joseph for Afrikaans children and housewives) by C. P. Hoogenhout was probably the very first Afrikaans publication of a Bible story (Roux 1994, 5).

5. A number of children's Bibles are available in Afrikaans in South Africa, but our focus will be restricted here to the older compilation of biblically based stories by Maxwell 1945 and the editions by De Graaf 1990, Hildebrand 1962, Nothnagel 1981, 1997, and Postma 1953.

6. South African children's Bibles are often in part or fully translated, and sometimes revised in some aspects, from other mostly Euro-American counterparts; e.g., Deist and Deist 1982 was originally published as *The Story of Jesus* (London, 1981); and the Olmstead 1975 series was originally published as *The Picture Bible for All Ages* by David C. Cook in 1973. The children's Bibles translated into Afrikaans derived from the Romantic tradition and were produced during an era of emerging nationalisms in Europe; generally these were carefully selected for their potential fit in and usefulness for the South African context (Barnard 2007, 3).

black, influenced in no small way by the ferocious status-conscious officialdom of the Dutch East India Company at the Cape, the importation of slaves, and the ambiguous status of free blacks, the relatively small white community became increasingly conscious about their identity. It would take another century, a *Groot Trek* ("Great Trek or Move"), and the establishment of *Boere Republieke* ("Boer republics"),[7] however, before such notions of nationalism would be expressed forcefully with the Anglo-Boer War of 1899–1902, followed shortly thereafter by the Rebellion of 1914. Moreover, together with the changing times of the period surrounding the two World Wars, the ever deteriorating relationship between a white and a fast-growing black population, the lingering effects of the destructive war at the beginning of the twentieth century, and the global economic crisis of some thirty years later—all contributed to a valorization of Afrikanerhood, enmeshed in political ambition and economic programs (Giliomee 2004, 39–42).

A common anthropological problem, it is in the case of the Afrikaners of South Africa a particularly complex task to describe the group along the lines of nation and nationalism. Afrikaners were the descendants, although not exclusively, from the Dutch, English, German, and other immigrants from Western Europe who arrived in the country mainly during the seventeenth and eighteenth centuries. Notwithstanding social sanction against such practices, liaisons with indigenous people, and Malay slaves in particular, ensured that the nature and profile of Afrikaner communities became rich and hybrid in various ways, with the Afrikaans language as probably the best example of such hybridity—one factor that probably gave rise to an enduring quest for both social identity as well as political power. The Afrikaners cannot therefore adequately be described racially or ethnically, since the construction of those people who became known as or referred to themselves as Afrikaners, took place over many decades

---

7. The *Groot Trek* refers to those Afrikaners who left the Cape colony during the first part of the nineteenth century in ox-wagons with their families, servants, and livestock in search of a better life, free from British rule; and also because of discontent with some of the Cape administration's laws and practices—no small items of which were the official end of slavery on 1 December 1838 as well as the growing sense of alienation of colonists through the continuing conflicts on the colony's eastern border. Eventually the Zuid-Afrikaansche Republiek or ZAR (South African Republic) was proclaimed in 1852 and the Oranje Vrystaat or OVS (Orange Free State) in 1854 (Giliomee 2004 108–11, 120–54).

as an intricate and complex history. A number of characteristics common to Afrikaners, and probably shared with other ethnic, linguistic, or other groups elsewhere in the world, can, however, be listed. A group that began to take shape in the heyday of modernity, Afrikanerhood was informed, for example, by the notion of progress and human intellectualism, as much as it was increasingly since the twentieth century defined over against (especially) English-speaking "whites" and indigenous or black people, and the secular notion of Afrikanerhood was from the beginning inseparably tied to Christian religious and biblical notions.[8] It is, given the focus of this contribution, the notion of otherness in a context of valorized sameness that will attract most attention in our discussion.

Although not aloof from the past, as was evident in the 1938 centenary celebrations of the *Groot Trek* and the 1949 inauguration of the *Voortrekker* monument, toward the middle of the twentieth century Afrikaner concerns increasingly focused on the future. The future orientation is also evident in a comparison of the 1938 centenary celebration of the *Groot Trek* with its concerns for defining the Afrikaner in distinction from all perceived foreign influences, and the tercentenary celebration of the arrival of Van Riebeeck in the Cape with its concern to locate political power in the hands of Afrikaners and other (read: English-speaking) whites allowed into their *laager* (van der Watt 1997, 3). With nationalist fervor late nineteenth- and twentieth-century Afrikaner historians (such as Gustav Preller) deliberately made use of inversion, displacement, and regression in their historical construal of the dichotomy of black savagery and white civilization, that would increasingly become a benchmark for Afrikaner nationalism, evident among others as a theme in Afrikaner art (van der Watt 1997). For many, the development of Afrikaner consciousness or Afrikanerdom came to fruition when the Nationalist Party, which was formed through and as a result of Afrikaner interests, took power in 1948, a move that heralded attempts at the consolidation of Afrikaner nationalism—as ideological construct of identity and consciousness, informed by a shared history and social culture—as well as the beginning of the infamous Apartheid times.

---

8. The relationship between religion and Afrikaner identity, and even more particularly the strong Calvinist influences that played a role in the formation of Afrikaner identity, have often been commented upon; cf. Barnard 2007, 18–23; van der Watt 1997; various essays in Kinghorn 1986.

Afrikaner Nationalism and Afrikaans Children's Bibles

Although a simplification of a more complex situation, Afrikaner identity was largely informed by two important considerations: in the first place, the lingering Dutch but especially British colonial influence and the attempt of Afrikaners to disentangle themselves from these colonial heritages; second, and increasingly prominent, the perceived threat of indigenous (black) people for Afrikaner identity, power and politics, economic livelihood, and social and cultural life. Both stood in conjunction to the will to power, as a result of dominance and suppression but also the aspiration (and even sense of pride) to demonstrate or prove the Afrikaners' abilities over against erstwhile masters.

Throughout the years Afrikaner nationalism has maintained strong bonds with religion, favoring a Calvinist Christian orientation that made much of the predestined role white Afrikaners had to play.[9] This role was racially defined, dependent on binaries such as civilization and savagery, progress and primitivism, chosen and doomed, and Christian and pagan. One corollary of the post-1948 racist Apartheid structure of South Africa was, unsurprisingly, the privileging of Christianity,[10] ostensibly with claims to its status as "majority religion" but covertly Christianity was also deemed to be in the interests of the ruling Nationalist Party. Ironically, as much as the Christian discourse was used to prop up the Apartheid state, liberation movements and those working for the dismantling of Apart-

---

9. Notwithstanding references to historical events during the *Groot Trek* and the taking of a vow at the Battle of Bloedrivier (which was a resounding victory for the *Voortrekkers* against overwhelming odds and a numerically superior Zulu army), often presented as both confirmation of a divine destiny as well as foundation for pursuing a missionlike divine purpose, evidence suggests the absence of sustained religious interpretation of the event until early in the twentieth century, when they became important themes in the development of Afrikaner nationalism (Giliomee 2004, 125–27; van der Watt 1997, 6).

10. Christianity was privileged, e.g., by the 1986 (final Apartheid) constitution referring in no uncertain terms to the Christian or biblical God; by an educational policy existing within the framework of Christian National Education; by having national media coverage by the SABC as public broadcaster biased toward Christianity (and only particular manifestations thereof) in the content of the programs broadcasted; by legislation regulating sport and recreation and economic activities on Sundays, done at the request of certain Christian denominations.

heid were equally heavily invested in Christianity, in its Protestant[11] forms in particular. The ambiguity of the situation was mirrored in the general acceptance of and, in other religious communities, tolerance for Christianity and its preferred status as official religion of the country.

The Bible has been an important document since the early days of the Cape Colony, initially often the only book to be read and studied (Giliomee 2004, 28) and to be included in the development of the Afrikaners as nation—with the claim to their exclusivity seen to be underwritten and justified by the Bible (Barnard 2007, 13–15). A *laager* mentality nurtured the sense of exclusivity with, on the one hand, togetherness and belonging as concerns and, on the other hand, the impulse to close the own group off from perceived external threats. With Afrikaner communities generally conservative and traditionalist, the axiom of the patriarchal, hierarchical context held: *Buig die boompie terwyl hy jonk is* ("Bend the little tree/ sapling while it is young"). Within Afrikaner nationalism it was considered important that children be taught self-discipline, self-control, self-improvement, and "Christian values" (Barnard 2007, 31). In the same way that "Bible story tellings narrate more than their own content; they tell stories from within the spirit of those who write them" (Bottigheimer 1996, 151), children's Bibles became important scaffolding for supporting the budding Afrikaner nationalism of the twentieth century. As Barnard suggests, Afrikaans illustrated children's Bibles both "encoded the principles of Afrikaner nationalism" and at the same time served as "didactic tools for the configuration of an exclusive national consciousness" (2007, 1–2).

Imagining the Other in South African Children's Bibles

For many people an obvious and identifiable difference between Bibles generally and children's Bibles is the use of pictures and other iconographical materials. "Because illustrations in children's Bibles function in close partnership with text, they provide internal exegesis and play a central role in resolving puzzles thrown up by the stories themselves" (Bottigheimer

---

11. In addition to the so-called Black Danger (stereotypical construal of black people as dangerous, inferior, morally suspect, etc.) and Red Danger (Marxist Communism), the Roman Danger (Roman Catholicism) was used more restrictively than the other two, but still robustly to warn Afrikaners against the *volksvreemde* (that which is foreign to Afrikaner people) and, therefore (it was reasoned), as that which threatened their existence.

1996, 57). Statistics suggests that since the Protestant inception of children's Bibles, illustrations were important to and formed an integral part of these Bibles and fitted into a general trend within publishing history, namely the illustration of printed religious material; already in the sixteenth and seventeenth centuries 83 percent of all illustrated books were religious (Bottigheimer 1996, 56).

The use of illustrations in Afrikaans children's Bibles is instructive in the choice for particular illustrations but also for how illustrations are made to highlight specific interpretations of an inherently multivalent text and to construct the self and the other. Along with a gradual unshackling from British colonialism, the hybrid Afrikaner national identity since the middle of the twentieth century found ways of justifying its own hegemony and dominance over others, through internal colonialism, xenophobia, chauvinism, and paternalism, and enforcing these through elaborate systems of monoculturality, suppression of other communities, and uneven development (Baines 1998, 2; Barnard 2007, 10). Identity in contemporary society is often ambivalent and hybrid. As postcolonial studies show, there is, on the one hand, the "amnesia of colonialism," the strong impulse of colonialism to impose a Western sense of identity. The hegemony of Western identity assists in the systematic erasure or marginalization of an indigenous (awareness of) identity through the destruction of local culture by the foreign culture (Hutcheon 1991, 167–89). On the other hand, with increasing globalization that requires people to come to terms with (the existence of) other (according to different categories) groups, the claim for an unadulterated, indigenous culture or identity is increasingly untenable.[12] This is certainly the case in South Africa, where the postcolonial situation has for long been characterized by the struggle of colonial settler communities for autonomy from the "mother country," as well as by the struggles of indigenous cultures against both the mother country and its settler communities—complicating notions of nationalism and national identity.

---

12. Similar notions are voiced from a postmodern perspective: "There is a right wing version of postmodernism in which every identity becomes irreconcilably pitted against every other, and a recognition of 'otherness' turns into a doctrinaire refusal to engage with others. A left-wing postmodernism, on the other hand, would suggest that we are always already constituted by traces of others from the past, and respect for others should lead to ethical forms of negotiation which recognise the particularities of social location" (Brett 1998, 313).

Such complications were, however, underplayed in twentieth-century Afrikaner nationalism, in part because nationalism harbors elements of the suggestive and the sentimental, which are useful in constructing and using symbols that serve as markers or descriptors of convictions and values. The sentiment expressed by symbols has in the past often resided in religion, particularly in a context like South Africa where religious conviction and political sentiment were connected in various, strong ways. Ultimately, within nationalism symbols are important for securing social cohesion, the legitimization of political authority, and the establishment of convictions and the regulation of behavior (Barnard 2007, 18–23). But as social-identity theory has shown, an intricate relationship exists between human psychological functioning and large-scale social processes and events that affect and are affected by the former (Tajfel 1982b, 2; Turner 1996, 4). People's view of themselves in relation to the surrounding social and physical world are in many respects influenced by their membership of social groups (Tajfel 1982b, 2). People often choose to define their social location according to selected group affiliations, due to processes of social influence that cause them to internalize certain social norms and to which they in a variety of circumstances consciously relate and model in their attitudes and social behavior. In short, people are part of a group because they choose to associate with the group. They are actively engaged in construing and constructing the world in which they live.

In issues of nationalism and othering, the unequal access to power for individuals and groups contributes to the differences that exist between dominating and dominated groups. Ascribing social categories to marginalized groups often impinges on their self-understanding as well as on their description by other groups. "The achievement or the *construction* for oneself of full individuality is the privilege of social differentials" (Tajfel 1982b, 5; Deschamps 1982, 85–98). Wrestling against British imperialism and its legacy as well as contemporary concerns and aspirations, twentieth-century Afrikaner nationalism illustrates such identity construction processes and claims to power—processes from which Afrikaans children's Bibles did not remain aloof. Like the use of headings in children's Bibles to steer meaning and the interpretation of stories (Bottigheimer 1996, 155), illustrations often served the same purpose, providing both image and the hermeneutical grid for understanding the story. In what follows a few instances of portraying the other in Afrikaans children's Bibles in ways complementary to Afrikaner nationalism are pointed out.

Claiming Jesus for the Cause: An Anchor Role in Identity

Although the precedent has been set centuries ago in illustrations in European children's Bibles, and even earlier in artistic impressions, in South African children's Bibles Jesus is also portrayed as a white, Caucasian man. The portrayal of Jesus came to play an important role in the ability to establish and maintain the self as essential for processes of othering. With Jesus put into an anchor role in many illustrations, a number of instances of othering are illustrative of the tendency to formulate group identity and self-identity according to biblical texts, by postulating a specific other(s) and by ascribing certain characteristics to them.

In an interesting example from *Oom Attie se Slaaptyd-stories*, a collection of stories fusing the biblical and the modern, a chapter called "Jesus het die Kinders van Alle Nasies lief" (Jesus loves the children of all nations) has a remarkable portrayal of characters (Maxwell 1945, 63). Jesus is seated, given the traditional portrayal of Jesus perhaps an unexpected pose, and he embraces children. Notwithstanding the claim, he is not surrounded by children of all nationalities, as the majority of them are portrayed as white with accompanying characteristics. A token black boy with stereotypical larger nose and flatter lips stands out among the white children, as an archetype probably used to represent the entire "black race." The black boy's white robe, which is similar to Jesus' robe, may suggest association but is probably rather aimed to contrast with his black body, while covering it. Within the ambit of Afrikaner nationalism the scene fits into the missionary impulse of the divine call on whites in general and Afrikaners in particular to Christianize the heathen, who could be identified by their black skins[13] (Barnard 2007, 36–38).

Generally, however, the portrayal of otherness in Afrikaans children's Bibles was not done in racial terms, maybe partly due to their nature as (often) imported and translated Bibles. Given the opportunities offered by the physiological traits of the people inhabiting the first-century Mediterranean world, the decision of editors against racial profiling of otherness

---

13. The mutual concern with social status and racial identity (purity) that characterized the West certainly since the eighteenth century was imported with the Dutch and English colonialist ventures in South Africa. By the beginning of the twentieth century, and especially following the devastation of the Anglo-Boer War (1899–1901) on material and psychological levels, particularly in the Afrikaner society, the emphasis on racial identity became pronounced.

in South African and other children's Bibles is nevertheless interesting. However, in Afrikaans children's Bibles it is possible that racial profiling of otherness is present; that otherness is indeed tantamount to blackness but implicitly and underlying the portrayal of sameness as "whiteness"— making blackness present in its absence.[14] Such notions may be involved in a next example.

In the chapter "Jesus, die Kindervriend" (Jesus, the friend of children) it is sameness rather than otherness that characterizes the portrayal of the characters in the illustration (Maxwell 1945, 322). The conventional or typical portrayal of Jesus is accompanied by children in modern-day attire, prim and proper middle-class clothes suggesting notions of morality and discipline, traits considered important within Afrikaner nationalism. But other treasured features are also strongly present. The toy airplane clasped by one boy suggests progress and development, invoking notions of industrialization and technology that were strongly associated with males and their perceived superiority. A girl with a doll leaves little doubt about its symbolic maternal image that, along with male strength and superiority, suggests the proper role for Afrikaans women as full-time wives and mothers. These stereotyped portrayals are borne out by the gender-specific clothes the children wear, with the hyperfeminine curled hair and ribbons, dresses, and frills of the girls and the plain clothes and short haircuts of the boys (Barnard 2007, 38–40).

Biblical Characters as Benchmarks

It is clear from Afrikaans children's Bibles that they set benchmarks for identity, whether taken over from children's Bibles from elsewhere or created afresh, such as to ensure the regulation of what constitutes sameness and otherness. A good example is the portrayal of Adam in *Aan Moeder se Knie* (Postma 1953, 14) in a figure entitled *Adam het die diere een vir een gestreel en elkeen 'n naam gegee* ("Adam stroked the animals one by one and gave each a name"). With a romanticist portrayal of

---

14. At least three elements are involved in such decisions by authors and editors (since editors are of course also narrators!): (1) the selection from what gets called reality with its many-sided and contingent nature; (2) the very selection that is co-determined by an author's or editor's predispositions; and (3) different authors and editors will make different choices (cf. Coles 1996)—although such considerations are rather common experiences, they are not always admitted as such.

Adam as a nude, muscular person without any specific racial skin tone but with decidedly white facial features, the image is one of the exotic human being in perfect harmony with nature. In fact, with one hand on a tiger, while holding an eagle with the other hand, Adam symbolizes not only harmony but also superiority over nature, the whole of creation (cf. Barnard 2007, 41–43). In the South African context this would have recalled notions of human power through the progress associated with development and industrialization and constituted a benchmark for the ideal human being. Furthermore, since white superiority was justified by Western culture that often relegated Africans to animals, male supremacy in the figure of Adam now conceivably also involves white supremacy. The idealized male complete with patriarchal trimmings as the mainstay of white Afrikanerhood is found back in Adam in Gen 1–3, while the worryingly ambiguous role of women, who are prone to succumb to the temptation of the ultimate other, Satan, is read back into Eve. In children's Bibles, Adam is often presented where he "stood singly in Paradise with a fawn and a bird, icons of guiltlessness, leaving Eve to be associated not with blissful innocence but with tainted knowledge" (Bottigheimer 1996, 209, also 197–215).

In a presentation in *Die Nuwe Kinderbybel*, Noah is portrayed as the stereotypical bearded man with a staff in hand, striking an ecstatic maybe even heroic pose (Hildebrand 1962, 12). Even more illuminating though is the portrayal of the surrounding context, which is ensconced in otherness, a desolate plain and mountain over all of which a threatening sky towers. Different motifs can be identified in the illustration, and the notion of taking control over nature through human progress and technology is present again. But here the whiteness of Noah and his religious fervor could not have gone unnoticed in the heat of Afrikaner nationalism in the midtwentieth century, underwriting the exclusivism claimed through Afrikaner Christian nationalism and their concomitant ostensible superiority (Barnard 2007, 45–46). The portrayal of biblical characters as exemplary figures by (over)emphasizing their virtues but omitting any reference to their transgressions or moral lapses gives rise to moralizing trends. In Afrikaans children's Bibles, the lives of characters in the Old Testament, such as Moses and David, are retold by focusing on their good attributes or the important role they played in the history of Israel, while failing to mention acts such as murder, adultery, deceit, and the like (Roux 1994, 39–40).

OTHERNESS AS A BROADER CONCEPT

The portrayal of identity through celebrating sameness and disclaiming otherness in Afrikaans children's Bibles involved the portrayal of certain characters, as much as certain contexts through binary lenses. The ultimate and archetypical other in all children's Bibles is probably Satan, and this is no exception in Afrikaans children's Bibles with the presentation of *Jesus en Satan* in *Ons eie Kleuter-Bybel* serving as good illustration (fig. 4.1; Nothnagel and McBride 1981, 161–62). With the lonely Jesus peering over a vast desertlike area, the presence of an ominous shadow complete with horn and pointed features against a rock on the right side of the page lends the second, pictorial image to accompany the story of Jesus' temptation as recounted in Luke 4:1–13; Matt 4:1–11; and Mark 1:12–13. Picking up on the theme of the desert symbolizing emptiness and danger to human life, the notion of a vast empty land to be brought under control, in the name of progress and prosperity would have resonated well in Afrikaner nationalism (Barnard 2007, 53–54). Not only is Satan associated with the negative of the desert, with danger and desolation, but he has literally become part

Fig. 4.1. Jesus and Satan (Nothnagel and McBride 1981, 162).

Fig. 4.2. The Israelites underway (Nothnagel and McBride 1981, 43).

of it through the shadow attached to the rock in the illustration. With this depiction of Satan as engraved in nature and the wilderness in particular, Afrikaner nationalism could make the link between Satan and the perceived wicked and malicious black savage.

Given the strong influence of reformed Christianity (and even Calvinism) in the formation of Afrikaner identity in the twentieth century, it can be understood that the boundaries between the political and the spiritual were fluid. Political otherness and religious otherness were interwoven so that the victory by the *Voortrekkers* over the Zulu warriors at Bloedrivier on 16 December 1838 was not just a victory of whites over blacks but of Christianity over heathenism as well, celebrated as a religiously focused public holiday, *Geloftedag* (Day of the Vow). Afrikaner political identity was formatted with biblical terminology and metaphor, with the *Groot Trek* compared to Israel's exodus from Egypt,[15] the liberation of the

---

15. Ironically, the strong alignment with the biblical Israel apparently did not register any dissonance with Jewry of later times, although since the Second World War anti-Semitic sentiments would sporadically surface among Afrikaner communities (Giliomee 2004, 392–95). Afrikaner theologians such as Bennie Keet, popularly known as BB, criticized the exegesis within Apartheid circles and reminded that not

Afrikaner people (cf. Barnard 2007, 18). It comes as no surprise then to find similarities in the portrayal of the one defining Afrikaner nationalist symbol, the *Groot Trek*, and the foundational element of the exodus in the Old Testament. In a chapter entitled "Die Israeliete trek" (The Israelites travel) of *Ons eie Kleuter-Bybel* (Nothnagel and McBride 1981, 42–43), the people of Israel are visually presented as traveling through a wasteland (fig. 4.2).

Running across a two-page spread, from bottom left to upper right corner, the Israelites are portrayed as a group in which the individuals are not recognizable. Without necessarily suggesting this as editorial intention, it is in the context of Afrikaner nationalism difficult to see that the image of the *Groot Trek* would not also have been evoked by such imagery. As if to underwrite such a claim, two midtwentieth-century advertisements for products as diverse as a health mixture (fig. 4.3) and gasoline (fig. 4.4) employed similar imagery (Barnard 2007, 51–53, 114–15).

In their "trekking," Afrikaner people were making a political statement and engaging in a sociocultural experiment, all of which were seen to be underwritten by their religious convictions. Like the biblical people of Israel, Afrikaners were believed to have had a divine purpose on the southern tip of the African continent—and like the Israelites, Afrikaners believed that the fulfillment of their God-given duties required the protection of their own identity through separation from others.

OTHERNESS, LANGUAGE, AND FEAR: THE TOWER OF BABEL

Otherness in Afrikaner nationalism was not about valorizing the exotic but rather exposing threats to the nation, as can be seen in the account of the tower of Babel. With various interpretations of Gen 11 over many centuries, the consensus that developed over time was that the dismantling events of the project should be connected to human imperfection rather than divine intention, to punishment for sin rather than God's capriciousness. The human perversion invoking divine retribution was perceived to have originated in the unsound intentions of the people and was mostly ascribed to human arrogance and pride, whether this

---

only were the Jews all Semitic but that the perceived Jewish exclusivity of biblical times was based on religion only (Giliomee 2004, 430).

Fig. 4.3. Andrews Lewersout advertisement (*Huisgenoot*, November 1938).

Fig. 4.4. Shell advertisement (*Huisgenoot*, November 1945).

was explained as the inspiration for aspiring to divine status or as merely acting out the (sinful) human impulse to autonomy, or even ascribed to people's longing for a communal and even urban existence, or, of course, ascribed to God's intentions and actions to disperse the world population over the earth, furnishing at the same time what amounted to an etiology for the world's different language groups (Bottigheimer 1996, 152–61). Human hubris is, however, not explicit in the biblical account, not even in Gen 11:4 where the intention to build a high tower (in wake of the flood) is expressed, which intended to prevent the dissolving of the community; there is no indication in the text of human awareness of God's desire to disperse people over the earth. The subtext of an etiology for different languages and for the range of human populations on earth is at best only implicit.

In South Africa the story of the tower of Babel provided what the midtwentieth-century architects of Apartheid required: divine sanction for difference, seen as forcefully underlined in different language groups failing to understand one another and thus providing legitimation for the invention of political, social, and other structures with which to enact this sociopolitical arrangement. The powerful influence of a reigning sociopolitical context is noticeable also in the interpretative framework of children's Bibles. In Europe, for instance, the interpretation of the tower of Babel in the wake of the Thirty Years War (1618–1648) in German children's Bibles, which experienced much of the devastation of the war, was to see it as an injunction against municipal enterprise and civic pride; in France, which suffered far less structural damage, the story served as a conclusion to the Noah narrative and, at the same time, was about the preparation of a place of asylum rather than hubristic revolt against God (Bottigheimer 1996, 159).

In *Die toring van Babel* (*The Tower of Babel*; Nothnagel and McBride 1981) the illustration does not portray confusion as much as fear, with frightened people running away from presumably the commotion ensuing from people speaking in different languages. In Afrikaner nationalism the threat of other people exemplified by other language groups was perceived as a real danger, presenting ready justification for separating people socially but also spatially and geographically. Especially when compared with another illustration from the translated *Die Nuwe Kinderbybel* (*The New Children's Bible*; Hildebrand 1962), which shows the industriousness of a building site and productive workers, the previous illustration's emphasis on bewilderment, disarray, and fear is prominent.

OTHERNESS AMIDST SEX AND RACIAL PURITY

The maintenance of sameness through insulating otherness led to concern about sexual matters, which was from early times also a problematic area for children's Bibles. With reference to the biblical narratives of Joseph and Potiphar's wife, and David and Bathsheba, with their sexual undertones, Bottigheimer (1996, 116–32) demonstrates how these stories were retold in children's Bibles of the eighteenth and nineteenth centuries in such a way so as to conform to the sentiment of the day. For example, the erasure of sexuality from the first narrative required alternative and effectively exogenous explanations for the sexual desire of Potiphar's wife, invented (following Josephus) eunuch status for Potiphar, and an enviable relationship of trust and companionship between Potiphar and Joseph. In twentieth-century European children's Bibles, which were also riding the antisexual tide of the time, protecting children's sexual innocence was a particular concern to the extent that it was deemed legitimate to censor narratives deemed sexually too explicit or unacceptable—lest this be interpreted as about sexual notions only, the tendency should be noted that such treatment of sex was often accompanied by the preferential treatment meted out to patriarchs (Bottigheimer 1996, 138–39).

In the middle twentieth-century South Africa the concern with race (and, to some lesser extent, class) played an important role in society and was accompanied by a strong religious influence that was informed by puritan values. The latter showed signs of the lasting effects of a nineteenth-century, Victorian-age sexuality as it washed over into the promotion of an antisexual attitude and the regulation of sexual liaisons in South African twentieth-century politics, and it is therefore not difficult to understand that some of the first Apartheid laws were the Prohibition on Mixed Marriages Act (1949) and the Immorality Act (1950).

It is also not surprising that although the interaction between Joseph and Potiphar's wife is mentioned in an Afrikaans children's Bible, the illustration focuses on the subsequent event of Joseph's imprisonment (Nothnagel and McBride 1981). The portrayal of Joseph (and, granted, Pharaoh's two workers as well) with white features sanitized the story for Afrikaners from racially complicating factors. Moreover, in twentieth-century South Africa the muting of sexual undertones was accompanied by a sociopolitical concern, namely racial pride and purity, avoiding the illustration of Joseph being put in a compromising situation by a married woman, who was also from another country. In Afrikaans children's Bibles a concern with children's sexual innocence was therefore met with an equally pressing concern to protect Afrikaner racial identity.

RECONFIGURING IDENTITY: OTHERNESS REVERSED OR REIMPOSED?

With the 1994 democratic elections and the dawning of a new era in South African politics, if not yet always on the social landscape, children's Bibles also felt the strain of different times with different national goals and aspirations. The presentation of two stories in the later (1997) English rendition of *Ons eie Kleuter-Bybel* as *My Very Own Bible for Toddlers* is evidence of such changes in children's Bibles. In the Afrikaans version, "Jesus se vriende het mekaar lief" (Jesus' friends love one another) the focus is on piety in the household, with an all-white group kneeling and an elderly man leading them is prayer (Nothnagel and McBride 1981, 175–76; fig. 4.5). Since in Afrikaner thinking the family was of specific importance as first bulwark against perverse political, social, and religious influences, it played a strong ideological role, and its invocation recalled important themes such as physical health, attractiveness, fertility, and progressive integration. However, in the reworked illustration of the 1997 English edition (Nothnagel 1997, 190–91; fig. 4.6), the same company of people are now portrayed as racially mixed!

In another story, "Jesus kom weer" (Jesus will return), the correlation between white and Christian identity is again evident, as subsequent to Jesus' parousia, heaven as the promised land of the idyllic future is portrayed as a place for white people (Nothnagel and McBride 1981, 190–91).[16] However, the racial complexion of the characters in the illustration is again changed in the post-Apartheid version of this children's Bible: now black children are also seen worshiping in the household and frolicking in heaven (Nothnagel 1997, 190–91; Barnard 2007, 54–55). Notwithstanding the differences between political regimes, South African children's Bibles apparently remain important elements in the social engineering of the day!

---

16. Cf. Giliomee 2004 on the importance in Afrikaner thinking of a "whitemansland," a goal to be achieved through the establishment and enforcement of Apartheid.

Fig. 4.5: Jesus se vriende het mekaar lief (Jesus' friends love one another) (Nothnagel and McBride 1981, 175).

Fig. 4.6. Jesus' friends love one another (Nothnagel 1997, 190).

Conclusion: Bibles according to Our Image

The choice or selection of stories, or sections thereof, for inclusion in children's Bibles is inevitably an indication of factors such as agency, hermeneutical presuppositions, theological convictions, and sociopolitical locations. While wanting to avoid claims to some moral high ground or to simplistic value judgments, the purpose of this inquiry was to provide a glimpse of the ideological setting and role of Afrikaans children's Bibles in Afrikaner nationalism in the twentieth century. In the end, if nothing else, this relationship should not be portrayed as either surprising or out of the ordinary! "More often than not, rewritings of Bible stories for child readers seem to proceed from clear social, if not political, intentions" (Bottigheimer 1996, 71). While Afrikaans children's Bibles were not first and foremost written as documents wanting to further Afrikaner nationalism (Barnard 2007, 28), they served a useful purpose toward the construction of Afrikaner social identity (Barnard 2007, 24). An important aspect of this was, without invoking crude or distasteful portrayals, the imperative to present the other—and therefore the self—in ways appropriate to the constructed identities.

In her discussion of how choices are made in the presentation of biblical narratives in children's Bibles, Bottigheimer refers to the adage that what a society wants its children to know is how a society wants itself to be: "Logic may fall by the wayside, sacred texts may be borrowed for secular purposes, reader credulity may outweigh textual credibility, but socially stabilizing messages return, in ever renewed form, in generation after generation of children's Bibles" (1996, 57). The notion that children's literature reflects societal ideals, or at least interests and desires, probably has to be expressed even stronger in the case of South African children's Bibles. The reciprocal relationship between children's Bibles and their originating communities exists on two levels, both past and future: as much as "a children's Bible is a memorial to ourselves and our habits of thought" (Coles 1996, 939), as much it can be taken on as a living yardstick to structure, to establish and maintain theological and accompanying sociopolitical interests. Part of the larger complex set of machinery that underwrote and maintained positions of dominance (Thomas 1993, 40), of a system that structured the powerful minority over against the oppressed and marginalized majority, South African children's Bibles reflected the interests of white, and in particular Afrikaner, communities during the twentieth century.

Works Cited

Adam, Ian, and Helen Tiffin, eds. 1991. *Past the Last Post: Theorizing Post-colonialism and Post-modernism*. New York: Harvester Wheatsheaf.

Baines, Gary. 1998. "The Rainbow Nation? Identity and Nation Building in Post-Apartheid South-Africa." Online: http://www.arts.uwa.edu.au/MotsPluriels/MP798gb.html.

Barnard, Louis H. 2007. "The Illustrated Children's Bible as Cultural Text in the Construction of Afrikaner National Identity." MPhil thesis, University of Stellenbosch.

Bottigheimer, Ruth B. 1996. *The Bible for Children: From the Age of Gutenberg to the Present*. New Haven: Yale University Press.

Brett, Mark G. 1998. "Locating Readers: A Response to Frank Moloney." *Pacifica* 11:303–15.

Coles, Robert 1996. Review of R. Bottigheimer, *The Bible for Children: From the Age of Gutenberg to the Present*. *Christian Century*. 113 (28): 937–39.

Crook, Zeba A., and Philip A. Harland, eds. 2007. *Identity and Interaction in the Ancient Mediterranean: Jews, Christians, and Others: Essays in Honour of Stephen G Wilson*. New Testament Monographs 18. Sheffield: Sheffield Phoenix.

De Graaf, Anne. 1990. *Die Kinder-Bybel*. Translated by O. Olwagen. Vereeniging: CUM.

Deist, Ferdinand. 1986. "Die Bybelverteller en die Eksegeet." Pages 70–82 in *Essays in Religious Literature for Children/Opstelle oor Godsdienstige Kinderverhale*. Edited by Pieter G. R. De Villiers. Pretoria: CB Powell Bible Centre.

Deist, Ferdinand, and Henrietta Deist; Victor Ambrus (ill.). 1982. *Toe Jesus op aarde was*. Pretoria: Van Schaik.

Deschamps, Jean-Claude. 1982. "Social Identity and Relations of Power between Groups." Pages 85–98 in *Social Identity and Intergroup Relations*. Edited by Henri Tajfel. European Studies in Social Psychology. Cambridge: Cambridge University Press.

Giliomee, Hermann. 2004. *Die Afrikaners: 'n Biografie*. Kaapstad: Tafelberg.

Hildebrand, Olivera. 1962. *Die Nuwe Kinderbybel*. Roodepoort: CUM.

Hutcheon, Linda. 1991. "Circling the Downspout of Empire." Pages 167–89 in Adam and Tiffin 1991.

Kinghorn, Johann, ed. 1986. *Die NG Kerk En Apartheid*. Braamfontein: MacMillan.

Maxwell, Arthur S. 1945. *Oom Attie se Slaaptyd-stories 1*. Cape Town: Sentinel.

Nothnagel, Juliana. 1997. *My Very Own Bible for Toddlers*. Cape Town: Lux Verbi.

Nothnagel, Juliana, and Angus McBride (ill.). 1981. *Ons eie Kleuterbybel*. Pretoria: NG Kerk Uitgewers.

Olmstead, C. Elvan, ed. 1975. *Prentebybel vir almal*. 6 vols. Kaapstad: Verenigde Protestantse Uitgewers.

Postma, Minnie. 1953. *Aan Moeder se knie: Bybelverhale vir Kindertjies*. Pretoria: Van Schaik.

Roux, Cornelia D. 1984. "Perspektiewe op Aspekte van Afrikaanse Kinderbybels." MA thesis, Stellenbosch University.

———. 1989. *Afrikaanse Kinderbybels*. Stellenbosch: Kindergodsdiensburo.

———. 1994. *Kinderbybels in Perspektief*. Stellenbosch: Kindergodsdiensburo.

Tajfel, Henri. 1982a. "Instrumentality, Identity, and Social Comparisons." Pages 483–507 in *Social Identity and Intergroup Relations*. Edited by Henri Tajfel. European Studies in Social Psychology. Cambridge: Cambridge University Press.

———. 1982b. "Introduction." Pages 1–11 in *Social Identity and Intergroup Relations*. Edited by Henri Tajfel. European Studies in Social Psychology. Cambridge: Cambridge University Press.

Thomas, Gladys. 1993. "Just Entertainment?" Pages 40–44 in *Towards More Understanding: The Making and Sharing of Children's Literature in South Africa*. Edited by Isabel Cilliers. Cape Town: Juta.

Turner, John C. 1996. "Henri Tajfel: An Introduction." Pages 1–23 in *Social Groups and Identities: Developing the Legacy of Henri Tajfel*. Edited By W. Peter Robinson. International Series in Social Psychology. Oxford: Butterworth, Heinemann.

Watt, Louis van der. 1997. "'Savagery and Civilisation': Race as Signifier of Difference in Afrikaner Nationalist Art." *De Arte* 55. Cited 29 May 2009. Online: http://www.unisa.ac.za/default.asp?Cmd=ViewContent&ContentID=725.

Veggies, Women, and Other Strangers in Children's Bible DVDs: Toward the Creation of Feminist Bible Films*

Susanne Scholz

Children's Bible Films and Biblical Studies: Introductory Comments

Films show us how to make sense of the world and how to think about social categories such as gender, race, ethnicity, class, and the geopolitical constellations in which we live, work, and move. Films are cultural products, undoubtedly "a crucial adjunct in the interplay of power relations between peoples, societies and cultures" (Gearon 2001, 290). They map, confirm, and reinforce prevailing sociocultural, geopolitical, economic, and religious paradigms. This is also true for children's films, secular and religious. These films "help to craft and restore certain perspectives for each new generation of young minds during the crucial years when children are 'acquiring the ability to understand stories'" (Doucet 2005, 291). Considering this significant function of films in our lives, it is surprising that neither secular nor religious children's films have received much scholarly attention. This neglect is even worse for children's Bible films, which have barely been studied at all. To date, Athalya Brenner is the only Hebrew Bible scholar who has done serious work in this area. She published an analysis of four diverse children's films on Gen 1–3 (2006).[1]

---

* I would like to acknowledge the Perkins Scholarly Outreach Award, which supported my research for this article in summer 2009.

1. See also Doucet 2005, 290: "To date, however, children's films have received very little attention" in the field of international relations. Doucet acknowledges several books that examined children's films, such as Bell et al. 1995 and Smoodin 1994.

Considering the plethora of children's Bible DVDs in U.S. Christian bookstores, the lack of scholarly engagement is puzzling and certainly should trouble anybody who agrees that "film and television have become influential moral and spiritual reference points for young people" (Rossiter 1999, 212). The scholarly disinterest in children's Bible films is only topped by the absolute dearth of children's Bible films written from explicitly feminist, womanist, *mujerista*, or other theopolitically progressive perspectives. The fact is that most currently available children's Bible films are written, produced, and distributed by religiously conservative organizations. They advance notions about biblical literature that seemingly disconnect religion from politics, economics, and "empire," as if biblical storytelling were detached from the economic, political, and social infrastructures of the world, past or present. Disguising biblical storytelling as an ahistorical and apolitical activity, they claim to serve as educational entertainment[2] that tells what the Bible says (Gearon 2001, 292–93).

This article exposes the illusion of theoideological neutrality in four animated children's Bible DVDs produced since 2002 and focuses on their embedded rhetoric of gender, race, ethnicity, and geopolitical constellations. The analysis is illustrative rather than comprehensive, but it indicates the challenges that many recently produced DVDs pose to the advancement of a progressive biblical hermeneutics. Four DVDs are not a quantitatively huge number, but these four films stand out for their technical quality, creativity, and innovation. They are fun to watch and surpass previous children's Bible films because they are extremely entertaining, colorful, and expressive. The music is attractive and includes contemporary rhythms and sounds. Sometimes the storytelling reaches midrashic qualities that make the films unpredictable and attention catching. The days are gone when children's Bible films consisted of mere recitations of the actual biblical text. Current DVDs represent attractive educational and entertaining venues that teach today's children about the Bible in technologically advanced and engaging ways.

Yet they lack what Elisabeth Schüssler Fiorenza calls "emancipatory biblical pedagogy" (2009, 13). Stuck in a literalist-positivist hermeneutics and "fundamentalist anxiety," the storytelling of these DVDs does not engage the hermeneutical insights developed by feminist and hermeneu-

---

As of 2010, the field of biblical studies has yet to produce a book-length publication on children's religious and Bible films.

2. For an exploration of this dynamic, see Gearon 2001.

tically progressive scholarship in biblical interpretation during the past forty years. Instead, predictable hierarchical, androcentric, and ethnophobic assumptions pervade the DVDs, as they did in older films. Thus not much has changed. Though their appearance is up to date, current children's Bible films still serve to map, confirm, and reinforce prevailing normative sociopolitical and theoreligious practices, even when they are sometimes presented with a twist.[3]

Considering that religiously conservative companies keep producing and distributing these films, the hermeneutical partiality of the DVDs is unsurprising. After all, films—whether for adults or children, whether they tackle secular or religious topics—construct biblical meanings within a specific moment in time and space. In other words, films are tied to larger discursive networks that are permeated by power dynamics historically grown, politically and socially shaped, and culturally justified. It is high time that biblical scholarship takes account of these dynamics in children's Bible DVDs. Yet, in the end, what will be needed are children's Bible films written from socioculturally and politically, religiously, and theologically progressive perspectives that broaden the spectrum of biblical storytelling in film, provide diverse perspectives in those retellings, create visibility of progressive theological hermeneutics, and offer transformative visions of alternative constructions of life on planet earth.

Gender, Race, and Otherness in Children's Bible DVDs

Stories play an important role in developing children's expectations about this world (Feinberg 2008, 147), and so too children's Bible DVDs contribute to a child's sense of a "prosocial identity" (King and Benson 2006, 386). Like other educational materials, Bible DVDs have "reordering powers" (386) over children's understanding of their social and spiritual contexts. These films present beliefs and values that, like all children's materials, aim to offer children a sense of belonging, form their identities, and give them tools to assert themselves in the world. Although children's films are usually "sold as mindless state-of-the-art entertainment and not as agents of socialization" (Lugo-Lugo and Bloodsworth-Lugo 2009, 177), animated films for children, including animated Bible DVDs, play a significant role

---

3. For an excellent analysis of how such twists play out in secular children's movies, such as *Shrek 2*, see Marshall and Sensoy 2009.

in forming children's notions about gender, race, and otherness, regardless of whether they address these issues explicitly. The way DVDs portray biblical characters communicates unspoken but plainly visible assumptions about sociopolitical and cultural-religious ideologies even when they are projected into a distant past. The following analysis of four children's Bible DVDs illustrates that these films reorder the world's power structure in favor of the status quo.

THE ANIMATED KID'S BIBLE—EPISODE ONE: CREATION

The DVD series *The Animated Kid's Bible* is produced by The Kids Bible Company LLC, a media and entertainment company that claims to be "passionately dedicated to reaching and engaging children of all cultures with Bible truths as presented by state-of-the-art 3D-CGI animation."[4] The CEO and producer is Australian-born Tom Broadbridge, who produced movies from *Bingo and Molly* (1997) to *The Coast Town Kids* (1980) before turning his attention to *The Animated Kid's Bible* (2005), a multivolume series on the book of Genesis. The six regular single DVDs—entitled *Creation, Voyage of the Ark, Towering Pride and True Lies, Rain of Fire, Brothers at War,* and *Joseph the Dream Reader*—include the film, a music video, a trailer, a fact file, a storyboard, and a family tree. Additionally, seven DVDs offer "Interactive Bible Lessons" that cover every chapter in Genesis, and six more DVDs provide "Home Education Lessons" for homeschooling children. The DVDs can be bought individually or as a package at a slight discount, ranging in price from $12.95 to $299.

The DVD series stands out among children's Bible films for its innovative animation technology, computer-generated imagery (CGI), also used by the famous U.S. animation studio DreamWorks and in many video games. This technology makes the series exceptionally entertaining, attractive, and enjoyable to watch, and the promotional web literature promises that *The Animated Kid's Bible* is "at least as cool as any video game your kid has!"[5] The series is, however, predictable in its theoideologically Christian Right perspective. The company's mission statement

---

4. Company mission statement. Cited 30 June 2010; online: http://www.animatedkidsbible.com/pages.php?cID=1&pID=2&osCsid. The website address changed to http://www.thekidsbible.com as of 19 October 2010; it does not contain the mission statement any longer.

5. Cited 30 June 2010; online: http://www.animatedkidsbible.com/product_info

discloses that Broadbridge "had a fervent desire to broadcast a fundamental Christian message to young people on an international scale whilst maintaining the integrity of the Bible itself."[6] In other words, a Christian fundamentalist film producer decides to make children's Bible films to communicate the "100% inerrant truth"[7] of the Bible to an international children's audience. Yet the actual cover of the DVD presents itself with a slick and colorful design unmarked by any explicit Christian fundamentalist vocabulary.

The first DVD, *Creation* (2005; 40 min.), begins with a prologue with which every story is introduced in this series. A table with a lit white candle, an ancient looking map, and a thick front cover of a brown book appears as the first shot that soon focuses on the book cover with golden letters saying "The Animated Kids Bible." Then a young person's voice, a boy or a girl, says the following two sentences while a Middle Eastern melody plays in the background: "Many stories begin with the words, 'Once upon a time,' but this story which is our story begins before there was a time. Our story comes from a book called the Bible and it begins with the words 'In the beginning.'" Then the scene ends (00:18–44).

The film continues with a black screen shot that shows only the title stating, "Genesis Episode 1: 'Creation,'" and the same child's voice reads Gen 1:1–2 in a simplified translation that describes the earth as having "no shape" and being "empty" instead of being a "formless void." Then the screen changes and light spheres appear while an older male voice, God's voice, says: "Let there be light."

The child's voice disappears and the seven-day creation story is read by the male voice representing God. Yet after God says: "Let us make people. They will be in our image, just like us," the child's voice reappears, saying: "Then God made a human being, a man who is like himself" (04:04–47). A human-shaped figure starts emerging from brownish desertlike earth and

.php?cPath=26&products_id=66&osCsid=5f408cbb1e445e248fc2e3ba70164989. Information no longer available. See n. 4.

6. See the company's mission statement. Cited 30 June 2010; online: http://www. animatedkidsbible.com/pages.php?cID=1&pID=2&osCsid. Information no longer available. See n. 4.

7. See the section entitled "Our Statement of Faith & Beliefs" of the company's mission statement. Cited 30 June 2010; online: http://www.animatedkidsbible.com/ pages.php?cID=1&pID=2&osCsid=a30927c3f6a4b64acc3f08db2875ec8b. Information no longer available. See n. 4.

increasingly morphs into a male-proportioned form. As a result, in the film the creation of humanity begins with one man, effectively substituting Gen 1:27 with 2:7.

Interestingly, however, the film takes seriously the visual representation of the man being made of earth (Gen 2:7). At first the skin of the man looks like raw clay and his face does not have real eyes and a mouth, only indentations, but as the storyline progresses the male earthling begins to look like a "real" man with a smooth lightly tanned skin, brown hair, and a muscular, athletic, and youthful body. Since the film is based on an edited and modified biblical text, the first creation story of Gen 1:1–2:4a moves seamlessly into the second creation account of 2:4b–3:24, as if they were one uninterrupted single-narrative account. This editorial decision is understandable because it would be difficult to explain the repetition in film. The film also shows the first man enjoying the garden with the animals and, encouraged by God, naming the animals. Only then does the film move on to the creation of the woman.

At this point the narrator disappears and direct speech between the male-voiced God and the man makes the film look like a "real" film in which the characters speak directly with each other. Even humor is built in. For instance, the man nods approvingly when God tells the man that he did well in naming all the animals. Then God informs the man: "Now every male animal has a female mate, except you. It is not good for you to live alone. I will make a female partner for you." This modified version of Gen 2:18 not only personalizes the pronouns from the biblical text's third-person singular to the film's second-person singular, but also makes two important modifications to the biblical narrative. First, in the film God states the need for companionship *after* the man named the animals and as an explanation for the creation of the woman. Yet in the biblical text the divine speech gives *haadam*'s need for companionship as the reason for the creation of the animals. It is when the animals appear not to be an appropriate *ezer* (helper) for *haadam* that God creates the woman. Second, the film adds the idea that the male human needs a "female partner" because all "male animals have a female partner." This correlation is absent in Gen 2:18, and so the film reinforces heterosexist standards in accordance with the Christian fundamentalist conviction of normative heterosexuality. Thus the film presents an *interpretation* of the biblical story despite its claim to merely depict the narrative as "it is."

Next, the film shows how the woman was created from the man's rib during the night (06:28–07:46). The scene ends with the man sleeping on the ground and the woman cuddled next to his left shoulder. She has long brown hair, a fair tan, and a young woman's body that remains discreetly hidden from the viewer's sight. The man wakes up and looks with amazement at her, and she in turn wakes up and coyly smiles at him, bending her head down just a little bit. He says: "My female partner has been taken from my own flesh and bone. I will call her woman because she has been taken out of man." The additional phrase, "my female partner," is peculiar, really funny in its clinical word choice. The phrase, of course, does not appear in the biblical text. The man then tells the woman about the prohibition not to eat from the tree, yet another addition in the film that is not part of the biblical narrative. There the prohibition is told only to the first created human, before the human couple is created. In fact, the addition of the explanation in the film establishes the primacy of male over female creation. The film also advances ethnic and age stereotypes. The man and the woman are portrayed as a white, young, and physically attractive couple, an assumption that has certainly prevailed in religious depictions of the story throughout the ages.

In the next scene, the man goes his own way, and immediately thereafter the serpent approaches the woman. Predictably, the serpent has a female voice and looks like a green dragon. Although the woman resists initially, as depicted in Gen 3:1–7, eventually she eats from the fruit. When the man reappears asking, "Woman, where are you?" she gives him the fruit silently, and he eats from it without any further comment. Then he throws the fruit behind him, which lands on the ground with a big bang, looks down on himself, gets frightened about his nakedness, and picks up some green leaves from the ground to cover himself. The woman does the same, and then they run off to hide behind a tree (08:04–10:35).

The filmic depiction of these crucial moments misses a great opportunity to present the famous story as innovatively in content as in technology. Grounded in fundamentalist Christian convictions, the film perpetuates the traditional Christian reading of Gen 1–3: a young white couple represents Eve and Adam, and she is secondary to him. Moreover, the serpent's representation with a female voice reinforces the idea of the feminine as dangerous and evil. The merging of the first creation account with the second reproduces a classic Christian and Jewish solution to the apparent literary duplication of the biblical story line. The company's goal of producing Bible films for "children of all cultures" must therefore be considered as failed. In short, androcentric, Western, and conservative Christian perspectives contribute to the perpetuation of problematic sociopolitical and cultural-theological assumptions. This is a considerable danger of this DVD, since it so successfully entices young and old viewers with its outstanding technological creativity and thoroughly engaging presentation.

BIBLE ANIMATED CLASSICS: RUTH

Another company producing numerous children's Bible DVDs in the past twenty years, NestFamily Entertainment, calls itself a "leading creator, producer, and distributor of engaging, inspirational, and educational consumer products and resources to homes, schools, libraries and churches."[8] Its products aim to "transform lives and positively impact our culture by developing children with positive character traits, spiritual strength and sound academic skills through our vibrant, fun and profitable company."[9] The adjective "positive" appears repeatedly but remains undefined. The company's slogan, "inspire, educate, entertain, nurture," sounds similarly innocuous because the underlying theoreligious convictions remain hidden. The ideological persuasion of NestFamily Entertainment becomes clear only when one carefully examines the background of the people serving on the company's advisory board. The website describes the advisory board as "independent" and consisting of "respected theologians" who "review all key elements of the NestFamily Bible story films, from the original script through the finished product." The website also explains that "the Board ensures that the stories provide the highest quality education, animation, and entertainment, and are worthy of your trust. The individuals are from various denominations and have extensive Bible, seminary, education, history and arts training."[10]

That is the claim, but a closer look uncovers the hidden agenda that comes as no surprise. NestFamily Entertainment adheres to a Christian Right position, as illustrated by the four members listed on the advisory board. One of them is Reg Grant, a professor of pastoral ministries at Dallas Theological Seminary in Dallas, Texas, which posts a "Doctrinal Statement" on its website stating: "Our faculty and board affirm their agreement with the full doctrinal statement (below)," which asserts "the authority and inerrancy of Scripture." Biblical inerrancy is, of course, a

---

8. See the company's website: http://www.nestfamily.com/About-Us-W7.aspx.
9. Thus stated in "Our Vision" (ibid.).
10. Online: www.nestentertainment.com/helptopics.aspx?Topic=advisoryboard.

classic marker of Christian Right theology. Another member comes from a similar Christian conservative position. Ed Decker is the president of a religious group called "Saints Alive in Jesus," which labels itself a group focused on "Apologetics," "evangelical in nature,"[11] and "a Christian non-profit corporation founded upon the call of God to witness Jesus to those lost in Mormonism and other cults."[12]

To an uninitiated observer, a third member of the advisory board seems to break with this Christian fundamentalist tradition. Rabbi Yechiel Eckstein gives the advisory board the appearance of moderation, since he represents the Jewish tradition. Yet he is the founder and president of the International Fellowship of Christians and Jews (IFCJ), a highly influential group that facilitates exchange between Israeli political movers and the Christian and political Right in the United States. It is thus likely that he would also support theopolitically conservative goals. The fourth member, Nathan Hatch, former provost at the University of Notre Dame and current president of Wake Forest University, is the most academically credentialed board member,[13] but in the past he too endorsed and contributed to the strengthening of Christian conservative perspectives and helped in founding evangelical institutes and scholarship initiatives.

In addition, Richard Rich, the writer of the particular DVD under consideration, is listed as "an American/Mormon film director, producer, writer and assistant director. He worked in various capacities, such as assistant director, coproducer, and related positions at Walt Disney Studio. He also serves as a bishop in one of The Church of Jesus Christ of Latter-day Saints in California."[14] Credentialed as producer and writer of the film on Ruth, he too is of a theologically conservative background.

In short, the NestFamily Entertainment team does not include any progressive or even mainstream theological scholars or thinkers. Instead, religiously conservative white males dominate. These are, in my view, astounding facts when one considers that the DVD cover does not disclose any of this information but merely presents the DVD's content as entertaining and educational material. The DVD back cover states that the film aims to nurture Bible knowledge. It also emphasizes that the film was directed by industry experts, such as Richard Rich, "former Walt Disney

---

11. Online: http://www.saintsalive.com.
12. Online: http://saintsalive.com/who-are-we.
13. See http://www.wfu.edu/president/.
14. Online: http://en.wikipedia.org/wiki/Richard_Rich_(director).

Productions director." As far as the buying public are aware, then, the DVD appears devoid of any particular religious-theological agenda and is simply a Bible film for children, when in fact the DVD advances a theopolitically conservative perspective.

The ideological background of the DVD team makes the cinematic story of the book of Ruth (2006; 45 min.) predictable. It turns into a love story between Ruth and Boaz that has a happy end and results into a growing family. At the very end of the film, the voice of a male narrator explains: "So Boaz took Ruth, the Moabite, and they were married. And it came to pass that Ruth bore a son and they called him Obed. Ruth's loyalty and courage was the beginning of Israel's greatest age. Her son Obed became the father of Jesse who was the father of David, a king who united Israel in righteousness."

The film assumes a stereotypical androcentric and geopolitical perspective that has rarely been challenged in public religious-Christian discourse, which is probably part of the success of these kinds of Bible film productions. In this particular film the biblical scene of Naomi claiming Ruth's son as her own is omitted (Ruth 4:16–17), and any other hermeneutical perspectives, as for instance articulated by feminist and postcolonial studies on Ruth (such as Nadar 2001), are excluded although they were widely available when the DVD was released in 2006. In this particular DVD, then, Ruth represents the ideal qualities of a future wife. She supports her mother-in-law, Naomi. After she and Naomi return to Bethlehem, Ruth works miracles and immediately repairs and cleans the abandoned house. She even helps the mice by feeding them and rescues a baby mouse from drowning in a bucket of water. Ruth also goes out to find food and humbly inquires about collecting grain from a field, which turns out to be Boaz's field. There she gleans with the other widows on the edges of the grain fields. When Boaz sees her, he falls instantaneously in love with her (12:30–14:15). He approaches her and invites her to take as much grain as she needs. He stutters and is very awkward, like an enamored man. Ruth thanks him graciously and seems also to be taken by him. When Ruth returns home in the next scene, she learns from Naomi that he who is "next in kin" must marry her. Ruth responds with slight embarrassment to Naomi's request to ask Boaz for marriage. Ruth feels awkward because she, too, has apparently fallen in love with him.

A long scene (15:20–17:00) depicts how Boaz and Ruth try to tell each other that they have fallen in love. Boaz does not manage to state his feelings because he worries about his age. Ruth fears that she is a

Moabite, a foreigner, who has little to offer to Boaz. Both wind up saying only "Nice day, isn't it?" or "Good morning!" and "Good Night!" to each other and depart without having told each other their true intentions. The entire scene is completely invented, as the biblical narrative does not include any of these conversations and encounters. Yet in the film the emphasis on the emotions strengthens the notion that the book of Ruth is a love story leading to marriage and the birth of a son, an ancestor of Jesus Christ.

In another scene, after serious encouragement from Naomi, Ruth approaches Boaz in the field in the evening. She tells him that "you are a near kinsman to me" whereupon he asks her: "You know what that means?" She says, "Yes, do you?" and he replies, "Yes, will you?" Ruth answers, "Yes," and Boaz then says, "Ruth, but there is a nearer kinsman than I, Jabesh." When she tells him that she has no possessions, that she is "worthless," he exclaims, "No, you are priceless!" (18:21–20:00). Boaz is then called by one of his male workers, and Ruth runs away into the darkness of the evening.

In the next scene Boaz works out the details with the other kinsman, Jabesh, who earlier in the film was portrayed as a greedy and crude money and property hunter. He relinquishes his first claim on Naomi and Ruth when he is told how much they would cost him (21:50–22:58). Boaz tells him that he would need to buy new clothes for this future wife and her mother-in-law, a new and larger house, and spend a lot of money for his future six to seven children. Jabesh, greedy and dumb, is portrayed as so thoroughly horrified about spending money that he begs Boaz to fulfill his kinsman responsibilities and to take Ruth and Naomi away from him. With a trick, then, Boaz is able to marry Naomi.

Exploiting the clichés of women's taste for new clothes, home decoration, and many children, the film presents the men as being in charge of property and legal arrangements while the women make sure to identify their next economic provider. In this retelling of the book of Ruth, love plays a central role although it is not spoken about publicly, only agreed upon in the night or between the young woman and her mother-in-law. Other women do not appear, except as silent widows on the margins of the grain fields. One wonders what would have happened to the two women if Boaz had not immediately fallen in love with Ruth. Would they glean grains from the edges of the fields like the other widows? The film teaches children that women better be smart in finding a husband so that they do not wind up without financial support from a man.

FRIENDS AND HEROES—A FRIEND IN HIGH PLACES (SAMSON AND DELILAH)

The DVD series *Friends and Heroes* integrates both Hebrew Bible and New Testament stories within a larger narrative about one boy, Mackey, and his friends living in Alexandria, Egypt, in the first century C.E. The series is produced by the British company, Friends & Heroes Productions Ltd., and it is perhaps the most creative of the DVDs discussed so far because the main bulk of the DVD does not consist of the actual retelling of Bible stories. Each episode centers on Mackey and his friends, especially Portia, the Roman niece of the Alexandrian governor; the sister of Mackey, Rebekah; and other characters. At opportune moments in their adventures one or another character is reminded of a Bible story that they then tell each other. In other words, biblical stories illustrate general principles, as they become pertinent in the lives of the main characters, Mackey and his friends.

In the case of Samson and Delilah, the second episode of the series (2007; 25 min.), Mackey's sister, Rebekah, is reminded of the biblical couple when she compares Portia's Roman with Delilah's Philistine identity. Rebekah refers to the story to emphasize that "certainly the Romans are not like us." In Rebekah's retelling, the Romans are like the Philistines and Delilah, whereas Samson and the Israelites are like Rebekah, Mackey, and their family and Christian and Jewish neighbors suffering under the Romans. Even though the film presents the biblical tale within a geopolitical comparison, Rebekah's belief is ultimately rejected when her mother repudiates it. Thus, in this appropriation, the biblical story functions as a negative illustration for the main characters, Mackey, Rebekah, and Portia, who become good friends despite their geopolitical differences. The film seems to suggest that these differences do not matter on a personal level.

The gender and racial stereotypes in the visual retelling of Judg 16 are also worth considering. For instance, Delilah's looks communicate clearly that she is nothing but trouble for Samson. The narrator's voice is Rebekah's, who characterizes Samson as "wild and handsome and really, really strong." Samson appears as a muscular, half-naked bodybuilder who throws away a lion and eliminates fighters surrounding and attacking him from all sides. He is deeply tanned with shoulder-length brown hair that makes him look like a nonwhite and intimidating warrior of ancient times, physically strong but with little intellect, a racialized view of Samson that reinforces racially charged notions about the brown and black male body. The narrator, Rebekah, explains: "Samson wasn't afraid of anything, not even the Philistines when they showed up. Naturally, the Philistines wanted to get rid of him." When he falls in love with Delilah, "even though she was a Philistine," Rebekah explains that "his enemies saw their chance." They went to Delilah and paid her to find out the secret of Samson's strength. Clothed in a sexy green dress, with green pearls in her hair and equally green eyes, she sets out to get the answer.

For the first time the film uses direct speech. While the screen shot shows a house from the outside at night, we hear Delilah's husky voice: "Tell me, Samson, why are you so strong? What makes you weak and help-less? Please, please tell me?" While she is asking, the camera moves inside the house and shows Delilah's face with her green eyes and green dress and green pearls, as she gives wine to Samson, reclining on a bed. Samson whispers back in a low-key voice: "Just tie me up with seven bow strings." Then he stretches and falls asleep while Delilah leaves the house under a huge full moon. The scene hints at her going to the Philistines although this encounter is not shown.

Instead, in the next scene Delilah is at the bed of the sleeping Samson with the Philistines surrounding the bed with drawn swords. Delilah claps her hands twice and calls out: "The Philistines are here." Samson wakes up and immediately defeats them. Yet "Delilah doesn't give up" and "kept nagging him," and so Samson tells his secret at her second attempt. The narrator's voice, Rebekah, explains: "This time Delilah knew he had told her the truth," and the film shows coins of silver falling down to symbol-ize Delilah's large payment for the deceit. Again Samson is seen sleeping, but this time he has a bald head. Now he is too weak to even get off the bed and the Philistines capture him quickly. They blind him, bind him, and throw him into prison. The narrator then explains that a year passed during which Samson's hair has grown back. When the Philistine crowd wants to see him in the temple, he comes and destroys the place by pray-ing to God to give him strength, and then he pushes the pillars away from underneath the roof. This ends the telling of Judg 16 (07:52–11:25).

The next screen shot is back in Rebekah's and Mackey's house where their mother states dryly: "Well, that's a cheerful story," while Mackey replies: "Rebekah, the Romans are not the Philistines." Thereupon Rebekah acknowledges: "Maybe. But if I were you, I wouldn't let that girl [i.e., Portia] anywhere near my hair." This comment demonstrates that Rebekah is jealous of Mackey's friendship with Portia and tells the Samson and Delilah story as a deceitful love story with geopolitical implications. Yet both her mother and brother reject Rebekah's view and scorn her for inappropriately comparing Judg 16 to the power dynamics of the Roman Empire. Hence, the film advances the notion that friends can safely ignore sociopolitical, cultural, and religious differences. It privatizes, personalizes, and sentimentalizes geopolitical structures of domination in the ancient world.

Stereotypes are abundant in this filmic retelling. Delilah has a curvy and sexy figure, green eyes and a green dress, a color that perhaps hints at her greed for money for which she betrays Samson, who is said to love her. The muscular build and dark skin of Samson depict his masculinity in a most stereotypical way. He speaks only two or three sentences to Delilah, answering her questions with the minimum of words, devoid of any emotional expression. His prayer in the temple is brief. Interestingly, the film also abbreviates the biblical text. Instead of making three attempts, Delilah learns Samson's secret already after the second round. Thereafter she disappears from the film, which rushes to the story's end so that the first-century friends and heroes can continue on their journey. It seems as if the telling of the Samson and Delilah story is included merely as a perfunctory obligation. The main characters seem relieved when the Samson and Delilah story is over, and they reject the story's relevance for their own lives. Viewers are left wondering why the inclusion of the biblical story was even necessary since Judg 16 is indeed not a very "cheerful story."

VeggieTales: Minnesota Cuke and the Search for Noah's Umbrella—A Lesson in Confidence

Since their creation in the 1990s, the popular English-language computer-animated children's films, VeggieTales, have aimed to communicate "positive biblical values" and that "God loves us."[15] Phil Vischer founded the company, Big Idea Inc., in 1989, which filed for bankruptcy in 2003 after intense business conflicts with a distribution company.[16] The company's first feature film, *VeggieTales: Where Is God When I'm S-Scared* (1993), led to many others, including the 2009 film, *VeggieTales: Minnesota Cuke and the Search for Noah's Umbrella—A Lesson in Confidence* (50 min.). The

---

15. So defined by Mike Nawrockie, vice president of Big Idea Productions, during an online radio interview: http://hiskids.net/player/?show=src&filename=http://media.hiskids.net/src/mike%20nawrocki%202009-02-15.mp3.

16.See, e.g., the explanations by Phil Vischer in his blog at http://www.philvischer.com/?p=38.

purchase of the DVD included a green children's umbrella so that children have a "real" prop that is prominently featured in the story of the film.

The cover promises "an ark-sized adventure" in which "Larry the Cucumber is Minnesota Cuke, a children's museum curator and part-time detective hired to find the famous Noah's Ark." The story is, however, convoluted and does not at all follow the biblical tale of Noah's ark. The central prop, the umbrella, which the DVD cover characterizes as "Noah's mysterious and powerful umbrella," is completely invented, as are all the events surrounding the hunt for Noah's umbrella. Hence this children's Bible DVD does not even try to present a detailed story of Gen 6–9, a characteristic rhetorical strategy of the VeggieTales. Predictably, the lack of biblical storytelling and the emphasis on abstract moral lessons do not find approval from Christian Right critics, who find the films "bloodless" and "trivializing the Incarnation" (Moore 2008, 18). They bemoan the absence of any Jesus-talk and the abstract focus on "moral truths," such as confidence, which allow the producers to broaden the appeal to non-Christian audiences.

The plot line of this thirty-eighth VeggieTales episode focuses on Minnesota Cuke, who searches for Noah's ark after he learns of the mysterious and powerful relic "Noah's umbrella." Joined by his best friend, Julia, and his former archenemy but now friend, Professor Rattan, Minnesota Cuke finds the umbrella before Rattan's twin brother, Wicker, uses it for his evil goals. The main characters in this VeggieTales film are, as always, Larry, the talking cucumber, and Bob, the talking tomato. Only one woman character is included: Julia, a friend of Larry (11:39–12:34). This time Larry performs as "Minnesota Cuke" and chases after Noah's umbrella in a bumbling fashion. His opponent is Wicker, who has a Spanish accent, a golden front tooth, and a thin upper-lip mustache. He is helped by a nontalking supporter who also has a stereotypical Mexican mustache and wears a wide straw hat. The film reinforces racist ideas about Mexican men, presenting them as untrustworthy, evildoing, and fighting on the wrong side. The good character, Larry, is the bumbling cucumber whose luck is abundant and crucial for surviving and solving the mystery hunt. Julia, the female character, supports him, often understanding the intrigues before her male friend gets it, but her lipstick friendliness does not take over the scene, and, in fact, she becomes the victim of abduction and is in need of her male friend's help. In the process all of them get caught, but with the help of Julia's hairpin and further luck the three friends succeed in solving the puzzle of Noah's umbrella against all odds and even against their own full comprehension.

Interwoven into the hunt for the ark and later the umbrella are references to Noah and the Bible. For instance, when Minnesota dislikes the instructions, worrying that people will laugh at him, his friend Martin (Bob the Tomato) reminds him of Noah (14:03–44): "Remember how Noah had to do things that seemed silly to the people around him? The Bible says there was no rain and no water nearby so building a giant boat seemed really strange to his neighbors. I'm sure he got lots of laughs! But he obeyed God's instructions." This is an intriguing and entirely midrashic observation based on creative imagination.

In the film, references to Noah carry the plot line and give the character, Minnesota, the courage to do the strange thing of hopping up the pyramid backward. When people start pointing at him and laughing, Minnesota gets embarrassed and frazzled. He turns around while Julia keeps staring to the ground below. At the very moment when she sees the secret sign on the ground (the umbrella), the silent Mexican gangster who followed them kidnaps her. When Minnesota turns around again, she is gone, and the search for Julia begins (15:23–16:41).

Another reference to Noah occurs when the friends are in the movie theater and Minnesota activates the projector. The screen shows animals two by two as a visual reference to Gen 6–9 (24:16–25:00; 25:22–43). Later Julia explains to Minnesota that "the Bible says, when we do the right thing, God's favor surrounds us like a shield. Noah was doing what God asked him to do. He was a righteous man.... When Noah did what was right, he felt God smiling at him and he could ignore all the laughing" (34:50–35:20). In other words, references to Noah appear throughout the film although they are not front and center. They illustrate that, like Noah, one can overcome feelings of embarrassment and do "the right thing" even when other people laugh about it.

Gender stereotypes abound. When Julia is locked up with Professor Rattan in a room, she and her hairpin prepare the way to find Noah's umbrella and even the ark. She opens the locked door with a hairpin, saying: "One girl's hairpin is another girl's get-out-of-jail-free card" (22:21–36). When Julia and Rattan leave the room, Rattan states approvingly: "That is one useful hairpin!" (23:31–36). Later when Julia, Rattan, and Minnesota escape from the movie theater, Minnesota advises that they lock the entrance door, and Julia responds: "Got you covered," and swings her hairpin in the air (27:11–17). These references suggest that a typical female beauty prop, the hairpin, is essential in guaranteeing the protagonists' success. Julia's presence is thus essential to Minnesota's overall victory, but Julia's contribution is limited to what is traditionally defined as a woman's prop. The film suggests that gender-characteristic behavior of women is welcome and even necessary to the smooth performance and triumph of men, who would never have the benefit of a hairpin without a woman friend.

Another scene advances stereotypes about gender, sexuality, and ethnicity. After Julia is abducted, Minnesota tries to find her. He stands in the streets, carrying her pink purse with the engraved letters "girl power," while trying to figure out what to do next. Meanwhile men on the other side of the street point at him, laugh, and comment on the kind of purse Minnesota is holding as a man. Minnesota responds trying to explain that the purse is not his but his friend's. He gets flustered and embarrassed, and at that very moment the Mexican-looking man who kidnapped Julia snatches the "top secret" guidebook from Minnesota's hand. In the film, then, the other men's homophobic laughter serves to distract Minnesota and teaches that men should not hold pink women's purses or else they might get into trouble. It is also important to note that the Mexican-looking thief never speaks, while Minnesota does not stop talking, worrying, and shouting: "Stop, stop. Thief! Call the police! That guy stole my book. Stop! He is fast. Oh, man, now I lost the instruction book, too!" He is portrayed in a feminized and helpless fashion while the ethnically identified perpetrator is successful and silent like a "real" man.

The film also promotes outright racial-ethnic prejudices about Mexican men. Wicker and Rattan look identical, as if to suggest that Wicker's characterization as evil is only accidental because the other identical-looking character turns out to be good. Yet the choice to paint both characters as accented foreigners with stereotypical Mexican looks reinforces the notion that one never knows whether a Mexican man is good or evil and one needs to carefully evaluate each situation. These messages are subtle but they are never absent.

The four DVDs reinforce mainstream notions about gender, sexuality, race, ethnicity, and geopolitical power dynamics. They also delegate religious convictions into the privatized and individualized realm and define the Bible as a storybook of the past. Privatized and individualized views characterize many people's ideas on religion and the Bible from childhood to old age, and the most current children's Bible DVDs ensure that yet another generation of children will take them for granted for the next seventy to eighty years.

SPIRITUAL DEVELOPMENT, SOCIOPOLITICAL CONFORMITY, AND CGI
TECHNOLOGY: THE NEED FOR FEMINIST BIBLE FILMS

Bonnie J. Miller-McLemore accurately observes that "over the last century, the subject of children has held minimal interest in the religious academy" (2008, 31). The same can be said about Christian popular culture and educational materials, such as the four children's Bible DVDs evaluated above. Countless children's Bible films exist, and none of them has been systematically analyzed by scholars of religious, theological, or biblical studies. Were it not for Athalya Brenner's 2006 article, not a single scholarly article would exist critically examining children's Bible films. A reason for this dire state of affairs certainly has to be sought in, even today, the field of religious, theological, and biblical studies largely presupposing an androcentric and empiricist-scientific hermeneutics that considers children's issues as beyond the realm of serious academic work. Miller-McLemore quotes Karl Rahner, the famous midtwentieth-century Catholic theologian, who maintained that the teaching and raising of children "cannot be the aim of a theologian" (2008, 37). The situation is equally problematic for films and movies of any kind. They have become artifacts of investigation in religious, theological, and biblical studies only in recent years (e.g., Aichele and Walsh 2002; Exum 2006; Kreitzer 1994; Marsh and Ortiz 1997; and Runions 2003).[17] Children's Bible films have obviously not even made it that far.

Consequently, when it comes to children's Bible films, the spiritual and educational development of children is largely in the hands of lay producers, directors, and advisory boards, all of whom are eager to articulate their particular theopolitical and religious agendas. The four children's Bible DVDs examined above illustrate how some of these agendas affect representations of gender, sexuality, race, ethnicity, and geopolitics. Unsurprisingly, they indicate the pervasiveness of conservative-literalist and Christian Right theological convictions that dominate public discourse about religion, Christianity, and the Bible in the United States. Thus, conformity to the sociopolitical status quo with its deeply androcentric, ethnocentric, and hierarchical practices shapes the storytelling in children's Bible DVDs. The production of these films by mostly conservative Christian companies

---

17. Interestingly, other academic fields are apparently also struggling with developing critical media literacy. For instance, Kellner and Share maintained that "critical media pedagogy in the USA is in its infancy" (2005, 373).

and the successful DVD distribution within the conservative Christian book distribution system ensure that in the first decade of the twenty-first-century children continue growing up with religious-conservative view-points on the Bible and Christianity. The only considerable difference is that this time the DVDs are unusually entertaining and technologically very advanced products. Created with CGI technology, children's Bible DVDs are fun to watch and attractive to a generation of children used to playing computer games. Yet none of the materials has been "held accountable for its outcomes as an educator of young children" (Hilty 1997, 80),[18] a situation also typical for nonreligious children's films and movies.

If progressive Christian theological and biblical discourse, as it has also developed in feminist studies, wants to reach beyond the narrow confines of the ivory tower and reach lay audiences effectively and consistently, we will need to find ways to produce feminist Bible films for children. They will need to adapt to some of the marketing strategies exhibited by the DVDs analyzed above. For instance, the DVD covers need to be designed to market these as children's Bible films that simply aim to educate and entertain children. Henry A. Giroux called this approach "the politics of innocence," which masks commercial and ideological interests (1995). References to the ideological hermeneutics of the films have to be omitted because, like other films, children's Bible DVDs are presented as entertainment free of ideology. They do not openly declare themselves as "agents of socialization," which is part of the appeal and "power" of this material to the wider public (Lugo-Lugo and Bloodsworth-Lugo 2009, 166, 177). The DVDs will also need to include additional resources, such as sing-a-long music, so-called curriculum lessons, short quizzes, or even "exciting episode previews." Most importantly, the DVDs have to be created with the newest technology available in animated film production. In other words, the production of feminist Bible films for children will require highly professional staff and lots of money. In my view, we need to encourage students to consider seriously going into this kind of business, and ideally, they would recruit partners and staff already working in the animated film industry.

This is no small feat. Yet it must be done if feminist Bible scholars want to stand a chance of communicating sociopolitically and culturally-theologically progressive views of biblical texts to lay audiences, including

---

18. Another scholar aims to hold Disney accountable for its commercial, ethical, and political interest in producing animated children's movies; see Giroux 1997. See also Giroux's extensive 1999 study.

children.[19] We cannot afford an attitude that dismisses educational entertainment of children as outside the realm of religious, theological, and biblical studies. Miller-McLemore says it well when she explains that "taking children seriously as a theological subject requires a movement across the conventionally separate disciplines in the study of religion" (41). She even suggests "an orientation toward practice" (41), although she probably did not have children's Bible DVDs in mind. To write, direct, produce, and distribute children's Bible films, grounded in a progressive and feminist biblical hermeneutics, will be a singularly important task. After all, as Giroux explains, "media culture has become a substantial, if not primary, educational force in regulating the meanings, values, and tastes that set the norms that offer and legitimate particular subject positions—what it means to claim an identity as a male, female, white, black, citizen, noncitizen" (1999, 2–3). As agents of socialization, films shape children's minds and emotions every day and for decades to come.

The creation of alternative children's Bible DVDs must also be part of a larger effort, as proposed by Douglas Kellner and Jeff Share, that "critically negotiate[s] meanings, engage[s] with the problems of misrepresentations and underrepresentations, and produce[s] … alternative media" (2005, 382). Alternative film will need to disrupt dominating theocultural representations of biblical literature as homogeneous, disinterested, authoritative, and universally valid meaning. They will present a "new cultural politics" that is both "deeply pedagogical" and "political in [the] attempt to revitalize the institutional and ideological conditions necessary for diverse forms of political [and shall we also include: theospiritual] activism aimed at sustaining democratic public life" (Giroux 1999, 58). As such, the creation and distribution of feminist Bible films for children will make a serious contribution to what Elisabeth Schüssler Fiorenza calls "the democratization of biblical studies." It is crucial to develop such materials soon.

Works Cited

Aichele, George, and Richard Walsh, eds. 2002. *Screening Scripture: Intertextual Connections between Scripture and Film.* Harrisburg, Pa.: Trinity.

---

19. The direction of communication is the opposite from what some scholars in Christian education advised in recent years; see, e.g., Allen 2008.

Allen, Holly Catterton, ed. 2008. *Nurturing Children's Spirituality: Christian Perspectives and Best Practices*. Eugene, Ore.: Cascade.

Bell, Elizabeth, Lynda Hass, and Laura Sells, eds. 1995. *From Mouse to Mermaid: The Politics of Film, Gender, and Culture*. Indianapolis: Indiana University Press.

Brenner, Athalya. 2006. "Recreating the Biblical Creation for Western Children: Provisional Reflections on Some Case Studies." Pages 11–34 in *Creation and Creativity*. Edited by Caroline Vander Stichele and Alastair G. Hunter. Sheffield: Sheffield Phoenix.

Doucet, Marc. 2005. "Child's Play: The Political Imaginary of International Relations and Contemporary Popular Children's Films." *Global Society: Journal of Interdisciplinary International Relations* 19:289–306.

Exum, J. Cheryl, ed. 2006. *The Bible in Film—The Bible and Film*. Leiden: Brill.

Feinberg, Jeffrey E. 2008. "Making Stories Come Alive." Pages 146–63 in *Nurturing Children's Spirituality: Christian Perspectives and Best Practices*. Edited by Holly Catterton Allen. Eugene, Ore.: Cascade.

Gearon, Liam. 2001. "A Spirituality of Dissent: Religion, Culture, and Post-Colonial Criticism." *International Journal of Children's Spirituality* 6:289–98.

Giroux, Henry A. 1995. "Memory and Pedagogy in the 'Wonderful World of Disney: Beyond the Politics of Innocence.'" Pages 43–61 in *From Mouse to Mermaid: The Politics of Film, Gender, and Culture*. Edited by Elizabeth Bell, Lynda Haas, and Laura Sells. Indianapolis: Indiana University Press.

———. 1997. "Are Disney Movies Good for Your Kids?" Pages 53–67 in *Kinderculture: The Corporate Construction of Childhood*. Edited by Shirley R. Steinberg and Joe L. Kincheloe. Boulder, Colo.: Westview.

———. 1999. *The Mouse That Roared: Disney and the End of Innocence*. Lanham, Md.: Rowman & Littlefield.

Hallbäck, Geert, and Annika Hvithamar. eds. 2008. *Recent Releases: The Bible in Contemporary Cinema*. Sheffield: Sheffield Phoenix.

Hilty, Eleanor Blair. 1997. "From Sesame Street to Barney and Friends: Television as Teacher." Pages 69–83 in *Kinderculture: The Corporate Construction of Childhood*. Edited by Shirley R. Steinberg and Joe L. Kincheloe. Boulder, Colo.: Westview.

Kellner, Douglas, and Jeff Share. 2005. "Toward Critical Media Literacy: Core Concepts, Debates, Organizations, and Policy." *Discourse: Studies in the Cultural Politics of Education* 26:369–86.

King, Pamela Ebstyne, and Peter L. Benson. 2006. "Spiritual Development and Adolescent Well-Being and Thriving." Pages 384–98 in *The Handbook of Spiritual Development in Childhood and Adolescence*. Edited by Eugen C. Roehlkepartain et al. Thousand Oaks, Calif.: Sage.

Kreitzer, Larry J. 1994. *The Old Testament in Fiction and Film: On Reversing the Hermeneutical Flow*. Sheffield: Sheffield Academic Press.

Lugo-Lugo, Carmen R., and Mary K. Bloodsworth-Lugo. 2009. "'Look Out New World, Here We Come'? Race, Racialization, and Sexuality in Four Children's Animated Films by Disney, Pixar, and DreamWorks." *Cultural Studies Critical Methodologies* 9:166–78.

Marsh, Clive, and Gaye Ortiz, eds. 1997. *Explorations in Theology and Film*. Malden, Mass.: Blackwell.

Marshall, Elizabeth, and Özlem Sensoy. 2009. "The Same Old Hocus-Pocus: Pedagogies of Gender and Sexuality in *Shrek 2*." *Discourse: Studies in the Cultural Politics of Education* 30:151–64.

Miller-McLemore, Bonnie J. 2008. "Children and Religion in the Public Square." Pages 31–44 in *Children, Youth, and Spirituality in a Troubling World*. Edited by Mary Elizabeth Moore and Almeda M. Wright. St. Louis: Chalice.

Moore, Russell D. 2008. "The Gospel's Bigger Idea: You Can't Tell the Story of Jesus without Jesus." *Touchstone: A Journal of Mere Christianity* 21:18–21. Online: http://www.touchstonemag.com/archives/article.php?id=21-08-018-f.

Nadar, Sarojini. 2001. "A South African Indian Womanist Reading of the Character of Ruth." Pages 159–75 in *Other Ways of Reading: African Women and the Bible*. Edited by Musa W. Dube. Atlanta: Society of Biblical Literature; Geneva: WCC.

Rossiter, Graham. 1999. "The Shaping Influence of Film and Television on the Spirituality and Identity of Children and Adolescents: An Educational Response—Part 3." *International Journal of Children's Spirituality* 4:207–24.

Runions, Erin. 2003. *How Hysterical: Identification and Resistance in the Bible and Film*. New York: Palgrave Macmillan.

Schüssler Fiorenza, Elizabeth. 2009. *Democratizing Biblical Studies: Toward an Emancipatory Educational Space*. Louisville: Westminster John Knox.

Smoodin, Eric, ed. 1994. *Disney Discourse: Producing the Magic Kingdom*. New York: Routledge.

PART 2
LEARNING HOW TO DEAL WITH THE OTHER

No Greater Love: Jonathan and His Friendship with David in Text, Tradition, and Contemporary Children's Literature

Cynthia M. Rogers and Danna Nolan Fewell

Ah wondrous *Prince*! Who a true *Friend* could'st be,
When a *Crown Flatter'd*, and *Saul threatned* Thee!
Who held'st him dear, whose *Stars* thy birth did cross!
And brought'st him nobly at a *Kingdoms loss*!
Israels bright *Scepter* far less glory brings;
There have been fewer *Friends* on earth than *Kings*.
(Cowley 1656, 2.120–25)

No one has greater love than this, to lay down one's life for one's friends.
(John 15:13 NRSV)

With this literature biased toward David, it is easy to choose David over Saul. Jonathan, however, had to choose much earlier, still in the midst of great ambiguity. The text invites us to reflect on the cost of loyalty and the terrible ambiguities within which loyalty must be practiced.

The story of Jonathan and David should not be used for a general celebration of the virtues of friendship. Rather, it is an exposé of the wrenching, risk, pain, hurt, and hope required as God brings God's new reign. (Brueggemann 1990, 153)

Despite the construction of Jonathan as an active and individualized character in 1 Samuel, subsequent commentary, artwork, and retellings have relegated Jonathan to a supporting role whose main functions are to amplify the conflict between Saul and David and to provide the friendly foil against which David rises to success. Children's literature also often assigns Jonathan a secondary part and turns him into the model friend of the more important David. In this piece we compare the biblical portrayal of Jonathan with those included in the illustrations and texts of children's Bibles and religious education curricula to explore the ways in which Jonathan is othered in efforts to translate a complicated story into a digestible, but perhaps misguided lesson for children.

The following discussion falls into four parts. First, we trace how Jonathan's friendship has been construed in select pieces of art and literature in the history of interpretation. We then examine how recent children's Bibles and children's biblical literature reflect or diverge from these interpretive trends. In the third section we present a modestly detailed reading of passages in 1 Samuel that feature Jonathan in an attempt to expose the complications of Jonathan's character and of his relationship with David. Finally, we conclude with suggestions about how the complexity of the biblical text could be productively reflected in contemporary children's literature.

DAVID'S FRIEND, JONATHAN[1]

The biblical Jonathan rarely stands on his own in the afterlife of critical, educational, literary, devotional, and artistic works that reference his name. As Saul's son and David's loyal friend, he embodies the connective tissue between the two as they vie for the throne. Biblical commentary, commonly reflecting the Bible's perceived preference for David, eagerly provides us with literary explanations for Jonathan's mediating position and theological rationales for his seemingly necessary abdication of kingship: Jonathan's affection for David, along with that of Michal, brings David into Saul's family, giving him a plausible place in line for the throne. Jonathan's allegiance to David in light of his father's paranoia intensifies the dramatic conflict between the divinely rejected Saul and divinely chosen David. Finally, Jonathan's love, however it is construed, prompts him to step graciously, conveniently out of the path of David's divinely ordained rise to kingship. In short, Jonathan's character gets absorbed into the Saul-

1. We thank the following people: Christopher J. Anderson, Methodist Librarian and Coordinator of Special Collections, and Sarah Ashley, Instructional Technology Specialist, both of Drew University, for help with image reproduction; Betsy Richardson, Director of Christian Formation for Children and Families, Union Congregational Church, Montclair, NJ, for assistance in navigating children's literature; David M. Gunn for consultation on history of interpretation; and He Qi for permission to use his work *David and Jonathan* (2001).

David plot, as he does what Saul cannot bring himself to do: he abdicates the throne, ending Saul's dynasty before it begins. Thus, Jonathan himself justifies David's rule as God's design for Israel's future (Jobling 1998, 93–101). Once he has fulfilled his duty to the plot, unequivocally declaring allegiance to David as king (1 Sam 23:17), he literally disappears from sight until his death alongside his father on Mount Gilboa (Jobling 1986; Gunn 1980, 89).

Jonathan's self-sacrifice has had many admirers in critical commentary, artistic and literary imagination, and religious catechetical materials. In the longest medieval treatment of friendship (*De Spirituali Amicitia*), the twelfth-century abbot St. Aelred of Rievaulx highlights Jonathan's selfless devotion in his advocacy of friendship as the highest of Christian virtues, warranting martyrdom if necessary. Even when verbally abused by his father,

> this youth, supreme in love, reverences the rights of friendship. Unflinching in the face of threats and unmoved by insults, unmindful of fame but mindful of kindness, he despises a kingdom for the sake of friendship. *"You will be king,"* he says, *"and I will be second after you."* …
>
> Here was genuine, perfect, stable, and lasting friendship, not spoiled by envy or weakened by suspicion or ruined by ambition. This friendship, although so attacked, after such a battering, neither yielded nor collapsed. Though shaken in many a siege it proved unbending, and after many a wound and injury, it remained steadfast. Therefore, *go and do likewise.* (*Spiritual Friendship* 3.94, 96)

In the Renaissance, Jonathan's self-sacrifice was lauded as a component of ideal neoplatonic friendship, a relationship governed by complete trust, consensual aims, ambitions, attitudes, and willingness to sacrifice self and possessions for one's companion (Pebworth 1980, 99; see also opening quote from Cowley above). In later centuries these ideals continue to hold sway. The fourth book of Edmund Spenser's *The Faerie Queene*, subtitled "Of Friendship," lists "trew" Jonathan and David among well-known pairs of ideal Greek companions, who

> on chast vertue grounded their desire,
> Farre from all fraud, or fayned blandishment;
> Which in their spirits kindling zealous fire,
> Braue thoughts and noble deedes did euermore aspire. (*Faerie Queene* 4.10.26–28)

In more contemporary treatments, Jonathan's love for David has been construed as fraternal devotion or brotherly love, a motif taken up in William Faulkner's *Absalom, Absalom!* (Ross 1980, 145–46), and as the fidelity expected of a comrade-in-arms, a political ally, or even an alter ego (McKenzie 2000, 84–85; Hertzberg 1964, 154–55, 172; McCarter 1980, 305).

But not all treatments have understood the two to be on equal standing. In their handbooks on education, Renaissance Christian humanists approvingly cited Jonathan's relationship to David as an example of princely behavior (Frontain and Wojcik 1980, 5), a sentiment echoed more recently in Hans Wilhelm Hertzberg's description of Jonathan as "a real nobleman of high sensibility" (1964, 172). In artistic tradition Jonathan's noble status has had prominent play, typically indicated by age, body position, gesture, and attire. From Rembrandt's elderly, princely Jonathan (*David and Jonathan*; 1642)[2] to Gustave Doré's regally protective Jonathan (*David and Jonathan* in *La Sainte Bible*; 1865) to He Qi's ceremonial warrior Jonathan whose awesome demeanor compels David's submission (*David and Jonathan*; 2001; fig. 6.1),[3] Jonathan's relationship to David has, at least in the eyes of some, been governed by distinct sociopolitical parameters and conventions, lending credence to the notion that his "love" is that of a political patron and protector (Thompson 1974; Nardelli 2007).

Alongside these readings, perhaps inspired by Michelangelo's, Donatello's, and Verrocchio's *Davids* as much as by the evocative language of the biblical text itself, there has been increasing attention to the homoerotic dimensions of Jonathan's attachment to David. There are several adaptations of this romance involving varying degrees of social equality and hierarchy: as mutual and open affection between actual historical personages (Horner 1978, 26–39), as a variation on well-known mythic relationships (Ackerman 2005, critiqued by Nardelli 2007), as a neutral literary reflection of homosocial (particularly, military) culture (Jennings 2001), and

---

2. Although Rembrandt's painting is entitled *David and Jonathan* where it hangs in the Hermitage, Rembrandt himself referred to it as *David's Farewell to Jonathan*. The seeming age and status differences between the two figures have caused some critics to propose alternative identifications—either David and Absalom or David and Mephibosheth (Pyper 2007, 46–47). However, two of Rembrandt's drawings (1642, the Louvre; 1655–1658, Rijksprentenkabinet, Amsterdam) labeled *David Taking Leave of Jonathan* also portray an older and clearly upper-class Jonathan. For a provocative reading of Rembrandt's versions of this scene and the father-son image it portrays, see Pyper 2007, 45–48.

3. For this and other works by Dr. He Qi, see online: www.heqigallery.com.

Fig. 6.1. He Qi, *David and Jonathan* (2001).

as the text's pro-David political construction of a womanly Jonathan in contrast to a manlier David (Fewell and Gunn 1993, 149–51; George 1997; Jobling 1998, 161–65; and Linafelt 2008). Jonathan's desire for, identification with, David, reciprocated or not, politically fabricated or not, compels Jonathan to act against his own interests, to "empty his heirdom into David" (Jobling 1986, 25; 1998, 98).[4]

Treatments more theological in nature tend to ignore the homoerotic possibilities and to set Jonathan's affection in the frame of divine providence. Not uncommonly, such readings accept compliantly textual claims of divine preference for Davidic ascendance. Even Brueggemann's reading, cited in our epigram, while fully cognizant of the text's politically laden theology

---

4. For a visual illustration of how this has been reflected in the history of Western art, see Pyper's 2007 analysis of the works of Cima da Conegliano, Rembrandt, Julius Schnorr von Carolsfeld, and Frederic, Lord Leighton.

and clearly sympathetic to Jonathan's individuality and pain, tends to genu-
flect to the text's construction of inevitable self-sacrifice in service of God's
greater plan. Gently nudged, the valorization of self-sacrifice slips across
the testamental divide, with Jonathan's devotion to David being compared
with following Jesus (Brueggemann 1990, 153) or even with Jesus' own pas-
sion—which also has a history of being couched in terms of "friendship."[5]
Thus, for many, a logical connection is forged between Jonathan's friendship to David and Jesus' friendship to all humankind. For example, in a
1950's volume devoted to church school education, we read: "The love of
Jonathan is in a way a prototype of Jesus' love for humanity. It was a stoop-
ing, bending, self-emptying love such as the Master of men expressed when
he divested himself of glory, left his Heavenly Father's home, and came to
this earth to become 'the friend of man'" (Maus 1954, 318). Consequently,
we find Jonathan's friendship with David serving a number of ideological,
political, and theological ends, both within the story world of 1–2 Samuel
and beyond. The pro-David slants of both the Bible and much subsequent
tradition seem content to leave Jonathan leaning toward, yearning for, for-
feiting family and future for David.

Contemporary children's literature taking up this text, while discreetly
avoiding the homoerotic possibilities and downplaying the social hierarchy, seems nevertheless firmly committed to magnifying Jonathan's loyalty
to David and holding it up as a model of friendship for all ages. Children's
Bibles including this story tend to use a number of presentational strategies to reinforce the theological inevitability of David's reign, while rel-
egating Jonathan to the role of "best supporting" friend.

CHILDREN'S BIBLES AND CHILDREN'S BIBLICAL LITERATURE

Admittedly, lines between children's Bibles, Bible storybooks, and catechetical literature can be quite blurred. Most children's publications
featuring or engaging the Bible have didactic goals that target religious
enculturation and character development; seldom do they present the

---

5. In the nineteenth century, "friendship" was an important theme in the portrayal of Jesus (Prothero 2003, 62–65). Children's religious education of that era was
designed to nurture "character development"; consequently, friendship was a reasonable topic, with Jesus, Jonathan, and David emerging as exemplars of friendship. As
we shall see, contemporary Christian education continues to be heavily influenced by
these nineteenth-century ideals.

biblical text without interpretation or commentary. Many contemporary children's Bibles and resources carefully select and freely retell stories to match varying levels of juvenile comprehension and to support particular learning objectives. Themes, events, and characters that sustain particular theological viewpoints or ethical programs are highlighted, while others considered to be less applicable are omitted. The miniscule nineteenth-century "thumb Bible" (Janes 1852–1856) is an early example of selectivity. Abridged in text and size to fit an adult's view of a child's hand and mind, this Bible contains (understandably!) passages about children that offer adventure and lessons on character building: "Moses in the Bulrushes," "Samuel Called of God," "Daniel in the Fiery Furnace," "Mary and the Child Jesus," "Prodigal Son," and "Timothy Learning the Scriptures." Reverend Janes believed children to be "naturally inquisitive" and hoped to steer children away from the popular press and toward a love of the Scriptures, "that their minds may be properly occupied, and their hearts rightly exercised" (Janes 1852–1856, 7–8). John Locke, likewise arguing for selectivity, included David and Jonathan among passages "which may be proper to be put into the hands of a child," but urged use of the "precise words of the scripture" (Locke 1683, §159), a practice also followed in Janes's miniature (Bottigheimer 1994, 74). Many children's Bibles today continue a highly selective approach. When they do include the story of David and Jonathan, they tend to spotlight only the portions of the text that illustrate Jonathan's devotion to David (1 Sam 18:1–5; 1 Sam 20).

When standard translations are used, textual selection, editorial prompts, and illustrations dictate what passages are read and how they are construed. The 2006 *New Revised Standard Version Children's Bible* is an unabridged text, but its sections are dotted with icons, signaling levels of importance and interpretive lenses: the label "God's Path" indicates especially significant texts that reveal "who God is" and how God wants us to live; "Finding the Path" designates suitable passages that can be applied to one's life; "Light on the Path" specifies passages worth committing to memory; and the tag "Points along the Path" marks (seemingly peripheral and optional) people and places to explore along the way. Moreover, the various genres and subjects in the Bible are collapsed into one all-encompassing rubric: "the story of God and the message of Jesus." Within 1 Samuel, passages about David warrant the icon for "God's Path," while those about Jonathan absent David are designated as the less significant "Points along the Path."

Another popular reading convention in children's biblical literature is the rubric of the "Bible as treasure." Religious educational materials that cultivate Bible study skills, such as Cokesbury Press's *Learning to Use My Bible* (2007), reinforce this idea through posters, songs ("I Treasure Your Words"), and memory verses ("I treasure your word in my heart"; Ps 119:11) that accompany maps, cards, and lists of biblical books. While both the path icons and the treasure motif are useful techniques designed to help children appreciate and navigate what must seem to be a rather strange and off-putting book, they encourage a consumerist mode of engagement. Reading becomes a matter of hunting for treasure; tangible, obtainable, containable keepsakes that promise happiness and delight; static object lessons waiting to be found, possessed, cherished, internalized by the industrious child. If the child misses the treasure, there are plenty of treasure maps and guideposts to chart the way ("God's Path") to the prize: pictures and captions direct the reading and imprint the imagination. Questions probe the degree to which the treasure has been secured, that is, the extent to which the children have absorbed the details of the story and have understood the underlying moral.

JONATHAN AND DAVID, A JUVENILE FRIENDSHIP

What do we find in versions of the Jonathan and David story that target children? This story, like others, falls prey to the desire for manageable, easily digestible, and recallable messages. Despite Brueggemann's plea, Jonathan is typically a one-dimensional figure exemplifying the virtue of friendship, and the story is easily condensed into a memorable platitude. In the ABCs of biblical knowledge,

> J is for Jonathan,
> David's good friend;
> Their friendship was tested
> And held till the end.
> A friend loveth at all times. (Prov 17:17)[6]

While earlier children's literature utilized classic biblical art to illustrate stories and lessons,[7] there has been a growing tendency in the last half

---

6. See the popular clipart illustrating biblical ABCs at http://thebiblerevival.com/clipart44.htm.

7. See, e.g., Sooy 1889, whose volume utilizes 178 illustrations by Gustave Doré (without attribution!).

century to depict Jonathan and David in a more youthful manner. So, for example, in the 1955 edition of Egermeier's *Bible Story Book* (235; fig. 6.2), the two young men are pictured as adolescents, younger than the biblical text suggests. However, their youth is juxtaposed to a battle scene in the background, and Jonathan's stance and elegant attire (reflecting the artistic traditions of Rembrandt and Doré) suggests princely concern for a lower class subject. In the *Golden Children's Bible*, published initially in 1962, Jonathan and David are again depicted as teenagers, but the violent context has been replaced by a benign wooded background, and the class distinction between the two is muted (Grispino 1993, 237; fig. 6.3). David, like Jesus in the *Golden Children's Bible's* New Testament illustrations, is golden-haired, blue-eyed, and centrally positioned, while the darker-haired Jonathan turns toward and reaches for David.[8] Jonathan's princely status is indicated with embellished tunic and laurel-wreath crown, but David wears royal red, signifying that he, not Jonathan, is true heir to Israel's throne. The picture downplays social difference, highlighting instead the understanding that the two are well-matched companions, an affinity that can be eagerly exploited in literature desiring to constrain friendships within certain social boundaries. For example, one publication targeting adolescents with the goal of "developing leaders for the world tomorrow" insists that the strength of Jonathan and David's friendship was grounded in common status, experiences, values, and above all a traditional construction of masculinity. Both were princes (one by birth, the other by marriage), mighty men of valor, reliant upon God, and respectful of the government: "They were real men, able to show the true, proper and right love of a brotherly friendship." Such a remarkable friendship is possible only with "others of like mind, who share the same goals, hopes and dreams."[9] But well-matched companions or not, one is clearly more

---

8. Led by an editorial board with Protestant, Catholic, and Jewish representation, the *Golden Children's Bible* was an ecumenical effort, with the sale of English-language copies reaching 4,625,000 by 1995. But despite its ecumenical appeal, its illustrations reflect Eurocentric ethnic stereotypes; hence Jesus is presented as golden-haired and blue-eyed, surrounded by people with dark hair and brown eyes (Bottigheimer 1996, 212), a tendency we see replicated in this illustration of David and Jonathan.

9. "Bible Personalities: David and Jonathan: A True and Lasting Friendship," *Ambassador Youth: A Publication by the Restored Church of God* (online: http://www.thercg.org/youth/articles/0201-jadatalf.html).

©Providence Lithograph Co.

Fig. 6.2. *Egermeier's Bible Story Book* (1955).

Fig. 6.3. *The Golden Children's Bible* (1962–1998).

deserving of attention, as is evidenced by the centered David and Jonathan's turned posture and obscured face, a visual trope with a long history.[10]

In interpretive traditions eager to make christological connections, Jonathan, as one willing to pass his mantle to one more worthy, is made to play John the Baptist to David's Jesus (e.g., Roper 1973, 2000). The associa-

---

10. Giambattista Cima da Conegliano's sixteenth-century *David and Jonathan* (ca. 1505–1510) is a common illustration in biblical literature, as is the more modern anonymous painting *Jonathan and David* (see Egermeier 1923, 239; Maus 1954, 319; Faris 1925–1928). In both of these works, the darker headed, slightly darker complexioned, Jonathan looks adoringly at David who stares off into the distance as if being summoned by a grander future. David the visionary and Jonathan the devotee have left their cultural imprint, paving the way for lessons about the value of selflessly promoting the interests of a friend out of mutual commitment to the will of God. See, e.g., the evangelical Bible study materials: "David and Jonathan: 1 Samuel 20:1–42," *Through the Old Testament in Two Years*, part 1, lesson 33 (Mission Arlington/Mission Metroplex, 2009; online: http://www.missionarlington.org/d/OT-09-33-DavidAnd-Jonathan.pdf).

Fig. 6.4. *Standard Bible Story Readers*, book 3 (1926).

tion of David with Jesus, invited by genealogy and reinforced by messianic tradition, is given a celestial radiance when the white-clad David gazes toward heaven or serenely receives Jonathan's sword as if it were a divine mandate (Faris 1925–1928; fig. 6.4). Once cast in a christological light, the friendship between Jonathan and David becomes an easy tool for Christian evangelism. For example:

> Jonathan could have been upset that David would be king instead of him. After all, he was the next in line. However, God had anointed David to be king and Jonathan knew that he must follow God. Jonathan loved David and was happy for him to be the next king. Friends are happy when others succeed…. They care and love at all times.

Jesus wants to be our Best Friend too. He loves us so much that he died for us on the cross.[11]

Lessons on Friendship

Cartoonlike characters have become popular in Bibles and Bible stories developed for very young children. *The Beginner's Bible: Timeless Bible Stories* strives to be age-friendly with colorful drawings of Jonathan and David (Henley 1993-2005, 188). By 2005 gender inclusiveness dictates that Michal also join the childhood chums (182; fig. 6.5). In this cartoon world, friendship simply happens, enhanced by goodwill and generosity. The relational triad of Michal, Jonathan, and David is devoid of any dynamics that smack of personal or political advancement on the part of David, or personal or political naïveté on the parts of Michal and Jonathan. The little girl Michal never grows up to become David's angry and abandoned wife, and young Jonathan's highly suggestive gifts of armor and clothing are nothing more than thoughtful tokens upon which the friendship is built.

The *Read and Learn Bible* (American Bible Society 2005) also uses cartoon illustrations to target children ages five to eight. Its chapter from 1 Sam 18–19, entitled "David's Friend," describes Jonathan's role in protecting David, but it keeps central David's character, safety, and reputation. David's social prominence is explained by the comment "God was with David," which may suggest to young readers that popularity is a sign of God's favor, and doing whatever is necessary to befriend the popular is a service to God. Missing is any emphasis on the mutuality and give-and-take of friendship. Rather, the lesson appears to be an endorsement of unidirectional care while questions of reciprocal responsibility, interpersonal relations, complicating circumstances are left unexplored. In a similar vein, *The Adventure Bible* (Richards) includes an application box entitled "Let's Live It!": "SHOWING FRIENDSHIP: Read about the friendship of David and Jonathan in 1 Samuel 20:1–42. After reading the story, name three ways that Jonathan showed his friendship with David. Name three ways you can be a friend to someone" (1984, 335).

---

11. This teachers' guide admonishes instructors to "please remember always to include the New Testament verses—this helps each child see how God's ultimate plan was fulfilled in Christ!" ("David and Jonathan," [online: http://www.missionarlington. org/d/OT-1YR-34-DavidJonathan.pdf). See also the article cited above: "You can have this kind of friendship with God and Christ" ("Bible Personalities").

David became friends with
King Saul's son, Prince Jonathan,
and Jonathan's sister, Michal.

Fig. 6.5. *The Beginner's Bible* (2005).

We might expect a fuller exploration of friendship in mainstream Sunday school curricula; however, as a general rule, David and Jonathan are portrayed much as they are in children's biblical literature. In a Methodist class packet geared to children age four to six ("David and Jonathan" in *Living Together* 1987), Jonathan and David are pictured as happy young adolescents. David, slightly foregrounded, looks eager to receive, as if new toys, the weapons and purple cloak Jonathan is handing him. He has nothing to offer Jonathan in return. The two figures serve as role models to exemplify the literature's main goal to instill in young children the values of friendly behavior, sharing, and cooperation.

While much of this literature targets children in particular age ranges, age differentiation may be impossible in a small Sunday school program. The Methodist *One Room Sunday School* curriculum is by necessity multiaged and defaults to the simple and the absolute. The "faith point" or central theme described in the 1 Sam 20 lesson is "friends should be loyal to one another and take care of one another" (2003, 88), while the accompanying Bible verse is the ever-popular "a friend loves at all times" (Prov 17:17). The notions of loyalty, caretaking, and love are presented as though self-explanatory, and one wonders whether typical class discussion encourages children to question what these terms actually mean. What paths might *loyalty* lead children to take? Should *love* result in behaviors that always serve the interests or desires of one's friend?

In contrast, the Methodist age-graded curriculum developed for older elementary students leaves 1 Sam 20 more open to complexity. The central message, "we respond to God's love by being a faithful friend," is slightly more nuanced, and the complementing Bible verse, "Some friends play at friendship, but a true friend sticks closer than one's nearest kin" (Prov 18:24), recognizes a range of motives that might underlie friendly behavior ("David and Jonathan" in *Exploring Faith* 2003, 82). Children are invited to consider Jonathan risking his father's anger as he defends David and plots a way to save David's life.

The accompanying illustration suggests some of the pain and ambiguity of Jonathan's plight (fig. 6.6). Here the figure representing Jonathan is older and feminized. Reminiscent of a protective older sister, s/he tightly, maternally, embraces the younger, masculine, but more vulnerable David. Both appear exposed and fragile, standing alone against the world in the vast wheat field setting of their exchange. Again Jonathan is the "true friend sticking closer" to David, an image of painful self-sacrifice, a human buffer against a father's violent rage.

If the Jonathan and David story is to serve as the model lesson on friendship, we must ask how children's biblical literature constructs both the biblical text and biblical messages about friendship. In a world of peer pressure, bullies, queen bees, wannabees, cliques, clubs, and gangs of all types, what do these renditions of the Jonathan and David story communicate? Are there no limits to loyalty in friendship? Is unquestioning trust always a good thing? Are some friends more deserving of devotion than others? Is popularity a sign of divine favor? Is it appropriate to ignore familial responsibilities, to repress one's own interests and talents, to sacrifice one's physical wellbeing or one's own future for the sake of a friend? Should an attachment to someone else be an individual's defining identity marker? Is true friendship possible only with those who share our theological, political, and social views?

Fig. 6.6. *Exploring Faith* (2003).

We would be the last to suggest that teaching children to value friendship and to act in friendly ways is misguided. Moreover, as educators, we understand the importance of pitching biblical study at developmentally appropriate levels. Nevertheless, we wonder if this tendency to reduce both the biblical text and the notion of friendship underestimates the moral, social, and political challenges that even young children face (see Coles 1997; Davis 2001; Parker 2003, 2006) and inhibits more mature ways of reading the Bible once they become older. Both verbal ideas and visual images can leave firm imprints in early childhood that are often difficult to augment or change as children become able to handle more complex ideas (Stein 2009).

As long as Jonathan and David are held up simply as models to emulate, as long as their friendship is idealized, as long as Jonathan's loyalty to David is glorified as exemplary self-sacrifice, then what becomes of the grittier details of their story? Rather than being annoying, and thus expendable, complications to simple lessons, perhaps those gritty details take on more urgency as maturing children find themselves in complicated worlds and relationships that saccharine versions of the Bible can no longer speak to. For children whose experiences require a more complex and individualized set of ethical responses, perhaps a fuller, more multifaceted examination of Jonathan and the challenges of friendship is in order.

Reviewing Jonathan

1 Samuel 13–14

The glaring commonality among the preceding readings is that Jonathan is never considered apart from David. David casts such a massive, dense shadow across tradition that Jonathan's independent presence is difficult to detect and even harder to assess. Moreover, because we read proleptically, with knowledge of the importance David will assume, we often fail to consider that there were other viable leaders in Israel's past and that those heroes, too, had a following among the populace and a special place in cultural memory (cf. McCarter 1980, 27; Hertzberg 1964, 19). The story is remembered primarily as David's story; other characters are supporting cast: foils, friends, helpers, and contextual chorus providing the backdrop and advancing David's plot. Nevertheless, the Bible does afford us, before David commandeers the stage, a momentary glimpse of Jonathan detached from both friend and father. In 1 Sam 13–14 we see an independent Jonathan who displays such courage that Saul pales by comparison, and David himself is hard-pressed to surpass it.

As many commentators note, Jonathan's initiative, assertiveness, and daring in both assassinating the Philistine prefect and attacking the Philistine garrison contrasts sharply with the sedentary, cautious, hesitant Saul. While Saul "sits" at Migron, apparently stymied by a lack of weaponry and warriors, Jonathan and his arms bearer scramble up a cliff face and wreak havoc on an entire company of Philistines. Indeed, if, as Keith Bodner notes (2008, 131–33), a character's first words indicate significant aspects of personality, then Jonathan's first speech act alone sets him apart from his father. While Saul's first utterance had been, "Come, let us go back" (1 Sam 9:5); Jonathan's is, "Come, let us cross over" (14:1, 6). If Saul's tenure is plagued by indecision, retreat, and distraction, Jonathan waits for no one, seizing opportunities as they present themselves. "Cross over" he does, fighting first a terrain of thorn (*bozez*) and tooth (*seneh*), then a garrison of taunting Philistines. By contrast, Saul fiddles around in camp, calling roll to identify the absentee warriors and attempting to consult the ark for guidance about what to do.

The next episode sharpens the contrast between father and son. Saul puts the troops under threat of curse if they eat before he is avenged of his enemies (14:24); Jonathan, however, either does not *hear* or simply does not *heed* the oath (Green 2003, 244), eats honey discovered in the forest, and is reinvigorated while the rest of the soldiers grow faint. When informed, or perhaps confronted, about Saul's oath, Jonathan openly criticizes his father's policy, insisting that such an oath is impractical and shortsighted. His father, he claims, "has *troubled* the land," an accusation that puts Saul in the inauspicious company of Achan (Josh 7), Jephthah (Judg 11), and Simeon and Levi (Gen 34), all notorious for impetuous behavior with deadly consequences. When the oath's breach is discovered, Jonathan is found to be in violation. He announces unapologetically what he has done, "Behold, it is me. I will die."

Is this the response of a "loyal soldier" refusing to question orders, to entertain rebellion, to consider escape? Of a devoted son reluctant to challenge his father (Fokkelman 1993, 74)? Is Jonathan's admission designed to expose the absurdity of the oath, to limit his father's violence, to allow Saul the opportunity to renege, to stir the people to intervene (cf. the discussion of Jephthah's daughter in Fewell 1998, 77; 2003, 79–80)? Whatever lies behind Jonathan's declaration, it carries no purchase with his father. The people, however, will have none of Saul's death sentence. "Should Jonathan die, who has brought about this great deliverance in Israel? Absolutely not!" Perhaps this defensive gesture indicates that the people sense Saul's impending madness (Fokkelman 1993, 74). Or perhaps it suggests that Saul's brand of piety and his view of what serves public interest are not shared by all (Brueggemann 1990, 105). Whatever the case, the public protest, like Jonathan's own earlier criticism of his father, intimates that Saul isn't acting with the people's best interests at heart.

By transferring admiration from father to son, the narrator may indeed be laying the groundwork for David's appearance and promotion. The next step is to transfer admiration from Jonathan to David, which Jonathan himself takes the lead in doing (Jobling 1998). However, in addition to presenting David as the object of Jonathan's affection and loyalty, the narrator has the more arduous task of establishing David as a credible competitor to Jonathan's valor. To accomplish this, the narrator is forced to import Goliath from some other hero's story (2 Sam 21:19) and to make remarkable claims for David's offstage activity—such as killing lions and bears (1 Sam 17:34–37) and capturing two hundred foreskins (18:27) from, we assume, quite unwilling Philistines.

But despite the narrator's valiant efforts to push David into the spotlight, Jonathan's exploits in 1 Sam 13–14 challenge the centripetal force of David's personality. Jonathan is the protagonist for a day. Time slows to accommodate his feats and to allow an unobstructed view of the ways in which he relates to political oppressors, to fellow soldiers, to his father, and to God. This brief portrait presents a young leader who fights oppressors because they are oppressors, who (unlike David) doesn't calculate personal gain (cf. 17:24–27, 30), who (unlike David or Saul) doesn't ask his troops to do anything he's not willing to do himself (cf. 22:17–19; 2 Sam 11), who (unlike David or Saul) has earned and can rely upon the support and protection of his followers (cf. 1 Sam 22:7–8; 23:12; 2 Sam 15–17). He is a son whose loyalty to his father also accommodates correction, critique, and confrontation; he is a religious person who values, but does not bank on, divine favor and who, moreover, is not paralyzed by divine silence. The stubborn memory of his heroism casts a critical shadow over David's character and reign, suggesting an ancient community politically divided and theologically mixed .

1 SAMUEL 18:1–5

In 1 Sam 18 Jonathan ends his solo career. His life (*nephesh*) becomes bound up with David's in more ways than one. David has killed the Philistine giant, without the help of Saul's proffered armor, and has been brought before the king. By the time David finishes speaking with Saul, Jonathan's *nephesh*, his "soul," his life, his desire, is "bound up" with that of David, and Jonathan loves him as his own *nephesh* (18:1). In children's literature, this exorbitantly ticklish language is tamed into terms of mutual friendship, a move that has its analogue in recent English translations. The New English Translation flatly states, "When David had finished talking with Saul, Jonathan and David became bound together in close friendship." The NIV, with its customary Christian slant, is not above resorting to evangelical cliché: "After David had finished talking with Saul, Jonathan became one in spirit with David." Both translations suggest a mutuality that is far from apparent in the Hebrew text and occlude any erotic, emotional, or political meanings commonly noted in critical commentary. Is Jonathan's life "bound" to David's in the same heartrending way as Jacob's is bound to Benjamin's after the loss of Joseph (Gen 44:30)? Does the "binding" (*qashar*) of Jonathan to David foreshadow the two's future conspiracy (*qashar*) against Saul? Does the "binding," as does the word "love," connote political allegiance and patronage that the heir apparent now extends to a special subject (see Thompson 1974, 334; Nardelli 2007)? Does Jonathan "love" David the same way Michal "loves" David? Is Jonathan's identification with David the narrator's attempt to set up David's eventual replacement of Jonathan (Jobling 1998: 95–96)? Whatever the language connotes, it does not reveal how David feels about Jonathan. The most we can glean is that whatever sort of bond Jonathan is offering, David accepts. *Why* he accepts, we are not told.

Further clouding David's response is the way in which Jonathan's bond and affection is narratively entangled with Saul's coopting of David's service. The text jockeys David back and forth between Saul and Jonathan, embedding Jonathan's regard in Saul's conscription, creating a web of political and personal patronage that David would be foolish to refuse. In the course of a few verses (1 Sam 17:58–18:5), Saul interrogates David, Jonathan loves David, Saul detains David for his service, Jonathan cuts a covenant with David and gives him his military gear, Saul puts David in charge of the troops. Saul provides the opportunities for David's advancement, while Jonathan equips him for success. Initially, David's success means success for the house of Saul and Jonathan, but as David's popularity grows, Saul increasingly views him as a rival—which spurs Jonathan to mediate between his father and his friend.

1 SAMUEL 19:1–7

By 1 Sam 19, Saul's jealousy and suspicion of David begin to spill over into his public discourse within the court. As he speaks somewhat vaguely about killing David, the narrator reports that Jonathan, in an echo of Saul's earlier scripted words (18:22), "delighted in David exceedingly" or, alternatively, "was exceedingly mindful of/attentive to David." The rich nuances of this language teeter between personal pleasure and political investment, and Jonathan's prior covenant with David (18:3) also stretches his motives for informing David of Saul's intent into the arena of responsible patronage. Consequently, Jonathan's incentives for protecting and defending David are linguistically stained with both personal fondness and social obligation.

Jonathan's willing intervention on David's behalf is commonly observed in discussions emphasizing the degree of his loyalty to his friend.

Indeed, the repetition of "son" and "father" language underscores the competing relational claims on Jonathan as he attempts to bring about a reconciliation. What is usually missed in such "lessons" is the way in which Jonathan reasons with "his father":

> The king should not sin against his servant David because he has not sinned against you. Rather, his deeds have been exceedingly good for you. He took his life in his own hands and struck the Philistine, and YHWH brought about a great deliverance for all Israel. You saw and rejoiced. Why would you sin against innocent blood—to kill David for nothing? (1 Sam 19:4–5)

Several things are worthy of note. First, although Jonathan speaks to Saul "his father," he addresses him as "the king," which casts the entire exchange in a political key. Second, like his father before him in 14:38, he cuts straight to the heart of the matter, bluntly labeling Saul's intended action as a "sin" without excuse. Third, he appeals to Saul's political self-interests: David's successes have been good for both Saul and the people. Finally, he returns to and intensifies the language of "sin," stressing "innocence" and killing for "no reason."

Jonathan's argument is driven by concerns for royal justice and the good of the people, not unlike his critique of his father in 14:29–30. There Jonathan rightly observes that Saul's decision was not made with the welfare of the people in mind. Here Jonathan points out that, not only would the killing of David be a detriment both to Saul and to all Israel, but that "kings" should not be in the business of killing loyal subjects. Jonathan builds upon, even embodies, the theme inherent in the people's initial request for a king. In 8:5, 6, 19 the people ask for a king who will judge, administer justice, for them. Jonathan is not only holding his father/king to this standard of justice, he is enacting, by pleading the cause of the innocent, the justice one should expect from a king. Persuaded by the arguments of his son, Saul relents, only to be stirred again to violence sometime later by an evil spirit from YHWH.

1 SAMUEL 20

This time it is David, in his first recorded speech to Jonathan (Alter 1999, 123), who must convince the unbelieving Jonathan that Saul devises evil and who invents a ruse to expose the king's true sentiments. Rather than confronting his father directly as he does in 1 Sam 19, Jonathan is persuaded by David to lie to his father regarding David's absence from the royal table. It is, as Robert Polzin notes (1993, 188–90), the first and only time Jonathan engages in any but the most straightforward of behavior, and he does so at David's direction.

The depictions of David and Jonathan in this chapter are highly ambiguous. While David's desperation seems genuine and his insights on Saul more apt than Jonathan's, we clearly see him capable of deception and wonder if such duplicity might characterize his relationship to Jonathan as well (Polzin 1993, 192). Jonathan himself seems naïve about his father and easily manipulated by David, or a more idealistic spin might praise his trust of both father and friend. One might, however, imagine a more complicated Jonathan who, in the course of 1 Sam 20, learns a painful lesson about the extent of his father's ambitions for him and what it means for one's friend to be the enemy of one's family (Green 2007). We might even suspect that Jonathan isn't as oblivious as he first appears to the machinations of both his father and his friend. After having nearly died at his father's command in 1 Sam 14, he is surely aware of his father's capacity for unwarranted violence (Miscall 1986, 107). And after David's remarkable military successes and public popularity, Jonathan is surely aware that David is a potential contender in the struggle for royal power, a bout that customarily takes no prisoners.

Moreover, Jonathan's initial protests may stem not from naïveté but from the constraints of his public surroundings and his social standing in relation to both Saul and David. The entire exchange is riddled with indicators of hierarchical distance between the two young men: David comes "before" Jonathan, petitioning him as a subject might petition a ruler; he speaks of having "found favor" with Jonathan, language that typically refers to a subordinate's favorable standing with one of higher rank; he alludes to himself as Jonathan's "servant" and appeals to the protection afforded by the covenant that Jonathan, as social superior, has initiated with him. This protocol suggests a public setting; hence, Jonathan's proposal that they "go out into the field" may be an attempt to escape the eyes and ears of the court (Bodner 2008, 216). Once in a remote location, Jonathan ceases to defend his father and grows deadly serious, not only promising to protect David, but insisting that David swear to preserve Jonathan's life and those of his descendants if, when, the tables are turned. In this revealing commendation, Jonathan's love for David and his love of his own life form a perilous equation tenuously balanced upon the oath repeatedly pressed upon David and upon Jonathan's knowledge of David's aptitude for deci-sive victories. Consequently, Jonathan invokes the name of Y<small>HWH</small> in mul-tiple ways: in blessing upon David ("may Y<small>HWH</small> be with you"; 20:13), as guarantor of David's success ("may Y<small>HWH</small> seek out David's enemies"; 20:15, 16, 22), and as warning to David to keep his oath ("Y<small>HWH</small> is between you and me forever"; 20:23, 42). Despite tradition's insistence upon Jonathan's absolute loyalty to David, Jonathan ultimately does *not* cast his lot with David. The two do bid farewell, an occasion marked by kissing and weep-ing, but finally punctuated with Jonathan's solemn reminder to David of the oath sworn between them. Jonathan returns to his family, his father, his people, to continue the fight against the oppressive Philistines under whom David will serve as mercenary.

What we find here is an extremely nuanced gesture of friendship, one that pushes the boundaries of familial ties and ethical principles, one that navigates, and for the most part maintains, social and political differences, one that recognizes the complicated moral spectrum within the human heart. It is a relationship heavily burdened with questions regarding intent, with calculations for self-protection, with demands for justice. While children's literature has endlessly rehearsed Saul's persecu-tion of and Jonathan's loyalty to David, it seems to have missed what Jon-athan's insistence on an oath and a covenant reveal about David: namely that David's loyalty is in doubt, and David is capable of the same kind of injustice and unwarranted violence of which he accuses Saul, charac-teristics that will emerge more starkly as his story unfolds. As he does in 1 Sam 14 on behalf of the people and in 1 Sam 19 on behalf of David, Jonathan here again pleads for justice, this time for his own family. Cast-ing off the starstruck, quixotic mantle of tradition, he emerges every bit a pragmatist (Edelman 1991: 158). And as a proponent of justice, he is, perhaps of all the characters in the books of Samuel, the most fitting figure to be king.

Concluding Reflections

The story of Jonathan and David has been presented primarily as an unequivocal story of friendship in both text and image for at least a mil-lennium. In children's Bibles and religious educational materials, it is offered as the template for children to emulate in their own friendships. "Friendship" may indeed be a natural *starting* point for children's engage-ment; however, as we have seen, the story's depiction of friendship is riddled with ambiguities, compromises, and questions of character. We wonder if it's time for children's literature to accommodate a more complicated picture.

Primarily, we would advocate that children's literature embrace Jonathan's individuality and complexity: Jonathan's leadership, military feats, fractured relationship with his father (both before and after he meets David), the decisions with which he wrestles—all provide rich material for children and adolescents undertaking a study of their religious heritage. A balanced treatment of what both Jonathan and David bring to the relationship also allows a fuller discussion of friendship, its demands, challenges, and rewards. But to achieve this, children's Bibles and literature must allow exploratory space and less directive texts and images.

The dynamic relationship between Jonathan and David is well suited to an educational approach that recognizes how children progress through different stages of cognitive growth and moral reasoning.[12] Kindergarteners and early elementary children will relate concretely to an example of friendship in the Bible. They can then be encouraged to shift to their own age-appropriate experiences through open-ended questions: What makes someone a friend? What does a friend do/say? Why are friends important? At the older elementary and young middle school age, peers and best friends take center stage in the child's social world. Older children can better appreciate the conflicting loyalties Jonathan faces and the dangers Jonathan's friendship poses to himself and David. But rather than forcing a template of selfless loyalty as a model for friendship at this stage, a developmental approach would facilitate discussions of the kinds of relationship issues and ethical dilemmas young adolescents face: peer pressure, family versus friends, loyalty, new friends versus old friends, popularity,

---

12. The moral development theory of Lawrence Kohlberg (1927–1987), built upon the work of psychologist Jean Piaget (1896–1980), is perhaps the best known cognitive developmental approach. Kohlberg articulated six stages of moral growth: (1) following rules backed by punishment; (2) following rules when it meets one's immediate interest and allowing others to do the same; (3) behaving according to the expectations of those close to you; (4) fulfilling the duties and laws of the institutions and social systems to which you have agreed; (5) acting out of awareness of one's social contract and commitment to the welfare and protection of all (social contract theory); (6) universal ethical principles of justice guiding personal response regardless of society's laws (Kohlberg 1981). According to Kohlberg, the moral reasoning of many people never reaches beyond levels 3 or 4, and admittedly, his theory has invited criticism (notably Gilligan 1982).

prejudice, materialism, bullying, mutuality, rumors, pushing boundaries, and so on. For older middle and high school adolescents who are developing the cognitive structures for abstract thinking and whose moral reasoning can stretch beyond peers to community and societal justice, there is rich biblical material to mine, such as Jonathan's defense of David to Saul in 1 Sam 19 and the covenant made between David and Jonathan in 1 Sam 20. What do we learn about each as leaders? What character traits do they demonstrate? To what extent does either argue for justice? What purposes does their covenant serve? Why might a covenant be necessary? Are similar "covenants" made between individuals and political communities today? What forms do they take, and how do they serve justice?

This developmental approach for older adolescents can also invite a deeper look at Jonathan and David's relationship. Power, status, and sexuality are highly relevant, and the considerable argument for a gay reading offers a textual arena where teenagers can wrestle with issues of sexual identity and may find support of homosocial lifestyles and acceptance. As we consider age-appropriate children's Bibles and religious education material, there is a critical need for literature that avoids narrow models, theological inevitability, didactic lessons and instead encourages interpretational breadth and questions about the text, the self, and what it means to live in relationship with others.

Works Cited

Ackerman, Susan. 2005. *When Heroes Love: The Ambiguity of Eros in the Stories of Gilgamesh and David.* New York: Columbia University Press.

Aelred of Rievaulx. 2009. *Spiritual Friendship.* Translated by Lawrence C. Braceland. Edited and introduction by Marsha L. Dutton. Cistercian Fathers Series 5. Trappist, Ky.: Cistercian Publications; Collegeville, Minn.: Liturgical Press.

Alter, Robert. 1999. *The David Story: A Translation with Commentary of 1 and 2 Samuel.* New York: Norton.

American Bible Society. 2005. *Read and Learn Bible.* New York: Scholastic.

Bible Personalities: David and Jonathan: A True and Lasting Friendship. Ambassador Youth: A Publication by the Restored Church of God. Online: http://www.thercg.org/youth/articles/0201-jadatalf.html.

Bodner, Keith. 2008. *1 Samuel: A Narrative Commentary.* Hebrew Bible Monographs 19. Sheffield: Sheffield Phoenix.

Bottigheimer, Ruth B. 1994. *Children's Bibles: Sacred Stories, Eternal*

Words, and Holy Pictures. Exhibition Catalogue, Houghton Library, Harvard University, 12 September–28 October 1994. Stony Brook: Bottigheimer.

———. 1996. *The Bible for Children: From the Age of Gutenberg to the Present.* New Haven: Yale University Press.

Brueggemann, Walter. 1990. *First and Second Samuel.* IBC. Louisville: Westminster John Knox.

Coles, Robert. 1997. *The Moral Intelligence of Children.* New York: Random.

Cowley, Abraham. 1656. *Davideis: A Sacred Poem of the Troubles of David.* Book 2 in *Poems.* Edited by A. R. Waller. Repr., 1905. Cambridge: Cambridge University Press.

Davis, Patricia H. 2001. *Beyond Nice: The Spiritual Wisdom of Adolescent Girls.* Minneapolis: Fortress.

Edelman, Diana V. 1991. *King Saul in the Historiography of Judah.* JSOT-Sup 121. Sheffield: JSOT Press.

———. 1992. "Jonathan Son of Saul." *ABD* 3:944–46.

Egermeier, Elsie E. 1923–1955. *Egermeier's Bible Story Book: A Complete Narration from Genesis to Revelation for Young and Old.* Anderson: Warner.

Exploring Faith: Older Elementary Students. 2003. Nashville: Cokesbury.

Faris, Lillie A. 1925–1928. *Standard Bible Story Readers, Books 1–5.* Illustrated by O. A. Stemler and Bess Bruce Cleaveland. Salem, Ohio: Schmul.

Fewell, Danna Nolan. 1998. "Judges." Pages 73–83 in *The Women's Bible Commentary, Expanded Edition with Apocrypha.* Edited by Carol A. Newsom and Sharon H. Ringe. Louisville: Westminster John Knox.

———. 2003. *The Children of Israel: Reading the Bible for the Sake of Our Children.* Nashville: Abingdon.

Fewell, Danna Nolan, and David M. Gunn. 1993. *Gender, Power, and Promise: The Subject of the Bible's First Story.* Nashville: Abingdon.

Fokkelman, J. P. 1993. *Narrative Art and Poetry in the Books of Samuel: A Full Interpretation Based on Stylistic and Structural Analyses.* SSN. Assen: Van Gorcum.

Frontain, Raymond, Jean Wojcik, and Jan Wojcik, eds. 1980. *The David Myth in Western Literature.* West Lafayette, Ind.: Purdue University Press.

George, Mark. 1997. "Assuming the Body of the Heir Apparent: David's Lament." Pages 164–74 in *Reading Bibles, Writing Bodies: Identity and the Book.* Edited by Timothy K. Beal and David M. Gunn. New York: Routledge.

Gilligan, Carol. 1982. *In a Different Voice: Psychological Theory and Women's Development.* Cambridge: Harvard University Press.

Green, Barbara. 2003. *How Are the Mighty Fallen? A Dialogical Study of King Saul in 1 Samuel.* Sheffield: Sheffield Academic Press.

———. 2007. "Experiential Learning: The Construction of Jonathan in the Narrative of Saul and David." Pages 43–62 in *Bakhtin and Genre Theory in Biblical Studies.* Edited by Roland Boer. SemeiaSt 63. Atlanta: Society of Biblical Literature.

Grispino, Joseph A., et al., eds. 1962–1998. *The Golden Children's Bible.* Illustrated by Jose Miralles. Racine: Western/Golden Books.

Gunn, David. 1980. *The Fate of King Saul: An Interpretation of a Biblical Story.* JSOTSup 14. Sheffield: JSOT Press.

Henley, Karyn. 1993–2005. *The Beginner's Bible: Timeless Stories by Zonderkidz.* Illustrated by Dennas Davis. Grand Rapids: Mission City.

Hertzberg, Hans Wilhelm. 1964. *I and II Samuel: A Commentary.* Translated by J. S. Bowden. OTL. Philadelphia: Westminster.

Horner, Tom. 1978. *Jonathan Loved David: Homosexuality in Biblical Times.* Philadelphia: Westminster.

Janes, Edmund S. 1852–56. *Miniature Bible: With Engravings.* Philadelphia: No. 2 Taylor's Alley.

Jennings, Theodore W., Jr. 2001. "Yhwh as Erastes." Pages 36–74 in *Queer Commentary and the Hebrew Bible.* Edited by Ken Stone. Cleveland: Pilgrim; Sheffield: Sheffield Academic Press.

Jobling, David. 1986. "Jonathan: A Structural Study in 1 Samuel." Pages 12–30 in *The Sense of Biblical Narrative: Structural Analyses in the Hebrew Bible I.* JSOTSup 7. Sheffield: University of Sheffield Press.

———. 1998. *I Samuel.* Berit Olam: Studies in Hebrew Narrative and Poetry. Collegeville, Minn.: Liturgical Press.

Kohlberg, Lawrence. 1981. *The Philosophy of Moral Development: Moral Stages and the Idea of Justice.* San Francisco: Harper & Row.

Learning to Use My Bible: A Special Study for Elementary Girls and Boys: Class Pack. 2007. Nashville: Abingdon/Cokesbury.

Linafelt, Tod. 2008. "Private Poetry and Public Eloquence in 2 Samuel 1:17–27: Hearing and Overhearing David's Lament for Jonathan and Saul." *JR* 88:497–526.

Living Together as God's People: Children's Bible Studies. Fall 1987. Nashville: Cokesbury.

Locke, John. 1693. *Some Thoughts on Education*. London: Churchill. Online: http://www.fordham.edu/halsall/mod/1692locke-education.html.

Maus, Cynthia Pearl. 1954. *The Old Testament and the Fine Arts*. New York: Harper.

McCarter, P. Kyle. 1980. *I Samuel: A New Translation with Introduction, Notes, and Commentary*. AB. Garden City, N.Y.: Doubleday.

McKane, William. 1963. *I and II Samuel: Introduction and Commentary*. London: SCM.

McKenzie, Steven L. 2000. *King David: A Biography*. Oxford: Oxford University Press.

Miscall, Peter D. 1986. *I Samuel: A Literary Reading*. Indiana Studies in Biblical Literature. Bloomington: Indiana University Press.

Nardelli, Jean-Fabrice. 2007. *Homosexuality and Liminality in the Gilgameš and Samuel*. Amsterdam: Hakker.

New Revised Standard Version Children's Bible. 2006. Nashville: Abingdon.

One Room Sunday School. 9 November 2003. Nashville: Cokesbury.

Parker, Evelyn. 2003. *Trouble Don't Last Always: Emancipatory Hope among African American Adolescents*. Cleveland: Pilgrim.

———, ed. 2006. *The Sacred Selves of Adolescent Girls: Hard Stories of Race, Class, and Gender*. Cleveland: Pilgrim.

Pebworth, Ted-Larry. 1980. "Cowley's *Davideis* and the Exaltation of Friendship." Pages 96–104 in Frontain and Wojcik 1980.

Polzin, Robert. 1993. *Samuel and the Deuteronomist: 1 Samuel*. A Literary Study of the Deuteronomic History 2. Bloomington: Indiana University Press.

Prothero, Stephen. 2003. *American Jesus*. New York: Farrar, Straus & Giroux.

Pyper, Hugh. 2007. "Love beyond Limits: The Debatable Body in Depictions of David and Jonathan." Pages 38–59 in *Between the Text and the Canvas: The Bible and Art in Dialogue*. Edited by J. Cheryl Exum and Ela Nutu. Sheffield: Sheffield Phoenix.

Richards, Lawrence O. 1984. *The Adventure Bible: A Study Bible for Kids*. Grand Rapids: Zondervan.

Roper, David H. 1973 (updated 2000). "Jonathan and David: 1 Samuel 18–20, 23." Peninsula Bible Church Library. Palo Alto, Calif.: Discovery Publishing. Online: http://www.pbc.org/files/messages/18136/18138_3056.html.

Ross, Stephen M. 1980. "Faulkner's *Absalom, Absalom!* and the David Story: A Speculative Contemplation." Pages 136–53 in Frontain and Wojcik 1980.

Sooy, J. L. 1889. *Bible Talks with Children; or, The Scriptures Simplified for the Little Folks, with Lessons Drawn from the Actual Sayings of Childhood*. Philadelphia: Parish.

Spenser, Edmund. 1882. *The Faerie Queene* IV from *The Complete Works in Verse and Prose of Edmund Spenser*. London: Grosart. Prepared by Risa S. Bear for Renascence Editions: University of Oregon, 1995. Online: http://darkwing.uoregon.edu/~rbear/queene4.

Stein, Valerie. 2009. "Know*Be*Do: Using the Bible to Teach Ethics to Children." *SBL Forum*. Online: http://www.sbl-site.org/publications/article.aspx?articleId=799.

Thompson, J. A. 1974. "The Significance of the Verb *Love* in the David-Jonathan Narratives in 1 Samuel." *VT* 24:334–38.

THE WORD BECAME VISUAL TEXT: THE BOY JESUS IN CHILDREN'S BIBLES

Melody Briggs

The only story in the canonical Bible that portrays Jesus as a child is his visit to the Jewish temple at the age of twelve, in Luke 2:40–52. While both Matthew and Luke contain birth narratives, only the Lukan account extends this narrative to include comments on Jesus' childhood development and a story to illustrate this development. It is not surprising then that this story is frequently selected for inclusion in children's Bibles: it provides child readers with their only view of Jesus at an age close to their own.

While identifying with Jesus as a child may draw child readers into the biblical world, it is adults—the authors, illustrators, and publishers of children's Bibles—who shape the contours of this world. Ruth Bottigheimer, a historian of children's Bibles, defines these texts as the "prose re-workings of the narrative sections of the Bible for child-readers" (1996, 4, citing Peter-Perrett 1991, 53). These rewritten Bible stories are an echo of the text, an interpretation that determines the form of the biblical text provided to children. Their production is generally guided by two aims: to communicate biblical content to children, rather than the actual words of Scripture, and to make the text relevant to its target readers (Bottigheimer 1996, 88).

This pursuit of relevance significantly influences what is communicated through a retelling. What is deemed relevant often derives from the way of life that the story's retellers would like to form in their readers; that is, the retellers seek to communicate the biblical story in a way that produces a certain response in their readers. While this response may or may not be an overt aim of the retelling, it is nonetheless a product of the ideological concerns of the reteller. This response is a function of the implied reader embedded in the text and can be detected through a close reading of the text. We will look at these potential responses in more detail in a later section.

The pursuit of relevance also impacts the retellings' representations of Jesus as a boy. In a volume concerned with the depiction of otherness in children's Bibles, it is notable how Jesus' otherness is all but eliminated from the retellings considered here. Although the Jesus of Luke 2 is a twelve-year-old Jewish boy, living in the first century, originating from northern Palestine, and steeped in the cultural and religious practices of his sociohistorical context, these characteristics are only minimally represented in the retellings. What is foregrounded instead are the aspects of the story that provide points of familiarity for contemporary readers, such as Jesus getting lost, engaging with his parents, and talking with a group of teachers.

Contemporary notions of childhood thus shape these representations of Jesus. Although the concept of childhood is a social construct that alters through history (see Ariès 1962), any differences between a first-century Jewish concept of childhood and a twenty-first-century concept are virtually erased in favor of maintaining the story's relevance for contemporary readers. According to Jewish custom, a Jewish boy came of age at thirteen years, and in this story, Jesus is twelve and thus on the brink of manhood. Yet the significance of Jesus' age is rarely addressed in the retellings, and, as we will see, some of them even cast him as a younger child.

Children's Bibles are generally illustrated books that communicate through both verbal and visual components; therefore, both their words and pictures require analysis in order to ascertain meaning. These two discourses convey different types of information and may even generate divergent meanings. According to the children's literature theorists Nikolajeva and Scott, "the visual text is mimetic; it communicates by showing. The verbal text is diegetic; it communicates by telling" (2006, 26). Analyzing Luke 2:40–52 in a children's Bible is not merely a matter of asking what illustrations have been added or what words have been chosen. Placing words and pictures "into relationship with each other inevitably changes the meaning of both" (Nodelman 1988, 199). It is this marriage of words and images on the page that forms the narrative and determines the impact of the story upon its reader.

In this article, I analyze the relevant aspects of the verbal and visual discourses of a variety of retellings of the story of Jesus in the temple to explore what they communicate to their readers. In order to provide background for these analyses, I turn first to a brief discussion of Luke

2:40–52. Then, I offer close readings of a number of retellings, examining their ideological functions. Finally, I consider a number of retellings that demonstrate how the narrative power of the Lukan text may be preserved. Here I argue that, rather than primarily confining the reader's response to the ideological concerns of its retellers, this approach has the benefit of enabling the reader to respond imaginatively to the text.[1]

READING LUKE 2:40–52

Before we can consider how children's Bibles retell the story of Jesus in the temple, we must first consider how the Gospel of Luke tells it. This is not the place for a full exegesis of this passage. However, a few comments on the structure and literary elements of the narrative will help to shed light on the shape it is given in children's Bibles.

Although the story actually begins in 2:41 and concludes in 2:51, 2:40 and 2:52 are included in this discussion because of the role they play in the passage as well as in children's Bibles. Luke 2:40 both concludes the previous section and provides a transition into this story, while 2:52 concludes the whole Lukan infancy narrative. These two verses form a frame around the story and draw attention to Jesus' development, particularly his developing wisdom or *sophia*. Luke 2:40 asserts that Jesus was "filled with wisdom," while 2:52 describes him as increasing in wisdom. In the latter verse, wisdom is the first aspect of Jesus' development that is mentioned, placing it in a position of primacy.

The story may therefore be intended as an illustration of that wisdom (Tannehill 1996, 77).[2] This raises an important question: Does the story demonstrate that Jesus, even as a child, already possessed great wisdom, or does it exemplify the development of Jesus' wisdom? Some children's Bibles, particularly those concerned with theological boundaries, use the story to demonstrate the former position: Jesus, as a child, was already wise. They represent Jesus as a static character, already formed at age

---

1. The Bible translation I use throughout is the NRSV unless otherwise indicated. The children's Bibles under consideration are all produced for the British market, although a number of these are American in origin.

2. While this is perhaps the dominant theological interpretation of the purpose of the story, the story may also be viewed as a depiction of Jesus' maturation or an assertion of his unique sonship, both of which are addressed in the discussion below. See, e.g., Green 1997; de Jonge 1978.

twelve, and the purpose of the story is to provide a portrait of that wisdom. Other children's Bibles retain more of the ambiguity of the text, portraying, for instance, the crucial exchange between Jesus and his mother, but not controlling the reader's interpretation of its significance.

The narrative begins in 2:41–42 with a brief description of the family's annual trip to Jerusalem for the Passover. These verses set the scene for the story, and the Lukan author assumes knowledge of the Passover festival on the part of his implied reader. Children's Bibles cannot do the same, and, as we will see, many seek to fill this gap in their target readers' knowledge base. The next four verses, 2:43–46, describe Mary and Joseph's search for their son, climaxing with their discovery of him in the temple debating with its teachers. The plot of the first half of the story concentrates on this search for Jesus, adding significant tension to the narrative. Although Mary and Joseph are the active agents, Jesus is the focal character: the plot begins with his trip to Jerusalem and then directs the reader's focus toward the search for him. Most children's Bibles recognize the discovery of Jesus as a key moment in the narrative, and virtually all of them visually depict this scene. Some of them even conclude the narrative here.

However, in the biblical text, this is not simply a story about Jesus as a lost boy. The second half of the story focuses on the nature of Jesus' wisdom, first describing people's responses to his words and then detailing the verbal exchange between Jesus and his mother. The narrative gives two angles on the missing boy: those in the temple see him as remarkable, a messianic character in the making. His mother, on the other hand, is more concerned with his conduct than his precocious intellect. First she questions his behavior, then she makes a statement clarifying the impact of this behavior on his earthly parents, those responsible for him. The text uses a strong term, "to cause pain," to describe this impact (Nolland 1989, 131). Mary's response calls into question the validity of Jesus' wisdom: is it merely good answers, or does it also translate into prudent conduct? As the Messiah, Jesus needs both.

Mary's veritable rebuke evokes Jesus' first words in Luke's Gospel, which are delivered in the form of two questions: "Why were you searching for me? Did you not know that I must be in my Father's house?" (2:49). The second question can mean Jesus would be "in my Father's house" or "about my Father's business" (Marguerat and Bourquin 1998, 117). The Greek phrase encompasses both meanings, and the biblical writer may have deliberately included this ambiguity in the text (de Jonge 1978, 353). Many children's Bibles eliminate this polysemy, drawing out one of the two possible interpretations, but not both.[3] Interpreting the phrase as "in my Father's house" provides a direct response to the question of Jesus' location, but Jesus' parents' inability to understand the phrase signals that the other meaning may also have been in view. This second meaning has to do with the nature of Jesus' relationship to his heavenly father and its implications for his life. While Mary refers to Joseph as Jesus' "father," in his response Jesus attributes this title to God, foregrounding the difference between his mother's perception and his own. This pinpoints a central issue in the biblical account: to whom does Jesus owe his "primary allegiance" (Green 1997, 156)? The remainder of the Gospel indicates that Jesus' allegiance is to God (cf. 8:19–21). Yet in this passage, Jesus is still a boy, and this encounter highlights the complexity of negotiating between his status as God's son and his role as the son of earthly parents (cf. Nolland 1989, 132).

The Lukan account concludes with a description of Jesus as an obedient son. Although Jesus' parents may not fully understand him, he submits to them. Jesus' conduct is altered, at least moderately, through this incident (Nolland 1989, 131). By returning with his parents to Nazareth and obeying them, Jesus enacts wisdom. He has even, perhaps, gained wisdom through this episode for, in his willingness to return, Jesus yields to his role as the son of Mary and Joseph, accepting that at the age of twelve he is not yet ready to engage in public ministry.

The story, then, illustrates Jesus' wisdom on two levels. It portrays Jesus as advanced in wisdom, even as a boy, and it also demonstrates how Jesus' wisdom was honed through his experiences as a child. While the text is open to either or indeed both of these readings, retellings of this story tend to reduce the narrative to just one of these meanings. We turn now to a consideration of how a number of children's Bibles portray this wise yet developing boy Jesus.

Taming the Text

While the Lukan purpose for the story of Jesus in the temple has to do, at least in part, with a portrayal of Jesus' wisdom, retellings of Luke 2:40–52 often reflect other areas of concern. These concerns may be defined by the

---

3. Indeed, any English translation must do the same, although English Bibles usually preserve some of the ambiguity by including a footnote containing the alternative meaning. For instance, the NRSV includes "Father's house" in the text and gives the alternative reading in a footnote.

type of implied reader they construct. Literary theorist Wolfgang Iser uses the term "implied reader" to refer to the "active participation" of the reader in a novel. The term encompasses both the "prestructuring of the potential meaning by the text" and the "reader's actualization of this potential through the reading process" (1974, xii). Our focus here will be upon the way retellers structure their version of the story of Jesus in the temple around a particular meaning, often in a way that excludes other potential meanings.

Some retellers use the story to foreground a particular social value, constructing an implied reader who needs moral guidance. I refer to this approach as *value-driven* retellings. Other retellers seek to protect the reader from theological error and so construct an implied reader who requires theological boundaries. I refer to these texts as *dogma-driven*. Others supplement the narrative with information that, while providing background to the story, is not central to the biblical version. The implied reader here appears to be in need of education, and I refer to this approach as *education-driven*. Finally, some retellers seek to maintain the ambiguity of the text while encouraging child readers to resolve this ambiguity. This implied reader is in need of stimulation to engage with the story, and I refer to these texts as *engagement-driven*. These uses of the story are not mutually exclusive, and many children's Bibles incorporate elements from more than one approach. But for the sake of clarity, we will consider each approach separately.

We will look at value-driven and dogma-driven retellings in this section and discuss the other two approaches in the following section. Both value-driven and dogma-driven retellings could be described as "taming" the text so that it aligns with a particular ideological or theological position. This taming is not just about the text; it also seeks a correspondent response in the reader.

Value-Driven Retellings

Bottigheimer (1996) demonstrates that children's Bibles invariably reflect the social values of the historical era, location, and confession that produce them. Some adults view the Bible itself as a repository of religious morals and children as the fundamental members of society in need of learning these morals. It is an easy step from this perspective on the Bible to treating children's Bibles as tools of socialization. The New Testament's only story of Jesus as a boy particularly provides fodder for those who wish to inculcate contemporary family values.

An obvious example is the way in which some children's Bibles use this story to teach children to obey their parents. The *One Way Bible* (2004) contains Bible stories selected from the New Living Translation. It appears, at first glance, to be an abridged version of a dynamic-equivalent Bible translation. However, the story of Jesus in the temple is framed by an introduction and epilogue that control its interpretation. The writers Emily Malone and Jeanette Dall, along with the illustrator Joe Van Severen, present Luke 2:40–52 on one doublespread, only about half of which is devoted to the biblical text. The top of the left-hand page (or verso) entitles the story "Jesus and His Parents." The story is thus set up as a narrative about the relationship between Jesus and his parents. Then come two sentences that narrow the parameters of meaning considerably: "Think of a time when it was hard for you to obey your parents. If obeying your parents is hard for you, imagine how Jesus felt. Mary and Joseph were his parents, but he was *their* God. See what Jesus did when his parents were upset with him" (2004, 122). Writing the introduction in the second-person allows it to address the implied reader directly. This introduction functions as a lens through which to read the story: the implied reader expects the story to address the difficulty of filial obedience.

All of this is printed in a bright orange font, while the biblical text that follows is printed in a smaller, black font. The epilogue returns to the orange font with, "Let's talk about it…" but then reverts back to the black font for the following: "Even though Jesus was God, he respected his parents by returning to Nazareth and obeying them. Jesus showed us how to be obedient to our parents and to do what they ask without complaining. When we obey and respect our parents, we are following Jesus' example" (2004, 123). Returning to the black font places the significance of this injunction on a par with the Bible story. Even though the introduction raises the interesting paradox of Jesus' incarnational status relative to Mary and Joseph, the epilogue treats this status as a mere plank upon which to erect a motive for filial obedience. Since Jesus is God, he is greater than the implied reader: yet even he submits to his parents. For the implied reader, what is significant is the way the story models Jesus' obedience to his parents. Jesus' wisdom, the Lukan framing idea, is thus replaced with Jesus' obedience. The conclusion of the doublespread underlines this by stating: "Honor your father and mother as the Lord your God commanded you. Deuteronomy 5:16 NLT." An Old Testament commandment about duty to parents is added to strengthen the authors' use of the narrative, regardless of the commandment's context. The Lukan tension between Jesus' allegiance to God and his duty to his parents as a child is eliminated; the only aspect of Jesus' otherness that is preserved is his deity, in order to present him as a model child.[4]

Another value that some children's Bibles attribute to Luke 2:40–52 is God's protection of children. In *My First Bedtime Bible* (2005), Mary Batchelor and Penny Boshoff present the story on one doublespread. The brief verbal narrative truncates the story, building from a short search for Jesus to Mary and Joseph's discovery of him in the temple. The written text is fully integrated with the story's one image, which depicts Jesus in the temple talking to the teachers while Mary and Joseph look on. This image shows Jesus safe and comfortable in the temple, surrounded by teachers and his parents—a familiar set of adults to any child. This book targets young readers, and the Jesus depicted here is a small child, with only his first-century clothing to hint at any difference between him and the reader. The authors conclude the verbal discourse with: "'Didn't you know I'd be here in my Father's house?' said Jesus" (2005, 149).

Each doublespread in this children's Bible includes a short prayer. Here the prayer is located after the story in the top right-hand (or recto) corner and reads: "When I get lost, you're always there, When I'm alone, you always care. Please keep me by your side, God. Amen" (2005, 149). While the written narrative leaves some of the ambiguity of Jesus' question intact, this concluding prayer disambiguates Jesus' response, by drawing the focus back to the search for Jesus and narrowing the meaning of the story to that of a child being lost. This could be viewed as an ironic counterpoint to the illustration, but casting the message in the form of a prayer suggests that it is not ironic, but serious. The prayer is the only part of the verbal discourse written in the second person, directly addressing the implied reader and therefore having the most personal significance.

Dogma-Driving Retellings

While the two children's Bibles discussed above instantiate the shaping of the story by particular values, another approach shapes the text for theological purposes. One common theological concern is that of guarding the

---

4. Notably, Malone and Dall's names do not appear on the title page of the *One Way Bible* but are hidden away in fine print on the reverse of the title page, which lists them as "project authors." This children's Bible thus gives the impression that it presents only the biblical text to its readers.

purity of Jesus' conduct in the temple, lest his perfection be brought into question. This can be seen in *The Lion Graphic Bible* (1998), which presents Bible stories in a comic-strip format. Its illustrator and authors, Jeff Anderson, Mike Maddox and Steve Harrison, provide their boy Jesus with an excuse for staying behind in Jerusalem. After Mary and Joseph find him in the temple, Joseph asks, "What are you *doing* here? This is the temple!" Jesus replies, in the next panel, "The caravan left without me. I knew I'd be safe here, and that you'd come sooner or later" (1998, 169).

This response effectively removes the weight of Jesus' decision to stay in Jerusalem from his own twelve-year-old shoulders and places it on the adults responsible for the caravan. Essentially Jesus responds, "You left without me, so I found somewhere safe to wait." Any hint of subversion on Jesus' part is erased from the text, and Jesus is presented instead as a sensible boy who acted wisely and, with a nod to the current mood of British society, placed safety first. It is not until the subsequent panel that Jesus states, "After all, didn't you know I would be in my *Father's* house?" (1998, 169). However, Jesus' initial statement so thoroughly answers Joseph's question that it makes this subsequent panel appear to be an afterthought. The authors also incorporate only the second of Jesus' two questions to his parents, as the first question, "why were you searching for me?" contradicts the motive that they have attributed to Jesus.

Another theological boundary evident in representations of the boy Jesus is the preservation of his deity and the attributes that accrue to it. Author Pat Alexander, in *The Puffin Children's Bible* (1991), attributes any failure in understanding to Mary and Joseph, keeping Jesus' understanding and wisdom intact. After Mary asks, "Why did you do this to us?" the author interjects a narrative clarification: "Jesus seemed almost surprised at her question" (1991, 176). The author then configures Jesus' reply in a way that indicates that it is Mary's question that is surprising, not Jesus' behavior, collapsing Jesus' two questions into one assertion: "But surely you knew I had to be here, in my Father's house." While the two Lukan questions may be rhetorical, they are also open ended; Jesus, as a boy, seeks to understand, and possibly even to appease, his parents. By turning these questions into a single statement, Alexander empowers her representation of Jesus, and his questions coalesce into a subtle rebuke.

The author then alludes to Jesus' authority by unpacking his parents' response: "Mary and Joseph were puzzled by Jesus' answer. They were forgetting that Jesus was no ordinary boy, that God was his Father" (1991, 176). This final sentence sets up a contrast between Jesus' parents and Jesus: while the former are forgetful, Jesus is a deity. Alexander's Jesus is above reproach. The story concludes: "They returned to Nazareth, where Jesus was obedient to them as he had always been before" (1991, 176). If the story had raised any questions about Jesus' obedience as a child, this final sentence quashes them. Jesus is not a child so much as God in a boy-suit. The reworked story preserves his knowledge and authority.

Landy points out that children's Bibles, in an attempt to be responsible, create a canon within a canon, which "adapts the Bible to our ethical needs." Landy considers this "an act of bad faith" (1997, 164); that is, such adult censuring displays a lack of faith in the text. In fact, authors who frame the text around an interpretation in line with a particular set of values or a theological position display a lack of faith in both the text and their readers. Although both the *One Way Bible* and *The Puffin Children's Bible* stress Jesus' obedience, the former uses it as a model for its readership while the latter foregrounds it as part of a theologically acceptable portrait of Jesus. The former is concerned with the behavior of its readership while the latter is concerned with their beliefs. Both frame the story in a way that guides their reader toward a particular response. In the next section, we consider two other uses of the story to guide the reader.

Guiding the Reader

Children's Bibles are designed, by definition, for their target readership, and the perceived needs of these readers are often not far below the surface of the text. In the case of the story of Jesus in the temple, these needs include the acquisition of information to enhance understanding of the story and stimulation to look for some meaning in the text. We will look at each of these approaches in turn.

Education-Driven Retellings

Children's Bibles often serve as tools for Christian education. The result of this for Luke 2:40–52 is usually the devotion of significant narrative space to depicting the story's primary background event, the Passover. But since most children's Bibles are restricted by space, many retellers then truncate another part of the narrative to make space for their educational information; the standard choice is Mary and Joseph's search for Jesus. As we saw earlier, the Lukan text builds up narrative tension through this search. In these retellings, the narrative tension is lost, and effective story-telling given second place to an education about Jewish customs.

For example, readers of *The Lion First Bible* (1997), by author Pat Alexander and illustrator Leon Baxter, may be led to believe that the story is primarily about the Passover. This retelling consists of three doublespreads on six pages. Each page contains written text and one picture. The top of the first doublespread displays the title: "Where is Jesus?" While this sets the story up as a search for Jesus, neither the focus of the first half of the verbal discourse, nor the illustrations support the title. The boy Jesus is not only in, but also central to five of the six illustrations, making it virtually impossible for the implied reader to wonder about his location. The entire first half of the story depicts the pilgrimage to Jerusalem and the celebration of the Passover. It is not until the recto of doublespread two that Jesus goes missing. This page contains the only image where Jesus is absent; then he is discovered immediately overleaf, on the verso of doublespread three. Luke's tightly woven account building up to Jesus' first encounter with the teachers in the temple is sacrificed to make room for a secondary story about the Passover, which distracts the reader from the original plot.

The verso of doublespread two includes an image depicting Jesus, Mary, and Joseph eating the Passover meal together. While the image does little more than portray the three family members consuming nondescript food from a large bowl, the written text defines the context, explicating the significance of the meal as a recalling of God's delivery of his people from Egypt. The author and illustrator even provide a footnote to their version of the exodus story located earlier in their children's Bible. If their intent were to foreground the narrative continuity between the Old and New Testaments and to locate the boy Jesus firmly within the Jewish tradition, this would have been theologically laudable and would have highlighted Jesus' religious and cultural otherness. However, the Passover meal is not portrayed in their earlier retelling of the exodus. Indeed, the meal's insertion in the New Testament narrative appears to be a way of making up for its omission from the Old Testament account.

Another topic of education is the Jewish temple. By far the most common picture included in visual depictions of Luke 2:40–52 is an image of Jesus in the temple, surrounded by the Jewish teachers and sometimes his parents. Children's Bibles that reduce the story to one doublespread visually summarize the story with this image, giving the scene the most narrative weight. If the child reader retains one image from this story, it will be this one. As we saw above, Mary and Joseph's discovery of Jesus in the temple is the climax of the first half of the Lukan story, so this visual representation retains some of the Lukan emphasis. In the Lukan account, Jesus locates himself in the temple as the place on earth that signifies the presence of his heavenly Father. The illustrators of children's Bibles usually depict the temple through its interior only, reducing it to colonnades, a stone floor, and a spacious hall. The referent for these visual metonyms is left primarily to the reader's imagination. Aware of this, authors often interject brief explanations into the verbal discourse.

In *The Big Bible Storybook* (Barfield et al. 2006) the story appears on one doublespread with a single full-spread image showing Jesus, the teachers, Mary, and Joseph in the interior of the temple. This interior functions as a backdrop and consists only of a tiled floor and two colonnades in earthy tones. The authors elaborate on this further in the written narrative, calling the temple, "the beautiful meeting place, where people could go to pray and sing to God" (2006, 130). The phrase "meeting place" affirms the subject of the visual discourse: Jesus' encounter there with the Jewish teachers as well as his parents. But the Jewish understanding of the temple as God's dwelling place is omitted, and the temple is represented as a place where people go to meet one another. The description "pray and sing to God" distances the temple even further from its Jewish roots, suggesting that it is like a church. The otherness of Jesus' location, with all of its implications for his identity, is eliminated in order to convey the central site of Jewish worship as a familiar setting.

Educating the reader is beneficial if it enhances understanding of the story of Jesus in the temple. As Nikolajeva and Scott point out:

> For many stories with a historical dimension, the correct and careful delineation of setting is both necessary and educational. The details of the setting can offer information about places and historical epochs that go far beyond the young reader's experience, and do so in a subtle, non-intrusive way that provides an understanding of unfamiliar manners and morals and the cultural environment in which the action takes place. (2006, 63)

The key critique here of children's Bibles is that their authors and illustrators sometimes fail to approach this education in "a subtle, nonintrusive way." When they use the story of Jesus in the temple primarily to educate their readership, they may obscure the actual story. Educational information needs to be limited to that which illuminates the story. The basic plot of Jesus in the temple is not dependent, for instance, upon a working knowledge of the Passover festival. As de Jonge points out, the Passover is not central to the story, providing little more than a reason for Jesus' location in Jerusalem (1978, 330). In contrast, some understanding of the Jewish temple may help the reader to grasp the tension that Jesus experiences between the locus of his father in Jerusalem and his parents in Nazareth.

ENGAGEMENT-DRIVEN RETELLINGS

In contrast to the other approaches we have discussed, engagement-driven retellings of Luke 2:40–52 tend to keep the interpretation of the story open, while concomitantly prodding the reader to wrestle with the story's meaning. Consequently the narrative structure is often preserved, and the reader empowered to interrogate the text.

Questions are commonly used to stimulate the implied reader's engagement. In the *Candle Read and Share Bible*, Gwen Ellis concludes the story with Jesus' statement to his mother: "You should have known I must be where My Father's work is!" (2007, 315). However, the final written element on the doublespread is a question framed and offset by a blue rectangle at the bottom of the recto. It is directed at the implied reader: "That was a strange thing for Jesus to say. What do you think he meant?" (2007, 315). The implied reader thus steps into the role of Mary, pondering Jesus' words.

Author Christina Goodings and illustrator Melanie Mitchell, in *My Little Bible Board Book* (2007), attribute this same question to Mary, weaving it into the story as the final line of their verbal discourse. Jesus says to Mary, "Didn't you know I would be here? … The Temple is my father's house." The text concludes: "What did he mean? Mary wondered." The written discourse leaves the implied reader with a query about the significance of Jesus' statement. However, any implication of difference in understanding between Jesus and his mother is removed by the visual discourse. The story occupies one doublespread, and the recto depicts Mary running open armed toward Jesus in the temple. The written text does not indicate Jesus' age, but the image suggests that he is about six years old. Mary and Jesus face each other, smiling broadly, and Jesus lifts one arm up to Mary, ready to be swept up into his mother's arms. Clearly this is a child who is glad to see his mother, casting Jesus in the role of a contemporary lost child.

While encouraging engagement with the meaning of the text is beneficial to any reader, it also sets the story up as a narrative that must be worked at. Even engagement-driven retellings are not content to let the story function on the merits of narrative alone. Their implied reader needs to actively engage with the text in order to discern some significance in the story. While these retellings may preserve the polyphony of the text, they maintain an expectation that the story has some significance and that that significance should be pursued. Nonetheless, this approach preserves an openness in its retelling that comes closer than any of the other approaches to the complexity of the Lukan text. We turn now to a consideration of how the narrative elements of Luke 2:40–52 may be given priority.

REDEEMING CHILDREN'S BIBLES

When the retellers of the story of Jesus in the temple shape the story around a particular concern, what child readers experience is not the polyphony and otherness of the biblical world, but a domesticated story that, while being perfectly safe, holds little challenge. This analysis has shown that it is not just the text that is tamed; it is also the reader. Indeed, it could be said that the text is tamed in order to produce a certain outcome in the reader. The text becomes a didactic tool, and narrative takes second place to function. When stories become repositories for teaching, their "narrative power" is often overlooked (Stephens and McCallum 1998, 16), and children are robbed of one of their primary motives for reading.

Children do not read in order to absorb approved ideologies. If child readers are to read the biblical text more than once, and in a variety of forms, it must be allowed to *be* narrative. When children's Bibles present the biblical text as a source of information or training, readers may be led to think, "I know that information or moral. I don't need to read it again." For readers to experience the text in such a way that they want to return to it, children's Bibles need to draw readers into the biblical world and leave them wanting to visit there again.

While all narrative has an embedded ideology, effective narrative enables the reader to engage with the story, not merely to work out its meaning but in order to experience its secondary world. Ellis and Smallman, in the *Candle Read and Share Bible* (2007), use both their visual and verbal discourses to draw the reader into their retelling of the story of Jesus in the temple. The story is contained on two doublespreads, with a paragraph of text at the top of each page and an image at the bottom. The title of the first doublespread is, "Where is Jesus?" and the focal characters are Joseph and Mary, who essentially enact the title. The first sentence establishes their centrality: "Every year Jesus' parents went to Jerusalem to celebrate the Passover feast" (2007, 312). Both pictures affirm their significance. The image on the verso shows them near the end of a line of travelers, walking along a road toward the right of the double spread. In the second image, they have reversed direction and are running back toward the left, while their fellow travelers continue toward the right. Here they are large scale, their facial expressions convey anxiety and their heads ringed with sweat drops emphasizing their effort.

Jesus is visually absent from this doublespread. A child reader attempting to answer the title question would find her- or himself in the same subject position as Jesus' parents, looking for, but not finding the child Jesus. The verbal text is bound closely to the visual, describing Mary and Joseph's discovery of Jesus' absence, their return to Jerusalem to search for him, and concluding: "They were afraid they had lost Jesus" (2007, 313). The words keep the focus on the search for Jesus, and the implied reader takes on the same role as Jesus' parents, effectively entering the narrative world.

The tension is resolved as soon as the page is turned, so that like Mary and Joseph, the implied reader makes a sudden discovery. The written text declares that Mary and Joseph find Jesus in the temple, and the verso image depicts Jesus talking with three teachers. Mary and Joseph join Jesus in the final, recto image, their faces conveying relief but their heads still ringed with sweat. This visual sequence forms a coherent narrative. If the verbal text were removed and only the images remained, the order of the pictures and their linear portrayal of Mary and Joseph communicate a basic message about two adults' search for a boy. The synergy of the verbal and visual discourses gives the reader an experience of the story.

Effective retellings will also be those that unlock the child reader's imagination. As Iser asserts, good literature does not provide everything for the reader; rather, the writer leaves gaps in the narrative so that the reader has to create and not merely observe (1974, 38–39). As we have seen, retellers frequently fill the gaps in the Lukan narrative with signposts to its meaning. When meaning is controlled, the reader cannot participate in what Iser calls the "game of the imagination," and the result is boredom and abandonment (1974, 275).

The reader's imagination is engaged when the retelling empowers the reader to negotiate between different meanings, as exemplified by the retelling in *The Lion Read and Know Bible* (2008), by author Sophie Piper and illustrator Anthony Lewis. This retelling occupies two doublespreads, and the image on the second doublespread occupies the top half of the recto and depicts Jesus sitting in the temple, in the middle of a semicircle with two teachers on either side. Jesus and the teachers are on the right side of the image, and they look back across the page at Mary and Joseph who are standing on the left, having just entered the temple. Mary's arms are raised and she leans toward Jesus. The visual focus thus draws the implied reader's eyes to Mary, who in turn draws the focus back to Jesus. The overall visual focus then is on the interaction between Mary and Jesus. This image foregrounds their dialogue, which accompanies the picture. The language used is informal, giving a sense of familiarity:

> "What are you doing here?" cried Mary, as she rushed to hug him. "We've been frantic looking for you."
>
> Jesus replied with genuine surprise. "Why did you have to look for me? Didn't you know I would be in my Father's house?" (2008, 252)

The written text follows the structure of the Lukan account, while expanding it to attribute emotions to both characters. Jesus' response is embroidered with surprise, a surprise that reflects his own position. Only now does he perceive the impact of his conduct upon his parents. Yet Jesus' questions also subvert the necessity of Mary's search. If she had recalled who Jesus' true father was, she may have found him much more quickly. This retelling retains the tension between Jesus' allegiance to God and his attachment to his earthly family, foregrounding his difference from other children. The visual discourse draws attention to this tension and provides readers with just enough detail to stimulate their imaginations. The implied reader is left to ponder the implications of Jesus' conduct as well as the nature of his relationship to his parents.

The openness of the Lukan story may also be preserved through an approach that critiques received values rather than inculcating them. According to children's literature theorist Lurie, the most popular children's texts "are subversive in one way or another" (1990, 4). This approach is appropriate to the Gospel of Luke, for in it Jesus repeatedly subverts the values of his society for the sake of God's kingdom.[5] Subversive retellings

---

5. For instance, he elevates poverty over riches, breaks rules in order feed his friends, and rather deliberately insults one of his hosts (see Luke 6:1–5, 20–26; 11:37–44).

encourage the reader to interrogate the ideas and conventions represented in the text, as well as those of their own world.

This can be seen in the *Manga Messiah* (2006), in the way author Hidenori Kumai and illustrator Kozumi Shinozawa draw out the contrast between other peoples' perception of the boy Jesus and his parents' reaction. After Mary and Joseph discover Jesus in the temple, Kumai and Shinozawa include four panels depicting onlookers praising the boy Jesus' intelligence. The final two of these panels occupy the top third of a page and are immediately followed by a slim rectangular panel that stretches across the whole page. This panel contains one word, "YOINK," and an image of Joseph's hand grabbing Jesus' right arm. Both the hand and arm are large scale, highlighting the severity of Joseph's action. The two panels below this one are smaller scale, depicting Joseph dragging Jesus away by his arm and an angry Mary delivering her rebuke to Jesus. The dichotomy between the different reactions to Jesus highlights the affective side of the story. Since the author and illustrator do not endorse either reaction, the reader is left to negotiate between them.

The page concludes with a large panel in the bottom right corner that depicts the top half of Jesus between two word bubbles. The first of these contains merely "…" indicating Jesus' confusion. In the second bubble, Jesus asks: "Why were you searching? I thought both of you would know that I had to be in my Father's house?" (2006, 45). On the following page, a narrative insert elaborates that "the father that Yeshuah meant was his Father God…. But his parents did not completely understand him at that time!" (2006, 46). The author fills in a Lukan gap in order to foreground the Lukan wordplay between Joseph and God as Jesus' father. This insert is integrated onto a page that depicts Jesus returning to Nazareth and obeying his parents.

Throughout, Jesus has the large eyes typical of manga comics, and he is referred to as "Yeshuah,"; that is, this representation of Jesus has a Japanese countenance and a Jewish name, both of which serve to accentuate his otherness. The result is a multilayered version of the story that subtly questions the adulations of the temple occupants, the actions of Jesus' parents, and Jesus' own conduct. This children's Bible targets slightly older readers, making this complexity particularly viable; however, even children's Bibles aimed at younger readers may maintain some of these qualities without complicating the story.

CONCLUSION

As John Rowe Townsend points out, children's picturebooks are often a child's "first introduction to art and literature" (1990, 315). Children's Bibles, comparably, may be a child's first introduction to the biblical text. If children's first experiences of the biblical world come through books that reduce the text to a social or educational tool, what will child readers deduce about the Bible? In contrast, retellings that draw the reader into the story bring the narrative world to life. And retellings that retain some of the subversiveness of the Lukan text equip the child to interrogate those very social and theological frameworks that are sometimes imposed upon them as readers.

As we have seen, the boy Jesus in the hands of his retellers is rarely subversive. At times, he is the picture of obedience, a child who models good behavior to those who encounter him. Sometimes he is the Messiah in a kid suit, his deity shining through despite the limitations of his age and of those responsible for him. Often he is a Western child dressed up in first-century attire, getting lost but acting sensibly given the circumstances. His otherness is consistently reduced as a means of instilling relevance into the story.

How children's Bibles represent Jesus influences how their target readers perceive him. Children's Bibles driven by a particular set of concerns may form the child reader around those concerns, but in the end it is the concerns that dominate this formation. The child may, for instance, learn what she or he is to believe about Jesus, without ever entering the world of Jesus. Only those children's Bibles that seek to empower child readers, rather than to form them, will enable their readers to imagine the biblical world, reimagine the world they live in, and visualize Jesus for themselves.

WORKS CITED

Alexander, Pat, and Leon Baxter (ill.). 1997. *The Lion First Bible*. Oxford: Lion.

Alexander, Pat, and Carolyn Cox (ill.). 1991. *The Puffin Children's Bible: Stories from the Old and New Testaments*. Rev. ed. Harmondsworth: Penguin.

Anderson, Jeff (ill.), Mike Maddox, and Steve Harrison. 1998. *The Lion Graphic Bible*. Oxford: Lion.

Ariès, Philippe. 1962. *Centuries of Childhood: A Social History of Family Life*. Translated by Robert Baldick. London: Cape.

Barfield, Maggie, et al.; Mark and Anna Carpenter (ill.). 2006. *The Big Bible Storybook*. Milton Keynes: Scripture Union.

Batchelor, Mary, and Penny Boshoff. 2005. *My First Bedtime Bible*. Milton Keynes: Authentic.

Bottigheimer, Ruth B. 1996. *The Bible for Children: From the Age of Gutenberg to the Present*. New Haven: Yale University Press.

Ellis, Gwen, and Steve Smallman (ill.). 2007. *Candle Read and Share Bible: More Than 200 Best-Loved Bible Stories*. Oxford: Lion.

Goodings, Christina, and Melanie Mitchell (ill.). 2007. *My Little Bible Board Book*. Oxford: Lion.

Green, Joel B. 1997. *The Gospel of Luke*. NICNT. Cambridge: Eerdmans.

Iser, Wolfgang. 1974. *The Implied Reader: Patterns of Communication in Prose Fiction from Bunyan to Beckett*. Baltimore: Johns Hopkins University Press.

Jonge, Henk J. de. 1978. "Sonship, Wisdom, Infancy: Luke ii.41–51a." *NTS* 24:317–54.

Kumai, Hidenori, and Kozumi Shinozawa (ill.). 2006. *Manga Messiah*. Wheaton, Ill.: Tyndale.

Landy, Francis. 1997. "Do We Want Our Children to Read This Book?" *Semeia* 77:157–76.

Lurie, Alison. 1990. *Don't Tell the Grown-Ups: Subversive Children's Literature*. London: Little, Brown.

Malone, Emily, Jeanette Dall, and Joe Van Severen (ill.). 2004. *One Way Bible*. Cincinnati: Standard.

Marguerat, Daniel, and Yvan Bourquin. 1998. *How to Read Bible Stories: An Introduction to Narrative Criticism*. Translated by John Bowden. London: SCM.

Nikolajeva, Maria, and Carole Scott. 2006. *How Picturebooks Work*. London: Routledge.

Nodelman, Perry. 1988. *Words about Pictures: The Narrative Art of Children's Picture Books*. Athens: University of Georgia Press.

Nolland, John. 1989. *Luke 1–9:20*. WBC 35A. Dallas: Word.

Peter-Perrett, Sybille. 1991. *Biblische Geschichten für die Jugend Erzählt*. Essen: Westarp Wissenschaften.

Piper, Sophie, and Anthony Lewis (ill.). 2008. *The Lion Read and Know Bible*. Oxford: Lion.

Stephens, John, and Robyn McCallum. 1998. *Retelling Stories, Framing Culture: Traditional Story and Metanarratives in Children's Literature.* London: Garland.

Tannehill, Robert C. 1996. *Luke.* ANTC. Nashville: Abingdon.

Townsend, John Rowe. 1990. *Written for Children: An Outline of English-Language Children's Literature.* 5th ed. London: Bodley Head.

DEPICTION OF THE DEVIL AND THE EDUCATION OF CHINESE CHILDREN: THE BIBLE IN THE TAIPING TRIMETRICAL CLASSIC

Archie Chi Chung Lee

The traditional *Trimetrical Classic* (TC) or *Three-Character Classic* is meant to be a kind of primer, written in poetic form with three Chinese characters to each verse.[1] It has been used as a primary education textbook in China for over a thousand years. This primer has a unique literary form to teach beginners to learn to read and write about a thousand words. When the Jesuit Mission arrived at the Chinese coast in 1583, they discovered this genre and followed the model and format to compose the *Catholic Trimetrical Classic* (CTC) with Catholic messages. This was followed by the Protestant missionaries, beginning with Robert Mission in 1807. A few versions of the *Protestant Trimetrical Classic* (PTC) have since been written and printed for circulation in Christian schools and Christian communities in China.

Yet another tradition was created by the Taiping Heavenly Kingdom, which was established in 1853 by Hong Xiuquan who claimed to be the second son of Shangdi, the Chinese rendering of the Judeo-Christian God of the Bible. This *Taiping Trimetrical Classic* (TTC) is a text of the religio-political peasant movement[2] of the Taiping (Great Peace) Heavenly Kingdom. It integrates biblical religion, traditional Confucian ethics, and a new interpretation of the history of China from the perspective of the utopian

---

1. The research in this paper was funded by the Hong Kong Research Grants Council for the project entitled "From a Foreign Book to Chinese Christian Scripture: Appropriation of the Bible in the Multi-Textual Milieu of China (1840–1919)."

2. Shih does not agree with the view to define the Taiping movement as essentially a peasant revolution; see the discussion in the introduction to his book (1967, ix–xix).

vision of Hong Xiuquan. The Taiping ideological construction in the TTC, presented as a primer for child readership, throws light on the interesting transmission of biblical messages to young children in traditional ways of didactic education in China. Functionally, the TTC is equivalent to children's Bibles in the Chinese context. Children are expected to memorize the text and effectively shape their lives according to its teaching. The theme of the devil and demonic spirits is central to the understanding of the TTC in the larger context of the Taiping Kingdom, referred to by the Chinese imperial government and the Western Christian world as the "Taiping Rebellion" (1853–1864). By depicting the devil in the TTC, the leaders of the Taiping Kingdom aim at achieving at the early stage of the children's development a clear mental perception of the other.

CHINESE PRIMERS, MISSIONARY IMITATION, AND EDUCATION IN THE TAIPING HEAVENLY KINGDOM

In its traditional form, the TC was used for the first level of education of children in basic reading and writing of Chinese characters. It is one of the three primers that were predominantly the only textbooks used in the elementary schools in China: the *Thousand Character Prose*, the *Trimetric Classic*, and the *Hundred Names*. There were several versions of each of the trio. The oldest of them is the sixth-century *Thousand Character Prose*, which contains one thousand different characters organized in couplets of four characters each. The subject matter varies from the origin of the universe to Confucian ethical values. The themes and content are not necessarily coherent. The *Trimetric Classic* originated in the Song Dynasty (960–1279) and uses three characters per couplet with a total of 1,416 words in 472 verses, while the *Hundred Names* consists of four hundred family names in China (Rawski 1979, 47). Together they help children in achieving the goal of acquiring the desired level of primary literacy with a vocabulary of around two thousand characters. These three primers also form the textbook to prepare children for enrollment in formal education in the Confucian classics.

The TC is believed to have originated with Wang Yinglin (王應麟, 1223–1296) of the Song Dynasty.[3] But the present form has gone through

---

3. The TC has been translated by the Protestant missionaries in the nineteenth and twentieth centuries. For an English translation of the text of TC by a sinologist, see Giles 1964, first published in 1910.

several revisions and editorial additions in the Ming and Qing dynasties (1368–1644 and 1644–1911, respectively). The most recent effort to update the content of the TC comes from Chang Binlin (章炳麟, 1869–1936). The content of the TC is very extensive, ranging from the cosmos to human life, nature (hills, rivers, seasons, plants and vegetation, and animals), social customs, and cultural practices. Since Confucius is the central exemplary figure in Chinese culture, imparting Confucian cultural values and moral ethics is therefore the main purpose of the TC in addition to learning the characters. The Confucian admonition to study earnestly and diligently also forms the core concern. One fifth (88 of 472 lines) of the traditional TC is on this theme. The TC also ends with the same note to urge children to recognize the importance of diligence.

The genre of using three characters to a poetic line is meant for children to recite and memorize the sentences by heart. Illustrations, pictures, and sketches are not considered necessary features of the genre. Its power is to imprint upon the young mind the ideology embodied in the text. Though it seems to go against the general Chinese assumption of literature written for children, being copiously illustrated and lively in style, the genre has proven to be appropriate, and it functioned adequately in China for children to learn the characters and be educated in the Confucian teachings.

The importance of education was inevitably taken up by the Taiping Heavenly Kingdom. Every youngster had to receive education in the Bible and other official Taiping publications.[4] An education bureau was set up to take care of children's education. It was stated clearly that twenty-five families were to be grouped into one section and in each section "all children must go to church everyday, where the sergeant is to teach them to read the Old Testament and the New Testament, as well as the book of 'Proclamations of the True Ordained Sovereign'" (Michael 1966–1971, 2:315). The term for "children" in the document is 童子, which does not specifically include girls. But taking the general policy of equality between male and female in the Taiping Kingdom, it is reasonable to assume that there is no distinction and separation between boys and girls in this document. Indeed, as the Chinese language has separate terms for "boys" (男童) and

---

4. See an important document of the Taipings: "The Land System of the Heavenly Dynasty" (1854) in Michael 1966–1971, 2:309–20.

"girls" (女童), "children" (童子) here may just be referring to youngsters in general (Chen 1995, 32).

Reforms and new practices were initiated by the revolutionary movement of the Taipings in terms of education of all children regardless of gender difference as well as the emancipation of women from the torture of foot-binding. Family education was also much stressed in the Taiping Kingdom. Lindley reports on his observation in areas ruled by the Taipings that each family has the Lord's Prayer written on a wooden board and hung in the most eye-catching spot in the house. He saw women teach children to recite the prayer every day (1866, 2:318). The Taipings surely followed the Chinese traditional belief in the value of education both within the family and in school. Education was considered essential in cultivating the original endowed good nature of human beings. It is the key to moral development, personal transformation, and cultural acquisition in China.[5]

Nevertheless, the Protestant missionaries had been critical of the Chinese primers used in the traditional education of children. Most of them considered that these books encourage the method of memorization and repetition in learning Chinese characters without anything in relation to rationality and morality (Rawski 1985, 142–44). They voiced the need to write new textbooks for the mission school curriculum in order to promote Christian values and do away with the traditional approach of pure memorization, but up until the 1890s the traditional TC was still being used in the mission schools. Mission presses also had the TC and the *Thousand Character Prose* printed even though missionaries were in general dissatisfied with these primers (Rawski 1985, 138, 145–46).

However, some missionaries affirmed that the TC could provide an efficacious mode for the dissemination of the Christian message. To capitalize on the popularity and familiarity of the TC among the Chinese, it is reported that Protestant missionaries imitated the style and wrote the PTC containing the Christian message for the use of students in mission schools in China (Rawski 1985, 146).[6]

---

5. For the Confucian understanding of the human being and the contribution of education to the cultivation of humanity, see Munro 1969.

6. Rawski listed five types of PTC now found in the American Board Collection of Chinese Language tracts in the Harvard-Yenching Library.

The Bible in the Taiping Trimetrical Classic

The TTC was written by Hong Xiuquan and his Prime Minister Lu Xianba (盧賢拔) in 1852 (Chen 1995, 35). It is comprised of 352 verses of three characters each, with a total of 1,056 characters. It can be divided into four sections. The content of the first section (148 verses) is taken mainly from Bible stories. The second part (60 verses) is devoted to the worship of Shangdi in ancient Chinese history and the blasphemous perversion of the emperors in leading the Chinese astray from Shangdi. This section functions to assert that Shangdi works not only in the history of Israel, but also acts in China. Shangdi is therefore not a foreign God. *Shangdi* ("The Lord on High") is a term found in the Chinese classical writings to refer to the highest object of worship and reverence in the ancient times.[7]

The abandoning of the worship of Shangdi in the second section serves to prepare for the discourse on the special mission of Hong Xiuquan to exterminate the demons and preserve the right way in the third section (76 verses). The devil is seen as embodied in the ruling emperor. The last section (68 verses) addresses children directly to admonish them to worship Shangdi and follow God's commandments in order to live an abundant life without calamities.

The TTC begins in the first twelve verses with the creation of heaven and earth:

The Sovereign Shangdi
Created heaven and earth,
Made land and sea,
All things ready.

In six days
All were created
Human dominates things
Endowed with glory.

Worship on the seventh day
To acknowledge heaven's grace;

---

7. On the missionary debates in adopting Shangdi as the name for the Judeo-Christian God of the Bible, see Lee 2004 and Kim 2004.

All of heaven and earth
Hold their hearts in reverence.[8]

The six-day structure of the creation story with the seventh day being kept as a holy day designated for the worship of the creator is basically followed. The biblical story of Gen 1:1–2:4a forms the backbone of the TTC and many of the Taiping religious ideas. There is, however, no mention of the fall of humanity as in the Christian interpretation of Gen 2–3. In "Taiping Songs on World Salvation," there is also no mention of the story of the garden in Gen 2–3. The sin of humanity comes to the world gradually in the loss of "human nature" (人性) and "true origin" (真源) (Michael 1966–1971, 2:239).[9]

The TTC stresses the significant belief in God's creation of the world and all human beings. The origin of humanity goes back to God's giving birth to humankind. This reflects the traditional view in Chinese writings that all men and women are born of Shangdi and are conceived of as being endowed with glory. This idea of God giving birth to humanity is expressed in quite a few Taiping writings. *The Imperially Composed Thousand Words Edict*, for instance, begins with the creation and birth of human beings:

The Supreme Lord and Great God
There is only one and no other.
In the beginning he displayed his power,
He created heaven and earth.
When the ten thousand things were completed
He gave life to human beings in the world.

From the creation of humankind, the TTC sums up the first section with the call for worship and response of gratitude to the sovereign Shangdi in verses 9–12. Skipping the rest of Genesis, the TTC immediately turns to the nation of Israel. The twelve tribes of the Israelites migrated to Egypt and, with the grace of God, multiplied. The people of Israel are introduced right after the story of creation as a foreign nation honoring

---

8. All quotations of the TTC are the new English translation from the Chinese original based on Franz Michael's rendering.

9. Michael's translation, which is claimed to be a moderation of that of W. H. Medhurst, does not bring out the exact meaning of the Chinese terms used here. His use of "men's minds" to render "human nature" is not appropriate.

God, but being oppressed by Pharaoh, who was said to be agitated by the devil in his heart (verses 13–28):

Once upon a time
A foreign nation was commanded.
Devoting to Shangdi
Its name was Israel.

All twelve tribes
Emigrating to Egypt,
Shangdi looked after them,
Their descendents gathered.

Then a king[10] came
Devil in human heart
Envied their prosperity
Inflicting pain and misery.

Ordered the girls to live
But not the boys.
The slavery was painful
And difficult to bear.

The Sovereign Shangdi
Showed mercy on them
And commanded Moses
To return to his native family.

Shangdi showed pity on Israel and intervened by commanding Moses and Aaron to petition Pharaoh for the people's release. The story of the ten plagues is accounted in detail, and stress is placed on the belief that they are miracles sent in God's anger. The TTC presents Pharaoh's oppression of the Israelites with hard labor and the biblical theme of the hardening of the heart of Pharaoh. The details of of the killing of all baby boys, the preservation of girls, and the ten plagues ending with the elimination of

---

10. TTC uses the character 狂 ("crazy or wild man") for "king" here. The Taipings reserved the Chinese character for "king" (王) for themselves. It is felt appropriate to render "king" instead of "crazy man."

the Egyptian firstborn sons are basically incorporated. The call of Moses and Aaron to press for the release of the people is God's compassionate response to Israel's pain and suffering.

The whole story of the exodus, the division of the Red Sea, the miraculous provision of manna and water, and the guidance in the wilderness with the cloud in the day and fire pillar at night are all briefly narrated. The consequence of the miraculous act of God is the exodus of the people from Egypt. The story is told as a saving act of God to redeem God's people. Israel's incredibly wonderful crossing of the Red Sea and the drowning of the Egyptians are said to be the display of God's mighty powers in preserving and redeeming God's people. For the wilderness tradition, the provision of manna for food is told. It is noted that the sending of quails is rightly seen as a result of the people's desires and lust for flesh (Num 11). God's promulgation of Ten Commandments at Sinai forms the climax of the Old Testament story.

From the giving of the heavenly law, the TTC concludes this whole section with humanity falling into the devil's hand and being caught by the evil schemes in disobeying God's commandments. This gives rise to God's compassion and pity on humanity by sending God's firstborn son, the Crown Prince,[11] into the world to redeem humanity from sin by Jesus's death on the cross and his resurrection on the third day:

> The Sovereign Shangdi
> Showed mercy to mankind,
> Sent his Crown Prince
> To descend on earth.
>
> He was named Jesus,
> The Savior of the world.
> He redeemed sin for mankind
> Truly suffered for them.
>
> On the cross
> His body was nailed.
> His precious blood was bled
> To save humanity on earth.

---

11. The title of "Crown Prince" (太子) is applied to Jesus.

Three days after his death
He came alive.
And for forty days
He deliberated on heavenly things.

The last two verses of the first section of the TTC stress Jesus as a teacher educating his disciples for forty days on the "heavenly matters" (天情) and commanding them to proclaim the gospel.

The TTC has a greater emphasis on creation and the exodus story in the Old Testament than on the story of Jesus: 120 verses are devoted to the Old Testament, compared with 20 verses about Jesus in the New Testament. Even so, the conquest of the promised land, the monarchical period of the kings, the prophetic tradition, and the exile are all absent. In a way, the TTC seems to cover only the Pentateuch: 8 verses on creation, 96 verses on the exodus, and 16 verses on the giving of the Ten Commandments and the subsequent disobedience of humanity.

It follows that in the final section of the TTC, children are admonished to choose the right path and live prudently with great discretion in order to ensure blessing from Shangdi. For the child readers, the exodus story with the miracles of the ten plagues and the crossing of the Red Sea is of utmost interest. The central thread running through the narration is the contrast between the devil's work and God's anger. The last section of 68 verses is devoted to the ethical teaching of the child readers of the TTC. The vocative phrase "little children" is adopted five times in the address. The call to worship Shangdi is of course the major imperative:

Little children,
Worship Shangdi;
Keep the Heavenly Commandments;
Not be disorderly.

Must train to be righteous;
Not to have a crooked heart.
The Sovereign Shangdi
Constantly keep monitoring.

Must train to be good
Not to be crooked.
Doing wicked deeds oneself

Is the first step to disaster.

To ensure a good end
Must make a good beginning;
An error of a hair's breadth
Leads to the loss of a thousand miles.

Be serious about the little
And careful with the small;
The Sovereign Shangdi
Is not to be deceived.

The doctrine of retribution in which the wicked will be punished and
the righteous rewarded is affirmed. The demand for reverence of God and
filial piety toward parents are linked closely. The child readers are repeatedly warned to behave themselves and avoid falling into the traps of the
devil. God watches over them and knows everything they do:

Benevolence descends upon the good,
Disasters descend upon the wicked,
Those who submit to Heaven are preserved;
Those who disobey Heaven, perish.

The Sovereign Shangdi
Is the Lord of the Gods;
The myriad things
Depend on him.

The Sovereign Shangdi
Is the Father of our souls;
Those who serve Him devotedly
Will be blessed.

Submit to the parents of the flesh,
And you will enjoy longevity;
Those who requite their parents
Will be rewarded with blessings.

Without the notion of the original sin, the Taiping ideology gives significance to the proper worship of God and the observation of God's commandments, which are often referred to as the "heavenly law" (天上法). To enforce obedience to God's commands, it must be underlined that God follows strictly the doctrine of retribution to reward the good and punish the wicked. The gift or deprivation of eternal life becomes the central message of the Taiping ideology.

The neglect of the Old Testament prophetic traditions in the TTC can be explained by their absence from the Taiping Bible. Only the Pentateuch and the book of Joshua were published. In the New Testament the story of the descent of Jesus to save the world is a direct response to human disobedience to the law given by God through Moses. The New Testament is therefore linked with Sinai, omitting the conquest tradition, the judges, the monarchy period, the prophets, the exile, and the rest of the Old Testament. Hong fulfils what is written in the New Testament, which he renamed as the "Former Testament" in the context of his own "True Testament."[12]

Shangdi in Chinese History and the Battle against the Devil in Hong's Vision

The second section of sixty verses is on Chinese history from the ancient time to the rule of the Qing Dynasty (1644–1911). At the beginning, the Chinese people walked the same way as the foreign nations in the worship of Shangdi. The ancient Chinese classical writings and literature record that all rulers before the Qin Dynasty (221–206 B.C.E.) served Shangdi:

China in the beginning
Was looked after by Shangdi;
Like the foreign nation
They walked the same path.

From Pan Gu
Down to the Three Dynasties,
They honored Shangdi,
As recorded in history.

---

12. On the Taiping reception and appropriation of the Bible, see Lee 2008.

But in the subsequent two thousand years since Qin Shihuang (259–210 B.C.E.) people were deluded by the devil. The worst of all comes with Hui (1082–1135) of the Song Dynasty, who changed the name of Shangdi to that of "Jade Emperor." That is why seven hundred years since Hui of Song till the present time, people have had no idea of who Shangdi is.

The Chinese had the same revelation as the foreign nation in their worship of Shangdi in the ancient time. But they were led astray by the Qin and Song emperors. No one nowadays seems to know Shangdi because of the evil act of the devil:

> Speaking about Shangdi
> People do not understand;
> While the Devil of Hades
> Acted most mischievously.

The theme of the devil deluding the people and corrupting them in rebellion against Shangdi is further underlined by giving him a new name: "Devil of Hades" (*Yanluoyao*, 閻羅妖). He is also called "Red Eyes" in the rest of the TTC.

If God's response to the scheming of the devil in the history of Israel is to send his firstborn son Jesus to the world in the biblical account, God will do exactly the same in the case of China by sending this time God's second son Hong Xiuquan. The full story (76 verses) of Hong's vision and commission with special emphasis on God's instruction of Hong in heaven is presented. This includes God's gift of his seal and sword, the endowment of authority to judge and rule the world, and the promise of the assistance of Jesus. This has been summed up in quite a few of the Taiping publications. It is a story that is meant to be owned and possessed by everyone in the Taiping Kingdom in order to establish political unity, social solidarity, and ideological concordance.[13]

The TTC has kept the tension of the role of Jesus and the mission of Hong. Both of them are sons of Shangdi. Apparently in the radical monotheistic faith of the Taipings it is not acceptable to see Jesus as God. As son, he is distinctive from Shangdi, who is the only true God, the Heavenly

---

13. The story is fully presented in "Gospel Jointly Witnessed and Heard by the Imperial Eldest and Second Eldest Brothers" (Michael 1966–1971, 2:7–18) and "The Taiping Heavenly Chronicle" (2:51–76).

Father. Jesus is therefore not God.[14] In the Confucian ethical order the father is not to be confused and mixed up with the son. Filial piety must be observed by the son in respect to the father. This explains why in some Chinese missionary work Jesus has not been the center of the Christian message (Malek 2002). The Taiping ideological construction sees both Jesus, the elder son, and Hong, the younger son, as human and therefore never on equal footing with the absolute divine Shangdi.

In the TTC Jesus is sent by Shangdi to descend to Judea to die on the cross in order to achieve salvation for all and bring humanity back to the monotheistic Shangdi. When it is China's turn, Hong is sent this time as God's son. He descends to this world to first read history and then ascends to heaven to be instructed by Shangdi in the true teaching. He was given authority and power symbolized in the granting of God's seal and sword. He was assisted by Jesus, his elder brother, and the divine messengers to fight against the devil.

In the presentation of Hong's vision in heaven and mission on earth the TTC portrays a concerted effort of the whole divine family in participating in God's plan for China. Every member of the family takes part in solidarity. The Heavenly Father and his wife, "Heavenly Mother" (天母), are both compassionate. Jesus is commanded to descend and his wife, called "Heavenly Elder Sister-in-Law" (天嫂), is very considerate and encouraging to Jesus. Both God and Jesus will descend to this world to assist Hong. The notion of a divine family with father and mother, brother and sister-in-law, is very imaginative. Hong also gives his son to Jesus as Jesus's stepson. To the child readers of the TTC, this family idea will not be offensive, although many Christians today would find it absurd.

The TTC is instructive in seeing China in the divine order of things and in connection with biblical history. Chinese history is interpreted "in light of this new understanding of China's place in the world" (Reilly 2004, 168). It is different from the traditional TC in which, almost exclusively, Confucian moral and ethical teachings are promoted. Children are imparted the traditional hierarchical social order and proper relations. There is in the TC a historical survey of the dynasties from the earliest to the Song (960–1279), when the TC was composed. There is, however, no mention of China's concern with the outside world and foreign history, as

---

14. Hong's annotations in the Imperial Edition of the Bible clearly spelled this out at Mark 12:28–34; see Michael 1966–1971, 3:229.

China represented the whole civilized world and the "barbarians" seemed not to be worthy of attention. The TTC puts ancient Chinese history in the same mode as the biblical history, and Shangdi acts in Chinese history as God does in Israel's history. The same word *ming* (命) for "command" or "commission" used five times in the biblical section is adopted for God's action in "Chinese history."

In the missionary PTC the basic doctrinal topics of the nature of God and God's creation, the fall of humanity, and the salvation achieved by Jesus in his death and resurrection are incorporated. The drastic difference between the TTC and PTC is apparent. Reilly rightly spots the contrast and characterizes both in these words:

> In this missionary version of the primer, there was not one mention of Chinese history or Chinese culture. Chinese students would learn that this true Divine Lord was concerned only with disembodied, ahistorical, culture-free souls. The Taiping version of the *Three Character Classic*, on the other hand, attempted to reclaim the Chinese past, placing that past in the more universal context of Shangdi's dealings with all humankind. (Reilly 2004, 169)

In comparing the TTC with the PTC, Franz Michael is of the opinion that the TTC intends to communicate a new religion based on both the Hebrew Bible and the story of Jesus, while the PTC refers mainly to the life of Jesus (1966–1971, 2:152). The new belief system divides humanity according to the Christian gospel preached by the missionaries into two largely defined categories of good and evil, but the division is politically interpreted. Instead of the traditional categories of believers and unbelievers, TTC sees the long history of ancient China with the emperors usurping the divine power of Shangdi as a record of "the Devil's evil plan in China."

Hong challenges the blasphemous presumptions of the emperors of the imperial empire to call themselves "Shangdi." To him, only Shangdi should be called "emperor" (*di*), and all earthly monarchs may be referred to as "king" (*wang*). Even Jesus, being the "Crown Prince" (*Taiji*), is only designated as Lord.[15] This view of the rulers of earth being called only "king" and not "emperor" or "sovereign" (*di*) applies to Hong as well. The

---

15. See "An Exhortation on the Original Dao for the Enlightening of the Age," collected in *The Taiing Zhaoshu* (Michael 1966–1971, 3:46). The rendering of "the

whole historical process since the Qin Dynasty has been blasphemous and idolatrous. All emperors assumed the absolute power and authority duly ascribed only to Shangdi. It is therefore not only individual emperors but the entire dynasty that the Taipings intend to overthrow. The people of Shangdi must stand up to fight against and to topple the Qing Dynasty. The TTC puts it clearly: "All were deluded by the Devil, those two thousand years" (Michael 1966–1971, 3:157). Reilly sums up the ideological thrust in the TTC and other Taiping writings as follows:

> This view of imperial history permeates all the major Taiping Documents. As the *Taiping Imperial Declaration* (Taiping Zhaoshu) emphasizes it was from the time of the Qin dynasty and the Han dynasty (202 B.C.E.–220 C.E.) that China began straying from the path of righteousness, and each succeeding emperor only added to the weight of that sin. When the Song emperors ascended the throne, they committed one of the most egregious sins yet: they changed the name of Shangdi. (Reilly 2004, 93)

The new interpretation takes the biblical salvation history and the new redemption history initiated by God's commission of Hong to rule the whole world as representing the compassionate plan of Shangdi to right the historical wrongs and restart history afresh. This new history is connected to the very history of China before Qin, when Shangdi was revered and worshiped by all Chinese people of the time. To the young readers of the TTC, this interpretation has a powerful ideological application, giving meaning to the current events of rebellious attempts to overthrow the barbarian Qin Dynasty. The Taiping movement is dignified in finding its root not in the Western Christian religion, but in a recovery of the worship of the very same God, Shangdi, in the remote past.

The Christian affiliation of the Taipings is therefore a two-edged sword. It is a foreign religion in close collaboration with the empire that destroyed the pride and dignity of an ancient kingdom since the Opium War of 1840. It is also a means that opens up a window to look at the spiritual power and military might behind the cannonballs. To dissociate with the "foreign" imperial power, Hong has to subvert Christianity and its sole claim on Shangdi. First, Shangdi must be indigenous. The Chinese must have worshiped Shangdi in the ancient time. Second, the devil must then

---

Original Dao" (原道) by "the Origin of Virtue" in the Michael translation is far from satisfactory.

be identified as embodied in the blasphemous emperors who claimed in the long Chinese history since Qin time to be Di (帝) and suppressed the popular worship of Shangdi. The ruling emperor of Qing is the embodiment of the devil, and his army is therefore devilish. He is considered as the last, but the most devilish of a series of pretenders.

This Taiping ideology is drastically different from the traditional Confucian context in which there is a rigid cultural dichotomy between the self and the other as well as between the civilized and barbaric. China is the central kingdom in the cultural sense of representing the civilized world. Everything else is classified as "foreign." In this way, too close a link with Christianity and foreign imperialist invaders is harmful to the kingdom. There should be some distance between the Taipings and the foreign nations. Maintaining an ambivalent association with the Christian West will also be healthy. A certain degree of ambiguity should be created to allow tensions and furnish potency to the Taiping Kingdom. The contemporary perception of the colonial powers as "foreign devils" is transformed into a devil within the Chinese territory. With the Christian depiction of the devil and the Taiping ideological construction of the Qing Dynasty as the devil, the Taiping depiction re-creates and refigures the devil as the enemy of Shangdi and the Heavenly Kingdom of Peace.

With the defeat of China in the Opium Wars and the subsequent series of unequal treaties from 1842 to 1860, the deep humiliation and wide discontent among the Chinese escalated to a record height that outbalanced the traditional mindset of supporting the orthodoxy and status quo. There is a quest for alternative means to bring about a better life for all. The promise of the Taipings in overthrowing the impotent and corrupt Qing government and establishing a kingdom of peace on earth with an eschatological vision of a paradise in heaven is too attractive to resist.

There is no doubt that this powerful image of the personified devil must be imparted to the young generation. Children must not only identify the living devil in their daily life, but also muster enough strength and energy to fight a victorious battle against it collectively. They have to first of all guard against themselves being turned into small devils and then be further equipped to kill and destroy all forms of devilish existence in society.[16] The Taipings classify humanity into two major categories: human

---

16. Different words are used in the TTC to convey the conception of the devil and his followers. The usual terms are "devil" (魔), "ghost" (鬼), "crooked and vicious" (邪), and "demonic spirit" (妖), sometimes used in various combinations. More spe-

beings and "demonic spirits" (妖). The TTC also goes along the same line. Children are admonished to pursue the right way and be human beings instead of demonic goblins:

> The correct are humans.
> The corrupt are devils.
> Little children!
> Seek to avoid disgrace.

The worship of Shangdi and obedience to the heavenly commandments are essential indicators of being human. Shangdi is portrayed in the TTC as "the Father of our Souls," a term created by Taipings to show the close link between humanity and Shangdi.

Learning the TTC by heart is the first step to get properly oriented in the long and persistent holy war against the enemies of Shangdi. In TTC, there is no separation between religion and politics in children's education. Children are initiated into the adult world of politics at an early age. It was reported that a children's army was part of the military structure of the Taiping Kingdom. Children were invited to join the army to put their ideology into practice.

Conclusion

Though what concerns us in this article is the educational presentation of the Bible to children in the TTC, we should be reminded that the biblical account in the first section is intertwined with the three remaining parts. The biblical stories of creation, the exodus, and the giving of the Ten Commandments are to be read in the context of the Chinese imperial history, Hong's heavenly vision, and his iconoclastic mission. The utopian vision of a new heaven and a new earth gives impetus and aspiration to the suffer-

---

cific designations are "Devil of Hades" (*yanluo*, 閻羅) or "Demonic Devil of Hades" (*yanluoyao*, 閻羅妖), "devilish serpent" (蛇魔), and "red eyes" (紅眼睛). According to *An Exhortation on the Original Dao for Awakening World* (原道覺世訓) there is the heretical and wicked belief that *Yanluoyao* determines life and death. "But this Demonic Devil of Hades is none other than the old devilish serpent, who is most mischievous and often transforms himself in order to deceive and entrap the souls of mortal human beings" (Michael 1966–1971, 2:38).

ings of the oppressed, which has a great impact on the ideological thrust of the Heavenly Kingdom of Peace.

The core of the TTC is the pledge for a decision to choose life rather than death. Only turning to Shangdi and living according to the commandments will ensure life eternal and a blessed life on earth. This central message has clearly been incorporated in other Taiping writings, including "An Exhortation on the Original Dao for Awakening the World": "Alas! Those who respect and worship the Sovereign God are therefore the Great God's children; in this life the Sovereign Great God will care for them, and after death their souls will ascend to heaven, to enjoy the eternal happiness of heaven. How blissful, how glorious!" (Michael 1966–1971, 2:46).

The giving of the commandments takes up a prominent place in the Taiping iconoclastic scheme and the worship of the monotheistic Shangdi, who is presented as writing the commandments by his very own hands and handing them to the people through Moses. Casting off demons, worshiping the true God, and obeying the heavenly commandments, according to Reilly, constitute the "standard three-part formula for following Shangdi" (2004, 97). Indeed, the Decalogue is taken by the Taipings as Shangdi's divine proclamation and therefore must be obeyed absolutely. There is a thread that runs through the TTC and connects the Old Testament stories of creation and redemption and Hong's vision and mission to carry out God's plan of salvation for China. He expects to return to the classical Chinese historical period when Shangdi was known and worshiped by all. In this sense he intends to restore the ideal past. He is a revivalist as well as a revolutionist and a rebel against the regime at that time. He aims to take China back to the ancient classical period at the point when China has fallen away from the worship of Shangdi.

The theme of divine battle between the Taipings and the devil embodied in the dynastic institution has attracted a lot of adherents who are being marginalized in society. Though the Taipings have not succeeded in overthrowing the old regime, its legacy to challenge the oppressing power continues to delegitimize the old imperial order. The biblical text has provided the language and framework for the Taipings to reinterpret Chinese history in the light of the salvation history and to see in the vision of Hong Xiuquan the constant iconoclastic struggle of Shangdi to eliminate the devil in the historical existence in China. The next generation of the Heavenly Kingdom of Peace was to be educated in its early stage of life and be equipped to bravely march on in the divinely sanctioned battle as the true children of the kingdom.

The TTC was definitely meant not to be an ordinary primer for children but an integral part of the program to prepare young ones in the utopian vision of the Taipings children who had been regarded as full members of the kingdom, incited to taking part in the ideological battle and military activities of the adult world.

Works Cited

Chen, Jingpan. 1995. *Education in Taiping Tainquo* [Chinese]. Hupei: Renmim.

Giles, Herbert A. 1964. *San tzu ching = Elementary Chinese*. Translated and annotated by Herbert A. Giles. Taipei, Taiwan: Literature House.

Kim, Sangkuen. 2004. *Strange Names of God: The Missionary Translation of the Divine Name and the Chinese Responses to Matteo Ricci's Shangti in Late Ming China, 1583–1644*. New York: Peter Lang.

Lee, Archie C. C. 2004. "Naming God in Asia: Cross-Textual Reading in Multi-Cultural Context." *Quest: An Interdisciplinary Journal for Asian Christian Scholars.* 3:21–42.

———. 2008. "The Bible in China: Religion of God's Chinese Son." *PSB* 29:21–38.

Lindley, Augustus F. 1866. *Ti-ping Tien-kwoh: The History of the Ti-ping Revolution, Including a Narrative of the Author's Personal Adventures*. 2 vols. London: Day & Son.

Malek, Roman, ed. 2002. *The Chinese Face of Jesus Christ*. Nettetal: Steyler.

McNeur, George Hunter. 1934. *China's First Preacher, Liang A-fa 1789–1855*. Oxford: Oxford University Press, China Agency.

Michael, Franz, in collaboration with Chung-li Chang. 1966–1971. *The Taiping Rebellion: History and Documents*. 3 vols. Translated by Margery Anneberg et al. Far Eastern and Russian Institute Publication on Asia 14. Seattle: University of Washington Press.

Munro, Donald J. 1969. *The Concept of Man in Contemporary China*. Stanford: Stanford University Press.

Rawski, Evelyn Sakakisa. 1979. *Education and Popular Literacy in Ch'ing China*. Ann Arbor: University of Michigan Press.

———. 1985. "Elementary Education in the Mission Enterprise." Pages 135–51 in *Christianity in China: Early Protestant Missionary Writings*. Edited by Suzanne Wilson Barnett and John King Fairbank. Cambridge: Committee on American-East Asian Relations of the Dept.

of History in collaboration with the Council on East Asian Studies/ Harvard University.

Reilly, Thomas H. 2004. *The Taiping Heavenly Kingdom: Rebellion and the Blasphemy of Empire.* Seattle: University of Washington Press.

Shih, Vincent Y. C. 1967. *The Taiping Ideology: Its Sources, Interpretations, and Influences.* Seattle: University of Washington Press,.

Wang, Zhongmin, ed. 1953. *Taiping Tianguo.* Shanghai: Shenzhou Guoguang She.

Conflating Creation, Combining Christmas, and Ostracizing the Other

Mark Roncace

The Bible is a collection of books written by many different people in a variety of places over a long period of time in multiple languages to diverse audiences in a plethora of social, religious, political, and economic contexts. Children's Bibles are different. They, generally, present the Bible as a single book and are written by one person in one place, time, and language to a fairly specific audience. Moreover, while the canonical Bible naturally features a diversity of stories from multiple points of view, children's Bibles do not. Instead, they harmonize the canon's disparate voices. This ubiquitous tendency among children's Bibles thus eliminates one of the richest and most pertinent aspects of the Bible: its inherent otherness.

Bibles for children are, of course, shorter than the canonical version, so it is to be expected that some of the diversity will be lost. It is difficult or impractical, for example, to include excerpts from every work in the Book of the Twelve or portions of every New Testament epistle. But still, abridged children's versions have plenty of opportunities to make the Bible's diversity apparent to its younger readers. Instead, they purposefully eschew such opportunities by blending the different stories or presenting only one of them. Two such instances are the differing accounts of creation in Gen 1–3 and the two different stories of Jesus's birth in Matthew and Luke. We will first consider how a number of recent English-language children's Bibles handle these two sets of stories before reflecting on the implications of homogenization.

Conflating Creation

It has long been recognized that Genesis features two separate stories of creation. The first (1:1–2:4a) recounts how God systematically spoke heaven and earth into existence, beginning with light on the first day, followed by the plants and animals, and concluding with the creation of man and woman in God's image on the sixth day. In the second story (2:4b–3:24), the Lord God first creates the man (Adam) from the dust and places him in the garden of Eden; then the Lord makes the plants and animals and finally the woman (Eve) from the man's rib. Finally, the serpent shows up and problems emerge. The two accounts, then, feature multiple differences: the order in which things are created, how humans are formed, the name of the deity (God versus Lord God), the image of the deity (transcendent and all powerful versus anthropomorphic), and the overall style (structured with no real plot versus a messy narrative).

While most readers of the present volume are presumably aware of the two disparate creation stories, the majority of people are not, as professors can attest by their students' lack of knowledge about these supposedly well-known passages. Perhaps children's Bibles are in part to blame, for they inevitably fail to present the two stories independently. Rather, their handling of the stories falls into one of the following four categories.

In the first approach the two accounts are combined by moving the creation of the man from dust and the woman from the man's rib from the second story to the sixth day of the first story. An example of this approach is *The Book for Children* by Kenneth Taylor:

> On the sixth day of creation God made animals that walk on land.... Then God made someone very special. God made a man! This is how God made him. He took some dust from the ground and formed it into a man's body.... God named the man Adam.... Then the Lord God planted a beautiful garden as a home for the man he had made, calling it the Garden of Eden.... Adam was the only person in all the world and he was lonely. God decided it wasn't good for him to be alone, so he made another person who would be with Adam and help him. This is how God did it. He put the man to sleep. And while he was sleeping, God took one of his ribs and made a woman from it.... Adam named her Eve.... Then God looked at all he had made in those six days, and he was very pleased.... On the seventh day God rested. (2000, 4)

The story then picks up with a retelling of Gen 3—the account of the snake and the forbidden tree.[1] Conflating the stories in this fashion omits the profound notion that male and female are created simultaneously and in God's image. Interestingly, however, all of the children's Bibles in this first category feature illustrations of the man and woman together; that is, there are no images in any of these books of the man by himself, even though he is created first.

A second approach opts to present only the first creation story in which the man and woman are created at the same time, before jumping ahead to the account of the snake and the tree. Thus, these children's Bibles essentially omit Gen 2 altogether, although they often name the first man and woman as Adam and Eve.[2] Perhaps these versions are preferable because they show the man and woman created simultaneously, rather than consecutively; nonetheless the omission of the second story leaves out the wonderfully anthropomorphic images of God, the notion of humanity's connection with the earth (man being formed from the dust), Adam's poetic outburst when he first sees the woman (2:23), and the comment about man leaving his mother and father and cleaving to his wife and the two becoming one flesh (2:24). There are indeed an abundance of rich theological, psychological, spiritual, and sociological elements that are lost in children's versions that omit Gen 2.

While the first two categories are, seemingly, reasonable ways to combine the two creation stories, a third approach does serious damage to the canonical accounts by portraying the creation of the man alone on the sixth day. For instance, the *Read with Me Bible* reads: "Then God said, 'Let us make man in our likeness.' So God created man in his own likeness. God saw that everything he had made. And it was very good.… On

---

1. Other books that take the same approach include *The Jewish Children's Bible: Genesis* (Prenzlau 1996), *The Eager Reader Bible* (Lucas 1994), and *My Book of Bible Stories* (Watchtower Bible & Tract Society 1978). Several others omit the man being created from dust and the woman from the rib, but they nonetheless depict only one creation of humans in which the man is formed first followed by the woman. These include *The Children's Bible in 365 Stories* (Batchelor 1995), *Children's Everyday Bible* (Chancellor 2002), and *The Preschooler's Bible* (Beers 1994).

2. These include *My Book of Bible Stories* (Rock 2003), *My First Bible* (Alexander 2002), *The Picture Bible* (Hoth 1998), *Classic Bible Stories for Jewish Children* (Kolatch 1994), *The Bible from Beginning to End* (Williams 2002), *My First Catholic Bible* (2001), which is an NRSV translation of select passages, and *The Pilgrim Book of Bible Stories* (Water 2003).

the seventh day God rested" (Rikkers and Syswerda 2000, 8–9). God then makes the garden for Adam and later a woman from the rib of the man. Fittingly, it features two pictures of the man sans the woman. I cannot help but note, in a Freudian mode, that in one of the images Adam is grasping the (curved upward) horn of a rhinoceros; and then when Adam and Eve are first pictured together, Adam is lying (naked, of course, with strategically placed plants) at the feet of Eve with a contented smile on his face. Eve indeed turns out to be a more suitable companion than the rhinoceros.

Similarly, *The Young Reader's Bible* says, "On the sixth day, God made living things for the land. Then God said, 'Let us make human beings. Let them rule over the fish of the sea, the birds of the air, and the living things on land.' God made the first human being from the dust. The first man was called Adam. God breathed into Adam the breath of life. God looked at all that he had made. It was very good! On the seventh day, God rested" (Bruno and Reinsma 1998, 18–19). In this version, apparently "human being" means "man." It includes two illustrations of the man alone. In the same way, the *New Catholic Picture Bible* reads: "On the sixth day God made all the animals that were to live on the ground. Then God said, 'I shall make man in My image. I shall make him to rule over all the things that I have created.' God formed man out of the dust of the earth. Then He breathed into him a soul that will never die. On the seventh day God rested from his work" (Lovasik 1981, 9). In stark contrast to the canonical version, here only the man—not the man and woman—is to rule over all creation, which implies that the man is to rule over the woman. In the biblical garden of Eden story, the same notion is present (3:16), but there the subjugation of woman is part of the deity's punishment for eating the fruit—it was not part of the original plan. In Lovasik's retelling, that the man alone has dominion over all creation is part of the divine design.

Karyn Henley's *Day by Day Kid's Bible* is a long—over eight hundred pages with no illustrations—and detailed book. It has ample space to feature both creation stories separately. Instead, day six begins with the creation of animals and then continues: "Then God said, 'Let's make people to be like us. They can be in charge of the fish and birds and cows. They can take care of the earth and all the animals.' So God made people like himself." But the plural "people" and "they" quickly vanish. It continues: "First he made a man from the dust. Then God breathed life into Adam, and he came alive" (2002, 4). God then tells Adam that he can eat all the plants for food. He then pronounces everything good and rests on the seventh day. Still no woman. She comes later, of course, after none of the animals is found to be a suitable helper for Adam.

A few more examples will illustrate just how common this approach is. Judy Healy's *Good News Bible Stories for Children* reports, "When all this was finished, God made man from the dust of the earth and called the man Adam. God looked at everything He had made and saw that it was very good. Then God took a rest!" (2004, 8). Again, the woman is created later. *My First Study Bible* tells the story from Adam's perspective. It begins, "I'm Adam, the first person God made. After God made me, He let me live in a very beautiful garden." A few sentences later, Adam reports, "He made a wife for me. Her name was Eve" (Loth 1994, 14). Not exactly what you find in the canonical account. *The Little Boys Bible Storybook* does not include the seven-day account; rather it begins with the creation of man: "God himself was moving the dirt! He was shaping it into his last and best creation—Adam, the very first man" (Larsen 1999, 10). So here the last and best creation is the man alone, not humankind together. Maybe that is what we should expect given the title of the storybook. But, by that logic, in the canonical version the notion of a "last and best" would clearly be reserved for Eve, the woman of the second story who is the culmination of creation. Not surprisingly, *The Little Boys Bible Story Book* features three illustrations of the man by himself.

Lest we think that this particular way of conflating the two stories emanates only from (conservative) Christian publishing houses, there is *The Bible Story* and *The Children's Illustrated Jewish Bible*. The former reads: "Last of all, God said, 'I will make man. I will make him in my likeness and after my image.' So out of the dust of the earth God formed the first man and breathed into his nostrils. And the first man, Adam, stood on the new earth and looked into the eyes of God. And he was not afraid" (Turner 1968, 5). It features one illustration of the man by himself. The latter book says, "And God made all the animals. And he created man in His own image, to rule over the fish and the fowl and every living thing. There was evening, and there was morning. The sixth day. The heavens and the earth were finished, and all of God's creations were done.... God saw that it was good. And the seventh day was blessed by God" (Brown and Hort 2007, 19). Evidently Eve was not part of God's creation—since "all" of creation was completed and there is still no Eve. In addition, here again is the idea that the man alone is to rule over all.

Much is already lost when children's Bibles harmonize the two stories, but to synthesize them in this particular fashion is quite troublesome. The

result is that there is now only one story in which the man alone is created in God's image, and only he is part of the creation that is pronounced
good. Adam is clearly primary; he alone has dominion over the created
order. He is created in the likeness of God, and the woman is created in
the likeness of man (the rib). Not only is the other story expunged, but the
woman becomes the other creation, clearly relegated to a secondary status,
part of the creation to be ruled by the man.

A fourth approach includes both stories, following the canonical
version, but makes a subtle attempt to conflate the two narratives. Several examples can be offered here. *The Children's Illustrated Bible* and *The
Illustrated Jewish Bible for Children* feature the same text by Selina Hastings. The books have "been carefully prepared with a panel of religious
consultants, historians, educators, and scholars." As advertised, they
contain maps, diagrams, pictures, and explanations of historical context.
These are no lightweight kiddy books. Their retelling of the creation story
follows the canonical seven-day account, with man and woman created
together on the sixth day. But when it comes to the second story, the creation of man from the dust is somewhat oddly omitted. Instead, God—
not the Lord God—simply places the man in the garden, suggesting that
the work of creating the man was already done in Gen 1. Also omitted is
the line from the biblical text that says that God formed all the animals
in hopes of finding a suitable companion for the man. Rather, Hastings's
text implies that the animals have been created, and God simply brings
them to the man so that he can name them, after which the deity creates the woman from the rib of the man. Thus, only some of the tension
between the two canonical accounts is permitted to remain; most of it is
editorially removed.

Trevor Barnes's "expert retelling has been fully approved by Catholic, Protestant, and Jewish theologians" (so the dust jacket). His book *The
Kingfisher Children's Bible* features gender-inclusive language, as well as
maps, diagrams, and historical notes. It makes two small editorial changes
to the second story that help to harmonize it with the first, though given
that it does present both stories, we cannot be sure that harmonization is
the intended effect. Rather than the canonical version's, "Then the Lord
God said, 'It is not good for man to be alone.... So out of the ground the
Lord God formed every animal of the field and every bird of the air'"; it
reads, "'It is not good for man to be alone,' said God, who had made many
animals and birds to keep Adam company" (2001, 14). The pluperfect
("had made") implies that the creation of animals had already been done

back in the first story. The second change is to retain the divine name God, instead of Lord God, which also provides consistency.

If Barnes can be excused for one pluperfect, there is no mistaking the harmonizing intentions of the pluperfects in the *Golden Children's Bible*, a book that has gone through numerous printings since its first publication in the 1960s and has sold millions of copies. It too has an editorial board consisting of a Catholic, a Protestant, and a Jewish scholar (Joseph A. Grispino, Samuel Terrien, David Wice). In a sense, this volume is a children's Bible only insofar as it includes selected texts. What it does present is more or less a straightforward translation—evidenced by its actually including the words Pishon, Gihon, Hiddekel, and Euphrates from Gen 2:11–13. While the *Golden Children's Bible* does include all of Gen 1–3, it harmonizes the two disparate stories by placing—and editing—2:4b–7 at the end of the first story and in the pluperfect tense instead of the simple past. In this way, it serves as a summary of the first story, instead of the beginning of the second one:

> God blessed the seventh day and made it a holy day, because on that day he had rested.
> This is how the Lord God made the earth and the heavens, and every plant before it was in the earth, and every tree of the field before it grew. And when God had made man, a mist had gone up from the earth, and had watered the whole surface of the ground. The Lord God had formed man of the dust of the ground, and had breathed into him the breath of life, and man had become a living soul. (1965, 15)

In order to link the two accounts, the editors eliminated the phrase at the beginning of 2:4b, "on the day" and the last half of 2:5, "for the Lord God had not caused it to rain on the earth and there was no one to till the ground." Including them would make it difficult to fit the two stories together. The pluperfects—six in two sentences—serve to suggest that the creation of man from the dust is simply a detailing of what already occurred on day six. Thus, in this retelling, the creation of man, not man and woman, is the climax of the first story. His creation is apparently the only one worth recapping in this concluding paragraph. So instead of man being God's first creation in the second story, he becomes the focus and pinnacle of the first story. The woman again becomes other.

True, there is nothing grammatically in Hebrew that prevents translating the tense as the pluperfect instead of the simple past, but, still, such a rendering seems to border on misrepresentation. Perhaps some of the authors and illustrators of other children's Bibles, who are not scholars, are themselves ignorant of the idea that there are two stories. But these three scholars certainly are not. Instead they employ some slick editing to unite the two different accounts. Furthermore, since no author is listed— they are merely the editorial advisory board—the illusion is given that the text is being transmitted/translated straight from the original Hebrew, as it would be in any Bible, but not necessarily in children's Bibles.

Finally, a couple of children's Bibles include both stories independently and relatively completely. They are both Jewish, not Christian, Bibles, which is perhaps not surprising since we are, after all, dealing with the Jewish Scriptures, and Judaism has a long, complex history of wrestling with its own sacred text. The only harmonizing redaction by the *JPS Illustrated Children's Bible* (Frankel 2009) is to retain the name God for the second story. *A Child's Garden of Torah: A Read-Aloud Bedtime Bible* (Grishaver 1998) significantly summarizes both stories for its audience, but does not blend the two accounts. It also features some surprisingly difficult questions for its young audience—for example, What do day one and day four have in common?—but none of these prompts a child to explore the differences between the two versions. In short, out of approximately thirty-five children's Bibles readily available in the United States, I was able to find only two that present both canonical creation stories. The rest conflate and eliminate.

Combining Christmas

A second instance in which children's Bibles harmonize the diversity of the canonical texts occurs with the Gospels. Rather than providing four separate accounts of the life of Jesus, nearly all children's Bibles attempt to blend them into one story. Most of them adopt the view stated explicitly in the introduction to the *Golden Children's Bible*: "In the beginning of the NT are found the four Gospels which tell the story of Christ's earthly life. They are four books by four authors—Matthew, Mark, Luke, and John— but as they contain one message, they are here combined as a single story." Anyone who has read the Gospels knows the great diversity among them. Mark's secret savior is virtually impossible to blend with John's otherworldly redeemer. Yes, it would be cumbersome to present four separate Gospels in children's Bibles, but still, young readers would benefit from gaining some sense of appreciation for the differences among the canonical accounts.

One place where the harmonization in children's Bibles is especially palpable is the presentation of a single Christmas story. Here children's Bibles splice together the birth stories of Jesus in Matthew and Luke. As with the two creation stories, it is not difficult to perceive the two irreconcilable birth narratives. Matthew features the announcement to Joseph, the birth of Jesus in Bethlehem (no census or manger), the visit from the wise men, the flight to Egypt, and the decision to live in Nazareth upon their return. Luke's version, by contrast, tells of the announcement to Elizabeth, the announcement to Mary, the meeting between the two mothers-to-be, the birth of the Baptist, the census and trip to Bethlehem for Joseph and Mary, the birth of Jesus in a manger, the proclamation to the shepherds, the presentation of Jesus in the temple where they encounter Simeon and Anna, and finally the return home to Nazareth.

The most common way in which children's Bibles combine the accounts is to intermingle them at the beginning to include both the angel's appearance to Mary (Luke) and to Joseph to allay his fears (Matthew). Children's versions follow Luke's story up until the shepherds visit the baby Jesus; then they switch to Matthew's account for the visit by the wise men and for Mary and Joseph's flight to Egypt before returning home.[3] However, when harmonizing the two stories, it is difficult to include Jesus's trip from Bethlehem to the temple in Jerusalem very soon after his birth, following Luke's chronology, since Jesus needs time to be in Bethlehem for the visit by the wise men and the escape to Egypt according to Matthew. Thus the most frequently excised material in children's versions is Luke's account of Jesus's circumcision (2:21) and his scene of Jesus's presentation in the temple, which is rife with Jewish customs, as is evident from its opening lines in 2:22–24:

> When the time came for their purification according to the law of Moses, they brought him up to Jerusalem to present him to the Lord. As it is written in the law of the Lord, "Every firstborn male shall be consecrated to the Lord." So they offered a sacrifice according to what is stated in the law of the Lord, "a pair of turtledoves or two young pigeons."

---

3. With some slight variations, all of the following take this approach: *The Eager Reader Bible*, *The Preschoolers Bible*, *The Picture Bible*, *Young Reader's Bible*, *Little Boys Bible Storybook*, *My Book of Bible Stories*, *My First Bible*, *The Children's Bible in 365 Stories*, *Good News Bible Stories for Children*, *The Bible Story*, *The Book for Children*, and *The Bible from Beginning to End*.

That is quite a bit of other information that complicates things: What and when is the time of purification? What does it mean to consecrate someone to God? Why turtledoves or pigeons? And what about the poor animals and all the blood? This is not part of the Christian Christmas story, is it? It must be from some other story. Indeed, Luke's only two quotations from the Hebrew Bible in Luke 1–2 appear in these verses; and five of the nine references to the law in Luke appear in the omitted scene of the baby Jesus in the temple. By deleting this scene in children's Bibles, Jesus's being a Jew and the events surrounding his birth following Jewish rituals is lost. The genealogies in both Matthew and Luke also establish Jesus's Jewish lineage, but, of course, these do not appear in children's Bibles. In short, Judaism becomes the other tradition that is absent from children's Christmas stories.[4]

A second group of children's versions depicts Jesus in the temple, but they make no mention of the end of the scene that states that when Mary, Joseph, and Jesus had finished their obligations in Jerusalem, they returned home to Nazareth (Luke 2:39). This allows room for the account of the wise men and subsequent escape to Egypt.[5] Such splicing of the two stories allows some tension to remain. Specifically, the attentive child reader or listener may wonder how or why Jesus, after leaving the temple in Jerusalem, went back to Bethlehem where he meets the wise men. The *Pilgrim Book of Bible Stories* (Water 2003) addresses the problem by omitting nearly all geographic references. It reports that Jesus was born in Bethlehem, but it glosses over the temple being in Jerusalem. Similarly, when the wise men arrive, there is no mention of Bethlehem—since Jesus apparently was able to go to the temple without leaving Bethlehem. The *Kingfisher Children's Bible* handles the geographic discrepancy by adding this note: "After the ceremony [in the temple in Jerusalem] Mary and Joseph went back to Bethlehem to collect their belongings and return home to Nazareth. They did not know that strangers were also making their way to

---

4. I am reminded of the *Seinfeld* episode in which Elaine is invited to a bris. She makes up an excuse as to why she cannot attend and goes to a baseball game instead. She says to George, "Who wants to see a circumcision anyway?" to which he replies, "Yeah, I'd rather go to a hanging." Likewise, children's Bibles would prefer to deal with something violent, namely, the crucifixion, which most of them include, rather than a circumcision.

5. The *Day by Day Kid's Bible*, *New Catholic Picture Bible*, *Golden Children's Bible*, and *Children's Everyday Bible* adopt this strategy.

Bethlehem at that very moment, having traveled from their homeland far away" (Barnes 2001, 150). So that explains how Jesus met the wise men in Bethlehem—his family had booked an extended stay in the stable and had decided to leave their stuff there.

Several Bibles present both Christmas stories separately, that is, they report that Jesus went home after his presentation in the temple. Then they pick up with the wise men. These include the *Read with Me Bible* (Rikkers and Syswerda 2000) and the *Children's Illustrated Bible* (Hastings 1994a), though the latter still intermingles the two stories by featuring the birth announcement to both Mary and Joseph. Similarly, *My First Catholic Bible* (2001), which presents excerpts from the NRSV from each of the four Gospels, includes both birth stories in their entirety. Thus the difference between the two accounts remains—the other is not expunged.

One more book deserves mention here. Every children's Bible that I examined included portions of Matthew and Luke's Christmas stories, with one exception. *My First Study Bible* (Loth 1994) ostensibly presents each book of the Bible separately, including the Gospels. According to the table of contents, the Gospel of Matthew begins on page 309, the Gospel of Mark on 341, and so forth. But what one actually finds is a conflation of the Gospels, and in the case of the birth stories, outright confusion. Remarkably, under the Gospel of Matthew, it tells of the announcements to Mary and Elizabeth, the birth of John the Baptist, the census, the trip to Jerusalem, the birth in the manger, and the angels and shepherds. There is nothing from Matthew at all! When you get to Luke, it has no birth story. *My First Study Bible*, then, is the only children's Bible that I found that features only one of the two stories—there is no mention of the wise men or the flight to Egypt, so there is no conflation—but it erroneously presents it as Matthew's account, not Luke's. In sum, as with the two creation accounts, only a couple of children's Bibles include both canonical Christmas stories.

OSTRACIZING THE OTHER

Harmonizing the canonical versions of creation and Christmas may make the story simpler. But in the process significant elements of the biblical text are sacrificed, and, more importantly, the very notion of diversity, of otherness, is compromised. Such compromise extends beyond the conflation of specific stories. Children's Bibles, as is well known, typically include only the narrative portions of the Bible. The law, wisdom, poetic, and prophetic books from the Hebrew Bible, as well as the New Testament epistles, rarely make their way into children's Bibles. Thus, these voices are not heard, their perspectives are excluded. While, on the one hand, such omissions are certainly understandable—it is, after all, challenging to present Leviticus and Isaiah to young readers—on the other hand, the exclusion of different genres is a significant loss. Encountering different types of literature challenges and extends readers' imaginations, awakens them to new ways of being, thinking, experiencing, and viewing the world. Indeed, "different genres are concerned to establish different world views" (Livingstone 1990, 155), which means that other perspectives on reality are absent from many children's Bibles.

The work of Russian literary theorist Mikhail Bakhtin can be used to reflect on the diversity of the Bible, its valuable inclusion of other points of view. Bakhtin refers to a "dialogic sense of truth" that "requires a plurality of consciousnesses" that "cannot be fitted within the bounds of a single consciousness" (1984, 81). Unlike a monologic conception of truth, which can be captured in one consciousness, or one perspective, dialogic truth exists at the place where multiple consciousnesses, unmerged voices, intersect. Truth, then, emerges in the conversation of separate and diverse perspectives. Texts, to be sure, are not conversations, but according to Bakhtin, one can produce a literary work that takes the form of a genuine dialogue, a mode of writing that he calls "polyphonic." In a polyphonic work, in contrast to a monologic one, the author creates several consciousnesses that are authentically independent of one another and of the author's perspective. In such a work, the dialogic exchange of the various perspectives invites the reader to participate in the conversation. As a descriptive category, then, Bakhtin's ideas provide a fruitful way to address the unmerged perspectives in the Bible, for instance in the two different creation stories or the four Gospels. Each voice can be deeply valuable as it contributes ideas and images, even if in paradoxical ways, to the conversation from which truth—dialogic truth—may emerge. By harmonizing the stories, then, children's Bibles reduce a polyphonic text to a monologic one. There is no longer a conversation. Children's versions tinker not only with the specific stories, but with the very nature of truth that the Bible expresses.

Moreover, the harmonizing of the Bible does not allow the child reader to participate in the conversation, to reflect on stories from different perspectives, such as the invasion of the land through the eyes of the Canaanites or the plagues from the Egyptian viewpoint. Historian Arthur

Schlesinger suggests that (hi)story "should be taught from a variety of perspectives. Let our children try to imagine the arrival of Columbus from the viewpoint of those who met him as well as from those who sent him" (1998, 15). In our globalized world, it seems self-evident that cultivating an understanding and appreciation of different views and ideas is an important task for parents and teachers. Children must learn to thrive among people of different races, languages, cultures, and religious traditions. The Bible, indeed, offers a wonderful resource for the facilitation of these skills and habits. Readers learn to listen carefully and attentively, to engage, evaluate, and interact with different voices in the text—that is, they learn to think critically and to be spiritually and ethically sensitive human beings. But those opportunities vanish when children encounter rewritten versions that conflate stories and omit the various genres present in the canonical Bible. Children's Bibles ostracize the other instead of offering its readers the chance to meet and learn how to treat the other.

Indeed, "literature helps us understand others. Literature lets us sympathize with their pain, it helps us share their sorrow, it helps us celebrate their joy. It makes us more moral. It makes us better people" (Ledwon 1995, 134). The Bible as literature can function not only in this way, but as polyphonic literature it can also serve as a model of conversation, showing us how other voices can and should be heard. The inclusion of multiple points of view can, likewise, nurture in children an acceptance of the tentative nature of knowledge, which in turn opens space for communication. Those who are aware of more than one perspective, who do not "know for sure" what the truth is, are more open to dialogue. The complexity, the polyphony, of the Bible reflects reality. Simplified children's versions do not.

The diversity of the Bible can serve as a wonderful resource not only for exploring with children the complexities of the world around them but also for preparing them to plumb the depths of the spiritual and religious life in the Jewish and Christian traditions. For example, both traditions include notions of the transcendence and immanence of God, which can be seen in the two creation stories. In the first story, God speaks creation into existence from afar. In the second account, the Lord God is pictured in anthropomorphic terms, as a potter shaping the man from the dust of the ground and crafting the woman from the man's rib. These two portrayals offer two wonderfully distinct ways that one might relate to God—both as an almighty, transcendent figure and as a more personal, intimate deity who is closely involved with humanity. God is the maker and ruler of the

universe (first story) and simultaneously the Lord who walks and talks with
Adam and Eve (second story). In children's versions one of these images
is inevitably subsumed by the other. As a result, the child's resources for
understanding and relating to the biblical God are diminished.

Furthermore, if one thinks of the wonderful diversity of the midrash,
then the many perspectives on the Bible are anticipated by the many
perspectives in the Bible. Richard Friedman, for example, points out the
richness of including two creation stories: "There are a hundred possible interpretations, some more reverent and some cynical. And that is
just the point. The mixing of the [two stories] into one text enriched the
interpretive possibilities of the Bible for all time" (1997, 236). Likewise,
a sense of appreciation for ambiguity and paradox may assist in reflection on the Trinity or the doctrine of the humanity and divinity of Christ.
As Parker Palmer says: "We invite diversity … because diverse viewpoints
are demanded by the manifold mysteries of great things.… We embrace
ambiguity … because we understand the inadequacy of our concepts to
embrace the vastness of great things" (1997, 110). If readers are allowed
to experience the tensions and ambiguities in the text, they may be more
prepared to do so in their "real lives" and to explore the mystery and vastness of great things in their spiritual lives.

So why do children's Bibles conflate and combine stories and stream-
line the narratives? Why do children's Bibles want consistency? After
all, "consistency is the last refuge of the unimaginative,"[6] as Oscar Wilde
said, and it is "contrary to nature, contrary to life. The only completely
consistent people are dead,[7] according to Aldous Huxley. "Foolish consistency is the hobgoblin of small minds," as Emerson said.[8] Well, maybe
that is just it: Writers and editors of children's Bibles think that the readers—those with small minds—want or need consistency. So they simplify the Bible because they are afraid that children cannot handle its
diversity, its paradoxical nature. On the contrary, Palmer observes that
"we arrive in this world with an instinctive capacity to hold paradoxes
together. Watch a young child go through the day, and you will see how
action and rest, thought and feeling, tears and laughter are intimate and
inseparable companions. In a child, the opposites commingle and cocre-
ate each other with the animal fluidity of breathing in and out" (1997,

6. Online: http://www.gutenberg.org/files/14062/14062-h/14062-h.html.
7. Online: http://en.wikiquote.org/wiki/Aldous_Huxley.
8. Online: http://en.wikisource.org/wiki/Essays:_First_Series/Self-Reliance.

66–67). Palmer continues by lamenting that as children grow into adults, they lose their natural inclinations to embrace paradox. Indeed, children's Bibles do not facilitate the development of the child's innate ability to negotiate ambiguity, to engage in dialogue, to appreciate the other.

Yes, it is more difficult to consider multiple stories, divergent points of view. It is much easier to listen to a lecture or sermon than to participate in a lively debate or argument. But the canonical Bible is much more akin to the latter than the former. Diversity of opinions and contrasting ideas are not only an inevitable part of life, they are, if Bakhtin is right, precisely what is needed to arrive at truth. Furthermore, the hard work required to wrestle with the various ideas in the Bible may very well be the hallmark of an authentic life of faith in the Jewish and Christian traditions. The very name Israel, after all, means to strive or contend with God. Readers of children's Bibles are not invited to engage in such a struggle. Rather, they are given the hobgoblin of small minds.

Perhaps another reason why children's Bibles blend the disparate canonical accounts is to avoid the "what really happened" questions. If writers and publishers of children's versions are committed to a belief in the historical veracity and reliability of the Bible, they may be averse to include two incompatible stories. If there are conflicting accounts about biblical events, is then one wrong and the other right? How do we know which is which? If some of the Bible is historically inaccurate, then what parts, if any, can be trusted as reliable history? Or maybe we should not read the Bible as a history book? These are, admittedly, difficult questions. But they are ones that an honest reading of the Bible forces a person to consider.

Parents and teachers might have an easier time explaining the presence of two conflicting creation stories than two irreconcilable Christmas narratives. The former could naturally be discussed in terms of religious, theological, or spiritual truths, rather than scientific or historical ones. Simply because the two stories do not agree does not mean that they are not true. As physicist Niels Bohr said: "The opposite of a correct statement is a false statement, but the opposite of a profound truth may well be another profound truth."[9] The creation stories fall easily enough into the category of profound truths; thus their differences do not deny—and perhaps even confirm—their truth. But the disparate Christmas stories raise

---

9. Online: http://en.wikiquote.org/wiki/Niels_Bohr.

another whole set of challenges for a tradition that is based, at least in part, on historical events in the life of Jesus. How these challenges are met is, of course, not the issue here, but rather the issue is that readers of children's Bibles are not given the opportunity to encounter such challenges.[10]

The tendency to harmonize goes all the way back to Tatian's *Diatessaron*. Children's Bibles, thus, are not unique in this regard. The tradition, however, rejected Tatian's work, opting for dialogue over monologue, polyphony over monophony, otherness over sameness. The Bible is indeed a book for the global community. It not only contains the Scriptures of two different major world religions, but it also has Egyptian, Babylonian, Canaanite, Persian, Greek, and Roman fingerprints all over it. It is a multicultural book. True, all of this may not be evident to a child reader. Nonetheless, its inclusion of a variety of voices could be made more salient simply by presenting both creation and Christmas stories. Unfortunately, most children's Bibles do not; thus they mute a rich and engaging aspect of the canonical Bible. Their intentions may be good, but harmonized children's versions rob the Bible of one of its most powerful, and certainly most germane, features. When children's Bibles ostracize the other—other stories, genres, and points of view—they sacrifice the opportunity to learn to value the other on the altar of simplicity.

Works Cited

Alexander, Pat, and Leon Baxter (ill.). 2002. *My First Bible*. Intercourse: Good Books.

Bakhtin, Mikhail. 1984. *Problems of Doestoevsky's Poetics*. Translated by Caryl Emerson. Minneapolis: University of Minnesota Press.

Barnes, Trevor. 2001. *The Kingfisher Children's Bible*. New York: Kingfisher.

---

10. Asking children to read and think carefully about the Bible—whether a children's version or the canonical one—is not a particularly radical idea. Here is advice given to parents by Bob Jones University Press, an ultraconservative, fundamentalist publisher, who no doubt reads the Bible as being literally and historically accurate: "Have your child analyze Bible passages with the same techniques he learns in literature courses. Distinguish genres in Scripture, such as poetry, narrative, and epistle. Look for characterization, plot structure, drama, and rhetorical devices" (online: http://www.bjupress.com/resources/articles/hsh/bible-the-center-of-education.php). When children truly read critically, they will see the diversity, the otherness.

Batchelor, Mary, and John Haysom (ill.). 1995. *The Children's Bible in 365 Stories*. Oxford: Lion.

Beers, Gilbert, and Teresa Walsh (ill.). 1994. *The Preschooler's Bible*. Wheaton: Educational Publishing Concepts.

Brown, Laaren, and Lenny Hort. Eric Thomas (ill.). 2007. *The Children's Illustrated Jewish Bible*. New York: DK.

Bruno, Bonnie, and Carol Reinsma. Jenifer Schneider (ill.). 1998. *The Young Reader's Bible*. Cincinnati: Standard Publishing.

Chancellor, Deborah, and Anna C. Leplar (ill.). 2002. *Children's Everyday Bible*. London: Dorling Kindersley.

Frankel, Ellen, and Avi Katz (ill.). 2009. *JPS Illustrated Children's Bible*. Philadelphia: Jewish Publication Society of America.

Friedman, Richard E. 1997. *Who Wrote the Bible?* San Francisco: HarperCollins.

Golden Children's Bible. 1965. New York: Golden.

Grishaver, Joel Lurie. 1998. *A Child's Garden of Torah: A Read-Aloud Bedtime Bible*. Los Angeles: Torah Aura Productions.

Hastings, Selina, Eric Thomas, and Amy Burch (ills.). 1994a. *The Children's Illustrated Bible*. London: Dorling Kindersley.

———. 1994b. *The Illustrated Jewish Bible for Children*. London: Dorling Kindersley.

Healy, Judy, and Sheilah Beckett (ill.). 2004. *Good News Bible Stories for Children*. New York: Kidsbooks.

Henley, Karyn. 2002. *Day by Day Kid's Bible*. Wheaton: Tyndale.

Hoth, Iva, and André Le Blanc (ill.). 1998. *The Picture Bible*. Colorado Springs: Cook Communications.

Kolatch, Alfred, and Harry Araten (ill.). 1994. *Classic Bible Stories for Jewish Children*. Middle Village NY: Jonathan David.

Larsen, Carolyn, and Caron Turk (ill.). 1999. *The Little Boys Bible Storybook*. Grand Rapids: Baker.

Ledwon, Lenora. 1995. *Law and Literature: Text and Theory*. London: Routledge.

Livingstone, Sonia. 1990. *Making Sense of Television: The Psychology of Audience Interpretation*. London: Pergamon.

Loth, Paul J., and Rob Suggs (ill.). 1994. *My First Study Bible*. Nashville: Tommy Nelson.

Lovasik, Lawrence G. 1981. *New Catholic Picture Bible*. New York: Catholic Book Publishing.

Lucas, Daryl J., and Daniel Hochstatter (ill.). 1994. *The Eager Reader Bible*. Wheaton: Tyndale.

My Book of Bible Stories. 1978. New York: Watch Tower Bible & Tract Society.

My First Catholic Bible. 2001. Illustrated by Natalia Carabetta. Nashville: Nelson.

Palmer, Parker. 1997. *The Courage to Teach*. San Francisco: Jossey-Bass.

Prenzlau, Sheryl, Zely Smekhov, Daniel Goldberg, and Lena Guberman (ills.). 1996. *The Jewish Children's Bible: Genesis*. Newark: Simcha Media.

Rikkers, Doris, and Jean E. Syswerda. Dennis Jones (ill.). 2000. *Read with Me Bible*. Grand Rapids: Zonderkidz.

Rock, Lois, and Carolyn Cox (ill.). 2003. *My Book of Bible Stories*. Oxford: Lion.

Schlesinger, Arthur. 1998. *The Disuniting of America: Reflections on a Multicultural Society*. New York: Norton.

Taylor, Kenneth, Richard Hook, and Frances Hook (ills.). 2000. *The Book for Children*. Wheaton: Tyndale.

Turner, Philip, and Brian Wildsmith (ill.). 1968. *The Bible Story*. Oxford: Oxford University Press.

Water, Mark, and Diana Shimon (ill.). 2003. *The Pilgrim Book of Bible Stories*. Cleveland: Pilgrim.

Williams, Derek, and Jacqui Thomas (ill.). 2002. *The Bible from Beginning to End*. Nashville: Abingdon.

PART 3
DESTROYING THE OTHER

"The Water's Round My Shoulders, and I'm—Glug! Glug! Glug!": God's Destruction of Humanity in the Flood Story for Children

Emma England

In the Genesis flood narrative (6:1–9:19) the narrator describes the destruction: the waters rose, the mountains were covered (7:17–20), and "all flesh died that moved on the earth" (7:21). The account is repeated with the addition of: "He blotted out every living thing" (7:23). The lack of God's name emphasizes the destruction as an event, while moving him to the background. As a result, God's direct involvement in the narrative is reduced during the destruction. Conversely, the death of those not on the ark is repeated three times (7:21, 22, 23) with the added clarification: "Only Noah was left, and those that were with him in the ark" (7:24). Most humans and animals clearly die. They die because God deems them wicked (6:5, 11–13). We never learn the exact nature of their crimes, crimes that God saw as warranting their destruction. The narrative is also silent about how people die and the extent to which they suffer.

When retelling the flood story for children, these are gaps the writer and illustrator will have to make decisions about. Specifically, they need to consider whether to include the destruction and to what extent, what God's role in it is, why humans deserve to be destroyed, and to what degree human (and animal) suffering is presented.[1] They use a variety of approaches, from ignoring the destruction to graphically visualizing

---

1. The terms "retold" and "retelling" distinguish the individual story from the object of publication. The term "children's Bible" does not accurately reflect the diversity of forms, including tracts, magazines, pamphlets, hymnbooks, and dictionaries. Stephens and McCallum claim there are three sorts of Bible retellings for children: traditional religious, literary, and secular humanist (1998, 31–32). Although this is an oversimplification, it is a useful reminder of the variety produced.

it. These approaches are a form of interpretation. They implicitly comment on the biblical narrative and transform it into something new. In this essay I present and analyze these approaches, focusing upon the relationship between word and image. This relationship is one of the most complex facets of retold Bible narratives for children, and how it affects the interpretation of biblical narratives is only just beginning to be considered. By concentrating on the relationship between word and image in the presentation of the destruction of humanity, it is also possible to uncover processes of othering in the retellings. These processes more specifically reflect identification markers based on gender, wealth, and behavior and are largely presented through invisibility or hypervisibility.[2] This othering also relates to children, both within the retellings and as (targeted) readers of them.

Humanity's Destruction in Word and Image

Readers familiar with the biblical narrative inevitably have what has been called a top-down approach to Bible story retellings (Stephens 1992, 19). In this approach assumptions are made based upon the readers' own knowledge of the underlying biblical narrative and their expectations of specific moral frameworks and the presence of the supernatural. These readers may be less likely to interpret each individual retelling as a narrative in its own right, because they evaluate the narrative based upon what they know from the biblical version. When a verbal text is accompanied by illustrations, this difficulty is compounded. Words and images have a complex relationship in children's books, and readers are likely to react to this relationship differently. Some may prioritize the words and others the images, but it is how they function together that forms the retelling's meaning and impression.

Academics working with children's Bible retellings also inevitably utilize a top-down approach: we cannot eradicate what we know. One possible way to try and overcome this is to develop a reading strategy that addresses the individual complexities of each retelling. For example, with picturebooks a reader could first read the words, then the images, before

---

2. Previous discussions of flood narrative retellings for children have offered overviews of the retellings (Piehl 1982, 80–86; Landy 2007, 351–76) and highlighted the use of Noah as a religious hero (Piehl 1989, 41–52) and model for obedience, goodness, and parental authority (Person and Person 2005, 56–89).

reading them together. This will often result in different narratives being uncovered, highlighting the significance of the word/image relationship.

In order to minimize impressionistic readings of children's Bible retellings as a group,[3] a more detailed and specific approach can be helpful, such as a quantitative content analysis: a research method for studying messages of communication that is replicable, reliable, and summarizing (Neuendorf 2002, 10; Krippendorff 2004, 18). Adopting this method, I broke the flood story into units (i.e., the animals enter the ark) and devised a classification system whereby for each retelling I could record which units were included visually and/or verbally. The results can be surprising: events and characters are frequently more or less popular than expected. In my work, I have undertaken an analysis of over three hundred English-language retellings of the flood story published in England between 1837 and 2007 for young children.[4] Based on this research, I have identified a range of approaches used by producers of the retellings to present the destruction of humanity. Here I present six approaches that highlight the significance of the word/image relationship and the destruction of humanity:

1. no verbal or visual reference
2. brief verbal reference and/or allusory visual representation
3. traditional verbal description, no visual representation
4. verbal elaboration, no visual representation
5. visual representation, no or brief verbal reference
6. visual representation, and traditional verbal description or verbal elaboration

---

3. Discussions of children's Bible retellings are often impressionistic, such as the idea that children's Bibles are "all the same" or that flood retellings never include the destruction. Such impressions are understandable; bookshops invariably include only a few examples, and many publishers share and recycle popular retellings. *The Lion Children's Bible* and *The Puffin Children's Bible* by Pat Alexander were published simultaneously in 1981 with illustrations by Lyndon Evans. They have identical contents but externally look different. In 1991 both titles were republished with new illustrations by Carolyn Cox.

4. It is difficult to state for what age group something is published unless it is explicitly referenced. Most retellings have no such statement, and when they do, the expectations for a five-year-old changes depending upon time and location. The use of "young," rather than a specific age, encompasses this change.

This essay considers all six of these categories, although there is a bias toward the last two because of my focus on the impact of the word/image relationship. These are represented by illustrated books and picturebooks. In illustrated books, the verbal text is the dominant narrative. Without the words the narrative would not be a readable story, whereas without the illustrations the narrative may be different but still a story. In contrast, picturebooks are a unique art form relying on "the interdependence of pictures and words, on the simultaneous display of two facing pages, and on the drama of turning the page" (Bader 1976, 1).[5] When the flood story is one of many in a "children's Bible" (*The Lion Children's Bible*, Alexander and Cox 1991a), it is usually illustrated. However, when it is in a single-story book (*The Story of Noah's Ark*, Smith 1905), that book will almost always be a picturebook.

No Verbal or Visual Reference

Many retellings do not reference the destruction of humanity (hereafter "the destruction") either in word or image. This includes nearly all of the concept books (e.g., alphabet and counting books) and novelty books (e.g., textured and bath books). One such example is *Noah and the Rabbits* (Kilroy 1992), a movable book (a book with moving parts), in this instance a lift-the-flap book.[6] In the book Noah has to find the talking rabbits a home on the already full ark. Noah, his wife, one son, the ark, and some rain are the only indicators of the source of the narrative.[7] This is typical of such retellings: they tend to focus on the idea of a large boat with a friendly grandfatherly figure looking after pairs of animals. The stories are often just set on the ark with little or no contextualization.

---

5. A growing number of texts offer alternative definitions and reading strategies to approach this unique and complex art form (cf. Nodelman 1988; Kiefer 1995; D. Lewis 2001; Nikolajeva and Scott 2001; Graham 2005, 209–26; Sainsbury 2005, 227–49; Sipe and Pantaleo 2008).

6. Movable books are a form of novelty book (they can also be concept books) and include pop-up, turn-the-wheel, and pull-tab books. They are also known as "toy books." This term can cause confusion because it also includes books that are toys, i.e., bags and soft toys incorporating books. The original use of the term was as nineteenth-century paper-covered picturebooks (Graham 2005, 217; Montanaro 2005, 562–64). The Genesis narrative has been re-created in all of these formats.

7. When Noah's wife is present, as in Kilroy's book, she is invariably cooking or cleaning.

Another example is the lift-the-flap book *Noah's Adventure in the Ark* (Mills 1996). It tells a recognizable version of the flood story but does not reference the destruction, concentrating on Noah saving his family and two of every creature at God's behest (1v).[8] Despite the absence of any apparent danger, Noah thanks God for keeping those in the ark safe (11v), and God promises never to send another flood (11v). The narrator tells the audience that God left a sign of his promise; the reader then lifts the flap to find the rainbow (12r).[9] In the biblical account, however, this rainbow is inextricably interwoven with God's promise never to drown the world again. What meaning can the rainbow and the promise have if there is no destruction? God's roles as creator, destroyer, protector/savior, and re-creator are effectively nullified. In the Genesis narrative the destruction, for all its narrated brevity, is essential to the story and cannot be ignored; neither can the question of why God destroys humanity, something that is clearly ignored when there is no destruction.

The decision to exclude humanity's wickedness, God's judgment, and the destruction avoids a variety of complicated moral questions about what wickedness is, who exactly is wicked, and why God made this violent decision. However, as a result of this exclusion the flood story undergoes a process of reversion in the form of a re-creation based on contextual and ideological configurations that are different from the source text (Stephens and McCallum 1998, 4). To an extent that all retellings undergo this process, we cannot know what the original configurations of the flood story were, but when the destruction is discarded it changes, if not removes, the central premise of the Genesis narrative: God's rela-

---

8. Most picturebooks do not include page numbers. Referencing pages is variously handled by scholars, including providing none (Nikolajeva and Scott 2001) to counting pages beginning with the title page (Graham 2005, 209). I count pages from the first leaf, irrespective of content. Front and back endpapers are not counted, although they sometimes have interesting content (Sipe and McGuire 2006). I also add "v" and "r" to the number to indicate whether the page is the verso (left-hand page) or recto (right-hand page). When no "v" or "r" is present, the page number is as designated in the book.

9. The last words of the book, prominently set on the flap covering the rainbow, are: "You can read about this story in the Bible. See Genesis 6:9–22, 7:1–24, 8:1–22, 9:1–17" (12r). Biblical references are not uncommon in retellings, although their purpose is often unclear. They appear to be an attempt to justify the retelling, validate it, locate it in religious tradition (particularly for religious publishers, as in this case), and/or encourage reading of the Bible (for the children or the adults?).

tionship with his creation. The biblical story presents the moment where God changes his mind: he transforms from being a God who punishes and destroys the inherent wickedness of his own creation to a God who accepts this and decides to deal with it (cf. van Wolde 1994, 75–83; Humphreys 2001, 72).[10]

By removing the moments that enable God to change his mind, particularly the (horrific?) destruction, God himself has been sent to the margins of his own story. The removal of the destruction subverts God's power both to punish and to protect humanity. Moreover, removing the destruction as an act that shows God's character in development affirms a normative understanding of God as immutable. The power balance shifts as the retellers take control of God's identity, or rather of the narrator (and the [implied] authors?), to suit their own purposes and ideologies. This shift may be as much about taking control from and shifting aside the narrators of Genesis as about the character of God. About half of the three hundred and more retellings I have read do not include the destruction, thus sending God to the sidelines. The remaining retellings do include the destruction as caused by God; the rest of this essay considers the variations in the presentation of the destruction.

Brief Verbal Reference and/or Allusory Visual Representation

The second category is largely based on absence rather than presence. A "brief verbal reference" is when the destruction has been mentioned but in the loosest possible terms, as in "Noah and His Ark" in *Genesis for Children* (Jewson 1950, 27–31): "But all the wrong thoughts that had caused the flood were washed away by it" (30). An "allusory visual reference" is when images do not include drowned or drowning people but do include motifs suggesting the former presence of humanity. This is most often indicated

---

10. The presentation of God and the central theme of the narrative is more complicated depending upon where the boundaries of the narrative are drawn and upon what intertextual references are used to interpret it. As reflected in this study, most producers of the retellings only use Gen 6:9–8:19; 9:8–17. Others include references to Adam and Eve (Gen 1–3), Cain and Abel (Gen 4), and the union between the daughters of humanity and sons of God (6:1–4), specifically as justification for the destruction. Yet others add the tower of Babel narrative (Gen 11) or references to Jesus. The former demonstrates humanity's continued wickedness and God's fulfillment of his promise. The latter may present Noah as a type of Christ or suggest what will happen if the reader veers from the Christian path.

by buildings under water, such as in *Noah and the Ark and the Animals* (Elborn and Gantschev 1984). The doublespread is in somber blue, gray, and greens.[11] In the bottom right-hand corner are four lines of text essentially ignoring the human dimension of the destruction: "And finally even the tallest mountains were underwater" (11r). The image shows lightning striking buildings and the buildings falling (10v–11r).[12]

These limited visual and verbal references are placed within the same category because they have a similar level of interaction with the Genesis narrative. They both acknowledge the destruction but are hiding it, effectively marginalizing it. The retellings with allusions to the destruction have a more complicated relationship with Genesis than retellings without the destruction. The relationship is more dependent upon the rest of the story.

For example, in "Why Did Noah Build an Ark?" in *Young Learner's Bible Stories* (Watson and Ferris 2007, 6–7) the doublespread covers Gen 1–10 in seven short paragraphs. The longest, "Noah and the Flood" roughly covers 6:5–8:4. It consists of ninety-two words, including: "Everything was destroyed apart from the ark" (7). This would clearly fit into the second category, as a brief verbal reference, were it not for the second sentence of the paragraph: "Finally, he decided to kill everyone in a flood" (7). To analyze the retelling as a brief verbal reference would not be fair to this specific retelling: a third of the total word count relates to the destruction. This increases the significance of the reference to the destruction

---

11. As terminology in picturebook analysis is still developing, the spelling "doublespread" is one of at least four used ("double spread," "double-spread," and "double-page spread" being the others), in addition to the word "opening." I use "doublespread" as it mirrors the now widely accepted spelling of "picturebook." It also emphasizes that the two facing pages should be regarded as a whole. The doublespread is often treated as one page, with the image(s) spread across the gutter (as is the case in all three figures in this article). The formatting of the verso and recto is key, and even if the image is only on the recto, with the text on the verso, the image will still catch the eye first.

12. The discrepancy between what occurs in the words and images is typical of heavily illustrated books and picturebooks. In this case the words offer a summary speeding up the flood, while the image presents a pause, a brief moment where the narratorial discourse (the illustration) interrupts the event (cf. Genette 1986, 95–112; Bal 1997, 99–111). The moment selected in the image often contradicts and challenges the words, thereby affecting their meaning and interpretation (Nikolajeva and Scott 2001, 157–61).

considerably.[13] On the other hand, if a retelling is long and detailed in other ways but makes a similarly minimal reference to the destruction, then the overall impact will probably result in the destruction having far less prominence. Even here, however, formatting can have an impact; if the destruction has a page of its own the dominance could be restored, further highlighting the complexities of children's Bible retellings.

Another element is introduced when retellings include both the verbal and the visual. The penultimate page of "Noah's Ark" in *God and His Creations* (Williams 2005, 10–13), a four-page sequential story (comic-book style), is split into forty-one panels. The largest depicts the ark floating with buildings under the water.[14] The accompanying reference to the destruction is: "Soon no other creatures were left alive, and the highest mountains were covered with water" (12). Although the word "creatures" is used, as with the previous example, God is explicit in his intention on the first page of the story: "I am going to put an end to all people" (10). Indeed, he is visualized looking cross and staring down at "the people" committing crimes. Nevertheless, the destruction image still requires extrapolation. The connection needs to be made between God's announcement and the destruction, which are separated by two large pages and numerous panels.[15] This specific example appears to have a careful interaction with, and consideration of, the Genesis narrative. Through the visual representation of God, it attempts to show his central significance while also enabling Noah and the animals to be foregrounded. Significantly, it shows a clear relationship between God and the destruction without having that relationship shown during the destruction itself, in a similar way to Gen 7:21–23.

The retelling is not without ideological othering. The author/illustrator Marcia Williams provides justification for God's judgment by including depictions of violent thieves. These thieves are all clearly poor and

---

13. It also demonstrates how identifying approaches through quantitative content analysis is useful, but best paired with qualitative analysis.

14. The other forty panels depict the ark floating in various scenarios, often with God helping it stay afloat. Forty is a reference to the length of time the rain is said to have fallen (7:4, 12, 17; 8:6).

15. This is exacerbated because of the complicated narration that involves frames within frames, borders overlapping frames (and vice versa), didactic narration, four different sorts of speech illustrated and typeset in different ways to indicate different voices, as well as verbal sound markers such as "Biff!" (10).

are illustrated in a variety of shapes and colors. Meanwhile Noah looks exactly like God, and Noah's family members all look like Noah. The "good" people are privileged by being not poor and are homogeneous in size, color, and clothing. The "bad" people are different from the good people in their heterogeneity. This kind of binary differentiation in the illustration may remind us that the flood narrative as recounted in Genesis is one biblical disaster where discrimination by race, class, gender, and age does not occur. Everybody except Noah and his family drowns, irrespective of who they are. In the retellings, othering based on ethnicity, class/wealth, and size is rarely so overt as in Williams's version, but it is nevertheless common. This is unsurprising given that, when visualized, Noah and the drowned need to be recognizable from each other beyond their actions. Difference thus becomes automatically embedded in the images.

Ultimately, retellings with a brief verbal reference and/or allusory visual reference to the destruction demonstrate the complexity of children's retellings because they show how difficult it is to analyze isolated motifs without referencing the whole structure of the narrative. By comparing isolated motifs across numerous retellings we can, however, achieve a useful overview of the complex varieties of interactions with the Bible.

TRADITIONAL VERBAL DESCRIPTION, NO VISUAL REPRESENTATION

Sometimes retellings are closely based upon the Genesis narrative; hence I label them "traditional." Many of these are in (near) complete Bibles such as *The Children's Bible* (Mee 1933). It was first published in 1924, and in the ten years that followed it had already been reprinted fifteen times. In it Mee uses the KJV. He removes the chapter and verse numbering and orders the Bible as a single narrative with subheadings such as "The Great Flood" (Gen 6:1–7:24; pp. 6–7) and "The Ark upon the Waters" (8:1–9, 15; pp. 7–8).[16]

In addition, numerous retellings rephrase one or more translations of Genesis.[17] When these sorts of retellings include illustrations they are par-

---

16. Gen 9:18–19 is in "The Tower of Babel" (8). Gen 9:20–29 is not included: Noah does not die. For an analysis of the "drunken Noah" narrative in children's Bibles, see Bottigheimer 1996, 103–15.

17. Some authors offer explanations as to which versions they used and why, as well as any other research they may have undertaken. For example, Michael McCar-

ticularly useful for demonstrating the significance of images because the words can broadly act as a control element. For example, "Noah and His Ark" in *The Usborne Little Book of Stories from the Old Testament* (Amery and Edwards 2007, 12–16) includes detailed paintings but none show the destruction. The words read: "Outside, the water rose until it covered the very tops of the mountains, and everybody and everything left on the Earth was drowned in the flood" (13). In comparison, *Noah's Ark* (Auld and Mayo 1999) uses a simplified version of 7:21–23 accompanied by a strong destruction image filling nearly the whole recto. The ark floats on the waters at the top right-hand side of the page. The rest of the page is a cross-section of the waters complete with numerous animals and five people sinking. The difference between these two retellings is stark: Amery and Edwards hide the destruction, whereas Auld and Mayo highlight it.

Retellings with a traditional verbal description but no visual representation of the destruction may appear to be more faithful to the Genesis narrative than retellings that remove or underplay it. In many ways, however, this apparent faithfulness proves problematic because of the role of God in the destruction and how that role is narrated in Genesis. Although God announces the flood (6:7, 13–17), he is silent for the duration of it (7:5–8:14). During the flood he only acts to shut the door of the ark (7:16), remember Noah (8:1), and make a wind blow (8:1). During the destruction itself, there is only one possible reference to him: "He blotted out every living thing" (7:23).

In order for a retelling to remain faithful to the biblical depiction of God's role in the flood, God has to actively state that he will destroy everything and then either physically or magically shut the ark and make a wind blow. He must also "remember" Noah, thereby implying that at some point he had forgotten him. This combination of factors is clearly challenging for producers of the retellings because they are rarely all present in any one version. As a result God's role in the retellings is diminished. This is particularly the case because references to other details such as God smelling Noah's offerings, his command to breed, and his demand for a reckon-

---

thy claims to have read several translations (including the RSV and NJV), commentaries (including *The Jerome Biblical Commentary*), and he was "especially inspired and educated by Robert Alter's new translation, *Genesis*" (2001, "Author's Note"). He also visited schools, libraries, and wildlife parks in order to "create a story that had the power and magic of the original, and would stretch the vocabulary and imagination of its listeners" (readers are not mentioned).

ing (8:20–9:7) are uncommon. Thus the narrative is essentially reduced to Noah, the ark, and the animals. God is demoted from being the primary character while Noah is promoted.

In the retellings, whether they include the destruction or not, Noah is the focalizer. The retellings make the flood story into the (abbreviated) story of Noah, a story that is different from the story of the flood (cf. J. Lewis 1968, 3; Peters 2008, 17–22; Stone, Amihay, and Hillel 2010, 1). In most retellings God is marginalized by his total or relative absence. The flood is no longer a means to an end for God; it is the tool by which the producers of children's books are able to present everything from learning the alphabet using animals to themes of environmental stewardship (Stephens and McCallum 1998, 54–56; Piehl 2005). With the rise of the centrality of Noah, the Genesis flood story is replaced in our cultural memory with "Noah's ark."

VERBAL ELABORATION, NO VISUAL REPRESENTATION

In some retellings additional material is provided to fill gaps in the Genesis account, particularly regarding human suffering. In recent years retellings have focused on the suffering of Noah and those trapped on the ark rather than the humans who drowned.[18] Throughout the nineteenth century and opening decades of the twentieth century the feelings and behavior of the victims of the destruction were more dominant. One such text is from the anonymous *Bible Stories in Simple Language for Little Children* (ca. 1894): "Then torrents of rain began to fall; the rivers overflowed; the sea rose over the land; the tops of the highest hills were covered with water; all men, women, and children were drowned. How dreadful it must have been!" (16).

This example appears to lead the audience (whether successfully or not) into empathizing with the drowning people. Emotive retellings have a complex relationship with the narrative. Thus, we could interpret the narrator as being didactic and appealing to the perceived sinner within each reader, or we could interpret the narrator as being critical of the act of destruction. Here again one needs to consider the overall structure of the narrative to decide. In *Bible Stories*, the narrator is being didactic; this can

---

18. "How terrible it must have been for Noah and his family to see before their horrified eyes the end of people they had known all their lives. For the Lord in his anger knew no mercy" ("The World Drowns" in Matthews 1979, 17–18).

be gleaned from the representation of 6:1–8, based on nineteenth-century interpretations of the verses (cf. Churton 1882, C5v–6r; Keil and Delitzsch 1864, 131): "And this son, who was called Seth, was very good; so were his children. But they foolishly married the daughters of Cain's sons, and in time they grew as bad as their new relations were. All the best men had died; there was only one good man and his family left: his name was Noah" (*Bible Stories in Simple Language* 1894, 14).

These Sethites and Cainites are presented in the narrative as a cause of the destruction. Despite describing them as "foolish" and "bad," the narrator also acknowledges how "dreadful" the flood was for them. This creates a bridge between the reader and the drowned. Typically, readers are encouraged to identify with Noah as part of the protected internal group. However, in this narrative (and those like it) the readers are being encouraged to identify themselves with the bad people who represent the wicked, violent, and corrupt of the Genesis story. This identification may minimize the difference between the self of the reader and the other of the drowned, or it may result in the reader identifying with the drowned. Attempts to create identification do not always succeed or work as expected though; indeed such subjectivity should not necessarily be encouraged (Nikolajeva 2010, 185–202). Nevertheless, giving a voice to those destroyed highlights the absence of the drowned from the Genesis narrative. By their very absence we see that the victims as a collective unit are marginalized through their lack of focalization, a lack that is part of the process of othering, an indicator that the reader of Genesis is encouraged to identify with the in-group of Noah's family.

Visual Representation, No or Brief Verbal Reference

One way to emphasize the significance of the destruction without having to describe it is to present its visual horror. In nearly all such examples, the destruction has a minimal verbal reference. In "The Flood and the Ark" in *The Youths' Bible and Commentator* (Cobbin 1873, 3–4), there is reference to God's decision to destroy "man" and his promise after the flood, but there is no actual account of the destruction. However, the image (signature unclear) consists of numerous drowning people and a few distraught people on rocks. Over a century later *Noah and the Ark* (1978) was published. The image of the destruction is a full doublespread with nine lines of text in the bottom right-hand corner. They describe the rising of the waters, the mountains disappearing, and the ark floating before: "Everything else drowned" (5v–6r). The image is very detailed, with over forty items including buildings, trees, animals, people sitting on houses, and one drowning, yelling, flailing man. Significantly, none of the people suffering the destruction are recognizable from the equally detailed earlier image of people committing the crimes for which humanity is destroyed (1v–2r). Thus, the perpetrators are not identified with those who experience the punishment.

Such retellings highlight the destruction motif at the expense of the protection/salvation. This is particularly the case in a short book such as this, where, of the nine doublespreads, four are directly connected with the destruction (criminals, people mocking Noah, the destruction, and the water with sunken buildings). In comparison, it is only on the last page that Noah thanks God and God makes his promise. Here the text dominates. The vibrant colors of the depictions of destruction are replaced with white. The image is small and unexpectedly includes iconography of the crucifixion clearly visible, but only to informed viewers. As the final image in the book, and accompanied by the promise and the rainbow, the message seems to show God as savior of humanity. However, the image is dull and is subsumed by the destruction, not least because it is presented on the final verso and does not even warrant a doublespread.

The message in this retelling is one of punishment, but the people being punished have not done wrong. Those that are depicted as engaging in crimes are not those who are seen being punished. Thus the causal link is not clearly narrated. With such dominance being given to an apparently unjustified punishment and so little to the protection, God becomes a tyrant. His role as the protector of humanity who changes his mind and ensures humanity's future is ignored.

By showing criminals as clearly different people from those who drown, we are left with a dichotomy. We must assume that the drowning people are also criminals, because if we assume they are innocent they do not deserve to be killed. If not, then God is clearly responsible for the death of innocent people. This question is also relevant for the next retelling.

The destruction image in "The Flood" (Hadaway and Atcheson 1973, 16–18) is one of the largest images of the destruction I have seen in any retelling. The doublespread is larger than A3 (6.5 x 11.7 in), and the image fills most of it. The entire retelling consists of only two versos and one recto. The ark is faintly visible in the background; the sky is almost black with clouds; dead and drowning animals and people float in the water. On

Fig. 10.1. Illustrator: L'Esperto S.p.A; the suffering of humanity (detail).

the left-hand side of the image is a rock swarming with exhausted people. This is mirrored on the right, but it is the bottom right corner, a detail a mere eighth of the original, on which I will focus (fig. 10.1).

A bedraggled looking woman, her mouth and eyes aghast, is looking to her left, the next page. As such, she acts as the pageturner.[19] When the page is turned, the viewer sees the only other visual motif in the retelling: the dove returning with an olive branch. It may be intended as an indication of peace, as a positive image with which to leave the narrative but it cannot possibly overcome the severity of the destruction image.

Another woman, also in red, holds a baby. This motif is influenced by an artistic tradition of depictions of the destruction where women cling to frightened babies.[20] This subject matter can also be seen in some nineteenth-century retellings, some using the same image occasionally colored, but this is the latest I have seen (cf. *Mamma's Bible Stories for Her Little Boys and Girls* in ca. 1862; *The Child's Own Book of Scripture Pictures* in ca. 1865). Such dramatic images of death and despair are not atypical for nineteenth-century children's books, but they are quite rare in twentieth-century books. The inclusion of it here may be even more of a shock than

---

19. A pageturner is a detail encouraging the reader to turn to the next page. Visual pageturners are usually in the bottom right-hand side of the image on the recto (Nikolajeva and Scott 2001, 152–53).

20. Cf. Michelangelo's *The Deluge* (1508–1509), Jan Brueghel the Elder's *The Flood with Noah's Ark* (1601), and Anne-Louis Girodet de Roucy-Trioson's *Scene of the Flood* (ca. 1806).

it might otherwise be because the representation of suffering of children is less common than it was even as recently as the Victorian period.

The baby being held by this woman in red is crying and is wearing pale blue, which may suggest that the baby's gender is male.[21] The boy and woman almost look to be fighting to get away from each other. The baby, although comparatively small, has a greater weight in the painting than any other figure (particularly when the picture is looked at as a whole). There are many reasons for this. His pale clothes immediately contrast with the dark colors of the rest of the image. The baby is small in comparison to the other foregrounded figures, which combined with his crying encourages the reader to feel empathy for him. He is facing the reader, with his eyes open, and human faces attract the gaze (Nodelman 1988, 100–101). The baby thus draws the reader into the narrative acting as a "visual intrusive narrator" by gazing directly at the reader (Nikolajeva and Scott 2001, 119, 123). Although the image includes many elements that the baby cannot see, this is the character directly communicating with the audience. Note also the other two figures in the detail: a man and a boy hugging. They appear to be at peace, or at least resigned, waiting for the end. In this detail they are prominent but in the full image they merge into the rock and background. They are the only peaceful beings in the image, and they are not directly communicating with the viewer as the (male?) baby is.

This image involves a complex process of othering. The women are excluded because of the baby's direct communication with the viewer and the peace of the man and boy. The baby, man, and boy are still going to drown and are thus automatically on the outside, excluded from the group being protected and saved. Nevertheless the man and boy do not appear to be victims, while the baby is clearly an unwilling victim. His direct communication with the viewer creates a bridge between the viewer and the drowning people in the image. It is uncomfortable to acknowledge an intrusive visual narrator as a victim, because this may make us a victim or a collaborator in creating their suffering. In this instance it is exacerbated by adult/child difference: accepting a presumably innocent baby as a victim is counterintuitive.

---

21. Very rarely, a retelling explicitly tries to justify the drowning of children. One such example is "The Flood" in *Stories from the Bible* (Wilson-Wilson 1916, 3r–4v): "But God knew that the fathers and mothers and grown-up people had grown so wicked that it was even better for the children to be drowned, and to go back to their Father in Heaven, than learn to do wickedness" (3v).

This, however, is the point. The baby is being differentiated precisely because he is hypervisible as a baby. The normative scenario for destruction images, including this one, is for adults to drown but here the baby is clearly in danger of drowning.[22] This challenges the aetonormativity of the scene, a normativity referring to child/adult power imbalance (Nikolajeva 2009, 13–24; cf. 2010: 8). The term reflects adults' colonization of children as expressed by Perry Nodelman, who claims that children's texts "assume the right of adults to wield power and influence over children; thus, they might represent a kind of thinking about less powerful beings that can be identified as 'colonial'" (2008, 78). By including a baby the illustrator has overturned the normal power structures by permitting a baby to drown and by using him to connect with the viewer. However, any overturning of power is only temporary, for although the baby has the power in this image, the baby cannot keep this power. In effect the baby as a symbol is being used by the adult illustrator to cause maximum anxiety.

By contrast, the boy in the man's arms never has any power. He does not fight to escape, as the baby does; instead he holds on to the adult male and seems to accept his fate, even though, or perhaps because, he is a child. In his case, the power remains with the adult. The composite image is thus a complicated set of otherings that have an ambiguous relationship with each other and the viewer. This is emphasized by the accompanying words: "Quite soon the ark began to float, but the water rose and rose, until it covered even the mountaintops and every living creature that was not on the ark drowned" (Hadaway and Atcheson 1973, 18).

This is the only verbal reference to the destruction in this version, and it is on the second verso. Hence the image is seen before it is explained. The retelling appears to be about the destruction but this is not necessarily the intention of the authors.[23] The words include a warm, caring God that says to Noah: "Don't worry" (Hadaway and Atcheson 1973, 17). This

---

22. Drowning babies are not as rare as one might think in the retellings. In *A Book about the Old Testament for Children* (Postgate and Hart 1922), the image by W. Lawson is dominated by three drowning or dead babies floating in the water. All are without clothes, and two are "nude" rather than "naked" (Nodelman 1988, 121–24). The only other objects in the image are the ark, waves, and two birds (cf. *Child's Own Book of Scripture Pictures* and Smith 1905).

23. This is the only truly horrific image in the book. It is likely that "L'Esperto S.p.A." is a society of artists commissioned to illustrate the book, and they chose images from their catalogue. This could result in the authors having little or no say in the images selected.

is clearly a different kind of retelling than the one illustrated. They do not function successfully together. In contrast, the final two retellings we shall consider offer a close relationship between words and images and offer an entirely different set of possible responses and interpretations as a result.

VISUAL REPRESENTATION, AND TRADITIONAL VERBAL DESCRIPTION OR VERBAL ELABORATION

There are relatively few retellings with both a verbal and visual elaboration. In comparison with the previous category, they tend to downplay the horror of the event. This is true of the book that supplies the title of this article: *Captain Noah and His Floating Zoo* (Flanders and King 1972). The doublespread of the destruction makes full use of the physical space of the book (8v–9r; see fig. 10.2). A tree placed across the gutter of the binding divides the space between the image and words. It creates a boundary, softening the effect of both by keeping them apart but simultaneously connecting them. One overweight man floats in an upturned umbrella while another man measures the depth of the water against his body with a ruler. Four people are in the tree: two on the verso who look desperate, while two on the recto smile happily. By itself the absurd image suggests vague concern but nothing life threatening. The text changes everything. The first two verses include the lines: "It looks like rain, / Now won't that just be jolly!" and "I shouldn't be surprised / If it was going to flood!"[24] The last verse is:

It looks like the sea
Is rising like a fountain!
It looks like—HELP!
I'm making for the mountain!
It looks like—AAAH!
The world's a brimming jug!
The water's round my shoulders,
And I'm—GLUG!
GLUG!
GLUG!

24. Originally the whole narrative poem was accompanied by music by Joseph Horowitz intended to be performed. Imagine the actions!

Fig. 10.2. Illustrator: Harold King; the comical, absurd destruction.

By itself this could be read in multiple ways, including as a piece of horror. However, the potentially horrific impact of the words has been lessened by the absurd image while the image has been clarified by the words. The image will always be the first thing seen but not necessarily "read." Different readers will read the words and images in various orders, perhaps even reading a verse and then looking more closely at the picture. The variety of ways of reading is considerable, but the permanent presence of both words and images ensures they always influence each other (Kiefer 1995, 20–22; D. Lewis 2001, 31–45). This makes reading complicated, particularly when we consider the hermeneutic circle that occurs upon multiple rereadings of the book.

The tree is the focal point, but if one follows the branches of the tree to the right and toward the text (not shown), then the reader will see the smiling people just before reading the text. However, if they look to the left and read the image, they will be guided in a circle around the people, probably finishing with the humorous man in the umbrella before seeing the ark and then reading the text. Either option leads one to be comforted before reading the verse. This is likely to change the way the poem is read so that the emphasis is on the humor: "I must go and get my brolly" or

The rain swelled the streams and sent them surging into the sea. The tide rose higher and higher and HUGE waves swept inland.

The people climbed trees, hills and mountains, but the water rose up and covered them all, while Noah's boat rocked safely on the waves until the rain finally stopped.

But then it began to rain. 'Perhaps Noah was right after all!' they wailed as they splashed about in the puddles and started to get very wet indeed.

Fig. 10.3. Illustrator: Steve Björkman; the guilty people drown.

"GLUG, GLUG, GLUG." This draws attention to the horror of the situation by presenting a fantastic reversal of the horror through humor. It presents the violence of the story in a way that simultaneously creates detachment through fictionalizing it with wonder and a sense of escape. This uncomfortably contrasts with the reality of violent death.

The final retelling is *A Boat Full of Animals* by Jennifer Rees Larcombe with illustrations by Steve Björkman. The destruction covers one doublespread (1999, 7v–8r; see fig. 10.3). The focal point is a man looking shocked and holding his head in despair. The man is in close-up, a rare device in picturebooks (Nodelman 1988, 151). It creates involvement with characters by dominating the page and drawing the reader's gaze. This man has already been seen in the retelling a few doublespreads earlier where he is seen mocking Noah. He is one of three people described as "bad" in a very large font. In that illustration he is the pageturner signaling the doom to come, but a pageturner with a difference. His finger is pointing toward Noah, who stands in the bottom left-hand corner of the doublespread.

Although he is breaking picturebook rules by pointing to the left, his arm completes the accepted convention of clockwise movement in picturebooks. The reader begins with Noah and returns to Noah (complete with circular blue sky and the frame of the ark). Even so, this man is pointing to the past, suggesting he is not looking toward the future, although Noah warns him, and the others, that they will be drowned if they do not repent. The back of the future victim's head continues into the space beyond. The significance of this man is also borne out by the coloring. He is painted over in a muted shade of green; nothing and no one else in the image is. That the prominent victim in the destruction image is discernible as this earlier actor demonstrates the intention in this retelling to offer a causal relationship between crime and punishment.

The image of the man drowning includes other people impressionistically painted in similar states of shock, fear, and worry. Three people are in the water struggling to get out while the ark is floating in the background. These people are given a voice: "'Perhaps Noah was right after all!' they wailed." On the one hand, the omniscient narrator is didactically showing that the victims have learnt the error of their ways, albeit too late. The narrator also uses "wailed," an interesting word choice, as it can have negative connotations of self-pity. This could increase the didactic perspective. On the other hand, it could be an objective narrator's assumption or an internal focalization. This would be matched by the use of the mocking neighbor as the primary victim.

The most unusual aspect of the retelling, however, is the dominance of the text. It uses as much space as the illustration and is set on the page explicitly in coordination with the image. The font is large and particular words are emphasized in size, boldness, case, and off-setting. These words highlight the situation, including "rain," "wailed," "very wet," and "rocked safely." The positioning and format of the text affects the focalization of the image: "very wet" is located above the man as the primary focal point, while "rocked safely" is placed directly above the ark (with a line just below, also comforting: "the rain finally stopped"). The ark is the only object on the bottom right-hand side of the page and is the new focalizer, acting as a pageturner, directing the narratee away from the despair of the victims.

The unpleasantness of the rain, flood, and nonspecified drowning starts, takes place, and stops on one doublespread, after which the rest of the narrative resumes. This is a rare example of a visualized destruction image that is structurally integrated into the whole narrative. It is also an example of how producers of a work can make it seem as if a character is treated fairly: the primary victim deserves his punishment because he admits so himself. Despite this, the overt narratorial presence, indicated with words like "wailed," suggests there is a bias at work. The criminal deserves his punishment, and as such he does not deserve to live. Effectively this excludes all criminals from being in the in-group, but given that the crime shown is mockery, one must wonder who it is that would not be excluded, othered, and thus condemned.

OTHERING IN WORDS AND IMAGES

In this essay I have demonstrated how producers of children's Bible retellings use a variety of approaches to present the destruction of humanity, from ignoring it to graphically visualizing it. I focused upon the relationship between word and image in illustrated books and picturebooks: how they fill each other's gaps, whether they complement or contradict each other, and their formatting on the page.

In my consideration of the approaches used and the relationship between word and image, I uncovered processes of othering in the retellings. When the destruction is removed from the narrative or when God's role within it is removed, God becomes a marginalized character. This could be because the producers are assuming that the child reader will be led by an adult using a top-down approach. It could be a way to sanitize the flood story, to make it more appropriate for children. The latter possibility could be counterproductive when the child reader finally encounters the Genesis flood story and discovers that God not only caused the flood, but that it destroyed all but the occupants of the ark. Their reaction may not be a positive one. Perhaps ironically, retellers who marginalize God's role in the destruction do not need to. Although God announces the destruction through direct speech (6:7, 13, 17; 7:4), God's only named act during the flood is to shut Noah in the ark (7:16), an act that can be interpreted as highlighting his role as protector.

When the destruction is included, different forms of exclusion and marginalization occur, based on gender, age, wealth, and behavior. The flood story has a ready-made in-group in the form of the occupants of the ark. In the retellings, the way this in-group is presented in comparison with the out-group sometimes leads to marginalization of people based on factors, including wealth. The reader's relationship with the various out-groups is ambiguous, as they themselves may feel part of the in-group or the out-group depending upon their own (self or imposed) identity and the narrative strategies present in the retelling. If the marginalization is based on behavior such as the drowning of murderers, this is likely to help develop feelings of identity with the occupants of the ark and perhaps even a sense of self-righteousness as well as a lesson for the future. If the crime is mockery, which many readers will have committed, the process of identification becomes more confused, with even less certain results. Not all children will relate their own behavior to that of the drowning people, but those who do, how will they feel? Their reaction to the narrative is likely to be ambiguous at best. Such ambiguities in the identification process and marginalization are also present when the visualization of the drowning people does not correspond with the visualized perpetrators of crimes. Not showing a correlation between those who drown and the criminals overlooks the punishment aspect of the destruction. This ambiguity reflects upon the Genesis narrative by reminding us how many victims there were, victims who by most standards would be considered innocent, especially children.

Children have a special role to play in the retellings. Externally, we should remember that these retellings are ostensibly produced for children to experience as decided by adults: adults create, manufacture, sell, and buy the retellings (not to mention analyze them). Their role within the retellings, particularly in the destruction, is more complicated. In the examples in this essay, we have seen a crying baby and drowning naked babies as the focalizers, as well as children performing bad acts that lead to the destruction. This inclusion of child criminals and/or victims in the retellings may result in a greater sense of identification with them, more than even those guilty of mockery. Nevertheless, in most retellings children are excluded, they are not represented at any point in the narrative, but such an exclusion may also prevent the child reader from identifying with the text. If there are no children or childlike characters, does this not marginalize the children, not only from the retellings but also from Genesis? This in turns mirrors the Genesis flood story, which never explicitly mentions children, but implicitly makes clear that children die. The type of presentation in the retelling will impact upon the understanding of the Genesis narrative for the child-reader. If they encounter a retelling with a particularly vivid representation of the destruction and later read the Genesis narrative, will they not be more likely to imagine the horrors?

This finally raises the question: should retellings include the destruction? The answer depends upon what is wanted from the retelling, and maintaining a balance between entertainment, faithfully representing the Genesis flood story, representing its perceived message(s), specific religious didactic messages, and nonreligious didactic messages. Producers of retellings will have their own intentions, although what an author, illustrator, designer, editor, and publisher intends may not be the same even for the same retelling at the moment of publication. How successfully their intentions are realized will vary, depending upon their own creative skills, their cooperation in the production process, and critically the individual reader's interpretation of the retelling. There is probably a place for most kinds of retelling, but the privileged adult needs to consider what explicit and implicit messages of morality and othering might be being expressed in the retelling. Even then, children are individuals with their own life and reading experiences, and while one may merely laugh at "the silly fat man in the umbrella" (fig. 10.2) another may cry when reading:

The water's round my shoulders,
And I'm—GLUG!
GLUG!
GLUG!

WORKS CITED

Alexander, Pat, and Carolyn Cox (ill.). 1991a. *The Lion Children's Bible*. Oxford: Lion.

———. 1991b. *The Puffin Children's Bible*. London: Puffin.

Alexander, Pat, and Lyndon Evans (ill.). 1981a. *The Lion Children's Bible*. Tring: Lion.

———. 1981b. *The Puffin Children's Bible*. Harmondsworth: Puffin.

Amery, Heather, and Linda Edwards (ill.). 2007. *The Usborne Little Book of Stories from the Old Testament*. London: Usborne.

Auld, Mary, and Diana Mayo (ill.). 1999. *Noah's Ark*. London: Watts.

Bader, Barbara. 1976. *American Picturebooks from Noah's Ark to the Beast Within*. New York: Macmillan & Collier Macmillan.

Bal, Mieke. 1997. *Narratology: Introduction to the Theory of Narrative*. 2nd ed. Toronto: University of Toronto Press.

Bible Stories in Simple Language for Little Children, with Numerous Illustrations. [ca. 1894.] London: Warne.

Bottigheimer, Ruth B. 1996. *The Bible for Children from the Age of Gutenberg to the Present*. New Haven: Yale University Press.

The Child's Own Book of Scripture Pictures Containing the Chief Scenes and Events of Bible History, Properly Arranged, and Adapted for the Delight and Instruction of Children: Old Testament. [ca. 1865.] London: Ward & Lock.

Churton, W. R. 1882. *Genesis: The Old Testament according to the Authorised Version with a Brief Commentary by Various Authors; The Pentateuch: Published under the Direction of the Tract Committee*. London: SPCK.

Cobbin, Ingram. 1873. *The Youths' Bible and Commentator; Being the Holy Scriptures Written in a Simple and Attractive Manner for the Young*. London: Blackwood.

Cox, Rosemary. 2000. *Using the Bible with Children*. Pamphlet B15. Cambridge: Grove.

Elborn, Andrew, and Ivan Gantschev (ill.). 1984. *Noah and the Ark and the Animals*. London: Neugebauer.

Flanders, Michael, and Harold King (ill.). 1972. *Captain Noah and His Floating Zoo*. Twickenham: Gluck.

Genette, Gérard. 1986. *Narrative Discourse*. Oxford: Blackwell. Reprint of *Narrative Discourse: An Essay in Method*. Translation by Jane E. Lewin. Ithaca: Cornell University Press, 1980.

Graham, Judith. 2005. "Reading Contemporary Picturebooks." Pages 209–26 in *Modern Children's Literature: An Introduction*. Edited by Kimberley Reynolds. Basingstoke: Palgrave Macmillan.

Hadaway, Bridget, and Jean Atcheson. 1973. *The Bible for Children Illustrated throughout in Colour*. London: Octopus.

Humphreys, W. Lee. 2001. *The Character of God in the Book of Genesis: A Narrative Appraisal*. Louisville: Westminster John Knox.

Jewson, Margaret J. [ca. 1950.] *Genesis for Children*. London: Foundational Book.

Keil, C. F., and F. Delitzsch. 1864. *Biblical Commentary on the Old Testament*, vol. 1: *The Pentateuch*. Translated by James Martin. Clark's Foreign Theology Library 3.22. London: Hamilton, Adams.

Kiefer, Barbara. 1995. *The Potential of Picturebooks: From Visual Literacy to Aesthetic Understanding*. Columbus: Merrill.

Kilroy, Sally (auth./ill.). 1992. *Noah and the Rabbits*. London: Puffin.

Krippendorff, Klaus. 2004. *Content Analysis: An Introduction to Its Methodology*. 2nd ed. Thousand Oaks: Sage.

Landy, Francis. 2007. "Noah's Ark and Mrs. Monkey." *BibInt* 15:351–76.

Larcombe, Jennifer Rees, and Steve Björkman (ill.). 1999. *A Boat Full of Animals*. London: Marshall Pickering.

Lewis, David. 2001. *Reading Contemporary Picturebooks: Picturing Text*. London: Routledge/Falmer.

Lewis, Jack P. 1968. *A Study of the Interpretation of Noah and the Flood in Jewish and Christian Literature*. Leiden: Brill.

Mamma's Bible Stories for Her Little Boys and Girls: A Series of Reading Lessons Taken from the Bible and Adapted to the Capacities of Very Young Children. [ca. 1862.] London: Griffith & Farran.

Matthews, Leonard. 1979. *The Children's Bible Treasury*. Maidenhead, Berks: Purnell.

McCarthy, Michael, and Giuliano Ferri (ill.). 2001. *The Story of Noah and the Ark*. Bristol: Barefoot Books.

Mee, Arthur. 1933. *The Children's Bible: The Greatest Book in the World in Its Own Words Illustrated from the Art Galleries of the World*. London: Hodder & Stoughton.

Mills, Peter (auth./ill.). 1996. *Noah's Adventure in the Ark*. Carlisle: Hunt & Thorpe.

Montanaro, Ann. 2005. "Movable Books (Pop-Up Books)." Pages 562–64 in *The Continuum Encyclopedia of Children's Literature*. Edited by Bernice E. Cullinan and Diane G. Person. New York: Continuum.

Neuendorf, Kimberly A. 2002. *The Content Analysis Guidebook*. Thousand Oaks: Sage.

Nikolajeva, Maria. 2009. "Theory, Post-Theory, and Aeto-Normative Theory." *Neohelicon: Acta Comparationis Litterarum Universalum* 1:13–24.

———. 2010. *Power, Voice and Subjectivity in Literature for Young Readers: Children's Literature and Culture*. New York: Routledge.

Nikolajeva, Maria, and Carole Scott. 2001. *How Picturebooks Work: Children's Literature and Culture*. New York: Garland.

Noah and the Ark. 1978. Illustrated by Stefan Lemke and Marie-Luis Lemke-Prichen. Translation of *Die Arche Noah* (Gütersloh: Gütersloher Verlagshaus Gerd Mohn, 1976). Bekhamstead: Lion.

Nodelman, Perry. 1988. *Words about Pictures*. Athens: University of Georgia Press.

———. 2008. *The Hidden Adult: Defining Children's Literature*. Baltimore: Johns Hopkins University Press.

Patterson Smyth, J. [ca. 1922.] *The Bible for School and Home: The Book of Genesis*. London: Sampson Low, Marston.

Person, Hara E., and Diane G. Person. 2005. *Stories of Heaven and Earth: Bible Heroes in Contemporary Children's Literature*. New York: Continuum.

Peters, Dorothy M. 2008. *Noah Traditions in the Dead Sea Scrolls: Conversations and Controversies of Antiquity*. SBLEJL 26. Atlanta: Society of Biblical Literature.

Piehl, Kathy. 1982. "Noah as Survivor: A Study of Picture Books." *Children's Literature Education* 2:80–86.

———. 1989. "'By Faith Noah': Obedient Servant as Religious Hero." *The Lion and the Unicorn* 13:41–52.

———. 2005. "Captain Noah's Environmental Voyage." Paper presented at the Sixth Biennial Conference on Modern Critical Approaches to Children's Literature. Nashville, Tennessee. April 1.

Postgate, Isa J., and Charles Hart. 1922. *A Book about the Old Testament for Children*. London: Alexander Moring/De La More.

Sainsbury, Lisa. 2005 "Picturebook Case Study: Politics and Philosophy in the Work of Raymond Briggs." Pages 227–49 in *Modern Children's Literature: An Introduction*. Edited by Kimberley Reynolds. Basingstoke, Hampshire: Palgrave Macmillan.

Sipe, Lawrence R., and Caroline E. McGuire. 2006. "Picturebook Endpapers: Resources for Literary and Aesthetic Interpretation." *Children's Literature in Education* 37:291–304.

Sipe, Lawrence R., and Sylvia Pantaleo. 2008. *Postmodern Picturebooks: Play, Parody, and Self-Referentiality*. Routledge Research in Education 16. New York/London: Routledge.

Smith, E. Boyd (auth./ill.). 1905. *The Story of Noah's Ark*. London: Archibald Constable & Houghton, Mifflin.

Stephens, John. 1992. *Language and Ideology in Children's Fiction*. London: Longman.

Stephens, John, and Robyn McCallum. 1998. *Retelling Stories, Framing Culture: Traditional Story and Metanarratives in Children's Literature*. Children's Literature and Culture. New York: Garland.

Stone, Michael E., Aryeh Amihay, and Vered Hillel, eds. 2010. *Noah and His Book(s)*. SBLEJL 28. Atlanta: Society of Biblical Literature.

Watson, Carol, and Julie Ferris (ill.). 2007. *Young Learner's Bible Stories*. London: Alligator.

Williams, Marcia (auth./ill.). 2005. *God and His Creations: Tales from the Old Testament*. London: Walker.

Wilson-Wilson, Theodora. [ca. 1916.] *Stories from the Bible*. London: Blackie.

Wolde, Ellen van. 1994. *Words Become Worlds: Semantic Studies of Genesis 1–11*. BI 6. Leiden: Brill.

SAMSON'S SUICIDE AND THE DEATH OF THREE THOUSAND OTHERS IN CHILDREN'S BIBLE STORIES THROUGH TWO CENTURIES

David M. Gunn

Samson's story, or some part thereof, is often retold for children, though no few authors also choose to bypass him entirely (and sometimes the whole book of Judges). My topic concerns the hero's violent end, his killing of some three thousand Philistines along with himself in the house of Dagon. Given the binary world of good and bad that we often encounter in children's stories, it is no surprise to discover that the Philistines are generally bad people. Storytellers, as we shall see, make sure that their young readers or listeners understand this fact. The biblical account, of course, is laconic. Philistines and Samson alike do what they do and say what they say. The narrator wastes no words on evaluative or affective adjectives. So retellers supply in their own texts what is missing in the Bible and clarify the reasons why the Philistines deserve to die.

Many stories of Samson for children include illustrations of Samson in the house of Dagon. How, then, do these pictures present Philistines? At first sight, on looking through numerous storybooks going back two centuries, I am struck by how ordinary the Philistines appear. Many look desperate and terrified, but then so they ought since sudden death is coming upon them. To be sure, occasionally, there are the caricatured ugly-frightened faces that are the staple of comic-book baddies and common enough in children's illustrations, but mostly what we see are fearful looks, falling bodies, and attempts to flee. Moreover, while some illustrations picture the doom of many Philistines, others show only a few figures, and some none at all—we see Samson alone. Why minimize the number of Philistines or remove them entirely from the depiction of destruction and the death they deserve? The illustration in a 1980 publication (Turner) shows people streaming from the temple, some looking as though they might just make it, while in a 2004 illustration (Hastings) Samson stands by himself under the crumbling superstructure and, in the right foreground, a small group of Philistines, men and women, appears visually to have made a successful escape. Why rescue Philistines?

It may not be easy for artists to make doomed Philistines look like wicked people. Illustrators work under various constraints, including the space and frame available, and such considerations may account in some cases for few Philistines and lone Samsons. But as the example of the escaping Philistines suggests, there are likely to be other factors involved in the design of these illustrations. One obvious factor is adult concern about presenting mass slaughter to children (let alone any respectable person). Jesse Lyman Hurlbut addresses this issue of visual violence in the preface to his *Story of the Bible*, a book that turned out to be one of the long-lived classics of twentieth-century Bible stories. "Many of the engravings have been designed expressly for this book," he writes, "and both the subjects for illustrations and the pictures themselves have been prepared with great care. The publishers have not allowed, in the book, scenes of blood or such as would be repulsive to people of taste" (1904, 12). As it happens, many children's Bible storybooks contain pictures that have not been prepared for the book with great care and some, moreover, make a poor match with the text. But I would suggest that Hurlbut's concern about violence has been a continuing one for many authors, illustrators, and publishers of the story of Samson's end, where presenting the denouement inevitably means choices about presenting violence, not only in illustrations but also in the retold texts. If so, the question of how Philistines are presented is likely bound up with the question of violence.

In her pioneering book *The Bible for Children from the Age of Gutenberg to the Present*, Ruth Bottigheimer shows how adults have shaped their stories for children in accord with their theological beliefs and cultural values. In the case of Jael, for example, Bottigheimer traces the sometimes conflicting responses to the heady mix of violence and (female) gender that adult readers have discovered in this text (1996, 141–51). While some Catholic and Reformed authors in eighteenth- and nineteenth-century Europe wrote admiringly of both Deborah and Jael as heroic figures doing God's work, the reaction of other Protestants to Judg 4–5 "ranged from perplexed confusion through reluctant acceptance to angry denunciation and outright erasure" (146). A woman "treacherously" killing a sleeping man did not belong among their paradigms of virtue. The solutions were to minimize the details of the Jael episode, tell no more than that she killed Sisera, leave out the Jael episode, or omit any account of Judg 4–5 entirely.

While Jael has made something of a comeback in recent years, as views of women's roles have undergone a major shift, the history of her fall from favor is instructive. In Jael's case, Bottigheimer shows clearly that it was not violence as such that was the primary problem for the storytellers but violence by the agency of a woman, and this conclusion is certainly borne out by a review of the commentary tradition on this passage (Gunn 2005, 74–84). In Samson's case, where retold texts are concerned, and leaving illustrations aside for the present, I would argue that here too it is not violence as such that is the primary problem but the particular nature of the violence. It could, of course, be deemed excessive and quite disproportionate to the offense against Samson. Of even more concern to commentators through the centuries have been two other dimensions of the act. First, it was motivated by revenge (Judg 16:28: "strengthen me, I pray thee, only this once, O God, that I may be at once avenged of the Philistines for my two eyes"); second, it involved suicide.

Thomas Scott's popular commentary—written in the late eighteenth century, edited and reprinted throughout the nineteenth—is typical in arguing that "the cause of Samson was that of Israel and God." Though Samson was justly delivered into the hands of Israel's enemies because of his transgression, the Philistines had treated him cruelly and blasphemed the Lord. Hence, though normally we should forgive and pray for fellow sinners, in this extraordinary case, at God's instigation, Samson was right to avenge both God and Israel. Moreover, since he acted not for himself but for Israel's deliverance from its enemies, he was like a soldier in battle whose death could not be called a suicide. As for the problem of the great slaughter, that was clearly God's doing (and thus justified): "We must ascribe to the same power, which enabled Samson to throw down the building, the decisive destruction it caused" (Scott 1816, 1:750). It seems reasonable to assume, therefore, that retellings of the story for children would likely reflect these concerns of the standard commentary tradition. Fostering alienation from the "cruel" Philistines would certainly help mitigate for children some of the story's moral and theological difficulties (as it clearly did for adults, like Scott). By the same token, garnering sympathy for Samson might aid the same cause.

Actually, Samson was much in need of garnered sympathy since the manner of his death was far from being his only problem. While some children's authors insisted on Samson's status as a hero of the faith (in line with Heb 11), others could not help but point out his failings. Sarah Trimmer, one of the pioneers of children's stories in English, sets the tone for many when (skipping over the Delilah episode) she recounts in her description accompanying a little book of prints, "But Samson was a very foolish man, and did not obey God's commands, so he suffered him to lose his strength" (1790, 59). Caroline Hadley, echoing the popular commentary of Methodist Adam Clarke (1833), makes an oft-repeated point: "But though he was a strong man, he was not a great man. He wanted what is called moral courage, that is courage of the soul" (1866, 196). Much-read author Elsie Egermeier was frank with her young readers: "Sometimes he behaved much like a naughty child; and this wrong behavior at last got him into great trouble. It even cost his life" (1927, 192). For Theodora Wilson-Wilson, writing for older children, "Samson's story is a sad one … as he was far too fond of pleasure and of enjoying himself" (1938, 176). And for older children, too, the Most Reverend Louis LaRaviore Morrow summed things up: "Dalila was the cause of Samson's ruin. She was a bad companion for him. We must keep away from bad companions so that we may not be ruined forever" (1950, 85).

Delilah is, for most, the insuperable problem (cf. Houtman and Spronk 2004, 39–64; Gunn 2005, 211–20), and, of course, most (though not all) accounts of Samson's end come as the conclusion to the story of his love of Delilah. So the episode is frequently glossed by the reteller to provide suitable guidance to the young audience about the hero's failure and its awful consequences. Given that the Delilah episode represents the nadir (up to this point) of Samson's life, for the reteller who wants to hang on to some shred of Samson, despite his faults, as national hero or faithful figure, there is need to begin the recovery process urgently. And this is the situation confronting many who would retell Samson's final episode even before they have to deal with vengeance, suicide, and slaughter.

Let me now turn to some texts and illustrations, to examine more closely how they deal with the difficulties presented by the story of Samson's violent end, and how, in the course of so dealing, they present the Philistines, not only generically as "people" but also as men and women, adults and children. If, as the cases of the minimized or escaping Philistines suggest, some authors and illustrators have been reluctant to confront children with mass slaughter, have they also been ready to hide or rescue some Philistines more than others? Put another way, if children are to learn that Philistines deserved to die, does that mean all of them?

The Rhetoric of Texts

I confine my inquiry largely to an analysis of the rhetoric, so to speak, of texts and pictures. The data are drawn from my own collection of over two hundred books for children or "youth" published in Great Britain (mostly England) and North America (mostly the United States) since the late eighteenth century. Just under two-thirds of these contain our story. The earlier books are more often English publications but, from the late nineteenth century on, the proportion of books published in the United States is much larger. The books have predominantly a Protestant audience in view, though there are also some Catholic and Jewish materials in the sample, and more recent publications are often nondenominational. Any results of my survey are strictly subject to the limits of the collection.

Mass Slaughter, Suicide, and Vengeance for Children

As a rule (though not an invariable one), storytellers choose not to add many details to the scene of death and destruction that the biblical narrator recounts with economy: "And the house fell upon the lords, and upon all the people that were therein. So the dead which he slew at his death were more than they which he slew in his life" (Judg 16:30 KJV). Storytellers simply repeat, or something close to, the biblical text (mostly, until the later twentieth century, the KJV). Or they may add some shrieks, screams, and groans to render the horror: "There were loud screams; then all was still" (Madison 1946). Commonly they add a word or two to define the manner of the people's demise, most frequently that they were crushed or buried. Occasionally one finds exceptions to the rule, but rarely. "He perished," writes J. H. Willard in his little book on Samson in Altemus' Beautiful Stories Series, "among the heaps of mangled priests and chiefs and people" (1906). Henry L. Williams Jr., whose book for boys first appeared in 1865, lets his imagination take flight as the galleries bent like a bow and the planks warped, screams arose and people leaped to their death, the idol crushed its priests, and the altar coals kindled the mounds of debris under which were buried three thousand dead, dying, and wounded (1900, 112). Walter de la Mare's version (1929) is elaborated somewhat similarly. Both books would be read by older children. In general, however, it would be fair to say that restraint in the renderings of death has been a characteristic of versions of this episode intended for children, at least where the text is concerned.

While it is clearly hard to tell the story of Samson's end without mentioning that his action brought on his own death (most retellers do mention this, though in the biblical text his death is an inference confirmed by his burial), it is not hard to avoid the topic of suicide as a moral issue. No reteller uses the word "suicide," and while some authors say that he killed himself, most choose to say rather that he "was killed" or simply "died" along with the Philistines. In recent decades, for some very young readers, Samson's death is simply omitted: "He knocked down a palace to punish God's enemies" (Taylor 1989, n.p.); "when his hair grew back, his strength came back, and he protected God's people again" (Baker and Helms 1995, 57).

The problem of vengeance is different. While the biblical text does not even say that "Samson died," let alone "killed himself," Samson's prayer explicitly expresses his desire for vengeance. For many authors the problem of vengeance is removed (wittingly or not) by leaving out the prayer altogether—as is the case with one in six of my sample, fairly constantly from the mid-nineteenth to the mid-twentieth centuries. Another solution is to curtail the prayer at the point where Samson asks for strength—as with close on one in three, constantly from the late-eighteenth century to the present. Yet another device is to modify the prayer so that Samson asks God for strength to aid him, to help him against his enemies, to conquer his enemies, to bring down the temple, to "do justice for myself and for your people Israel" (Armstrong 1949, 140), with no mention of vengeance—as with about one in eight, constantly through both centuries. In sum, in about two thirds of the sample vengeance is not mentioned at all. The majority of the authors who use the term do so in the course of quoting or closely paraphrasing the biblical text, often in line with the style of their book, and even some of these authors omit "for my two eyes," leaving the motivation for vengeance less personal.

Whether vengeance is mentioned, authors, particularly in the mid-twentieth century, often find ways of signaling that the deed was for the best. Such rhetoric has the advantage of mitigating not only the call for vengeance, if expressed, but also any sense on the part of readers that the scale of death was excessive. Eleanor Boyd, who goes on to give her readers the KJV prayer in full, first alerts them to Samson's silent praying, as he stands, "silent, blind, immovable, bound in fetters of brass, while they heaped every manner of insult upon his poor bowed head." But pray he did, "and while his prayer seems a strange one to us, we must always remember that in the days I am telling you about, God punished evil people very often immediately for their wickedness" (1921, 104). Other mitigations are often simpler. Thus he had been given his last great strength "for the good of his people" (Krottjer 1925, 94).[1]

Descriptions of Samson as a hero who vindicates God and delivers his (God's and Samson's) people obviously serve to cultivate sympathy for, and confirm the young reader's alignment with, Samson as the story's hero. Another way to cultivate sympathy for Samson is to show him having emotion that sets him in sharp contrast to the Philistines. He patiently suffers while they rejoice in cruel behavior.

POOR SAMSON AND THE CRUEL PHILISTINES

Not all stories elaborate on the capture and the prison episode, but many do, if only by adding the word "cruel" to the biblical account of the Philistine's actions, particularly putting out his eyes (16:21): His eyes were "cruelly put out," writes the author of *Mother Stories from the Old Testament* (1908, 58; see also Fryer 1924, 150). The term "cruel" also characterizes the Philistines' treatment of Samson generally. Esther Hewlett, for example, speaks of Samson's "cruel enemies" (1828, 2:55); "very cruelly they treated him," writes Reuben Prescott in *Grandfather's Bible Stories* (1897, 165).

Another strategy is to make more graphic the putting out of his eyes (no doubt, for some, with Rembrandt's famous painting in mind): "They spat upon him and kicked him, and finally they thrust red hot irons through his eyes and put them out forever" (Boyd 1921, 103). Fulton Oursler moves from the physical description to Samson's suffering: "A dozen Philistines crowded over him with hot branding irons and put out his eyes. He screamed in pain" (1949, 1955, 138). Kenneth Taylor puts it a little more gently for very young readers: they "made him blind by hurting his eyes" (2002, 142), bypassing the branding irons or white-hot rods and going directly to the pain—and in a way that young readers will instantly recognize as wrong: they hurt him.

A glimpse into a feeling, suffering Samson is a common addition. In *The Story of the Chosen People*, H. A. Guerber writes, "Samson suffered

---

1. See also: "God had used Samson to free his people" (Morton 1927, 56); "the enemies of God and God's People were killed in the ruin" (Lord 1943, n.p.); "Samson had done a brave deed: he gave his life to destroy God's enemies" (Madison 1946, 24); "he freed the Israelites from the Philistines" (Schoolland 1953, 65); "he was a hero" who killed "the enemies of Israel" (Maryknoll Sisters 1955, 225); "he defeated the enemies of Israel" (Stoddard 1983, 107).

untold agonies while thus in the enemy's power" (1896, 111). Sulamith Ish-Kishor describes Samson during his captivity: "The misery of Samson's heart was terrible, and he longed to die. He became so weak and thin and worn-out" (1933, 38).

If the keyword for the Philistines is "cruel," probably the keyword for Samson is "poor"—as in "poor Samson!" Says young Lucy to her aunt at hearing of Samson's being blinded, bound, and made to "work hard in the prison-house": "How mortifying this must be to poor Samson!" (Neale 1817, 140). The expression—sometimes taking the form of "poor blind Samson!" (e.g., Pollard 1937, n.p.)—is used over and over again, constantly through two centuries.

Among the minority of writers who mention Samson's desire for vengeance, Harold Begbie does so in a way that is plainly designed to elicit sympathy and to wring the heart of his readers. As Samson hears the song and taunts of the Philistines, and as he remembers what he once had been, how he had thwarted God's intentions for him, a sob rises in his throat. In turn, "the memory of his mother rose in his heart. The days of his childhood returned, sweet and beautiful. Once, once he had been pure. Once he had been devoted to God! His arms tightened around the pillar; the sob broke in his throat" (1912, 126).

The biblical narrator uses only one term for describing how the Philistines treat Samson at the festival: "Call for Samson, that he may make us sport ... and he made them sport." The retellers all spell this out. Most common are three terms: they mocked, laughed at, and tormented him. One Sunday School Union writer commenting upon Samson's "cruel enemies" makes the point explicitly that it is "very wicked to laugh at poor afflicted people" (*Bible History for the Least and the Lowest* 1854, 29). Boyd even makes a comparison that may have been familiar to most of her readers: the "wicked Philistines" tormented Samson as a cruel cat torments a poor mouse (1921, 104). Torment occasionally shades into torture. Thomas Gaspey reports that the temple "crushed in its fall the heartless persecutors, who had tortured him and mocked his woe" (1851, 104). James Baldwin tells that "he was to be taken into the temple, where they would make a kind of public show of him. It is likely that they intended to torture him, and then offer him to Dagon as a sacrifice" (1895, 185).

Another way of stressing the poetic justice of the mockers' end is to set the hateful enjoyment of the merrymaking crowd against the emotion they experience in their ending. Mocking and merriment turn to fear, glimpsed through the sounds of the dying, in *A Treasury of Scripture Sto-*

ries (1869, 13): the temple fell "amid shrieks, and groans, and curses." Or as Madison puts it: "There were loud screams; then all was still" (1946, 24). As noted earlier, however, such additions are not the norm.

KILLING WOMEN AND CHILDREN

We have now seen that suicide is not an issue, vengeance can be reframed, and mass slaughter mitigated. Our sympathy lies with Samson and the tormenting Philistines deserve to die. There is, however, a complication. The biblical text says: "Now the house was full of men and women" (16:27 KJV), and a little later it specifies that upon the roof were "three thousand men and women." What do the retold texts say when they tell of these deaths? Do the writers have any aversion to speaking of Samson killing women, albeit Philistine women? Up to this point in the story, he has only killed men, and the only woman killed has been the Timnite woman, burnt to death by the Philistines.

Many authors follow the biblical story and speak of three thousand men and women assembled, and then, as in the KJV, use the gender-neutral term "people," or some equivalent, at the end—for example, "Philistines," "everyone," or "all who were there." From about the mid-twentieth century there is a tendency to drop the reference to "men and women" in the accounts of who gathered in the temple and who were killed; in other words it becomes harder to find the term "women." Even apart from the last fifty years, about half my sample drop "women" from the story, and such a rate of omission remains constant from the later nineteenth century. That might suggest some conscious or unconscious reluctance to tell children that the biblical hero killed a large number of women. Sparing women and children, rather than killing them, has been the cultural norm (whatever the reality) throughout these past two centuries. Drop the term "women" in the text and perhaps the question will simply not arise. If, that is, the illustrator plays along—to which question I'll return. Alternatively, for the Maryknoll Sisters, the women can remain but only as aristocrats (cf. Judg 16:27): the lords and ladies of the Philistines gathered for the feast, and accordingly "the lords and ladies of the Philistines were crushed at the banquet table" (1955, 225).

But then the other question arises, What about children? Did Samson kill children in the temple of Dagon? One author, John Williamson Tyler, writes that the house of Dagon was full of people, "men, women, and children; and about 3000 of them were upon the roof," but reports at the end simply that "all died" (1901, 126–27). However, that listing of children among the crowd is highly unusual, though Baldwin substitutes boys for women among the three thousand on the roof, perhaps because he was sure that in the East the men and boys would be separated from the women; he also avoids all mention of women in the temple or being killed (1895, 185).

Certainly it is common for storytellers to mention one child: the boy (or lad) who led Samson into the house and guided him to the pillars. But I have come across no writer who speaks of the boy's death, bar one, Fanny L. Armstrong, who wrote of him in a book entitled *The Children of the Bible* (1884). In Armstrong's account, Samson asks a boy to let him lean against the pillars. "The kind-hearted boy, willing to accommodate him, and fearing no evil, consented." Samson decides on revenge. "Now there were about three thousand men and women—no children mentioned, but I suppose there were some, as it is such a pity for so many to go into the presence of God without any to be saved eternally." Armstrong describes Samson bringing down the building, crushing himself, "three thousand men and women, and the kind-hearted little boy, to death" (84). "Samson's leader," she goes on to say,

> was a Bible-child—because he did a kindness for one of God's afflicted ones.... What a contrast between his kindness and the hard-hearted malignity of the haughty lords of the Philistines! He was sorry for the tired man. Ah! little did he know, when he agreed to that seemingly small request, that the black-winged angel of death was in the atmosphere, ready, with one fell swoop, to gather up the whole crowd. How little he dreamed that in a few moments he would lie a mangled mass of flesh, and blood, and bones, so near the man he so generously favored! He little thought his young soul would go up to the God of Samson amid the shrieks of horror—the wails of the dying—but such was the case. I hope he was too young to be lost. I hope the dying moments of the departing Samson were spent in asking a blessing on him. God grant that the persecuted judge and innocent boy together were borne on the broad, white wings of sympathizing angels to the home of the blest! (85)

Fanny Armstrong was a rare soul in going beyond simply noticing the boy to contemplating his fate and trying to turn that fate to some good in the education of her young readers. We may be struck by the cultural and theological sensibilities of this woman of an earlier age—no mangled mass of flesh, blood, and bones messes up most children's Bible stories of the past century. But her investment in the unnamed boy has its counterparts during the past decade or so in feminist-inspired explorations of the Bible's unnamed women and children.

One of the ideological effects of Armstrong's reading is to complicate the hard and fast division between Israelite and Philistine. Perhaps he is a Philistine, thinks Armstrong, and with that thought blurs the notion that all Philistines are wicked. Harold Begbie is another who sees the boy's action positively and so, too, complicates the binary: a tired-out Samson asks to rest, to lean upon the pillars. "In mercy," writes Begbie, "the boy guided the prisoner to the pillars of the great house" (1912, 51). But there Begbie leaves the lad.

The Rhetoric of Illustrations

Although not all the books in the sample have a picture to accompany their account of Samson's end, the majority do so. Most show Samson in the act of bringing down the building. Of the moral problems that may have concerned the storytellers—suicide, revenge, and mass slaughter—it is really only the last that is likely to have concerned the illustrators. That Samson is about to perish along with the Philistines will be as obvious in a picture as in a text, or, if there is any doubt, the text will confirm his death. Whereas storytellers have various ways of distracting readers from a potentially troubling question, there is little the illustrator can do to show Samson's act and at the same time steer viewers away from possibly seeing a problematic suicide. Nor can illustrators convey Samson's motive for the action even if they wanted to, so that choosing whether to depict his motive as revenge is not an issue; comic books that incorporate text into the design are an exception. All illustrators can certainly choose, however, the way they present the slaughter.

As already noted, there are three main ways of depicting the scene. One is to show the big picture, with Samson between the pillars and people tumbling from above and/or looking up with terror from below. Another is to show Samson between the pillars, closer up but still with some people in view. A third way is again to show him close up, but this time alone, straining on one or two pillars, but with no people, or only a hint of them, in view. Departures from this choice of scene are few. One notable exception is a picture, used between 1893 and 1911, showing Samson standing beside a pillar, his hands clasped apparently in prayer, with the lad sitting at his feet and, in the background, other people at a banquet table (see fig. 11.4 below, middle left).

Clearly, the praying picture has the advantage of avoiding the violence while drawing attention to the figure of faith. Not surprisingly, the lone Samson is a favorite for books for very young children, especially in recent decades; these books often use simplified designs and only hint at the violence. The other two main patterns convey varying degrees of violence depending upon the specific design and its conventions.

It is not possible in this essay, given constraints of space, to track in detail how illustrators have variously presented the violent scene through two centuries. Rather, I shall give examples of some of the ways illustrations of Samson's violent end may relate to the manner in which the storybooks present the Philistines. Together with the question of how much violence against the Philistines is actually depicted, I shall briefly explore the question of how different pictures relate to their host texts. Are pictures and texts consonant in their presentation of violence?

Doré and Schnorr von Carolsfeld

As it happens, for most of the nineteenth century, and well into the twentieth, the illustrations in the sample were dominated by designs originally intended for adult or at least family viewing. That is, they started out as designs in suites of Bible pictures, illustrated Bibles, and Bible histories with adults as the primary readership. The two most influential such designs come in the second half of the century from German artist Julius Schnorr von Carolsfeld and French artist Gustave Doré.

Schnorr's designs (fig. 11.1, top) were published in folio editions as a series of pictures with explanations (1852–1861). By the time an octavo version targeting children specifically appeared in Philadelphia (1884), publishers in the United States had begun borrowing them for use in children's Bible storybooks and continued to use them for another fifty years (even occasionally in the second half of the twentieth century).[2]

Doré's illustrations (fig. 11.2, top left) appeared first in 1866 in a massive French Bible and then in an English Bible published initially in parts (1866–1870). Cheap quarto versions appeared about a decade later (Doré 1879; *Bible Gallery* 1880), and soon Doré's pictures too found their way

---

2. Modified versions also appeared, such as the one in J. H. Willard's *What Is Sweeter Than Honey? The Story of Samson* (1906), the simplified design on the cover of *Mother Stories from the Old Testament* (1908), or the pared-down picture in *Bible Stories for Little Folks* (1918).

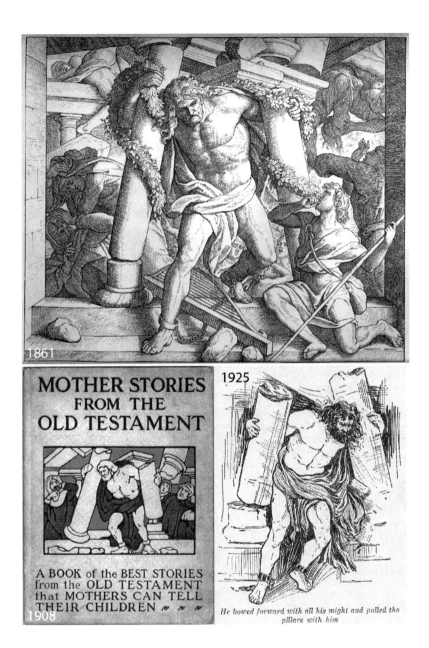

Fig. 11.1. Variations on Schnorr von Carolsfeld's classic design. (See the end of the essay for a full key to the illustrations.)

Fig. 11.2. Picturing many or few.

into children's books, remaining common, especially in the United States, well into the twentieth century. The design has continued as an influence in other pictures, such as (on a grand scale) those by Feodor Rojankovsky (Werner 1946; fig. 11.2, top right) and Eric Thomas (Hastings 2004) or, on a smaller scale, that in Worm (1958), each in distinctive ways.

Schnorr's style is formal and classicizing, with architectural forms and human figures reminiscent of Renaissance art. His expressed intent was to show the ideal, the essential religious value, of his subject. His close-up Samson is wholly intent on his task; he has a (discretely draped) body worthy of Michelangelo's interest; the lad at his feet looks up toward him with wonderment, perhaps, or even admiration, but certainly not the fear that fills another's face; discarded between Samson's feet and dividing his chained ankles is a stringed instrument—a symbol of abandoned merrymaking, perhaps; distinctly festooning the pillars and Samson (who clutches it with one hand) is a long leafy garland—the Philistine festivity is turning into Samson's victory, the triumph of true religion. One can imagine an adult forming such an interpretation of the picture and pointing out this or that element to the child beside her or on her knee. There are fear and falling bodies in the picture, to be sure, but strictly in the background. Foremost in this compact composition is the garlanded, powerful body of Samson between the pillars and the gazing boy who directs our gaze back to the hero.

Doré's scene could hardly be more different. The scale of the temple is immense, the collapsing pillars and superstructure vast; a stream of falling bodies is picked out against distant, sunlit (and still standing) columns, while a melee of frantic people spills into the foreground; tiny in relation to all this, but plainly the agent of destruction, is a briefly clad Samson, one leg planted, a knee on a pillar, arms outstretched, and hair a-flying. There is no escaping the death and destruction in this picture; the enormous havoc created by one lone, small figure is what is being illustrated.

Given the original provenance of these popular designs, one would probably not expect to find a particularly close correlation between them and the details of the texts in whose company we now find them. It is possible, of course, that the texts were written to conform to the pictures, but this seems not to have normally been the case. Generally speaking, however, Schnorr's picture usually fits better with its accompanying text, partly because, rather than standing upright and pushing as in the Doré design, Schnorr's Samson leans forward, pulling the pillars. That posture better conforms to the Bible's "bowed himself" (Judg 16:29), often taken by the storytellers to mean "bent forward." As regards the portrayal of violence, here too Schnorr's containment of the visual evidence of destruction and imminent death is more in accord with the tendency of the stories to be relatively restrained in their descriptions of death and destruction than is Doré's extravaganza.

With Doré's picture, the relation of illustration to text varies on the matter of violence. In contrast to the devastation of the illustration, Mrs. D. C. Weston, writing for young children, relates very simply that the house fell upon the lords, and the men and women in it, and killed them all (1883, 106).[3] More graphic is J. W. Beuel: "The entire building was overthrown, crashing down and burying in one common ruin three thousand men that were in the temple" (1889, 180). Also more graphic is Henry Neil who describes how "the roof and the entire building came down on the heads of the thousands of people in the temple," so that Samson and "all the vast multitude around him" were killed (1892, 85). Neither author, however, mentions one of the most dramatic elements of Doré's design, namely the slew of falling bodies.

Few Philistines

For all that it is less monumentally violent than the Doré picture, Schnorr's design does, of course, present terrified people and falling bodies. Some illustrators, however, reduce the visual elements of mass death by focusing largely on Samson and eliminating, or nearly so, other people. So the Philistines disappear. Often, though not always, these illustrations belong in books that are simply told and directed at younger children; accordingly, they tend to match their host text's economy. Samson may be a lone figure, pictured from behind, leaning in against the pillars, as in the "ABC" illustration in *Routledge's Scripture Gift-Book* (ca. 1866) or, with just a few figures added to the background, as in *Favourite Bible Stories for the Young* (1893). The ABC's accompanying ditty relates simply how Samson "pull'd down the pillars, and the house fell on [all his foes] that day," while the version in the *Favourite Bible Stories*, almost as economically, says that the pillars broke, "the house fell, and all the lords of the Philistines were killed in the fall of it" (1893, 58). A highly simplified version of Schnorr's

---

3. Josephine Pollard, in words of one syllable, says that "the house fell, and most [*sic*] of the Phil-is-tines were killed" (1888, 98). Adelaide Bee Evans (1911) follows the spare text of the KJV.

design appears in *Bible Stories for Little Folks* (1918) and Hurlbut, *Bible Stories Every One Should Know* (1925), in both cases accompanying Hurlbut's text from *Story of the Bible* (1904). This picture shows Samson alone, arms around the pillars, straining forward (fig. 11.1, bottom right). No doubt Hurlbut, concerned about scenes of blood and such, would have been gratified that here was a picture that matched the moderate tenor of his text and met the taste test. Other pictures of Samson alone, or nearly so, often align in similar manner with an accompanying text that mitigates the violence or at least does not elaborate the biblical text's sparse narration of the deaths. Such illustrations may be found throughout the twentieth century.

The inclusion of the odd falling body or terror-stricken face in an otherwise Samson-alone illustration may still be consonant with a writer's minimal presentation of violence. Annabel Spenceley illustrates a new edition of Taylor's *The New Bible in Pictures for Little Eyes* (2002) with a prominent Samson framed by pillars, but she includes, merged into the left background, two small terrified faces—one is tiny (143)! Taylor's text (from 1956) uses the device of a narrator (ostensibly) talking about the picture: "He is asking the men [*sic*] to let him stand by the two posts that held up the house. He is pulling the house down and Samson and the people will all die" (142). Careful little eyes will no doubt discover the faces and understand their terror. But, if they are troubled by any of this, they will be reassured by the prayer that runs along the bottom of the page: "Thank You, Lord, that You love us even when You let bad things happen to us."

Lu Kimmel's brightly colored and stylized illustration (O'Donnell 1936), borrows directly from Doré (cf. Samson's posture and the background columns) but reduces Doré's large frame down to Samson and the immediate pillars. Instead of the multitude of tumbling bodies, we see strikingly silhouetted against the bright background a small solitary falling figure (fig. 11.2, bottom right). There is no panicked crowd in the foreground. The many are represented by a token. Thomas O'Donnell tells the story in four sentences, but though he too does not mention the three thousand, he is direct about death: "All within it were killed, and Judge Samson with them" (27). To the reader who does not know the biblical text, O'Donnell's "all" helps amplify the significance of Kimmel's single falling figure. Here, then, text and picture may work together for an approach to presenting the biblical story's violence that is direct but minimal.

Occasionally a picture of mostly Samson (with pillars and masonry) and a minimum of doomed Philistines is set within a text that routinely elaborates the story including the details of its violent moments. Walter de la Mare's popular *Stories from the Bible* is such a text—people watch appalled as pillars bend and crack and topple, and the walls and roof descend upon images, priests, and the assembled throng "in a horror of lamentation and confusion" (1929, 266). The first U.S. edition includes Theodore Nadejen's brightly colored picture, in deco style, of Samson among collapsing pillars and falling building materials while dust rises behind (250). Careful examination, however, reveals two tiny figures in silhouette in postures of predicament (fig. 11.2, bottom left). Despite clear differences between this picture and that of Lu Kimmel (above), the similarities in design invite a comparison of the way each relates to its context.

Kimmel's picture, which sits beside a text that expresses the violence minimally, has one small but striking silhouetted reference to imminent death. Nadejen's picture, which sits beside a text that adds circumstantial detail and language of horror to the biblical account, has two silhouetted figures, not immediately obvious but discoverable, whose postures indicate alarm and flight. The design is subtle. Death is explicit in Kimmel's design, subtly implicit in Nadejen's. If the latter works with de la Mare's text, it is because a reader/viewer fills the picture with de la Mare's detail, so that the two become many, and alarm and flight turn to no escape and death. In this respect, despite the subtle differences between the pictures and the big differences between their contexts, both may fulfill a similar function for their readers/viewers. While Nadejen's picture may at first sight appear to mitigate the violence, it may also be seen, in context, as feeding off the text's explicit expression of violence and horror. In that case, while both of these pictures go out of their way to minimize the visual presence of the Philistines, both could also be said to remain consonant with their very different host texts.

WOMEN AND CHILDREN

Pictures of later twentieth-century publications vary in their explicit depiction of violence. Perhaps fewer people fall from above, and remarkably few are crushed, but many are about to be. According to the texts, and occasionally a caption, they are Philistines, enemies of (variously) Samson, Israel, and God. No authors suggest explicitly that some or all may not deserve to die. Yet implicitly, as we have already seen, authors may suggest, by excluding their mention, that some Philistines might properly have been excluded from the death sentence—notably women and children. Illustrators, whether conscious of it or not, have had the same option. Schnorr chooses to depict a woman falling from the balcony (in the upper right of fig. 11.1, top), and this figure is made more noticeable, in part by coloring her dress pink, in a later adaptation (Sandison 1924, n.p.; *One Hundred Bible Stories* 1948, 79). Doré's picture includes, distinctively, a mother and baby in the lower left foreground. In other black and white illustrations (often cheaply printed) from the end of the nineteenth and the early twentieth century, however, the men and women in the murky backgrounds are sometimes hard to discern, while women are often absent from the color plates of the 1920s and 1930s in the sample.

The tendency among texts from the later twentieth century to drop mention of women, noted earlier, is matched, curiously, by a tendency among illustrations since the 1950s to show women more prominently than they had often been shown earlier in the century, especially in the larger volumes of Bible stories, copiously illustrated in color, that were marketed from the 1960s on (fig. 11.3). In more than two thirds of those books published between 1950 and 1990 where women are as noticeable as men in the sample, women (as in "three thousand men and women") are not mentioned in the text. It also is the case that most of the authors are women and most of the illustrators men. One might speculate that the women are protecting the Bible from the accusation that it condones killing defenseless women or that men are responding, in a subliminal reflex, to the growing power of women in British and American society, postwar and especially in the late sixties and seventies. (So let them go back where they belong—in the temple of Dagon in the company of a strong man.) Or was this parity of men and women at the festival of Dagon a byproduct of Cecil B. DeMille's *Samson and Delilah* (released in January 1950), with its cast of convivial thousands, men and women alike, showing what things really looked like in biblical times? The medium does matter. Whereas authors have the option of speaking generically of people or Philistines, illustrated people must be men or women (or indistinct—not a usual style). Perhaps it is the constraints of the medium that have led illustrators (not just men) to express a different cultural concern than authors, over women's roles in society, by casting death as an equal opportunity. Whatever the cultural case, these pictures of men and women stick literally with the biblical text.

Apart from the lad who guided Samson, children are generally absent from the pictures of Samson's end in these Bible stories. One exception I have already noted, namely Doré's baby (fig. 11.3, top center). Another

Fig. 11.3. Women and children.

picture that jumps out (fig. 11.3, top left) is from an amazing suite of plates designed by Clément Pierre Marillier for a twelve-volume Bible published in Paris in 1789–1804 (see 3:79). The young lad is there by the pillar, and other children in evidence include a little girl in the foreground, bottom left. The design is used in Alexander Fletcher's *Scripture History for Youth* (1839); and much later, well after the advent of graduated age-related publishing, it is borrowed in the United States for *My Mother's Bible Stories* (Vincent 1896)—"designed for family use during 'the children's hour' around the evening lamp"—and in Reuben Prescott's *Grandfather's Bible Stories* (1897). In the texts, Mother does mention the "little boy" who led Samson, and Grandpa Reuben speaks of "a lad," but neither, of course, mentions any other children in the house of Dagon. One wonders whether the picture ever prompted any of the children around the lamp to wonder about the death of those other, Philistine, children.

The boy himself does not appear in illustrations as often as might be supposed. He is not found in the ubiquitous Scripture histories of the first half of the nineteenth century, but does appear occasionally later in the century (fig. 11.4). He is not obvious in Doré's picture but quite prominent, as a youth rather than a young boy, in Schnorr's design (fig. 11.4, top right). He is again prominent, as an older youth, in the "prayer" picture from the turn of the century (fig. 11.4, center left), but then hard to find except for the occasional illustration, including a few from the 1960s that also bring women into the picture (Goodhue 1961 [fig. 11.4, center] and *Children's Bible in Colour* 1964). Illustrators who have chosen to narrow the focus to Samson have already excluded the lad by default. But most of those who present a bigger picture have likely made a choice to drop from view the boy or youth Samson caused to die. If Samson's killing women could be accommodated, culturally, his killing a lad has proved a more difficult proposition.

Among the comic books that depict the boy, *The Picture Bible* (Hoth 1978) stands out (fig. 11.4, bottom). Like Armstrong, script writer Iva Hoth and illustrator André Le Blanc not only notice the boy, which most of the comic strips do, but they develop a picture of gentle kindness, and furthermore they write in Samson's reciprocating gesture: "Run, boy," he says, his hands on the pillars, "and don't stop until you're outside the temple" (223). Perhaps not all Philistines were irredeemably cruel and wicked. Perhaps not all Philistines deserved to die, after all. Perhaps some even merited rescue.

Fig. 11.4. The boy.

CONCLUSION

Of the three concerns about Samson's death expressed in the commentary tradition—suicide, vengeance, and proportion—we have seen that in texts suicide is unspoken, and vengeance often dropped or rephrased. As for proportion, some authors write of the three thousand, others settle for "many," while occasionally for the very young in more recent times there are no dead at all. While some authors elaborate on the scene of destruction, more often they confine their descriptions. Illustrators, unable to address the first two concerns, do have options in depicting the extent and manner of the slaughter. Doré's popular design, with its deluge of bodies, still finds muted imitation in recent decades. Schnorr's more restrained depiction has also been long lasting, often simplified to show but a few Philistines or Samson alone. As with many designs, these sometimes match their host text's account of the violence, and sometimes, particularly with Doré's picture, do not. In the case of the more restrained design, however, the mismatch does not necessarily undercut the tenor of the more elaborated text.

Consistently in the texts Samson's past failures and present deeds are framed and ameliorated by accounts of his cruel treatment at the hands of his (and God's) mocking enemies, along with assurances that his death was for his people's good and/or God's vindication. That is, poor Samson deserves our sympathy, the cruel Philistines deserve to die. Yet perhaps not all Philistines. We have also seen that many authors drop mention of the women present, increasingly so in the latter half of the twentieth century, reflecting, one might conjecture, a cultural aversion to the idea of a childhood hero who kills women. At about the same time, however, illustrators show women more prominently, suggesting a different cultural concern, over the roles of women, which might reflect differences in gender between authors and illustrators or stemming perhaps from the different constraints of print and visual media.

Though the biblical text introduces the boy into the scene, authors rarely include other children, and only Fanny Armstrong (1884) writes of the boy's death. In striking fashion, she hopes for his redemption. With rare exceptions (Doré is one), other children are absent also from illustrations. The boy, though prominent in Schnorr's picture, is elsewhere less present than women, especially over the past fifty years. His death is increasingly avoided. As if to rub the point in, *The Picture Bible* makes sure that the lad escapes, rescued by no less than the hero himself.

No, not all Philistines deserve to die.

WORKS CITED

Armstrong, April Oursler, and Jules Gotlieb (ill.). 1949. *Bible Stories for Young Readers*. Garden City, N.Y.: Junior Deluxe Editions.

Armstrong, Fanny. 1884. *The Children of the Bible.* New York: Fowler & Wells.

Baker, Carolyn Nabors, Cindy Helms, Danny Brooks Dalby (ill.). 1995. *The Beginners Bible for Toddlers.* Dallas: Word.

Baldwin, James. 1895. *Old Stories of the East.* New York: American Book Company.

Begbie, Harold. 1912. *The Children's Story Bible.* New York: Grolier Society.

Beuel, J. W. 1889. *The Beautiful Story: A Companion Book to the Holy Bible.* Richmond: Johnson.

The Bible Gallery, illustrated by Gustave Doré, with descriptions by Talbot Chanbers. 1880. London: Cassell, Petter & Galpin.

Bible History for the Least and Lowest. 1854. Philadelphia: American Sunday-School Union.

Bible-Picture Stories. 1953. Lajos Segner (ill.). Racine, Wis.: Whitman.

Bible Pictures and Stories. 1893. Philadelphia: Altemus.

Bible Stories for Little Folks: The Principal Facts of the Bible, the Lives and Adventures of Its Heroes, Retold in Simple Language for Children. Illustrated. 1918. Philadelphia: Winston.

Bottigheimer, Ruth. 1996. *The Bible for Children from the Age of Gutenberg to the Present.* New Haven: Yale University Press.

Boyd, Eleanor H. 1921. *How Granny Told the Bible Stories.* New York: Book Stall.

The Children's Bible in Colour. 1964. London: Hamlyn.

Captivating Bible Stories for the Young. 1895. [U.S.A.]: J. R. Jones.

Clarke, Adam. 1833. *The Holy Bible, Containing the Old and New Testaments: The Text.* New York: Waugh & Mason.

Doré, Gustave (ill.). 1866. *La Sainte Bible.* Tours: Mame & Fils.

———. 1879. *The Doré Bible Gallery.* New York: Fine Art.

Egermeier, Elsie E. 1927. *Bible Story Book.* Anderson, Ind.: Gospel Trumpet.

Evans, Adelaide Bee. 1911. *Easy Steps in the Bible Story.* Takoma Park: Review & Herald.

Favourite Bible Stories for the Young, with Numerous Illustrations. 1893. London: Nelson.

Fletcher, Alexander. 1839. *Scripture History, Designed for the Improvement of Youth*, vol. 1. London: Virtue.

Foster, Charles. 1884. *The Story of the Bible: From Genesis to Revelation. Told in Simple Language.* Philadelphia: Foster.

———. 1886. *Bible Pictures and What They Teach Us.* Philadelphia: Foster.

Fryer, Jane Eayre, and Edwin John Prittie (ill.). 1924. *The Bible Story Book for Boys and Girls*. Philadelphia: Winston.

Gaspey, Thomas. 1851. *Tallis' Illustrated Scripture History for the Improvement of Youth*. London.

Goodhue, Mary Pearson. 1961. *Mighty Samson*. Garden City, N.Y.: Know Your Bible Program.

Grainger, Muriel. 1971. *365 Bible Stories and Verses*. London: Hamlyn.

Guerber, H. A. 1896. *Eclectic School Readings: The Story of the Chosen People*. New York: American Book Company.

Gunn, David M. 2005. *Judges*. Oxford: Blackwell.

Hadaway, Bridget, and Jean Atcheson. 1973. *The Bible for Children*. London: Octopus.

Hadley, Caroline. 1866. *Stories of Old: Bible Narratives for Young Children*. London: Warne; New York: Scribner, Welford.

Hastings, Selina, Eric Thomas, and Amy Burch (ill.). 2004. *The Children's Illustrated Bible*. New York: Dorling Kindersley.

Hewlett, Esther. 1828. *Scripture History*, vol. 2. London: Fisher.

Hoth, Iva, and André Le Blanc (ill.). 1978. *The Picture Bible*. Elgin: Cook.

Houtman, Cornelis, and Klaas Spronk. 2004. *Ein Held des Glaubens? Rezeptionsgeschichtliche Studien zu den Simson-Erzählungen*. CBET 39. Leuven: Peeters.

Hunt, Patricia, and Angus McBride (ill.). 1981. *Bible Stories*. New York: Crown.

Hurlbut, Jesse Lyman. 1904. *Hurlbut's Story of the Bible. Profusely Illustrated*. Philadelphia: Winston.

———. 1925 [orig. 1904]. *Bible Stories Every One Should Know*. Philadelphia: Winston.

Hurlbut, Jesse Lyman, Ralph Pallen Coleman (ill.), and Steele Savage (ill.). 1957. *Hurlbut's Story of the Bible for Young and Old*. Philadelphia: Winston.

Ish-Kishor, Sulamith. 1933. *Children's History of Israel*, vol. 2: *From Joshua to the Second Temple*. New York: Jordan.

Krottjer, A. Gertrude, and Joseph Eugene Dash (ill.). 1925. *Favorite Bible Stories: Old Testament*. Chicago: Whitman.

Lord, Daniel. 1943. *New Catholic Bible Stories: Stories from the Old Testament*. St. Louis: Hirten.

Madison, Marian, and Warner Kreuter (ill.). 1946. *Picture Stories from the Old Testament*. Chicago: Wilcox & Follett.

Mare, Walter de la, and Theodore Nadejen (ill.). 1929. *Stories from the Bible*. New York: Cosmopolitan Book Corp.

Marillier, Clément Pierre (ill.). 1791. *La Sainte Bible, III*. Translated by Maistre de Saci. Paris: Defer de Maisonneuve.

Maryknoll Sisters. 1955. *Crusade: The Story of the Bible Retold for Catholic Children*. Chicago: Crawley.

Morrow, Louis LaRaviore. 1950. *My Bible History in Pictures*. Kenosha: My Mission House.

Morton, Elizabeth. 1927. *The Illuminated Bible Story Book for Young People*. Philadelphia: Winston.

Mother Stories from the Old Testament. 1908. Philadelphia: Altemus.

Neale, H. 1817. *Sacred History in Familiar Dialogues for the Instruction of Youth*. London: Gardiner.

Neil, Henry. 1892. *Bible Stories for Children … Designed to Interest and Instruct the Young in God's Holy Book. Illustrated*. Introduction by Russell H. Conwell. [U.S.A.]: Henry Neil.

O'Donnell, Thomas C., and Lu Kimmel (ill.) 1936. *The "Tell Me Again" Bible (Old Testament)*. New York: Gettinger.

One Hundred Bible Stories. 1948. St. Louis: Concordia.

Our Home Bible Story Book. 1960. JoAnne Brubaker (ill.). Chicago: Moody Press.

Oursler, Fulton, and Jules Gotlieb (ill.). 1949, 1955. *Bible Stories for Young Readers*. Garden City NY: Junior Deluxe.

"Patriarchus." 1892. *Sacred Pictures and Their Teachings: Grand Old Stories from the Good Old Book for Young and Old. Profusely Illustrated*. Philadelphia: Keystone.

Pollard, Josephine. 1888. *History of the Old Testament in Words of One Syllable*. New York: Burt.

————. 1937. *Wonderful Stories of the Bible*. Akron: Saalfield.

Prescott, Reuben. 1897. *Grandfather's Bible Stories*. Chicago: Stanton.

Routledge's Scripture Gift-Book. [ca. 1866.] London: Routledge.

Sandison, Geo. H. 1924. *The Great Stories of the Bible for Children*. New York: World.

Schnorr von Carolsfeld, Julius (ill.). 1861. *Die Bibel in Bildern*. Leipzig: Wigands. English edition: *The Bible in Pictures*. 1869. London: Blackie.

————. 1884. *Die Bibel in Bildern. The Bible Illustrated*. Philadelphia: I. Kohler.

Schoolland, Marian. 1953. *Marian's Favorite Bible Stories*. Grand Rapids: Eerdmans.

Scott, Thomas. 1816. *Commentary on the Whole Bible*. 6th American, from the 2nd London edition. Hartford, Conn.: Sheldon & Goodrich and Loomis.

Stoddard, Sandol, and Tony Chen (ill.). 1983. *The Doubleday Illustrated Children's Bible*. Garden City, N.Y.: Doubleday.

Taylor, Kenneth N. 1989. *My First Bible in Pictures*. Wheaton: Tyndale.

Taylor, Kenneth N., and Annabel Spenceley (ill.). 2002. *The New Bible in Pictures for Little Eyes*. Chicago: Moody Press.

Treasury of Bible Stories. 1995. [U.S.A.]: Publications International.

A Treasury of Scripture Stories. 1869. New York: Hurd & Houghton.

Trimmer, Sarah. 1790. *A Description of a Set of Prints of Scripture History: Contained in A Set of Easy Lessons*. London: Marshall.

Turner, Philip, and Brian Wildsmith (ill.). 1980. *The Bible Story*. New York: Oxford University Press.

Tyler, John Williamson. 1901. *The Bible Story Newly Told for Young People. Profusely Illustrated*. [U.S.A.]: Whitford.

Vincent, John H. 1896. *My Mother's Bible Stories*. Philadelphia: Globe.

Weed, Libby (ed.), and Jim Padgett (ill.). 1984. *Read-n-Grow Picture Bible*. Fort Worth, Tex.: Sweet.

Werner, Elsa Jane, ed., and Feodor Rojankovsky (ill.). 1946. *The Golden Bible*. New York: Simon & Schuster.

Weston, D. C. 1883. *Old Testament Stories*. New York: Dutton.

Willard, J. H. 1906. *What Is Sweeter Than Honey? The Story of Samson*. Altemus' Beautiful Stories Series. Illustrated. Philadelphia: Altemus.

Williams, Henry L., Jr. 1865 [8th edition, ca. 1900]. *Boys of the Bible*. Chicago: Donohue.

Wilson-Wilson, Theodora. 1938. *Through the Bible*. London: Collins.

Worm, Piet. 1958. *Stories from the Old Testament II: From Joseph to the Prophets*. London: Collins.

KEY TO ILLUSTRATIONS

Figure 1. Variations on a classic design.
1861, Julius Schnorr von Carolsfeld, *Die Bibel in Bildern* (Leipzig).
1908, *Mother Stories from the Old Testament* (Philadelphia).
1925, Jesse Lyman Hurlbut, *Bible Stories Every One Should Know* (Philadelphia).

Figure 2. Picturing many or few.

1866, Gustave Doré, *La Sainte Bible* (Tours).

1946, Elsa Jane Werner, ed., *The Golden Bible* (New York); Feodor Rojankovsky (ill.).

1929, Walter de la Mare, *Stories from the Bible* (New York); Theodore Nadejen (ill.).

1936, Thomas C. O'Donnell, *The "Tell Me Again" Bible (Old Testament)* (New York); Lu Kimmel (ill.).

Figure 3. Women and children.

1839, Alexander Fletcher, *Scripture History for Youth* (London); Marillier (ill.) 1791.

1883, Mrs. D. C. Weston, *Old Testament Stories* (New York); Doré (ill.) 1866.

1892, "Patriarchus," *Sacred Pictures and Their Teachings* (Philadelphia); Schnorr von Carolsfeld (ill.) 1861.

1953, *Bible-Picture Stories* (Racine, Wis.); Lajos Segner (ill.).

1957, Jesse Lyman Hurlbut, *Hurlbut's Story of the Bible* (Philadelphia); Steele Savage (ill.).

1958, Piet Worm, *Stories from the Old Testament II* (London); Piet Worm (ill.).

1960, *Our Home Bible Story Book* (Chicago); JoAnne Brubaker (ill.).

1961, Mary Pearson Goodhue, *Mighty Samson* (Garden City, N.Y.); Maurice Bower (ill.).

1964, *The Children's Bible in Colour* (London); Fabbri Studios, Milan (ill.).

1971, Muriel Grainger, *365 Bible Stories* (London).

1973, Bridget Hadaway and Jean Atcheson, *The Bible for Children* (London); L'Esperto, Milan (ill.).

1981, Patricia Hunt, *Bible Stories* (New York); Angus McBride (ill.).

1984, Libby Weed, ed., *Read-n-Grow Picture Bible* (Fort Worth, Tex.); Jim Padgett (ill.).

1995, *Treasury of Bible Stories* [U.S.A.].

2004, Selina Hastings, *The Children's Illustrated Bible* (New York); Eric Thomas and Amy Burch (ill.).

Figure 4. The boy.

1884, Charles Foster, *The Story of the Bible* (Philadelphia); R. N. Snyder (ill.).

1886, Charles Foster, *Bible Pictures and What They Teach Us* (Philadelphia).

1893, *Bible Pictures and Stories* (Philadelphia).

1895, *Captivating Bible Stories for the Young* [U.S.A.]; Schnorr von Carolsfeld (ill.).

1961, Mary Pearson Goodhue, *Mighty Samson* (Garden City, N.Y.); Maurice Bower (ill.).

1964, *The Children's Bible in Colour* (London); Fabbri Studios, Milan (ill.).

1978, Iva Hoth (script), *The Picture Bible* (Elgin, Ill.); Andre Le Blanc (ill.).

TRANSLATING THE BIBLE INTO PICTURES

Rubén R. Dupertuis

I became interested in the intersection of comic books and Bibles for children as a part of my attempt to make some sense out of the *Brick Testament*, a web-design project illustrating scenes from biblical stories entirely in the medium of Lego blocks. Despite the ostensibly child-friendly nature of the images—Legos are, after all, a children's toy—the project has a sharp critical edge to it. We catch a glimpse of it in the index, which has content ratings alerting viewers to which scenes contain "Nudity, Sexual activity, Violence and Cursing." Indeed, what Smith chooses to illustrate from the Bible emphasizes its "adult-themed" content by highlighting the violence, sexuality, and oddity of its content. Much of the material typically omitted or cleaned up for children's editions of the Bible is not only present in the *Brick Testament*, but is illustrated in great detail. One finds, for example, scenes illustrating the rape of Dinah (from Gen 34:1–34), Noah's drunkenness (9:18–29), and the beheading of John the Baptist, including an image of John the Baptist's recently severed head on a platter (Mark 6:20–29; Luke 3:19–20).[1] Thus, given Smith's illustration choices, it is hard to see the *Brick Testament* as a children's Bible. That said, in my judgment the *Brick Testament* is not unrelated to the tradition of illustrated Bibles. Because many if not most of the illustrated Bibles produced in the twentieth century are meant for children, the *Brick Testament* can be read as a critique of or reaction against ways in which the Bible is presented to children.

Regarding the purpose of the project, Smith states that, in the end, "illustrating the Bible in Lego has been, for me, a chance to retell these stories in a way that's more faithful to the text than the other illustrated Bibles I've seen" (James 2003). If the *Brick Testament* is a reaction to this tradition, it is worth looking at it alongside some examples of illustrated Bibles

---

1. Online: www.thebricktestament.com.

for children. I have chosen Bibles that fall generally into the category of comics because, while the *Brick Testament* is not technically a comic book, it is clearly borrowing the general form, language, and esthetics of that medium by the use of sequential frames to convey a story through the use of images, captions, and word and thought bubbles. I have also chosen to focus on the presentation of the story of Cain and Abel from Gen 4:1–16 in several different Bibles, in part because this story regularly features in most relatively recent Bibles for children, but also because it is a narrative that presents any translator with a number of difficult decisions.

In what follows I first address my approach to comic-book Bibles and the *Brick Testament* principally as translations. I then examine the presentation of Gen 4:1–16 in three comic-book Bibles before turning to some aspects of the *Brick Testament* in general and its presentation of the Cain and Abel Story in particular.

COMIC-BOOK BIBLES AS TRANSLATIONS

While a number of different approaches to this material would be fruitful, including retelling and adaptation among many, I have chosen translation for several reasons. The first is the nature of what can be referred to generally as "the comics medium" itself. The wide range of what has been considered and presented as children's Bibles includes retellings of a handful of stories, catechisms, epitomes, summaries, and various illustrated and picture Bibles (Bottigheimer 1996, 3–13). Comic-book Bibles, a relatively recent phenomenon, certainly fit within the tradition of illustrated or picture Bibles, but they also present some distinctive features and challenges.[2] Clear definitions of "comics," "comic books," and "graphic novels"[3] are notoriously difficult to come by, but one of the most useful and well known is that of McCloud, for whom comics are "juxtaposed pictorial and other images in deliberate sequence, intended to convey information and/or to produce an aesthetic response in the viewer" (1993, 20). It is worth emphasizing the image-driven nature of the medium, as is thinking of images or icons in broad terms. While for some, comics are a combina-

---

2. While precursors abound, comics emerge in force in the twentieth century. For a very brief history of the medium, see Saraceni 2003, 1–3; for a more extensive history, see Harvey 1996.

3. I use these terms interchangeably, although I recognize that many will draw more fine distinctions.

tion of language and images (Saraceni 2003, 5), for McCloud and others the images, icons, and symbols used to convey meaning in the medium are signs in the same way that the letters of an alphabet are. The comics medium is, in fact, increasingly being viewed as a language system that has developed a set visual vocabulary that requires a particular literacy on the part of the reader.[4]

It is also worth noting that in comics the images or pictures do not simply illustrate the text or the story, but are a central means through which the medium conveys meaning. Comics can, in fact, be thought of as a "hybrid word-and-image form in which two narrative tracks, one verbal and one visual, register temporality spatially.... Highly textured in its narrative scaffolding, comics doesn't [sic] blend the visual and the verbal—or use one simply to illustrate the other—but is [sic] rather prone to present the two nonsynchronously; a reader of comics not only fills in the gaps between panels but also works with the often disjunctive back-and-forth or *reading* and *looking* for meaning" (Chute 2008, 452). If the comics medium consists of a language, then presenting or telling a Bible story in this medium can be considered a translation.

A second reason lies in the fact that what little critical attention comic-book Bibles have received has all been relatively recent and has, in one way or another, addressed translation issues. Beard and du Toit (2005), for example, examine children's Bibles, including "picture" Bibles, in South Africa explicitly as translations through the framework of cognitive poetics. Burke and Lebrón-Rivera (2004) explore the possibility of reading a recent graphic-novel production of the story of Samson as midrash. They never use the term "translation," but their central concern is with the "transfer of Scripture" into the graphic-novel format, evaluating the level of accuracy of the graphic novel by comparison to the story of Samson in the Masoretic Text. Responding to Burke and Lebrón-Rivera, Clark also takes up the analysis of recent graphic-novel versions of the story of Samson. The concern with the "faithful transfer" of Scripture is even clearer here, as

---

4. Examples of this visual vocabulary include the ways in which "motion lines" or "zip ribbons" have been used to connote movement in a single frame, the use of posture and gesture, and even the use of particular icons to indicate certain types of speech (word balloons versus thought balloons). For a discussion of the challenge of representing movement in the comics medium, see McCloud 1993, 108–17. For the use of posture and gesture, see Eisner 2008, 103–14.

Clark (2007) notes places where the transfer of meaning was "unfaithful" and where it hits the mark.

A third reason is that fidelity in translation is also a goal of many of the comic-book Bibles themselves. This is the case, for example, in the comic-book Bible series put out by the United Bible Society. In an article published in *Bible Translator* with the aim of introducing potential translators to the conventions of comics, Mundhenk says that "the series of Bible comics is an attempt to adapt the message of the Bible in a way that is both faithful to the message of the Bible and also faithful to the comics format" (2002, 413).

The self-presentation of most of the comics I examined for this study also invokes fidelity to Scripture. The back cover of one comic-strip version of the Hebrew Bible attributes the following endorsement to a prominent Christian leader: "Parents will do their children a real spiritual service by providing them with *Picture Stories from the Bible*. The stories follow the text of Scripture very closely" (Gaines 1979). Another authority says of the book: the author "has put the Bible stories into the modern comic form without sacrificing the accuracy of the Biblical text, and with all due reverence." Although less explicit about being a translation, the *Comic Book Bible* also presents itself as a kind of Bible starter kit translated into "picturebook" form in order to be attractive and understandable to children (Suggs 1997, back cover). And as I noted above, fidelity to the biblical original is also part of the *Brick Testament*'s presentation. Smith says of his project: "For me, it's all about making the content of the Bible more accessible without changing that content" (James 2003). Although, as I note below, Smith's purpose in accurately representing the content of the Bible may ultimately be ironic, the claim of accuracy is there, thus legitimating the project by evoking popular notions of translation.

My own interest in approaching these texts as translations is twofold. The first concerns the type of translation that comic-book Bibles represent. Jakobson distinguished three kinds of translation: (1) interlingual translation—what is typically thought of as "translation proper"—in which the signs from one natural language (such as Hebrew or Greek) are interpreted by means of signs in another natural language (such as Spanish or English); (2) intralingual translation, in which the signs of one language are interpreted by means of other signs in the same language—essentially paraphrasing; and (3) intersemiotic translation, the interpretation of verbal signs by means of a nonverbal sign system (1959, 233). Comic-book Bibles are, or at least can be, all three types of translation. While the potential for interlingual translation exists, most comic-book Bibles start with an existing English language translation.[5] What parts of the biblical text they render in what Jakobson calls "natural language," whether that be rewording, paraphrasing, retelling, or something else, could be seen as intralingual translation. Certainly the use of images and icons would qualify as an intersemiotic translation. This last type is probably the most useful of the three for our purposes, but it is worth noting that the comics medium defies simple characterization.

I am also interested in the models of translation invoked, or better yet, assumed, when discussing comic-book Bibles. The focus on the fidelity of comics in their representation, retelling, or translation of biblical stories often appears to assume a rather simplistic model of translation that, in my judgment, may be overly optimistic about the possibility of capturing the objective essence of the original into the target language or medium. Indeed, one of the central developments of translation studies in the last few decades has been dispelling the notion that the mark of a good translation is whether it is accurate (Williams 2004). Much of recent translation theory reflects the understanding that translations are always complex cultural transactions (Porter 2001). As Venuti puts it, translations are "the site of many determinations and effects—linguistic, cultural, economic, ideological" (1995, 19). But if the undistorted transfer of meaning is not fully possible, what then is the role of the translator, and what makes a good translation? For Venuti, while some violence is unavoidable in the act of translation, translators have a choice between two tendencies. One possibility is performing what he calls a "domesticating" translation that privileges the values and cultural assumptions of the target-language reader. Domesticating models of translation, Venuti argues, are dominant in English-language translation. This applies to most contemporary English translations of the Bible, perhaps especially those aimed at niche markets. In addition to presenting the biblical texts in attractive, accessible,

---

5. See the discussion of this issue in the context of the production and translation of children's Bibles in South Africa by Beard and du Toit (2004, §4.5). In regard to the *Brick Testament*, Smith notes on his site that in earlier stages of the project he drew almost exclusively from the NJB, but because of copyright issues, he changed the wording based on translations in the public domain and the recommendation of friends with knowledge of the original languages (online: http://www.thebricktestament.com/faq/index.html). The biblical quotations that appear on every page of the *Comic Book Bible* appear to be taken from the KJV.

and understandable ways, they erase the cultural distance between the Bible and the present day, enlisting it (and the attendant authority of the Bible) in the maintenance and reification of contemporary cultural structures and ideologies.

For Venuti, the other possibility is foregrounding the cultural distance from and otherness of a source text by adopting a "foreignizing" translation. This is not a claim to be able to capture objectively some essence in the source text, because in the end the text's otherness is still rendered by means of the terms of the target language. The point, however, is "to develop a theory and practice of translation that resists dominant target-language cultural values so as to signify the linguistic and culture difference of the foreign text" (1995, 23). With these possibilities or tendencies in mind we can take a look at how the Bible is translated in comic-book Bibles for children.

Cain and Abel in the Primeval Epic and Comic-book Bibles for Children

I will focus on the story of Cain and Abel in Gen 4:1–16, a staple of recent children's Bibles. While there are numerous interpretive difficulties in this little story—as evidenced by the complex history of interpretation[6]—in my reading of the story there are four issues in particular to which I want to pay attention. The first is the apparent arbitrariness of God's choice of Abel's sacrifice over Cain's. The choice is not explained or justified in the Hebrew Bible. Both Cain and Abel make offerings from what is appropriate to their occupation—Cain the farmer, Abel the shepherd. As Brueggemann notes, "The trouble comes not from Cain, but from Yahweh—the strange God of Israel. Inexplicably, Yahweh chooses—accepts and rejects" (1982, 56).

The second interpretive issue is the first interaction between God and Cain immediately after the latter's sacrifice is not accepted and "his countenance fell" (Gen 4:5). In the wake of God's arbitrary preference for Abel's sacrifice, the reminder that doing well leads to acceptance, while not doing well opens one up to sin is hardly comforting since it is unclear what Cain did wrong in the first place (4:6–7). At best this, too, is another enigmatic

---

6. See, e.g., the discussion of Gen 4:1–16 in Westermann 1984, 279–320. See also Lohr 2009, who traces the history of interpretation of this passage as far back as the Septuagint translation of the Hebrew Bible.

feature of the story. At worst, God is not playing fair and is toying with Cain (Brueggemann 1982, 57). The third issue is God's second interaction with Cain, in which Cain is cursed, his connection to the ground severed, and he is destined to live as an exile and a wanderer. Cain's protest results in a form of accommodation: a mark protecting him from harm. The literary function of this mark on Cain is "two edged. On the one hand, it announces the guilt of Cain. On the other, it marks Cain as safe in God's protection" (Brueggemann 1982, 60). And the fourth issue I want to highlight is the violence that is at the heart of the first murder in the Bible. As with much in this terse, brief narrative, the pivotal moment is striking for its brevity: Cain invited Abel to a field where he "rose up against his brother Abel, and killed him" (4:8 NRSV).

Of the numerous publications that would fit under the category of comic-book Bibles, I have chosen to focus on three. The first, the *Comic Book Bible* by Rob Suggs, is a Christian publication (as are the other two examples on which I focus) that aims at an audience of children from ages eight to twelve and tells selected stories from both the Hebrew Bible and the New Testament.[7] In the *Comic Book Bible* the story of Cain and Abel is told in six panels on one page. At the top of each page is a Bible verse related to the story, a choice that may be related to an anxiety often seen in illustrated or picture Bibles over the relationship to the text of the Bible (Bottigheimer 1996, 39). In this case, the words selected from the Cain and Abel story are from Gen 4:4–5: "And the LORD had respect for Abel and his offering, but unto Cain and to his offering he had not respect." This choice highlights the importance of God's preference of the sacrifice of one brother over the other, which in the Hebrew Bible is enigmatic if not arbitrary.

In the *Comic Book Bible*, however, God's preference for Abel's sacrifice is anything but arbitrary. One way in which this is achieved is the dialogue supplied to the characters. In the first frame of the story Abel says, "I'll offer the best of my flock"; while in the next frame, Cain states, "Abel is always sacrificing. Maybe this old plant will do for me" (fig. 12.1). The order in which the sons are introduced and offer their sacrifices is reversed from the order in the Hebrew Bible, effectively making Cain play catch-up and introducing the notion of jealousy. The words ascribed to

---

7. Unless otherwise noted, all references to the *Comic Book Bible* are to p. 13, which contains the six frames of the story of Cain and Abel.

the brothers emphasize the importance of the proper attitude during worship. In addition to making clear the superior quality of Abel's sacrifice, the story also suggests that God's choice is understandable. In the second frame Cain says, "Abel is always sacrificing"; and in the third he thinks, "As usual, God liked Abel's sacrifice better, well I'm sick of it." In this story Abel apparently sacrifices more often, his offerings are better, and God routinely chooses the sacrifice of Abel over that of Cain. The justification of God's choice is also done visually. Abel is introduced in the first frame as the cute, bright-eyed younger brother active in tending his flock, while Cain bears a droopy moustache (a permanent frown?) and stands idle in the background leaning up against a tree. We see Abel's face again in the third frame—again he is smiling while his brother, watching him out of the corner of his eyes, thinks jealous thoughts. Whatever insight Cain's thoughts and words give the reader about his motivations, visually he is typed throughout as a villain.

Fig. 12.1. *The Comic Book Bible* (Suggs 1997, 13).

The first interaction between God and Cain before the murder of Abel is omitted entirely, while in the presentation of the second there is no indication that God's punishment of Cain for the murder of his brother with exile is accompanied by a way of protecting him against those who would do him harm. Here it is simply a punishment. This story is about a young man with a bad attitude (and bad facial hair) who succumbs to jealousy, kills his brother, and suffers a corresponding punishment. Finally, the *Comic Book Bible* avoids the violence in the story, showing a frame of

Cain's ambush of Abel, then going directly to God's second encounter with Cain. This is not surprising, as violence and perceived amoral actions in children's Bibles have been reworked or omitted for the better part of the last two centuries (Bottigheimer 1996, 54; Schine Gold 2004, 124–33).

An earlier comic-book Bible for children touches on many of the same themes. Published originally in 1942, *Picture Stories from the Bible* by M. C. Gaines has stories from both the Old and New Testaments in two separate volumes. Its version of the story of Cain and Abel is longer, told over fourteen frames (1979, 8–10). As is the case in the *Comic Book Bible*, in *Picture Stories* the reason for God's choice between Cain and Abel is made abundantly clear. After the brothers and their respective occupations are introduced, a caption states: "One day Abel decided to make an offering to the Lord—Cain pledged an offering too, but his heart wasn't in it." Below the caption is a scene of Cain and Abel flanking Adam at the dinner table in which Abel says, "For God's goodness I feel I should sacrifice a lamb from my flock to him!" Cain, however, states, "Oh well, I can offer him some of my fruit." The next frame depicts Cain watching Abel prepare his sacrifice, thinking, "I'll not be outdone by my brother." The frame in which God's choice is conveyed begins with the following caption: "God, looking into their hearts, commends Abel but not Cain."

Here the point is that attitude matters and that jealousy is the reason for God's rejection of Cain, and again the order in which the brothers offer their sacrifices is reversed. An interesting aspect of this Bible is the emphasis on God's ability to see into the brothers' hearts, something noted specifically in the caption and underscored by visual representation of the brothers. Unlike the *Comic Book Bible*, where the superiority of Abel is clear visually, here the two brothers are from the beginning virtually identical. The initial frame of the story depicts them as young children, featuring Cain climbing a tree while expressing his desire to watch things grow when he grows up, and Abel expressing his desire to be a shepherd while on the ground petting a sheep. All subsequent frames have the boys as adults; they are thickly muscled, idealized, and indistinguishable from each other except for Cain having a thin headband. Their physical similarity serves to call attention to God (who like the comics reader is privy to the characters' thoughts) knowing people's hearts and not being fooled by outward appearances.

Other choices in *Picture Stories* are also worth noting. The first interaction between Cain and God is presented here, but it is framed by Cain "slinking" away, muttering jealous words—something both visually depicted and stated in a caption—and a running Cain shouting, "You just wait." Cain's murder is here portrayed in more detail than in the *Comic Book Bible* in a frame with a caption reading, "They came to a field and suddenly Cain attacked and killed Abel." Below the caption Cain has Abel in a headlock with one arm, while in the other is a large stone ready to strike. The actual moment of Abel's murder is not shown, and the story quickly moves on. *Picture Stories* is one of the few comic-book Bibles for children to present the double-edged nature of God's second and final encounter with Cain. The final frame of the story depicts a downcast Cain protesting his punishment, particularly his fear that being a "fugitive and a vagabond" would get him killed, and a response from God: "I shall set a mark upon you lest they do this, and it shall be the brand of Cain." The brief explanation feels a bit more like an etiology for the "brand of Cain" than an emphasis on the idea that Cain is both punished and protected. Furthermore, the protection by God is necessary given the *Picture Bible's* choice to narrate the story of Cain taking a wife and becoming the father of Enoch. The inclusion of this material drawn from Gen 4:17 is unique in the comic-book Bibles for children I examined.

A very different treatment of the story of Cain and Abel can be found in the recent *Manga Bible* series from Zondervan, which has a volume dedicated to Genesis and Exodus entitled *Names, Games, and the Long Road Trip* (Lee and Hwang 2007). A more cartoony version clearly aiming at humor, this Bible is much more self-conscious in being a representation of biblical stories and is missing the somber tone of some of the other versions. The *Manga Bible* lingers over the events of Gen 4:1–16, devoting to it thirty frames over four and a half pages (for comparison, the much longer story of the flood in Gen 6–9 gets only thirty-five frames over six pages). Like the *Comic Book Bible*, the *Manga Bible* makes the superiority of Abel visually clear. Cain, drawn as an adult with angular features and spiky hair, is an unhappy thug. The first frame depicting Cain as an adult has him reaping grain with a sickle while complaining that "farming is too hard." The much younger Abel, on the other hand, is a cute kid with a round face and bowl haircut who is introduced to the reader in a frame depicting him holding a small sheep and saying, "Sheep are so cute." The only frames in which Cain is smiling are those in which he is planning and carrying out his plan to kill his brother and believes he has tricked God by hiding the body of the murdered Abel. Given the clear visual labeling of Cain as a bad guy, God's preference for Abel's sacrifice is not surprising. Aside from the rather generic labeling of Cain as a villain, the reason for God's prefer-

ence for Abel's sacrifice is more narrowly defined as Cain's greed. Here the
issue is not necessarily the right attitude or what is in one's heart, but how
much one gives to God: Cain is shown reconsidering how much to give to
God as a sacrifice, finally offering a minimal amount after reasoning that
he couldn't "give [God] an empty dish." While humor is clearly the aim,
the message is clear: Cain's sacrifice was unacceptable in its quantity, not
its quality.

The first interaction between Cain and God immediately following the
rejection of Cain's sacrifice is represented in the *Manga Bible* in four frames
that stand out for their more sophisticated use of the language of the comics
medium (fig. 12.2)—motion or zip lines indicate Cain's confusion at the
rejection of his sacrifice, sound effects indicate his anger as he cracks his
knuckles, and finally God's voice irrupts into a frame asking Cain questions
that are a paraphrase of Gen 4:6–7. Tired of being picked on, Cain decides
that God's disfavor is Abel's fault and begins to plot his murder.

Fig. 12.2. *The Manga Bible* (Lee and Hwang 2007, 14).

Here, too, the violence of Cain's murder is presented more graphically
than in the *Comic Book Bible*, but it is still suggested rather than shown.
Four frames portray Cain luring Abel out into a field, a fifth shows only
the top of Abel's head while above him looms Cain with a large rock in his
hands. Finally, while the *Manga Bible* does suggest that Cain is both cursed

and protected, it appears to be uncomfortable with God's protection of Cain and has him earn it with "tears of repentance."

As translations these Bibles are clearly on the domesticating end of the spectrum, but that is precisely the point. The stated goal of these comics is, in some way or another, to make the Bible accessible and fun for children. Several aspects about how this is done are worth noting. What is portrayed, including how it is portrayed, is filtered through contemporary beliefs about what is appropriate for children. This includes the decision to turn stories full of ambiguity into clear articulations of contemporary morals. But since what is deemed appropriate social behavior varies, it is worth noting the different reasons given for God's refusal to accept Cain's sacrifice. Both the *Comic Book Bible* and *Picture Stories* emphasize Cain's lack of appropriate attitude and jealousy, while the *Manga Bible* highlights Cain's laziness and, in particular, his greed—he simply did not give enough. Particular details may differ, but that these Bibles serve to reify contemporary values and morals places them squarely within the long tradition of children's Bibles (Bottigheimer 1996).

The visual aspects of how the biblical stories are represented are also clearly shaped by the concerns of the contemporary target culture. That almost all comic-book Bibles are in color says something about the younger audience these publications are targeting. Historically, most comics are in black and white. The exceptions are the more recent publications, including the *Manga Bible* series by Zondervan, which appear to be designed specifically to appeal to readers already interested in the comics medium. One could argue that giving all of the biblical characters some measure of recognizable ancient clothing represents a foreignization of sorts, highlighting the distance between the biblical and our contemporary worlds. The effect, however, is one of domestication as the foreign or ancient clothing works along the lines of contemporary notions of what is ancient or primitive (much like the elaborate sets of the "sword and the sandal" films produced by Hollywood). Furthermore, all biblical characters are portrayed as recognizably white, despite their ranging from fairly detailed to relatively abstract.[8]

This last point is worth elaborating. When it comes to the use of the comics medium, my initial judgment was that these comics are not very

---

8. Again, the *Manga Bible* may be the exception. Clear identification of the ethnicity of the characters is difficult, which may, of course, be intentional.

good—at the very least they do not represent a very sophisticated use of the comics medium. This is less applicable to the more recent publications that appear to be much more aware of and willing to make use of the lexicon of the medium. Of the comic-book Bibles discussed above, I would highlight the *Manga Bible* as the most sophisticated. But even the rather simplistic art of the others can have a particular function in the comics medium. McCloud argues that one of the key aspects of good comics art is identification on behalf of the reader with particular narrative characters. Identification, something that is also a part of exclusively textual narratives, is complicated in this case by comics typically visually representing people, and not all of us look the same. He argues that the more specific and detailed a representation of a particular person becomes, the fewer the number of people who can readily identify with the character (1993, 24–59).

Applied to comic-book Bibles, it might be argued that the rather simplistic art functions as a way of allowing greater identification. This does not necessarily work for *Picture Stories*, where the decision to render Cain and Abel in identical, adult, hypermasculine bodies and fairly detailed facial features does not facilitate identification. If anything, Cain and Abel represent a distant, idealized past. As I noted above, that the brothers are nearly indistinguishable also underscores the point that God knows people's hearts and that proper attitude is what determined God's preference of Abel over Cain. Identification is key, however, in the other two comic-book Bibles, where the character of Abel is much younger and drawn more simply or even abstractly than his brother. In the *Manga Bible*, for example, the character of Abel is a cute, somewhat generic good kid, while the character of Cain is so wholly other, so monstrous, that any possible sympathy, let alone identification, is made impossible.

Critiquing the Illustrated Bible Tradition
by Illustrating the Bible

Because Bibles for children, including illustrated or picture Bibles, are for the most part produced for didactic purposes, they tend to follow fairly consistent patterns in the stories they select and how these stories are presented. The *Brick Testament*, Smith's ongoing web-design project illustrating biblical stories using only photographed Lego blocks, can be read as a critique of this tradition. Begun in 2001, by 2003 the site had received enough interest to lead to the publication of a coffee table book entitled

The Brick Testament: Stories from the Book of Genesis. Smith published two more books in 2004 and has continued to add scenes to his online site. The website, which is my focus here, now has illustrations for much of the Bible.[9]

While Smith notes that his images are often used in church settings for educational purposes, the critical, if not satirical, edge of his project is readily apparent. What is of interest here is how this critique is carried out. The *Brick Testament* inhabits a carefully negotiated space at the intersection of a number of genres, styles, and sensibilities. Part comic book, part Bible illustration, part photography, part interactive online experience, Smith intentionally plays off of the conventions of all of these genres and media. But he plays with these conventions, particularly those of the comics medium, in ways that highlight the cultural otherness, occasional oddity, violence, and clearly "adult-themed" content of much of the Bible. It is, in a way, a sustained project of foreignization.

I take two of its central ideas to be a critique of literal readings of the Bible and an emphasis on the otherness or foreignness of the Bible. Smith critiques literal readings of the Bible by adhering to a strict literalism himself. In every frame the image is accompanied by the text being illustrated, effectively functioning as a caption. This can be read as a desire to follow Scripture closely; indeed, Smith claims that his illustrations remain "true to the text of the scriptures."[10] In most frames, however, this literalism creates a redundancy that effectively stilts the narrative. Because the comics language depends on both a textual and visual register, in this medium adaptations of biblical narrative that keep much or most of the wording of a biblical account are rare.[11]

In the *Brick Testament's* version of the Cain and Abel story, the encounter between God and Cain immediately after the murder begins with a frame illustrating the following part of Gen 4:9: "Yahweh said to Cain,

---

9. To my knowledge, changes to the website have typically been limited to illustrations of new material. Recently, however, Smith has revisited some of his early illustrations of Genesis, including his treatment of the story of Cain and Abel. My study of Smith's work is based on the original illustrations of Genesis that were displayed on the site from 2001 to 2010.

10. Online: www.thebricktestament.com/faq/index.html.

11. Giving potential translators of the United Bible Society comic-book Bibles guidelines on how to translate into the comics medium, Mundhenk recommends that when possible, the story should be carried by illustrations alone, with balloons being preferred over captions (2002, 406).

'Where is your brother Abel?' 'I don't know,' he replied." In the illustration above the text the dialogue is placed in word balloons, thus reproducing it twice on the page.[12] The effect of this redundancy is magnified in the remaining frames, which reproduce the final encounter between Cain and God almost in its entirety, including instances of rather lengthy speech by God. The end result is humorous in part because of its clumsiness and redundancy. As comics narrative, however, it is awkward if not just plain bad. But because Smith is presumably carrying out a narrative illustration that is "faithful" to the text of the Bible, the ultimate source of the awkwardness, then, is presumably the Bible itself.

Smith also appears to delight in capturing those places where this literalism produces surprising, odd, or humorous results. Such is the case in his illustration of Gen 9:28–29. Smith illustrates the majority of these two verses, which note the years that Noah lived after the flood and the total number of years he lived, in one frame in which Noah and his wife stand next to each other holding hands. The next frame illustrates the words "and he died" in a scene in which Noah is lying on his back while his wife, still standing, looks down on him. Literalism followed to absurd ends can also be seen in Smith's illustration of Mary's hymn of praise in Luke 1:46–55. Smith illustrates each of the attributes ascribed by Mary to God. The words "he has scattered the proud and arrogant," he illustrates with an image of God shooing a number of people away; "He has cast down rulers from their thrones," he illustrates with an image of God throwing a king off a chair; and that God "has raised up the lowly," is accompanied by an image of God holding three men with tattered clothing above his head. By following literalism to a fault, Smith is able to highlight just how much typical translations (and illustrations) do to make the text intelligible in our contemporary contexts.

The emphasis of the *Brick Testament* on what might be called the otherness of the Bible itself comes through in its retelling of the Cain and Abel story. Where most comic-book Bibles work hard to make the story relevant to contemporary sensibilities, particularly along the lines of what is deemed acceptable for children, the *Brick Testament* seems to push in the opposite direction. By the midtwentieth century, traces of sexuality were removed not just in Bibles for children but in children's literature more generally (Schine Gold 2004, 127–28). Accordingly, direct representations

---

12. Online: www.thebricktestament.com/genesis/cain_and_abel/gn04_09a.html.

of Adam's "knowledge" of Eve and her subsequent conception of Cain in Gen 4:1 are usually avoided in Bibles for children.

Smith, however, begins by sidestepping the euphemism of 4:1, preferring to depict the first couple having sex.[13] As noted above, the violence in the story is typically omitted or downplayed in children's Bibles; however, the *Brick Testament* focuses on it. The text of 4:8 is, "Cain said to his brother Abel, 'Let us go out to the field.' And when they were in the field, Cain rose up against his brother Abel, and killed him" (NRSV). Smith illustrates this one verse over three frames, the first depicting Cain asking Abel to join him in the field while concealing a knife, the second showing Cain attacking Abel, and the third frame corresponding to the text, "And he killed him," showing the slain Abel in a pool of blood (represented by blocks of translucent red Legos). Not only does Smith depict the primeval epic's first murder, but he seems to linger on the violence of the narrative.

What remains of the story is told in seven frames, all of which portray the final encounter between Cain and God. In four of the seven the slain body of Abel is visible in the background.[14] The ambiguity in the story, both in God's preference for Abel's sacrifice and the double nature of the mark given to Cain, is kept. This is due, in part, because Smith has chosen to illustrate almost all of 4:1–16. But it is worth noting that the interpretive difficulties of the ambiguity suit Smith's agenda well.

Judged in terms of the conventional application of the comics medium, Smith's translation of the Bible is a bad one, but intentionally so. What aspects of comics he appropriates, he appears purposefully to use ineffectively—the redundancy of the captions and the text in the word bubbles, for example—in order to highlight the otherness of the Bible. He uses the esthetics of the medium to illustrate that if followed closely the Bible itself is very different from what one expects. He consistently highlights instances of sex and violence in the Bible, but he also illustrates nonnar-

---

13. The English translation below the illustration also avoids the euphemism: "The man had sex with his wife Eve" (online: www.thebricktestament.com/genesis/cain_and_abel/gn04_01a.html).

14. A similar approach is taken in the *Brick Testament*'s version of the flood in Gen 6–9. Smith emphasizes that some animals did not make it into the ark. He also emphasizes the human loss in the story: the frame illustrating the moment in which Noah and his family emerge from the ark as the waters recede showcases the skeletons of those who did not make it into the ark.

rative material not typically part of the tradition of children's Bibles.[15] The legal materials in the Hebrew Bible do not translate well into comics narrative, but they do give Smith the opportunity to illustrate an instance of bestiality.[16] Smith's project appears designed to force people to take a look at what is really in the Bible. And the shock value of much of the *Brick Testament* depends on fairly stable patterns in the presentation of the Bible for children. This is emphasized by the choice of a medium often associated with children and the use of Lego blocks.

The *Brick Testament* can be fairly viewed as an extended project of foreignization in the sense that Smith is able "to signify the linguistic and cultural difference of the foreign text" (Venuti 1995, 23)—in this case the Bible. But the thrust of Smith's project is a reaction to contemporary translations, retellings, and interpretations of the Bible that he feels have misrepresented what is in it. This reaction is a domestication in its own right, because the force of the critique, the oddity and otherness he is trying to point out in the Bible, depend on contemporary assumptions of what is culturally acceptable and normative, what is odd and weird. It depends also on the absence of context.

Conclusion

The *Brick Testament* is at times very funny, smart, and even insightful in some of its critique. At its best, Smith effectively highlights how much modern translators/interpreters have to do to make the Bible intelligible and applicable in contemporary contexts. And Smith is right, too, in pointing out the adult-themed content of much of the Bible. That the Bible is not a children's book is clear to anyone who has wrestled with telling some of its stories to astute, young interpreters. A recent reminder of this came as I read one of the comic-book Bibles I studied for this project with my five-year-old daughter and I found myself trying to explain why Jesus could throw tables in the temple when he was angry but she couldn't. Smith is right, of course; the Bible is not a children's book, but here I sympathize with the attempts of the comics and other children's Bibles to present some of these stories to children in interesting ways. The problem, for

---

15. The working definition of children's Bibles adopted by Bottigheimer from Sybille Peter-Perrett: "Prose re-workings of the narrative sections of the Bible for child readers," makes clear the emphasis on narrative in the tradition (1996, 4).

16. Online: www.thebricktestament.com/the_law/bestiality/lv18_23a.html.

me, comes in the claims to accuracy and fidelity. Given the authority of the Bible in many contemporary settings, these claims are probably rhetorically expedient, but ultimately not very helpful—translation is far too complex a phenomenon for that. So is there a place for comic-book Bibles for children? In my judgment there certainly is. But perhaps the *Brick Testament* is reflecting frustration with the fact that for many the Bible is not allowed to grow up.

WORKS CITED

Beard, Luna, and Jaqueline S. du Toit. 2005. "A Proactive Approach to the Translation of Bible Stories for Children." *META: Translator's Journal* 50.4. Online: http://id.erudit.org/iderudit/019830ar.

Bottigheimer, Ruth B. 1996. *The Bible for Children from the Age of Gutenberg to the Present.* New Haven: Yale University Press.

Brueggemann, Walter. 1982. *Genesis.* Interpretation. Atlanta: John Knox.

Burke, David G., and Lydia Lebrón-Rivera. 2004. "Transferring Biblical Narrative to Graphic Novel." SBL Forum. Online: http://sbl-site.org/Article.aspx?ArticleID=249.

Chute, Hillary. 2008. "Comics as Literature? Reading Graphic Narrative." *Publications of the Modern Language Association* 123:452–65.

Clark, Terry Ray. 2007. "Biblical Graphic Novels: Adaptation, Interpretation, and 'Faithful Transfer.'" SBL Forum. Online: http://sbl-site.org/Article.aspx?ArticleID=641.

Eisner, Will. 2008. *Comics and Sequential Art: Principles and Practices from the Legendary Cartoonist.* New York: Norton.

Gaines, M. C. 1979. *Picture Stories from the Bible: The Old Testament in Full-Color Comic-Strip Form.* New York: Scarf.

Harvey, Robert C. 1996. *The Art of the Comic Book: An Aesthetic History.* Studies in Popular Culture. Jackson: University Press of Mississippi.

Jakobson, Roman. 1959. "On Linguistic Aspects of Translation." Pages 232–39 in *On Translation.* Edited by Reuben A. Brower. Harvard Studies in Comparative Literature 23. Cambridge: Harvard University Press.

James, Meredith. 2003. "Building a Colorful, Accessible Bible, Brick by Lego Brick." *Chicago Tribune*, 30 November 2003. Online: http://www.thebricktestament.com/press/chicago_tribune_03_11_30.html.

Lee, Young Shin, and Jung Sun Hwang (ill.). 2007. *Names, Games, and the Long Road Trip: Genesis–Exodus.* The Manga Bible 1. Edited by Bud Rogers. Grand Rapids: Zondervan.

Lohr, Joel. 2009. "Righteous Abel, Wicked Cain: Genesis 4:16 in the Masoretic Text, the Septuagint, and the New Testament." *CBQ* 71:485–96.

McCloud, Scott. 1993. *Understanding Comics: The Invisible Art.* New York: HarperPerrenniel.

Mundhenk, Norman A. 2002. "Translating Bible Comics." *BT* 53:402–13.

Niditch, Susan. *Chaos to Cosmos: Studies in Biblical Patterns of Creation.* Scholars Press Studies in the Humanities 6. Chico, Calif.: Scholars Press.

Porter, Stanley E. 2001. "Some Issues in Modern Translation Theory and Study of the Greek New Testament." *CurBS* 9:350–82.

Saraceni, Mario. 2003. *The Language of Comics.* Intertext. New York: Routledge.

Schine Gold, Penny. 2004. *Making the Bible Modern: Children's Bibles and Jewish Education in Twentieth-Century America.* Ithaca: Cornell University Press.

Smith, Brendan Powell. 2003. *The Brick Testament: Stories from the Book of Genesis.* Philadelphia: Quirk.

———. 2004a. *The Brick Testament: The Story of Christmas.* Philadelphia: Quirk.

———. 2004b. *The Brick Testament: The Ten Commandments.* Philadelphia: Quirk.

Suggs, Rob. 1997. *The Comic Book Bible.* Uhrichsville: Barbour.

Venuti, Lawrence. 1995. *The Translator's Invisibility: A History of Translation.* Translation Studies. New York: Routledge.

Westermann, Claus. 1984. *Genesis 1–11: A Commentary.* Translated by John J. Scullion. Minneapolis: Augsburg.

Williams, Alan. 2004. "New Approaches to the Problem of Translation in the Study of Religion." Pages 13–44 in *Textual, Comparative, Sociological, and Cognitive Approaches.* Edited by Peter Antes, Armin W. Geertz, and Randi R. Warne. New Approaches to the Study of Religion 2. New York: de Gruyter.

Samson's Hair and Delilah's Despair: Reanimating Judges 16 for Children

Caroline Vander Stichele

At the end of her essay on Bible films based on Gen 1–3 for Western children, Athalya Brenner notes that "popular culture can be used as an ally rather than mourned as an aberration. We'd better get involved in it if we want biblical studies to survive in higher education, beyond seminaries and religious institutions" (2006, 34). Her perception, it seems, is still valid, not least because popular culture as an object of scholarly work is often not taken seriously in the academy and even less so is material designed for children.[1]

In this essay I want to focus on another popular biblical story that has come out in animated form for children more than once: the story of Samson and his dealings with a woman called Delilah (Judg 13–16). The animated films I discuss in what follows are *Samson and Delilah* (2004; ca. 50 min.), which appeared in the series Greatest Heroes and Legends of the Bible hosted by Charlton Heston, and *Samson and the Philistines* (2009; ca. 22 min.) on the DVD entitled *The Judges* in the series The Old Testament Bible Stories for Children (produced by Under God's Rainbow). In my analysis of these animation films I focus on the elements that portray Delilah as Samson's other and the way these elements, more specifically her gender, ethnic and social identity, and class function in the different retellings of the story. In the second part of my essay, I compare these

---

1. That the scope of biblical studies needs to be broadened beyond a narrow historical-critical orientation in order to address reception history at large is also advocated by John Lyons (2010). In his perception, too, the viability of the discipline is at stake. Although Lyons envisions New Testament studies in the first place, his diagnosis applies to the discipline at large, at least in Western Europe.

retellings with the underlying biblical story as well as with other interpretations thereof.

Although the biblical text and its interpretation serve as point of reference in my discussion of this material, my aim is not to determine to what extent these films are somehow faithful to the biblical text, but rather to explore the interpretative possibilities presented in these cultural appropriations of the story. Compared to written media, such as children's Bibles, animation opens up new possibilities in adding movement, action, and sound to an otherwise still and silent medium.[2] As a result, animation operates at the intersection of textual and visual media. On the one hand, textual pretexts inform these retellings, from the Bible itself to its interpretations and from children's literature in general to children's Bibles in particular. On the other hand, animation films also relate and hark back to visual predecessors, both static, such as paintings, and dynamic, in this case feature films. Since it is impossible to discuss all these elements in one single essay, I will use these two animated films as case studies and refer to other media when relevant to my point against the background of these wider issues.

With the advent of modern media, such as radio, film, and television, new possibilities emerged of bringing the biblical stories back to life. In her book *The Bible for Children*, Ruth Bottigheimer mentions how E. R. Appleton's 1932 after-tea Bible story broadcasts on the BBC were advertised as telling "the old Bible stories in such a manner that they come right home to the child listener in a form so very dramatic and picturesque that they will never be forgotten" (1996, 55). Similarly, *The Old Testament Bible Stories for Children* advertises that "the Bible comes alive in this delightful animated series."[3] The question can, however, be raised whether the increased sophistication of these new media also applies to the message delivered, or if old wine is simply served in new skins. A close analysis of the material under discussion can provide at least a partial answer to that question.

---

2. To a certain extent comic strips also display features of both. See the essay by Rubén Dupertuis in this volume.

3. Back cover of *The Judges* DVD (2009), one of twelve DVDs from Under God's Rainbow, a division of Allegro Corporation.

Reanimating Samson and Delilah

Greatest Heroes

The Greatest Heroes version (GH), called *Samson and Delilah*, in fact covers the whole story in Judg 13–16, starting with the announcement of Samson's birth until his death. This retelling of the story is introduced by Charlton Heston, who in turn introduces two animated characters, Simon and his camel, serving as guides throughout the story.

In this retelling it is made explicit that Samson's unusual strength has been there from the very beginning. More specifically his hair is identified as the source of his strength, and therefore it should never be cut. The grown-up Samson has dark, long hair, bound in seven locks. He is a muscular man, with the features of a bodybuilder and strong facial features. He is also gendered as a straight heterosexual male. Not only is he "especially popular with young women" (09:14), but he himself also shows an interest in women, as becomes clear from both his attraction and marriage to a pretty Philistine woman (09:43–22:23) and his visiting a "woman of the night" in Gaza (31:34–40).

If his masculinity is undisputed, so is his ethnicity. He becomes the anointed leader of the Israelites and, after his ill-fated wedding, fiercely opposes the Philistines as his people's enemies and oppressors. They, in turn, call him a "poor Danite" and treat him as a lower-class person. This difference in class and status is further visualized in that Samson appears barefooted, while the Philistine soldiers wear sandals.

Samson's encounter with Delilah takes place in what is called "the Philistine valley of Sorek," where he catches the thief who stole her money (32:00–33:54). Delilah is explicitly identified as a Philistine woman. She is a village girl who lives on her own. The money stolen from her represents her whole fortune, thus suggesting that she is rather poor. She is, however, an attractive young woman, with blondish, long hair and large, almond-shaped, brown eyes. She appears in a more favorable light than Samson's unfortunate wife and the woman of the night from Gaza, who have similar facial features and long, red hair. As a result they look more seductive. As Brenner notes in her analysis of the animated creation stories, red hair often marks women as temptresses and is a recurrent element in the depiction of Eve (2006, 17, 29). In contrast, Delilah looks more innocent. That she is dressed similarly to the woman of the night may, however, suggest that she is in the same profession. Both are wearing a top with a skirt and a scarf, leaving their belly naked, while the other women appearing in the story wear dresses.

Samson falls in love with Delilah, which does not go unnoticed. Appealing to her loyalty for her people, the Philistine soldiers urge Delilah to find out what makes him weak. Initially she resists, but gives in when promised a reward (34:03–45). After three failed attempts (with bow strings, new ropes, and a loom), she finally persuades Samson to tell her his secret (34:46–38:35). In this scene, Samson is portrayed as totally unsuspicious in his love for Delilah, while she appears caught in the middle between her feelings for him and the pressure put on her by the Philistines to deliver him into their hands. When Samson finally tells her his secret, Delilah at first stops him by covering his mouth with her hand and tears up. When the Philistines come in to shave his head, she sighs and whispers, "Dear Samson, will you ever forgive me?" She bursts into tears when the barber starts cutting his hair and falls on her knees when Samson wakes up powerless, exclaiming, "Samson, I had to tell them. I'm so sorry!"[4] Moreover, when she receives her reward from the Philistine commander, she throws it back at him (38:52–41:25).

Delilah makes one more appearance later in the story, when Samson is brought into the Philistine temple. There she expresses her regret at what has happened to him: "If I had known you would torture and humiliate him, I would never have done it!" She is also there when the temple collapses, but it is unclear what happens to her, whether she survives or dies. However, since the last two close-ups are first of her and then of Samson, the suggestion is that she also died (43:15–46:12).

As far as the representation of Delilah in this retelling is concerned, she is shown to care for Samson, but is put under pressure by the Philistine soldiers to find out his secret. The big sum of money promised to her as a reward is clearly attractive to her as she gazes at the money offered to her in a purse similar to the one that was stolen from her but much larger. In return she asks them not to hurt him. After three failed attempts, she is urged by the military leader of the Philistines to use her "*womanly powers of persuasion*" because "*your people* are depending on you." Both her gender and ethnic identity are foregrounded here, but function differently in that her ethnicity relates her to the Philistine soldiers, while her

---

4. The barber is not explicitly identified as such. He is, however, a distinct character from the soldiers who escort him, because he is dressed differently, carries the knife, and shaves off Samson's hair.

gender sets her apart. In the same vein, the Philistine king praises her later at the temple, saying: "You accomplished something that even a thousand armed men couldn't. Enjoy the moment. It's yours!" After the Philistines have captured Samson, Delilah is told that she served her country well, a remark that again stresses her ethnic identity as a Philistine. This identity is not made visual in other ways, although some Philistines appear to have a slightly darker skin, while none of the Israelites do.

To this animated retelling of the biblical story, layers of interpretation are added by Heston in his introduction to the film and by the animated narrator, Simon, who appears in the story itself. Heston's introduction is situated in a room featuring bookshelves, antiques, rugs, and an ancient globe, suggesting a learned environment. The camera moves from the globe to an old book in black leather named *The Holy Bible* and from there to a book on the shelves entitled *Samson and Delilah*, before focusing on Heston himself, who takes the book from the shelf and addresses the viewers.

According to Heston, the story of Samson and Delilah is "a story of love and betrayal, failure and triumph, and ultimately a reminder that all men, no matter how great, can be brought down by their own flaws" (00:34–44). In his summary of the story Heston identifies the love in question as that of Samson and the betrayal as Delilah's, since only Samson is said to fall in love twice, while no emotions toward Samson are mentioned in the case of Delilah. To the contrary, the suggestion is that she is rather cold and calculating. As Heston puts it: "Sensing that *she can be bought off,* the Philistines tell her that they will pay her dearly if she can uncover the secret of Samson's strength and reveal it to them. She *readily agrees* to try and after three failed attempts she is successful.... Later that night, when Samson falls asleep, Delilah *informs* the Philistines of her discovery and they promptly shave his head" (02:34–03:03, emphasis added).

As appears from these quotes, Heston's introduction already offers a particular reading framing the animated film that follows. As a result, (adult) viewers are more likely to interpret the film in that light, because the introduction is directed in the first place at them, the child's parents or caretakers, who would also be aware that Charlton Heston played Moses in Cecil B. DeMille's *The Ten Commandments* (1956). Heston also features prominently on the cover of the DVD, which advertises the series as "hosted by Charlton Heston," clearly targeting the adult audience that is supposed to buy the DVD. Apart from this commercial interest, that Heston lends his aura to this production also authorizes his summary of the story and the retelling that follows.

Heston in turn introduces Simon, the animated narrator of the story. This boy not only appears in the story itself, but his narrating, and sometimes even singing, also interprets the different actions and characters involved. Simon, for instance, explains that although he became a judge in Israel, Samson "still took time to seek out pleasure with the women" (31:12–20) and that "Samson quickly fell in love with Delilah, but Delilah had *other things* on her mind" (34:47–53). This statement again rules out a love interest from her side. Moreover, after Delilah finds out Samson's secret, Simon sings: "He fell fast asleep with his head in her lap, like a child without a care, but when he passed out, Delilah made a shout: 'Come on in boys and get rid of his hair!' " (38:37–46).

On the one hand, Simon's interpretation of the characters thus confirms the reading already offered by Heston, of Samson as victim and Delilah as perpetrator, but on the other hand it also creates a tension with the presentation of Delilah within the story itself, as both her own words and facial expression show her affection for Samson. She, for instance, confesses to the leader of the Philistines: "It's not like I don't like him." Moreover, in the end, she refuses the reward offered to her and throws it back, a gesture that is actually contradicted by Simon's comment that "Delilah took the gold and the soldiers took his locks" (41:30–34).

As a result, in the narrative itself Delilah appears as a more complex character than suggested by both Heston and Simon. Her loyalties are divided between Samson and the Philistines, and in the end she shows regret at what she has done. Nevertheless, she dies when Samson destroys the Philistine temple.

UNDER GOD'S RAINBOW

The second portrait of Samson and Delilah appears on a DVD entitled *The Judges*. This animated film includes three stories from Judges: "Deborah and Gideon," "Samson and the Philistines," and "Samuel: A King for Israel." The story about Samson is about twenty-two minutes long, roughly half the length of the GH version, but equally covers Samson's whole life as told in Judg 13–16. The part that deals with Delilah is about eight minutes long, compared to sixteen minutes in the GH film, which is proportionately slightly longer.

In this animation film, Samson meets Delilah at a well in the valley of Sorek and asks her for some water to drink. Then he inquires who she is and tells her how beautiful she is and that her eyes are wonderful. She replies that she is a Philistine and invites him into her father's house. Samson falls in love with Delilah and stays with her for some time (11:55–12:55). Again, this does not go unnoticed. Delilah is approached by friends of her father, later identified as lords of the Philistines, who tell her to seduce Samson and find out his secret. Delilah objects that Samson will never disclose his secret to her, but they threaten her, saying that she will lose her father if she refuses. They promise her a reward of eleven hundred silver pieces if she finds out the secret of Samson's strength (12:56–13:57). Delilah tries desperately, but Samson makes fun of her. Finally, she reproaches him that he jealously protects his secret like a child, after which he discloses that his strength is in his hair (13:58–14:52).

Once Samson has fallen asleep, Delilah cuts off his hair with a huge knife and calls for the Philistines, who blind him and take him away to the prison of Gaza, where he is forced to turn the millstone (15:16–16:44). One of the onlookers mocks him, saying: "He was the strongest man in the world, and a woman was enough to reduce him to this?!" (16:54–58). When Samson is brought to the temple of the Philistines, Delilah goes up to him and asks: "Do you recognize my voice, Samson?" But he rejects her, saying: "Delilah, yours is the voice of sin and betrayal." She replies: "I'm no longer afraid of you, Samson. Today it's your turn to be afraid because you will be sacrificed to our God," to which he answers: "Don't exult in your victory, Delilah. Look at my hair. It grew back!" (19:40–20:15). He goes up to a pillar and pushes until the whole building collapses and covers everyone in it. Samson's body is taken back home by his people, and, although no word is said about Delilah's fate, the suggestion is that she died in the temple too.

In this animated film both Samson and Delilah are depicted as adults. Samson is good looking and muscular. He has sleek, dark, long hair, with twelve locks as a mark of his consecration to God, and brown eyes.[5] Delilah equally has dark hair, but blue eyes. His tan is darker than that of Delilah's and most of the other characters in the story. Still, although there are some varieties in skin color with the other characters, all are basically white people. No clear ethnic distinction is made between Israelites and Philistines. Variety in color of hair exists, but denotes age rather than ethnic identity.

---

5. The number twelve is at odds with the "seven locks" mentioned in Judg 16:19.

From their first encounter Samson and Delilah's different ethnic identity is stressed. She identifies herself as Philistine, while Samson explicitly relates his ethnic identity to his religious identity: "I'm an Israeli and I'm faithful to my God" (12:34–37). This statement is relevant against the background of what is mentioned by the narrator (male voice) at the beginning of the film: Jehovah is punishing his people by giving them in the hands of their enemies because they abandoned the way of their fathers in worshiping other deities. Samson, to the contrary, is portrayed as sticking to the faith of his fathers. In a dialogue with his parents about the Philistine woman he wants to marry, his father objects: "But she's a Philistine. She worships gods of stone. She's different from us," to which Samson replies: "She'll learn to worship the true God, I'm sure" (04:50–55).

As for Delilah, it can be noted that although she says that she lives in her father's house, no family members are ever shown. This is also the case with her attempts to find out Samson's secret. It is just stated in general that Delilah used every possible means to discover his secret. She is whining and sobbing to put pressure on him. No positive emotions are expressed by Delilah. She is absent when he is taken away and shows no regret at what she has done. When Samson is captured, he calls for Delilah, but one of the soldiers tells him: "It's useless calling her. Delilah betrayed you, Samson" (15:46–50). However, she shows up again later in the Philistine temple, stating that the roles are now reversed. Again, she explicitly identifies herself as Philistine as she refers to Dagon as "our God."

Apart from Delilah, Samson's bride is the only other Philistine woman mentioned in this retelling. She, too, is put under pressure, in this case by her father, who forces her to explain Samson's riddle to the guests. Afterward she tells some other women at the party: "And so I revealed the solution" and laughs (07:30–45). As a result, both Samson's bride and Delilah are ambiguous characters. On the one hand, their actions are explained and excused to the extent that they are put under pressure from outsiders, but on the other hand they show no regret at what they were forced to do. They appear callous, as they show no concern for the consequences of their acts for Samson. Delilah even ends up making fun of him at the temple. Another feature that Samson's bride and Delilah have in common is that they are dressed similarly. Moreover, as with most of the women explicitly identified as Philistine, they cover their heads. This marker of identity is clearly gendered, as no specific dress code exists that makes it possible to identify the Philistine men in the story except for the Philistine soldiers.

Overall, the portrayal of Delilah in this animated film is less sympathetic than in the GH version. However, in order to get a better sense of similarities and differences between these portrayals, in what follows I compare the two.

A Comparative Reading

Although the depiction of Samson is largely the same in both animated films, he appears as less of a womanizer in the Under God's Rainbow version (UGR). Also, his visit to a prostitute in Gaza is left out. When it comes to Delilah, he takes more offense at her insisting on knowing his secret than in the GH version, where he takes it more lightly. Their relationship is also less affectionate. Samson is not lying on her lap and Delilah is not showing any remorse at what she has done. She also appears more domesticated than in the GH version, in part because she does not live alone but in her father's house and because she serves Samson water at the well and later wine. The most important difference between both animated films, however, is that Delilah herself cuts Samson's hair with a big knife in UGR, rather than a barber doing it as in GH. As a result, she plays a more active role in Samson's demise.

Nevertheless, the two Delilahs also have much in common. Both are pretty village girls, dressed in pink, who give in to the pressure to collaborate in exchange for a reward. In both cases, Delilah is identified as a Philistine woman, and loyalty to her people plays a role in the way she acts toward Samson. Her loyalties are, however, more divided in GH than in UGR, and she is less directly involved in Samson's demise insofar as his hair is cut by a barber rather than by herself. As a result, the relationship between Samson and Delilah appears more antagonistic in UGR than in the GH version. Ethnic differences are played up by linking them more explicitly with religious differences and contrasting Jehovah, the god of Israel, with the gods of the Philistines.

Both Samson and Delilah appear more domesticated in UGR, as Samson does not have a weakness for women and Delilah is safely located in her father's house, rather than living on her own. By consequence, gender roles appear to be more traditional in UGR than in GH, where Delilah's social status is more of an issue, as she lives on her own and supposedly makes her own living, although it is never made explicit how. She tells Samson that the money stolen from her is her whole fortune, a motif that explains why the reward promised by the Philistines appears so attractive to her. However, no specific amount is mentioned as is the case in the UGR version, where she is offered eleven hundred silver pieces.

Delilah gets her reward in GH only after delivering Samson into their hands, but at that point she no longer wants the money. Instead, she throws it back and shouts: "I don't want your blood money!" This response builds a link with the betrayal of Judas, who is portrayed in the Gospel of Matthew as equally regretting what he has done to Jesus and bringing back the thirty pieces of silver he received from the chief priests and the elders: "But they said, 'What is that to us? See to it yourself.' Throwing down the pieces of silver in the temple, he departed; and he went and hanged himself. But the chief priests, taking the pieces of silver, said, 'It is not lawful to put them into the treasury, since they are blood money'" (Matt 27:4–6 NRSV).

Delilah thus combines the gesture of Judas, in throwing down the money, with the words of the chief priests in calling it "blood money." As a result, Samson is indirectly identified with the betrayed Jesus and Delilah with Judas, as his betrayer. The comparison with Judas is itself not original. It was, for instance, also made by Erasmus, who compared Delilah with Joab and Judas because all of them used their tongue for evil purposes (Gunn 2005, 212). Moreover, as Exum points out, what Delilah and Judas have in common is that their very names have come to signify betrayal as well as their doing it for money (1996, 176).

An intertextual link is also established in the UGR version, but with a different type of story. In this film, Samson meets Delilah at a well and asks her: "Excuse me, I'm thirsty. Will you give me some water?" This line sounds very similar to the request of Abraham's servant addressed at Rebekah in Gen 24:17: "Please let me sip a little water from your jar" (NRSV), but also to that of Jesus in John 4:7: "A Samaritan woman came to draw water, and Jesus said to her, 'Give me a drink'" (NRSV). At this point, gendered, ethnic, and religious differences intersect in a way very similar to that between Jesus and the Samaritan woman. Adult viewers who are familiar with these biblical stories may pick up such intertextual connections, but it is unlikely that children will. In addition, both links reveal a decidedly Christian interest, as Samson is effectively identified with Jesus and Delilah with either Judas or the Samaritan woman. No need to say that the first comparison does not exactly work in her favor.

Far from being a one-way process, elements that relate to the visual elaboration of the story, such as its depiction of characters and scenes on the one hand, and elements from textual elaborations, such as commentaries and retellings on the other hand, intersect. This is also the case in these animations, insofar as they reflect interpretations of the story that occur in textual and/or visual media. By analyzing the similarities and differences in the interpretative choices made between these two films and comparing them with other material, I seek to determine in what follows to what extent they confirm or subvert traditional interpretations. I discuss in more detail the interpretative choices that are made in the animated films in order to determine how Delilah is otherized. First, I examine how gaps in the biblical story are filled and ambiguities in the text resolved. Next, I situate the interpretative choices made in these animated films against the background of the biblical story's reception history, including its cultural appropriation in art and popular media, especially film.

DEALING WITH DELILAH

The first major gap we encounter in the biblical story, and a very important one at that, relates to Delilah's identity. In the biblical story the only information given is that she lives in the valley of Sorek (Judg 16:4), a rather vague indication of the area where she should be situated. It is a problem that interpreters often seek to resolve by specifying Delilah's ethnic identity. Thus, in both animation films Delilah is situated in this valley, but further identified as Philistine. This specification is highly relevant, as it allies Delilah with the enemies of Samson and his people and thus firmly locks her in the position of ethnic other. To identify her as Philistine also consolidates a long-standing tradition and ultimately contributes to a negative evaluation of Delilah's role in the story.[6]

Earlier dramatic portrayals of Delilah as Philistine can, for instance, be found in Camille Saint-Saëns's opera *Samson et Dalila* (1876), where she is a Philistine priestess, and in DeMille's film *Samson and Delilah* (1949), where she happens to be the sister of his Philistine bride. In the film *Samson and Delilah*, directed by Lee Philips (1984), she is identified with the (often equally presumed Philistine) prostitute from Gaza, and in Nicolas Roeg's 1996 version of the story, she is the cousin of the Philistine

---

6. Delilah is most often considered to be either Philistine or Israelite. Arguments for both options are given by Exum 1996, 184–85. See also Klein 1993, 62–66, who is in favor of a Philistine identity, and Amit 2002, for arguments in favor of identifying Delilah as Israelite. Other possibilities are ruled out in the process, notwithstanding that other groups are mentioned elsewhere in Judges. For the way in which the narrative casts the opponents of Israel in the role of the other, see Kim 2007.

King Hanun. In all these cases her being a Philistine is essential for the further development of the plot.

Apart from being a Philistine, Delilah is often also identified as a prostitute. According to Susan Ackerman "Delilah, in her role as Samson's mistress, is depicted in the text as very prostitute-like in her behavior" (1998, 231). Ackerman points to the similarities between Delilah, Tamar, and Rahab in that these women use sex to secure their own destiny. This is at most suggested in the first animation film but totally absent in the second. To identify Delilah as a prostitute is, however, a dominant interpretation in both textual and visual material (Gunn 2005, 212–17; Exum 1996, 184–96).[7]

That this view is not reproduced in these animated films may be less motivated by there being no substantial evidence for this identification in the biblical text than by the target audience being children. The second film goes even further in also leaving out Samson's visit to a prostitute. Such forms of censorship are, of course, by no means new. What Bottigheimer observes with respect to German Protestant children's Bibles from the eighteenth century may well apply here too: "What authors believed unsuitable for children's eyes was silently excised, especially within Old Testament stories" (1996, 41).[8]

The contrast with the feature films could hardly be greater here. DeMille's Delilah (played by Hedy Lamarr) may not be a prostitute, but she is a femme fatale. Turning her back to Samson after delivering him into the hands of the Philistines, she coldly declares: "No one leaves Delilah." In Philips's version, Delilah (played by Belinda Bauer) is a wealthy courtesan who does not accept that Samson wants to leave her for his people. These women don't take no for an answer, and they use their beauty and sex appeal to prevent Samson from going away. Roeg's film presents us with a different Delilah (played by Elizabeth Hurley) insofar as she is used by the Philistines as the bait to catch Samson, although she willingly obliges: "I am proud to serve my people in return for financial consideration." In all

---

7. In a later article Ackerman compares Delilah instead with two other women warriors, Jael and Judith, the major difference being that Delilah sells out to the enemy, rather than the other way around as in the case of Jael and Judith (2000). An alternative interpretation to identifying Delilah as a prostitute is to identify her as Samson's wife; see Amit 2002, 62–64.

8. See also the analysis of Dutch educational material, including children's and family Bibles, in Houtman and Spronk 2004, 108–32.

three cases, Delilah's fatal attraction is a major feature of her character, and Samson is the one who can't resist her charms.[9]

A further aspect of Delilah's identity that remains unclear in the biblical story concerns her social status. In the first animated film Delilah is depicted as a rather poor woman who lives on her own. In the second film she still lives in her father's house. In both cases, however, she appears as a village girl of rather modest means and as such is far removed from the glamorous incarnations in all three feature films. As already noted, in the first animation film Delilah appears in an outfit similar to that of the prostitute in Gaza. This outfit, which leaves arms and belly bare, is orientalizing and reminiscent more specifically of the outfit Delilah wears when she first meets Samson in DeMille's version.[10] Her outfits in the other feature films are hardly less orientalizing.

In the biblical story it remains unclear what Delilah's feelings for Samson are. Although it is explicitly stated that Samson fell in love with Delilah (Judg 16:4), no information is given about her feelings for him, thus leaving ample room for speculation about the motives for her actions. Most interpreters tend to attribute negative motives to her, such as greed, patriotism (when she is identified as Philistine), and carnality (Gunn 2005, 211–17). Some, however, point to her economic status as an independent woman who has to provide for herself. Thus Danna Nolan Fewell draws a parallel between Delilah and the prostitute in Gaza, mentioned a few verses earlier, who "uses her sexuality as a means of feeding and clothing herself" (1992, 74; also Ackerman 1998, 231).

At this point the animated films draw different pictures of Delilah. In the GH version she is emotionally involved, although her loyalties are divided between Samson and the Philistines. In UGR she is more distant and even tells him later in the temple that she is no longer "afraid" of him. In both animations, however, she is put under pressure by her Philistine countrymen and even threatened, elements that are absent from the biblical story. The result is that Delilah is excused for her action, because what she did was not an act of free will, but that interpretation also reduces her to an instrument of the Philistines and puts her in a position of depen-

---

9. For a more detailed comparison between DeMille's and Roeg's versions, see Exum 2002 and Houtman and Spronk 2004, 228–46.

10. See also the outfit of dancers from the early twentieth century, which was heavily influenced by the orientalism of that time period and inspired by Western representations of belly dancers (see Buonaventura 1994, 117–46).

dence rather than independence. Again, there is a clear contrast here with the feature films, in which Delilah has a will of her own, even if more so in DeMille and Philips, where she herself offers to deliver Samson into their hands, than in Roeg, where she is "hired" for her services.

In the GH animation Delilah's emotional involvement with Samson is most apparent in the scene where Samson tells her his secret. At the moment he wants to disclose what the source of his strength is, Delilah covers his mouth and says, "Ssshh … in a moment … let me look at you a little longer." A remarkable parallel to this scene can be found in DeMille's film, where Delilah equally covers Samson's mouth and says: "No, Samson, no! I don't want to be armed with a weapon to destroy you." The lines may be different, but the dramatic gesture is the same, as well as the emotional involvement of both Delilahs, even though the animated version is no match for the range of emotions displayed in DeMille's version. The motive of revenge that drives Delilah in the versions of both DeMille and Saint-Saëns, for instance, is totally absent in the GH animation film.[11]

In both the GH animation and DeMille's film Delilah tells the Philistines that she does not want him to be hurt. When she agrees to deliver him into their hands Delilah tells the soldiers in the animation film: "All right, but promise not to hurt him and let him go if you're wrong." In DeMille's version Delilah tells the commander before she leaves: "No drop of his blood shall be shed. No blade shall touch his skin." In this case the promise is kept quite literally, in that indeed no blood is spilled and his skin remains intact when Samson's eyes are burned out. In both cases Delilah shows remorse when she finds out what happened to Samson. In the animated film she tells the Philistine king at the temple: "If I had known you would torture and humiliate him, I would never have done it." In both DeMille's and Philips's version, Delilah is devastated when she finds out that Samson has been blinded. She visits him in prison and expresses her love for him. Roeg's Delilah is present when Samson is blinded. Here too, his eyes are burned out, but Delilah shows no regret.

Apart from these gaps in the story, an important ambiguity in the biblical text relates to who does the actual cutting of Samson's hair, Delilah herself or someone else. The NRSV suggests that "a man" cut Samson's hair:

---

11. For a discussion of Delilah's depiction in Saint-Saëns's opera, see Clanton 2009, 65–78, as well as Houtman and Spronk 2004, 171–216 for a discussion of this and other operas and oratorios devoted to this story and 217–27 in the same volume for a discussion of Samson and Delilah's representation in popular music.

"She let him fall asleep on her lap; and she called a man, and had him shave off the seven locks of his head" (Judg 16:19). The Hebrew text does indeed mention a man (*ish*), but the following verb is in the third-person singular feminine, indicating that Delilah herself is the one who does the shaving. Who the man is, however, remains unclear. According to Boling, Delilah called a man to bring her a razor and maybe to help her in shaving Samson's head (1975, 250), while Sasson suggests that Samson himself is the man in question and that Delilah calls him in order to check if he is indeed asleep (1988, 336–38; Exum 1996, 183).

That the man may be a barber is suggested by both the Septuagint[A] and the Vulgate translation, which identify the man as such (*koureus* and *tonsor*, respectively; Septuagint[B] has *anēr*). As a result, the text has often been interpreted this way. This reading turns Delilah into more of a passive witness than an active executor of Samson's shaving. The interpretation of Delilah as witness is also reflected in numerous depictions of this scene and is also followed in the GH animation.[12]

In the UGR animation, however, Delilah herself cuts Samson's hair with a big knife. This interpretation is also well represented in visual representations of this scene.[13] In both DeMille's and Philips's films Delilah cuts Samson's hair after he falls asleep because she has put drugs into his wine to prevent him from leaving.[14] Roeg differs from both the biblical

---

12. See, for instance, the illustrations discussed by Gunn (2005, 216–19) and the painting *Samson and Delilah* by Peter Paul Rubens (ca. 1609–10) discussed by Exum 1996, 192–93. Other examples are paintings by Francesco Morone (ca. 1500–1525), Sir Anthony Van Dijck (ca. 1618–1620), Rembrandt Harmenszoon Van Rijn (1628), in which a man arrives carrying a pair of scissors, and Jan Lievens (ca. 1630), in which Delilah hands a pair of scissors to a man, who makes a gesture with his hand as if he refuses to do the job. The gesture mirrors the other hand of Delilah, which is held up in similar fashion. In this painting it is unclear who will do the cutting. They both seem unwilling to do so. The painting thus opens up the possibility of an alternative interpretation of the text in which Delilah called a man to do the cutting, but he refused, so that she had to do the cutting herself. Some of these (and more) illustrations can be found on online at http://www.biblical-art.com/index.htm.

13. See Gunn 2005, 217–21. Paintings entitled *Samson and Delilah* in which Delilah does the cutting were made, e.g., by Lucas Cranach the Elder (ca. 1529–1530), Andrea Mantegna (ca. 1505), Gerrit van Honthorst (1615), Pompeo Girolamo Batoni (1766), Oscar Pereira da Silva (1893), and Max Lieberman (ca. 1902; cf. Dijkstra 1986, 374). For a detailed discussion of Mantegna's painting, see Hunt 2006.

14. That Samson fell asleep because Delilah made him drink too much wine was

story and other interpretations in that Delilah viciously cuts Samson's hair when he wakes up.

After this dramatic event, Delilah disappears from the biblical story, but not from the films. In the GH animation, Delilah is present when Samson is taken captive by the soldiers, and she is still there when his eyes are put out. This is not the case in the UGR version, where she is gone when Samson wakes up and is seized by the soldiers.[15] The actual putting out of his eyes is not shown, but suggested. The biblical story does not give any details about the way this is done. In the GH version, the Philistine leader lashes out at him with his fingers, saying: "I don't want him to ever see a beautiful woman again." In the UGR film, one of the soldiers uses a knife.

In all three feature films Samson's eyes are burned out. DeMille may well have set the example here. In his film the Philistine commander tells Samson when Delilah walks out: "Look at her, Samson. Look well. Remember her beauty. Never forget her treachery. Burn her image in your memory, Samson. She's the last thing you'll ever see." In Roeg's film, Delilah is present when his eyes are put out. This scenario is rarely represented in Bible illustrations (Gunn 2005, 215). A notable example of this scene is the painting by Rembrandt (1636), where a soldier puts out one of Samson's eyes with a knife, while Delilah flees from what looks like a cave, holding his hair in one of her hands.[16]

The Bible is also silent when it comes to Delilah's presence later in the temple, but in both animation films, as well as in the feature films, she appears to be there. In the GH film, Delilah is seated on the floor at the feet of the Philistine king. In the UGR film, she is standing with the audience and walks up to Samson to address him. In both cases she literally sides with the Philistines, although she expresses her regret at what has happened to him in the GH version, but mocks him in the UGR version. In both cases the suggestion is that she dies when the temple collapses.

---

already suggested by Pseudo-Philo, *Liber Antiquitatum Biblicarum* 43.6; see Houtman and Spronk 2004, 119.

15. Examples of paintings where Delilah is present when Samson is taken captive are *Il Guercino* (Giovani Francesco Barbieri), *Samson Captured by the Philistines* (1619), and *Samson* (Solomon Joseph Solomon; ca. 1886; see discussion in Exum 1996, 194–96).

16. See further Bal's discussion of this painting (1991, 331–46). Less known is the painting of this scene by Peter Paul Rubens (1609–1610).

In the feature films Delilah also comes to the temple. In both DeMille's and Philips's films she makes her entry with pomp and circumstance. She walks up to Samson and guides him to the columns. In Roeg's version, Samson is brought to the temple at Delilah's request in order to have him displayed. In both DeMille's and Roeg's versions, she dies when the temple collapses. Only Roeg shows explicitly how she is covered by falling stones. Philips has her escape from the temple in time, but she comes back later to recover Samson's body and to bring it back to his people. This is the only case in which Delilah survives.

DIFFERENT DELILAHS?

To conclude, I want to address two questions: what picture(s) of Delilah emerge from the animated films under discussion, and what are the repercussions of these depictions? As I noted before, there are a number of significant similarities in the way Delilah appears in both films, but there are some remarkable differences as well. Many of these are far from original, in that they reflect interpretations that have been around for a long time. That is the case, for instance, with the dominant tradition that identifies Delilah as Philistine. Some differences, however, also reflect ambiguities that originate from the biblical text, such as the identity of the person who cuts Samson's hair. Nevertheless, certain elements that both animations share may rather be informed by the genre and intended audience of these films. It is here, I think, that the comparison with the three feature films is most relevant for our purpose.

One important difference between the animation and feature films is that the latter play up the love interest, while the former play it down. If Delilah is portrayed as a sensual woman with a will of her own in the feature films, she is more of a pretty girl/woman in the animation films instead of one that signals danger. This may not come as a surprise in view of the target audience, but the question remains if that is an improvement. I will come back to this issue.

Another significant similarity between both animated films that sets them apart from the feature films is that Delilah is put under pressure and even threatened by the Philistines to deliver Samson into their hands, while in the feature films she either takes the initiative to deliver Samson (DeMille and Philips) or is more than willing to comply (Roeg). The result is that she appears as more of an instrument than an agent in the plot of the animated films.

A third issue of importance for the evaluation of her character in the animations is one that these films have in common with at least the feature films of DeMille and Roeg: that she too dies when the temple is destroyed. The exception here is Philips's version, where she not only survives but escorts Samson's body home to his people. As a result, this ending casts her in a more positive light.

If feature films are mostly meant to entertain a general audience, the animated films have the additional intention to educate their young viewers as well, at the least in familiarizing them with biblical stories. Some of the lessons they learn, however, may not be intentional at all. I want to come back here to my question at the beginning of this essay: do these films serve old wine in new skins? The answer to that question is yes and no. Old wine, yes, insofar as earlier interpretations are simply reproduced in these films. New wine, too, insofar as Delilah is no longer represented as a femme fatale and thus a dangerous woman, but this may well be a mixed blessing. Normalizing in a way makes her even more dangerous. *Any* woman you (boys) trust can bring you down. It only takes some pressure (from other men) to get her that far. The "good" news, however, is that women like that have no future. When push comes to shove, they will get their just desert. So there is a moral to this story. Normalizing Delilah then is not much of a blessing for girls, the more so if she also loses her agency in the process. In that case, there is little left for women to gain. The feature films hardly represent an alternative here, as Delilah's agency is tied to her female sexuality, thus locating the power of women in their bodies.

Moreover, while mighty Samson is a biblical hero and as such the character that male viewers are most likely and willing to identify with, Delilah is associated with his enemies and as such is firmly cast in the role of the other. In both animated and feature films she is identified as Philistine, but her otherness is also stressed by orientalizing her. This is expressed in the animated films through her clothing, be it in very different ways. In line with the feature films the GH version reproduces stereotypical depictions from the beginning of the twentieth century of oriental women as sensual through the partial display of nudity, while the UGR version does so in exactly the opposite way, by covering their heads and bodies.

In all this, Delilah's gender is far from accidental. It is also key to Samson's downfall. However, maybe the most troubling lesson for both boys and girls to learn from these animated films is that violence is an important feature of such others, be they male or female.[17] Samson is betrayed, shaved, captured, and blinded by Philistines, while Delilah is put under pressure by her own people to deliver him into their hands. Even when she shows regret in the GH animation, in the end she still dies. There is no way to redeem herself. Only Samson can do so.

These animated films then, and others too,[18] do much more than just familiarize children (and adults) with stories from the Bible. As cultural artifacts, they inform us about what biblical stories are considered important for children to know, and what views, values, and interests are communicated through the retelling of these stories. As I have shown, this also includes cultural stereotypes regarding the oriental other and gender stereotypes prevalent in their own culture. From a gender-critical perspective so much is still left wanting that Delilah's despair may easily turn into despair about Delilah. Nonetheless there is hope because, as we have also seen, there are enough gaps in the biblical story to leave room for a different Delilah.[19]

Works Cited

Ackerman, Susan. 1998. *Warrior, Dancer, Seductress, Queen: Women in Judges and Biblical Israel.* New York: Doubleday.

———. 2000. "What If Judges Had Been Written by a Philistine?" *BibInt* 8:33–41.

Amit, Yairah. 2002. "I, Delilah: A Victim of Interpretation." Pages 59–76 in *First Person: Essays in Biblical Autobiography.* Edited by Philip R. Davies. London: Sheffield Academic Press.

Bal, Mieke. 1991. *Reading Rembrandt: Beyond the Word-Image Opposition.* Cambridge: Cambridge University Press.

Boling, Robert G. 1975. *Judges.* AB. Garden City, N.Y.: Doubleday.

Bottigheimer, Ruth. 1996. *The Bible for Children from the Age of Gutenberg to the Present.* New Haven: Yale University Press.

Brenner, Athalya. 2006. "Recreating the Biblical Creation for Western Children: Provisional Reflections on Some Case Studies." Pages 11–34 in *Creation and Creativity: From Genesis to Genetics and Back.* Edited

17. See also the essay by David Gunn in this volume.
18. See further the essay of Susanne Scholz in this volume.
19. See, for instance, Amit 2002.

by Caroline Vander Stichele and Alastair G. Hunter. BMW 9/ASBR 1. Sheffield: Sheffield Phoenix.

Buonaventura, Wendy. 1994. *Serpent of the Nile: Women and Dance in the Arab World*. London: Saqi.

Clanton, Dan W. 2009. *Daring, Disreputable, and Devout: Interpreting the Bible's Women in the Arts and Music*. New York: T&T Clark.

Dijkstra, Bram. 1986. *Idols of Perversity: Fantasies of Feminine Evil in Fin-de-Siècle Culture*. New York: Oxford University Press.

Exum, J. Cheryl. 1996. *Plotted, Shot, and Painted: Cultural Representations of Biblical Women*. JSOTSup 215/GCT 3. Sheffield: Sheffield Academic Press.

———. 2002. "Lethal Woman 2: Reflections on Delilah and Her Incarnation as Liz Hurley." Pages 254–73 in *Borders, Boundaries and the Bible*. Edited by Martin O'Kane. JSOTSup 313. London: Sheffield Academic Press.

Fewell, Danna Nolan. 1992. "Judges." Pages 67–77 in *The Women's Bible Commentary*. Edited by Carol A. Newsom and Sharon H. Ringe. Louisville: Westminster John Knox.

Gunn, David M. 2005. *Judges*. Blackwell Bible Commentaries. Oxford: Blackwell.

Houtman, Cornelis, and Klaas Spronk. 2004. *Ein Held des Glaubens? Rezeptionsgeschichtliche Studien zu den Simson-Erzählungen*. CBET 39. Leuven: Peeters.

Hunt, Patrick. 2006. "Andrea Mantegna's Samson and Delilah." Online: http://traumwerk.stanford.edu/philolog/2006/02/.

Kim, Uriah Y. 2007. "Postcolonial Criticism: Who Is the Other in the Book of Judges?" Pages 161–82 in *Judges and Method: New Approaches in Biblical Studies*. Edited by Gale A. Yee. 2nd ed. Minneapolis: Fortress.

Klein, Lilian R. 1993. "The Book of Judges: Paradigm and Deviation in Images of Women." Pages 55–71 in *A Feminist Companion to the Book of Judges*. Edited by Athalya Brenner. FCB 4. Sheffield: Sheffield Academic Press.

Lyons, John. 2010. "Hope for a Troubled Discipline? Contributions to New Testament Studies from Reception History." *JSNT* 33:207–20.

Sasson, Jack M. 1988. "Who Cut Samson's Hair? (and Other Trifling Issues Raised by Judges 16)." *Prooftexts* 8:333–39.

Responses

CHILDREN'S BIBLES HOT AND COLD

Timothy Beal

This outstanding collection of essays pushes the field forward on many fronts. Especially striking to me is the force with which they move us beyond the history of children's Bibles as a kind of reception history, in which these widely varying works would be treated as interpretive receptions, translations, and abridgments of the (original) Bible, as if there is such a thing. Beyond such an approach, we are compelled to consider children's Bibles as Bibles in and of themselves. They are creations of the biblical in specific cultural contexts.[1] What Michel Foucault said about other subjects of historical research, such as medicine and the state, may also be said of the Bible and the biblical: it is not a given or self-evident intellectual object that is particularized, incarnated in different interpretations through the centuries, but a historically given discursive object, constantly changing as it is made and remade through different cultural productions of meaning (Hunt 1989; O'Brien 1989). Biblical essence is inseparable from biblical particularity as it takes form and effect in particular cultural contexts. Children's Bibles do not receive and interpret the Bible, as though it were a transcendent word to be incarnated in particular cultural-historical moments; they *are* the Bible, whose message, as Marshall McLuhan understood (1994, 8–10), is not simply its literary contents

---

1. It is a double privilege to respond to such an impressive collection of articles when they are dedicated to such an impressive, indeed formidable, scholar, colleague, author, and editor as Athalya Brenner. I am very pleased to have this opportunity to join in honoring her career thus far and to express, at least in a small way, my profound gratitude for her support of my own work, especially when I was just starting out. At my very first Society of Biblical Literature meeting, she invited me to publish my paper on Esther in her *Feminist Companion to Esther, Judith, and Susanna*. That paper grew into my dissertation, which in turn grew into my first book. No doubt many others have similar stories about Professor Brenner's encouragement of their careers.

but also and especially its social effect, what it does to us personally and collectively.

One major effect of the Bible as generated in and by children's Bibles is its contribution to the cultural production of Christian faith as black-and-white certainty and religiosity as right-and-wrong morality. The Bible, as cultural icon of this supposedly childlike faith, is the book of books, the authoritative, authorial, univocal, comprehensive, final, graspable, and readable word of God. God publishes it to answer questions about the meaning and purpose of life, putting them to rest in the name of its divine author. It is the manual and guidebook for finding happiness with God in this world and salvation in the next.

This cultural iconicity of the Bible is pervasive, perhaps especially in the United States, where most children's Bibles and other biblical products are published. According to the Pew Forum on Religion and Public Life, 78 percent of all Americans say that the Bible is the "word of God," and almost half of those believe that, as such, "it is to be taken literally, word for word." Polling data from the Barna Group indicate that nearly half of all Americans agree that "the Bible is totally accurate in all of its teachings" (86 percent of all "born-again" Christians believe the same), and the Gallup Poll finds that 65 percent of all Americans believe that the Bible "answers all or most of the basic questions of life" (Gallup and Simmons 2000).[2] These statements are shorthand descriptions of the idea of the Bible as God's magnum opus, the first and last word on who God is, who we are, why we are here, and where we go after this (and where *they* go, too).

Yet, as David M. Gunn's comprehensive study and analysis of the rhetoric of visual and literary representations of Samson's death in more than one hundred children's Bibles makes especially clear, the biblical circulates through culture and consciousness not in the form of narrative wholes but

---

2. The Pew Forum's 2006 survey report indicates that 35 percent of respondents agree with the statement: "The Bible is the actual word of God and is to be taken literally, word for word"; another 43 percent agree with the statement: "The Bible is the word of God, but not everything in it should be taken literally, word for word." Thus 78 percent understand the Bible as, in some sense, the word of God. Gallup's 2011 polling data correlate closely with the Pew data. On the popular view that "the Bible is totally accurate in all of its teachings," see www.barna.org. On the popular view that it contains "all or most of the basic questions of life," see Gallup and Simmons 2000. This data and its relation to the cultural iconicity of the Bible are discussed in greater detail in Beal 2011, 3–12.

as snippets and fragments that come together to form constellations of so-called biblical values that in turn produce this cultural icon of the Bible with its "binary world of good and bad" and, by extension, self and other. The Bible is not a thing, let alone a text, but a somewhat nebulous idea that integrates itself into this larger, culturally internalized sacred canopy of faith in blessed social cohesion over against any otherness that might threaten it. Much like Peter Berger's description of the social construction of religion as a dialectical process, in which we produce the culture that produces us (1967, 3–4), the Bible is not something historically given, "there" for us to take and read, but a cultural production that produces biblical culture.

Because a children's Bible is often one's first Bible book, these Bibles are indeed especially formative, making profound impressions of the biblical on tender ears and eyes. Indeed, not only might a children's Bible be "a child's first introduction to the biblical text," as Melody Briggs rightly emphasizes; for many who leave the pews and Sunday school rooms behind by early adolescence, it might turn out to be the one and only embodiment of the Bible and biblical values in print form. It is with this power and influence in mind that the essays collected here critically examine some of the ways children's Bibles work to construct a binary moral universe of self and other.

In the process of critical analysis, moreover, these essays often begin to raise a more subversive question: How do, or how might, a children's Bible work against that world, teasing at its cracks and fissures in a way that could begin to undo the otherness of the other, as well as the secure sameness of the self? What potentials are there for children's Bibles to open spaces in which a kind of deconstruction of that binary world can be hosted? In what follows, I would like to unpack this question with an eye not only on what is possible in the medium of the print book during these, its twilight years, but also on what might be possible in a digital networked environment like the Internet.

In a chapter called "Media Hot and Cold" from his 1964 book *Understanding Media*, Marshall McLuhan drew a basic distinction between what he described as "hot" and "cold" media. A hot medium is one of "intensity" or "high definition," which he defined as "the state of being well filled with data." A cold medium, on the other hand, is one of "low definition ... because so little is given and so much has to be filled in" by the hearer, reader, or participant (1994, 22). A photograph, then, is a hot medium, whereas a cartoon is a cool one. A light bulb is a hot medium, whereas a candle is a cool one. A lecture, he writes, is hotter than a seminar, because it is well filled with data and thereby leaves little room for participation. And, at least in his time, the well-filled, high definition audio-visual experience of the movie was hotter than the pixilated mosaic of the television image, which "the eye must act as hand in filling in" (29). "Hot media are, therefore, low in participation, and cool media are high in participation by the audience ... the hot form excludes, and the cool one includes" (23).

Along these lines, the literary medium of a Hebrew biblical narrative of Cain and Abel or Jael would be cool, that is, not well filled in, riddled with gaps, "fraught with background" and "dark and incomplete," as Erich Auerbach famously put it (1953, 18). The parables of Jesus are likewise cool, generating metaphorical tensions that require the reader to engage actively in the process of meaning making and unmaking.

With very few exceptions, children's Bibles are *hottings-up of the biblical*, revising and filling in both literary and visual data in such a way as to remove ambiguities, tensions, and gaps that otherwise leave biblical texts cool and invite participation from their young audiences. In the process, they "reduce the text to a social or educational tool" (Briggs) and "reify contemporary values and morals" (Dupertuis).

There are numerous examples of this kind of hotting-up among the essays collected here. Cynthia Rogers and Danna Nolan Fewell show how children's Bibles play down sexual undertones in the relationship between Jonathan and David—heating up the moral Bible by cooling off the homoerotic tones of their love, we might say. Melody Briggs reveals how most children's Bibles fill out the Lukan boy Jesus, textually and visually, in ways that reduce his rebellious dimensions and make him into a model of youthful obedience, thereby ruling out a child's imaginative participation in his cool complexity. Similarly, Mark Roncace draws our attention to the ways children's Bibles smooth over or harmonize contradictions and tensions in different biblical creation stories and accounts of Jesus's birth, filling in gaps and integrating them into singular narratives that leave no room for the kinds of questions young readers would otherwise inevitably bring to the table. Likewise David M. Gunn's analysis of "the rhetoric ... of texts and pictures" in children's versions of Samson, whose story is notoriously morally cold, especially on account of his vengeful violence and suicide. "Philistines and Samson alike do what they do and say what they say. The narrator wastes no words on evaluative or affective adjectives." Cool stuff. Children's Bibles fill in and hot up their biblical values, supplying clear moral reasoning and clarifying why the Philistine's deserve such violent deaths. Their literary narrations work to alienate biblical readers from the Philistine enemies, accentuating their cruelty while emphasizing the abject suffering of "poor" Samson. At the same time, their visual rhetoric minimizes the number of Philistine victims (often to one or two) and hides or "rescues" innocence by suggesting that some, especially women and children, survived.

Some find instances that interrupt this general tendency to heat up their Bibles morally and work to create a cooler, more participatory Bible, one that might host deconstructions of self and other. Dupertuis's essay on the *Brick Testament* is a wonderful example. And Briggs finds a cooler, more open depiction of the boy Jesus in *Manga Messiah*, a manga Bible published by Tyndale House in collaboration with NEXT, a group of evangelical Japanese manga artists and media-savvy professionals whose aim is to create high-quality, innovative Christian mangas for teens and young adults in many languages.

Another cool example, albeit not explicitly marketed to children, is *Bible Illuminated*, a large-format, glossy art-magazine Bible by a media-savvy Swedish company called Illuminated World, whose aim is "to present traditional things in a non-traditional way" in order to "drive an emotional reaction and get people to think, discuss, and share," and thereby "trigger bigger moral questions" (Beal 2011, 139–40). The first volume in English, ironically titled *The Book: New Testament* (2008) and also available in a free online version (www.bibleilluminated.com), uses the American Bible Society's Good News translation, laid out in four columns per page, without notes or commentary and without verse numbers. Interspersed throughout are visually rich, provocative photographic images whose relations to nearby texts are suggestive yet far from obvious. Sometimes, a nearby biblical passage, highlighted in a yellow box in the main text, will also appear on the same page with the image, like a caption. On a low-angle shot of a young boy pointing a handgun directly at the camera, for example, is this saying of Jesus from Matthew: "Do not think that I have come to bring peace to the world. No I did not come to bring peace, but a sword." Its provocatively ambiguous interplay of word and image "illuminates" in a cool way that undermines the cultural iconicity of the Bible and calls for a reader's imaginative participation.

Now, in the twilight of the media regime of the book and the dawning of digital networked culture, the greater questions concern what possibilities and potentials are opening up, and closing down, for children's Bibles with new media technologies like the Internet. On the one hand, the

Internet has been highly participatory and in that sense a cool medium. The world of blogging, commenting, sharing information (including officially censored information), and the cutting, pasting, and mashing up of digital texts, images, and sounds is a world of creative engagement that can work to blur boundaries, including those of canonical and extracanonical, insider and outside, self and other. On the other hand, the Internet is hot and getting hotter, saturating our lives in high definition, filling our sensory channels of seeing and hearing to the max, and increasingly turning Internet users into consumers rather than collaborative, interactive creators.

In *The Master Switch* (2010), Tim Wu shows how, throughout the twentieth century, every seemingly democratizing media revolution has been followed by corporate takeover, a "master switch" that centralizes and consolidates power and control of information. With the Internet, such mastery is sought by means of vertical integration, gaining control of production of digital information, the network infrastructure on which that information circulates, and the gateways of access to that information. The evangelical Bible business, which is largely responsible for the production of children's Bibles and the biblical values that the essays in this volume critically examine, would love to get hold of that master switch and is aggressively engaging in digital media technologies that will enable it to continue to thrive as producer of the cultural icon of the Bible in the Internet age.

Where does this media-historical horizon situate those of us who want to encourage and empower subversively creative interventions in the cultural production of the biblical? How can we do more than simply apply ideological critiques to biblical consumer products for children once they are already bestsellers? Getting there might call for a revolution in the culture of the academic humanities, itself very much a product of print culture, especially in its promotion of scholars as individual authors of linear article- and book-length texts. That is to say, such interventions might require new kinds of collaboration, not only with other scholars but also with digital artists, designers, and media technicians. I am reminded of scholarly collaborations on massive polyglot Bible projects in the early years of print culture: the six-volume Complutensian Polyglot (1522), for example, which involved numerous scholars and was as much about visual and tactile design, fonts, and layout as it was about translation and textual criticism. Doing scholarship was a matter of media invention, exploring the new potentials introduced by the media technology of the print book.

Indeed, insofar as message and medium are inseparable, we too must move beyond putting content into preformed media, namely print articles and books, to learn new media technologies that might enable heretofore unimagined modes of creative academic intervention and open participation. That would be pretty cool.

WORKS CITED

Auerbach, Erich. 1953. *Mimesis: The Representation of Reality in Western Literature*. Princeton: Princeton University Press.

Beal, Timothy. 2011. *The Rise and Fall of the Bible: The Unexpected History of an Accidental Book*. New York: Houghton Mifflin Harcourt.

Berger, Peter L. 1967. *The Sacred Canopy: Elements of a Sociological Theory of Religion*. New York: Doubleday.

Gallup Poll. 2011. "Religion." Online: http://www.gallup.com/poll/1690/Religion.aspx.

Gallup, Alec, and Wendy W. Simmons. 2000. "Six in Ten Americans Read Bible at Least Occasionally." Online: http://www.gallup.com/poll/2416/Six-Ten-Americans-Read-Bible-Least-Occasionally.aspx.

Hunt, Lynn. 1989. "Introduction: History, Culture, Text." Pages 1–24 in *The New Cultural History*. Edited by Lynn Hunt. Berkeley: University of California Press.

Illuminated World. 2008. *The Book: New Testament*. Sweden: Forlaget.

McLuhan, Marshall. 1994. *Understanding Media: The Extensions of Man*. Cambridge: MIT Press. [orig. 1964]

O'Brien, Patricia. 1989. "Michel Foucault's History of Culture." Pages 25–46 in *The New Cultural History*. Edited by Lynn Hunt. Berkeley: University of California Press.

Pew Forum. 2006. "Many Americans Uneasy with Mix of Religion and Politics." Online: http://pewforum.org/Politics-and-Elections/Many-Americans-Uneasy-with-Mix-of-Religion-and-Politics.aspx.

Wu, Tim. 2010. *The Master Switch: The Rise and Fall of Information Empires*. New York: Knopf.

The Otherness of Children's Bibles
in Historical Perspective

Ruth B. Bottigheimer

Children's Bibles are a simple fact of literary life in today's book market. With lively illustrations and edited stories, they simplify the canonical Bible for young readers. Martin Luther provided a good reason to edit Bible stories before giving them to children when he observed that the Bible makes a fool of the wisest men. A century later, an English Bible editor labeled several Old Testament stories "the hard parts," tacitly acknowledging their ethically and morally problematic nature and implicitly justifying either amending or emending their plots and contents. From the early 1700s onward, teachers and preachers edited Bible stories intrusively and often fundamentally, shifting blame and responsibility in directions more socially acceptable than those in the canonical Bible.

Despite centuries of value-driven, dogma-driven, education-driven, and engagement-driven rewritings, in Melody Briggs's concise conceptualization in her contribution to this volume, and despite the manifest past and present existence of hundreds of children's Bibles, the fact of *editing* stories from the Bible remains a vexing problem, if as was long believed, the canonical Bible was God's own word. Why should children read edited Bible stories rather than the canonical Bible itself? An easy answer is that young, and even adolescent, children are simply unready for the cultural and theological complexities of the Bible's narratives. Hence, it is sensible to offer appropriate assistance. At the simplest level of clarification, educators (whether in church, in school, or at home) explain unfamiliar words to make God's message understandable.

As God became redefined in the course of the eighteenth century as an embodiment of justice and lovingkindness, the unyielding moralities and harsh punishments of some Old Testament stories undermined contemporaneous enlightened church and school teachings. Earlier preachers and theologians had dealt with problematic Bible stories by reading and explaining them not as divine narratives in and of themselves, but as elaborately constructed figurations of greater social, moral, and divine truths. This strategy, devised in the Middle Ages, survived into the 1600s, but by and large, the heavy, convoluted, and virtually unreadable explanations that they bred crushed the stories they were supposed to explain and made them unsuitable for the simplified texts of children's Bibles.

By the 1700s English authors and publishers of Bible stories for children had the gracefully written Bible stories of the Port Royalist educator Nicolas Fontaine readily available in English to provide a template for a children's biblical text that was acceptably close to the canonical biblical text. Consequently, when eighteenth-century educators rewrote the Bible in their own image, they needed only to translate and edit Fontaine's stories to do so. Nonetheless, eighteenth-century editors of Bible stories still had to face inescapable questions that every author and scholar of Bible stories continues to face, questions that inform the essays in this volume: What content should be included in Bible stories as a whole? Nearly every essay touches on this question, but Hugh Pyper addresses it frontally. What details are, or should, be included in individual Bible stories and for what purposes might they be adapted? Archie Chi Chung Lee, Mark Roncace, Susanne Scholz, Jaqueline du Toit, Cynthia Rogers, and Danna Nolan Fewell take on these problematic aspects. How will, and do, children respond to individual stories? Laurel Koepf implicitly addresses this question. How are Bible stories illustrated, and to what extent is their illustration appropriate to the text they are meant to depict? Melody Briggs, Jeremy Punt, and David Gunn explore this question. In what medium do and can Bible stories appear, and how does the choice of medium affect the story that is communicated, whether in text alone, in static image, in moving image, in static Lego constructions, or in the moving images of a DVD or a film? This question surfaces repeatedly, with particular attention paid to theory (Briggs), film (Scholz and Vander Stichele), and Lego (Dupertuis).

Answering the questions in the paragraph above makes it imperative to acknowledge the presence of a notably large elephant in the living room, namely the rationale for the telling of edited Bible stories to children. Responses to *this* question about edited Bible stories resemble the structure of a Russian doll. The outer doll is visible, but unseen within it lies another doll, within which further dolls nest. A first approach to this question ignores the question of editing and focuses instead on the conviction that children growing up in nominally Jewish or Christian environments need to learn about the Holy Bible, because it is a cultural and religious icon. Even the most religiously unobservant parents—those who never attend church, meeting, temple, or synagogue—are likely to accept this cultural premise and to present their young sons and daughters with simple books of Bible stories as birthday or holiday gifts and with successively more complex versions of Bible content as their reading comprehension broadens. Generation after generation, the reasoning in this paragraph has resulted in the production of Bible excerpts for children, some of which are edited narratives, others of which are excerpts from canonical text.

As far as specific Bible content is concerned, most adults in the population at large know that the Ten Commandments prohibit killing and stealing. They also know that after "thou shalt not kill" and "thou shalt not steal," there are directives about respecting God and parents, with prescriptions about neighbors' wives, cows, and sheep following close behind. In discussions following talks for lay audiences, I have observed an overwhelming conviction that Bible stories provide ethical directives for children, and whatever the level of adults' biblical knowledge, they believe that these, and other, biblical rules of conduct are self-evidently valid for everyday life. For centuries, this kind of reasoning has resulted in carefully choosing among stories to be included in Bibles for children.

A sizeable, and different, portion of adherents to the idea that children should read Bible stories believe in the Bible as a revelation of God's salvific will for humanity and as a warning about the horrible consequences that follow inevitably upon contravening or simply not following the divine intentions expressed in the Bible and its stories. For these believers, it is objectively pragmatic to foster a familiarity with Bible content in order to learn how to achieve a guaranteed happy rather than an everlastingly miserable eternity. This reasoning spawned numberless children's Bibles, beginning in the nineteenth century, that consisted only of New Testament material.

Although the salvational aspect of the Bible resides for Christians principally in the New Testament, the Old (and chronologically pre-Jesus) Testament is an unavoidable fact and is moreover God's word, just as surely as is the New Testament. The relationship between the two Testaments has repeatedly been rationalized in Christian terms by understanding the people of the Old Testament as diachronic progenitors of Jesus in the New Testament. Hence the enormous importance from the Middle

Ages onward of the tree of Jesse and the stories about David the earthly king as Jesus's ancestor.

A very different reading of the relationship between Old Testament stories and the Christian New Testament is similarly rooted deep in the medieval period. In this reading, Old Testament figures like David were understood not in terms either of their historical or of their ancestral significance, but were conceptualized as both symbolic and actual pre-figurations of Jesus, an approach that supported a belief that Jesus existed, or inhered, within Old Testament stories. By this token, Adam's striking the head of the serpent that snapped at his heels in the book of Genesis was simultaneously the Old Adam of the Old Testament and the Jesus-the-New-Adam of the New Testament. In narrative terms, the Old Adam suffered from the devil's malice by being expelled from the garden of Eden, while in eschatological terms the New Adam repulsed the devil and gained admittance to the kingdom of heaven for all people. Absent from today's bookstore shelves, children's Bibles that inserted Jesus into the Old Testament have nonetheless been intermittently published in the last five centuries.

The reasons outlined above for Christian children to read Bible stories (I won't pursue either the history or the purposes of Jewish children's Bibles here) can be summarized as follows:

1. Children need to be familiarized with the Bible.
2. Bible stories show children what to do and what not to do.
3. The Bible reveals God's will.
4. Old Testament Bible stories show the preparation for Jesus's coming.
5. Old Testament Bible stories show how Jesus was prefigured within the Old Testament.
6. Old Testament Bible stories show how Jesus was present in the Old Testament.

This list begins with a religiously neutral stance and moves toward religiously determined formulations of reasons for providing Bible stories for children. (That the Bible's stories should be edited before being presented to children has long seemed indisputable.) This list is not exhaustive, nor is it meant to be. It simply illustrates that underlying and possibly unarticulated reasons for exposing young children to Bible stories steer the ways in which those Bible stories have been and will continue to be edited. It also demonstrates the broad historical spectrum on which contemporary children's Bibles take their place. What contemporary children's Bibles exemplify is well and broadly discussed in these essays. What they do *not* exemplify, which is also a defining characteristic, is equally important to understand.

The point at which many essays in this volume interact with the question "For what purposes are Bible stories to be told to children?" is at number two on the list above, with authors' individual analyses searching out alternative understandings for prescribed behavior based on contemporary visions of race, class, religion, gender, and colonialized status. In so doing, the essays' arguments juxtapose mainstream scholarly and lay values, and secular humanist views and religiously Bible-centric ones. In other words, the scholarly views can be as culturally overdetermined as are some of the texts being examined. Once we accept the cultural specificity of historical rewritings of Bible stories, and once we accept the likelihood that the mentality of the present day (as it addresses Bible stories edited for children) will itself inevitably be viewed by future generations as consisting of peculiar preconceptions and assumptions, we can begin to imagine that we, too, share in the cultural contingency of our observations and convictions about the place of Bible stories in children's lives.

Children's Bibles as Books

Let us begin by turning to the simple physical object, a book of Bible stories edited for children. And let us not take the existence of that book for granted, but let us examine the emergence of this cultural artifact. Let us also consider the ways in which children's Bibles fit into categories as different as the Western biblical tradition, European understandings of what constituted "the Bible," and European and American publishing practices. In the contemporary world it seems clear enough that a children's Bible should consist of stories from the Bible. It seems self-evident, because that is a form—and format—with which we are now familiar. But for the first few decades in which "Bibles" were printed for children's eyes, books that had the words "Children's Bible" on their title pages offered a broad variety of instructive texts, some of which included only the Ten Commandments with illustrations that were more or less appropriate for each one.

Children's Bibles emerged, as a genre, from a tidal wave of catechisms. The sixteenth century was inundated by "short," "long," "new," "revised," and "improved," catechisms. The tide began to ebb a hundred years later, halving in the seventeenth century, and halving once again in the eighteenth. Moreover, many catechisms were called a "Bible" in the original sense of the word *biblion*, meaning "book," and since they were meant to instruct children in the tenets of each church's faith, they were further titled a "Children's Bible" or "Bible for Children."

A typical catechism provided catechetical questions with answers taken from Holy Writ and identified by chapter and verse. In contrast to their simple format, their titles were often as florid as Ambrose Rigge's *Scripture Catechism for Children. Collected Out of the Whole Body of the Scriptures, for the Instructing of Youth with the Word of the Lord in the Beginning ... That They Might Be Taught Our Children, and Children's Children ... Presented to Fathers of Families, and Masters of Schools, to Train Up Their Children and Scholars, in the Knowledge of God, and the Scriptures* (1702). The content of Rigge's eighteenth-century English catechism differed but little from Martin Luther's sixteenth-century Small Catechism (*Parvus Catechismus*), whose language suggests, and the rest of whose title (*Pro in Schola, nuperductus*) clearly demonstrates that this catechism was meant for educationally privileged schoolboys. Other catechisms addressed girls and/or poor children, for whom the vernacular was appropriate, and they posed simpler questions, for which simpler answers to be memorized were provided. In an age that appeared to believe in the power-immanence of biblical words (because they were presented as God's own words), memorizing biblical phrases may well have been highly valued because it put eminently powerful (because they were divinely uttered) words at the believer's service. Whatever the perceived reason, memorization remained a goal set for young Christians, and it was fostered by including a few phrases from Holy Writ itself along with the Ten Commandments or the catechism in so-called children's Bibles. It goes without saying that contemporary children's Bibles differ profoundly from this sense of a children's Bible as a beginning acquaintance with power-immanent words emanating directly from God himself.

When Bible stories burgeoned as a publishing phenomenon in the later seventeenth century, one of the early ones produced in France called itself "a historical catechism." "Historical" meant a set of questions-and-answers based on biblical narratives, with the questions and answers aggregating into a complete "history." The first historical catechism was composed by Claude Fleury, a tutor to Louis XIV's heir apparent. Later translated into English as *An Historical Catechism Containing in Short the Sacred History and the Doctrine of Christianity*, its translator recounted a father's setting his three-year-old son on his lap and telling him about Abraham's willingness to sacrifice his son Isaac, while pointing out "the several incidents in a book of prints" (iv).

As the image of a father telling Bible stories to a small child well shows, a catechetical presentation of Bible stories is a quintessential two-person exchange, and children's Bible authors from the sixteenth to the nineteenth centuries adapted Bible narratives into dialogue form. For instance, Sebastian Castellio included only those stories that consisted of dialogic exchange (see Bottigheimer 2004). Marie Leprince de Beaumont incorporated Bible stories in a fluid catechetical form into her instructional *Tea-Table Dialogues between a Governess and Mary Sensible, Eliza Thoughtful, Jane Bloom, Ann Hopeful, Dinah Sterling, Lucy Lively, and Emma Tempest*. In this volume of miscellaneous instructional matter, Ann Hopeful tells the story of Adam and Eve, as she has memorized it (11–23), to which the governess, Mrs. Goodwill, adds a tale of a conversation between a gentleman and two poor people to demonstrate the truth of God's judgment on Adam, Eve, and the serpent.

Rewritings of children's Bibles demonstrate that it was not only the tale of Adam and Eve in the garden of Eden that needed rechanneling so that it would communicate a correct understanding of its contents. The same was true for any Bible narrative that showed a revered patriarch lamentably giving in to base inclinations, or for one that—perhaps more dangerously—named a woman like Judith, Jael, or Miriam as an active shaper of Old Testament history. Brave and bold heroines have been rarities in the overall history of children's Bibles, more often a problem to be disposed of than an example to be stressed.

It was a great leap of faith to put Bible stories before children's eyes and into children's hands without the guidance provided by questions and set answers, or by tutors' discursive correctives to children's nascent understanding of biblical texts. What becomes evident from the children's Bibles cited above is that children's Bibles as they are treated in the essays in the present volume themselves came to represent something other than the primordial catechetical format from which they emerged. We can trace a family tree for the contemporary phenomenon, children's Bibles, back through the centuries until we reach Petrus Comestor's *Historia Scholastica* in 1170. But it is equally true to declare that the genre of children's Bibles took centuries to define itself and finally did so to the exclusion of other forms only sometime in the 1700s. That is a respectably long history, but taking the long view, with 1170 as the starting point, we must recognize that a children's Bible consisting only of Bible stories was only one of several possible children's Bibles and that it has existed in this sole form for only three centuries.

It is also worth considering how broad in age and social condition the readership for simplified Bible content has been over the centuries. Comestor's *Historia Scholastica*, a book that was later used as a family Bible for the well-to-do and in the late 1400s as a grammar school instructional text, was originally aimed at university students. Bourgeois and farm-owning families and their entire households were targeted by Martin Luther's *Passionalbüchlein* (1529 et seq.), while beginning child readers and unskilled adult readers were grouped together as the intended market for Wendelin Rihel's *Leien Bibel* (1540). Children alone were addressed as readers of edited Bible stories only from the late 1600s and early 1700s onward, while in the late 1700s and early 1800s a new genre of edited Bible stories, so-called family Bibles, emerged for parents to read and explain to their households. Children's Bibles, then, represent a segment of a large body of edited Bible content prepared for a number of different readerships.

From the very beginning of their print production, the authors of children's Bibles viewed the project of writing biblical stories for children as providing children with alternative, and better, reading material than they routinely read. In 1690s England, for instance, one children's Bible author railed against chivalric romances, which he wished to replace with Bible stories; in 1890s Germany, it was violent and gory *Schundliteratur* that religious pedagogues wished to dislodge and replace with Bible stories. In both instances, the authors and publishers of children's Bibles regarded their products as other and better.

CHILDREN'S BIBLES: SELECTED SCHOLARSHIP, 1999–2011

In 1999, two Protestant professors of religious education, Rainer Lachmann at the University of Bamberg and Gottfried Adam at the University of Vienna, issued a book of essays (*Kinder- und Schulbibeln: Probleme ihrer Erforschung*, 1999) introducing and examining research problems in the genre of Bibles that had been rewritten for home and for school use by children.[1] In the same year a second volume of essays about children's

---

1. The following topics are covered in this volume: the classic Bible illustrations

Bibles appeared, discussing representations of God (Körtner and Schelander 1999). It explored issues ranging from visions and versions of God, through religious instruction, to evolution in the relationship between the Old and New Testaments in children's Bibles.

In 2003, Gottfried Adam, Rainer Lachmann, and Regine Schindler edited a number of essays that explored the ways in which Christian educators and Bible story authors had presented stories from the Old Testament and, in particular, the manners in which these stories had challenged their interpretations over time.[2] A 2004 volume of essays on the Bible as an educational book, edited by Volker Elsenbast, Rainer Lachmann, and Robert Schelander, incorporated articles on Noah (Norbert Mette), Moses (Martin Jäggle and Wolfgang Wagerer), Ruth (Wolfgang Langer), as well as individual children's Bibles such as Luther's *Passional* (Christine Reents) and Castellio's long-seller *Dialogi Sacri* (Ruth Bottigheimer).

With a volume on illustrations in children's Bibles from Luther to the internet (2005), Adam, Lachmann, and Schindler addressed a single subject.[3] This volume is of particular interest for studies of illustrations like

---

of Julius Schnorr von Carolsfeld (Christine Reents); sequential illustrations in Bible comics (Philipp Wegenast); the changing image of God in children's Bibles (Ruth Bottigheimer); the manners in which Jesus was envisaged after 1948 (Hilde Rosenau); the limits and definition of the genre (Bottigheimer); an assessment of rewritings based on literary theory (Josef Braun); a critical-constructive analysis of children's Bibles (Anneli Baum-Resch); joined descriptions and analyses of individual German children's Bibles (Rainer Lachmann, Gottfried Adam, Anneliese Pokrandt, Reinmar Tschirsch) and Hungarian (Hermann Pitters) and Austrian ones (Ernst Hofhansl).

2. The volume addresses issues such as whether the Old Testament was an independent document or was to be Christianized in the eyes of children's Bible editors and authors (Christine Reents); Jewish readers (Judith Suliman) and Jewish children's Bibles (Ruth Bottigheimer); the overall rewriting by the eighteenth-century Swiss author Johann Caspar Lavater (generally known for his writings on physiognomy); examinations of the creation (Reinmar Tschirsch) and of problematic stories (Irmgard Weth); and the individual story traditions of Rebekah (Anneli Baum-Resch), Noah (Josef Braun), and Abraham (Christoph T. Scheilke). It also includes essays by a children's Bible illustrator and a children's Bible storyteller, in addition to a consideration of digital interactive Bible stories (Winfried Bader), Bible comics (Philipp Wegenast), and recent children's Bibles (Reents).

3. Overall and theoretical pieces (Reinhard Mühlen, Ruth Bottigheimer) open the volume, followed by examinations of specific children's Bibles (Rainer Lachmann, Reinmar Tschirsch), national traditions, and individual subjects such as Jewishness (Regine Schindler), the depiction of families (Lachmann), children's responses to

those in the present volume. For example, Reinhard Mühlen's "The Brick Testament: Eine Kinderbibel mit einer Welt aus Legosteinen selbst entwerfen" addresses the same subject as Rubén Dupertuis's "Translating the Bible into Pictures," but the two authors focus on different aspects: Mühlen examines the religious educational potential of children's constructing three-dimensional illustrations for Bible stories, while Dupertuis understands the *Brick Testament* as "a critique or reaction against ways in which the Bible is presented to children." Clearly, there is a dialogue waiting to take place. Similarly, this volume's essays on comics and film offer perspectives that are germane to explorations of the same subjects in the present volume.

Essays on children's Bibles continued in 2008, with an exploration of the contents of children's Bible and the criteria for their inclusion.[4] Gender, religion, and education were the subjects singly and as a group in a study devoted to a gender-inclusive religious pedagogy. Published by the Comenius Institute in 2009, its editors, Annebelle Pithan, Silvia Arzt, Monika Jakobs, and Thorsten Knauth, invited examinations of gender discourse, the relative weightings of male/female identity, differing male/female reception of Bible texts. In 2011 the study of children's Bibles found a place next to the canonical Bible in the essays of *Retelling the Bible: Literary, Historical, and Social Contexts*, edited by Lucie Doležalová and Tamás Visi. One of this volume's participants, Jaqueline du Toit, contributed an essay on the subject of editing, and Kayko Driedger Hesslein discussed supercessionism in children's Bibles.

More recently, the Zurich-Bamberg-Vienna team that produced several of the volumes of essays noted above has also edited a volume on ethics and morality in Children's Bibles that came out in 2011. The group's 2012 symposium will be devoted to children's Bibles, children's literature, and literary criticism. Scholarship crosses linguistic boundaries at a lamentably slow pace. More research has been carried out among

---

illustrations (Irene Renz), Jesus in Bible comics (Rüdiger Pfeffer), the *Brick Testament* (Reinhard Mühlen), and a computer children's Bible (Andrea Klimt).

4. Edited by Gottfried Adam, Rainer Lachmann, and Regine Schindler, *Die Inhalte von Kinderbibeln: Kriterien ihrer Auswahl* examines individual children's Bibles from the sixteenth through the twentieth centuries (Jens Trocha, Adam, Lachmann, Christine Reents), included contributions by children's Bible authors (Rainer Oberthür, Schindler, Martina Steinkühler), a report on children's reception of children's Bible illustrations (Dávid Németh), and of internet versions of Bible stories for children (Roland Rosenstock, Daniel Schüttlöffel, Reinmar Tschirsch).

German-speaking researchers than in any other language group, which is why I have listed these many volumes devoted to the subject of children's Bibles. In the age of the internet, googling any of the scholars named above together with keywords like "Kinderbibel" or "children's Bible" will bring up titles that may well extend researchers' purviews and will speed them on their way.

WORKS CITED

Adam, Gottfried, Rainer Lachmann, and Regine Schindler, eds. 2003. *Das Alte Testament in Kinderbibeln: Eine didaktische Herausforderung in Vergangenheit und Gegenwart.* Zürich: Theologischer Verlag.

———, eds. 2005. *Illustrationen in Kinderbibeln: Von Luther bis zum Internet.* Jena: IKS Garamond.

———, eds. 2008. *Die Inhalte von Kinderbibeln: Kriterien ihrer Auswahl.* Göttingen: Vandenhoeck & Ruprecht.

Bottigheimer, Ruth B. 2004. "Sebastian Castellio and His *Dialogi Sacri.*" Pages 331–46 in *Die Bibel als Buch der Bildung.* Edited by Volker Elsenbast, Rainer Lachmann, and Robert Schelander. Vienna: LIT.

Doležalová, Lucie, and Tamás Visi, eds. 2011. *Retelling the Bible: Literary, Historical, and Social Contexts.* Frankfurt: Lang.

Elsenbast, Volker, Rainer Lachmann, and Robert Schelander, eds. 2004. *Die Bibel als Buch der Bildung: Festschrift für Gottfried Adam zum 65. Geburtstag.* Forum Theologie und Pädagogik 12. Vienna: LIT.

Fleury, Claude. 1740. *An Historical Catechism Containing in Short the Sacred History and the Doctrine of Christianity; by Abbe Fleury, Author of the Ecclesiastical History. Translated from the French, and Reformed for the Use of the Church of England by a Clergyman. Necessary for All Families.* London: James Bettenham for T. Cooper.

Fontaine, Nicolas. 1780. *An Abridgement of the History of the Old and New Testament, Interspersed with Moral and Instructive Reflections Chiefly out of the Holy Fathers.* Translated from the French by J. Reeve. Exeter: B. Thorn/London: T. Lewis.

Körtner, Ulrich, and Robert Schelander. 1999. *Gottes-Vorstellungen: Die Frage nach Gott in religiösen Bildungsprozessen. Gottfried Adam zum 60. Geburtstag* (= special issue of *Religionspädagogische Zeitschrift*).

Lachmann, Rainer, and Gottfried Adam, eds. 1999. *Kinder- und Schulbibeln: Probleme ihrer Erforschung.* Göttingen: Vandenhoeck & Ruprecht.

[Leprince de Beaumont, Marie.] 1806. *Tea-Table Dialogues between a Governess and Mary Sensible, Eliza Thoughtful, Jane Bloom, Ann Hopeful, Dinah Sterling, Lucy Lively, and Emma Tempest*. London: Darton & Harvey.

Luther, Martin. 1539. *Parvus Catechismus, Pro Pueris in Schola, nuperductus per Marti. Luth*. [Wittenberg: Georg Rhau.]

Pithan, Annebelle, Silvia Arzt, Monika Jakobs, and Thorsten Knauth, eds. 2009. *Gender—Religion—Bildung: Beiträge zu einer Religionspädagogik der Vielfalt*. Gütersloh: Gütersloher Verlagshaus.

Rigge, Ambrose. 1702. *A Scripture Catechism for Children. Collected out of the Whole Body of the Scriptures, for the Instructing of Youth with the Word of the Lord in the Beginning ... That They Might Be Taught Our Children, and Children's Children ... Presented to Fathers of Families, and Masters of Schools, to Train Up Their Children and Scholars, in the Knowledge of God, and the Scriptures*. London: T. Sowle.

Schlag, Thomas, and Robert Schelander. 2011. *Moral und Ethik in Kinderbibeln: Kinderbibelforschung in historischer und religionspädagogischer Perspektive*. Göttingen: V&R Unipress.

What Does a Child Want?
Reflections on Children's Bible Stories

J. Cheryl Exum

I would like to begin by congratulating the editors for a stimulating collection that brings the critical investigation of children's Bible stories to the wider attention of biblical scholars. Already flourishing in the social sciences and literary studies, the study of childhood and children's literature is only beginning to take its place among the many approaches biblical scholars currently employ, and this volume will provide an impetus for much needed further study. The fruits of such study will benefit not only the field of biblical studies but other disciplines as well, where the Bible's otherness (a topic that comes up frequently in this volume) can seem a stumbling block for nonspecialists. One hopes such research will in some way benefit children too.

A major problem with children's Bible stories, the contributors agree, is that they erase the Bible's otherness and the otherness of biblical characters, whether a Daniel (Pyper), a Jesus (Briggs), or even the occasional child (Koepf). Another is their lack of cultural diversity. They all too often fail to represent difference (gender, race, ethnicity, class, levels of disability), a failure that inevitably has an influence on the child's perception of self as well as other. Illustrations have an important role to play here, and, as these essays show, the relationship between text and illustration is complex. Often, as many of the authors point out, illustrations reinforce or intensify the process of othering, giving biblical characters physical characteristics not mentioned in the story. Although illustrations are reworked to reflect social changes (Punt), there are many examples here (not all reproduced) of illustrations that perpetuate the image of the white, fair-haired, and blue-eyed Jesus; picture foreigners, enemies, and lower classes as dark skinned; and ignore girls and women or show them in stereotypical roles. Illustrations also have the potential to make a story more inclusive, though the examples discussed here rarely do this. Surely there are some children's Bibles that portray children with disabilities, so that young readers who are physically challenged are not made to feel excluded, but typically, I imagine, characters are able-bodied, or miraculously cured because they have faith. Illustrations can either downplay or foreground scenes of violent destruction (see, especially, the examples of both techniques given by England and Gunn), and thereby make a gripping story boring for some children or distressing for others. They can be at odds with the story, as Briggs, England, and Gunn, in particular, illustrate, and as Vander Stichele shows in her discussion of different views of Delilah presented by a Samson-and-Delilah animated version, on the one hand, and its presenter Charlton Heston and the animated narrator Simon, on the other. I shall have more to say about the power of illustrations, and their disruptive potential, below.

I enjoyed all these articles, and, as someone whose interest lies primarily in the text itself, I especially liked reading about how particular biblical stories were retold for young readers: Daniel (Pyper), Samson (Gunn, Vander Stichele, Scholz), Jonathan and David (Rogers and Fewell), the flood story (England, Scholz), Naaman's young slave in 2 Kgs 5:1–15 (Koepf), the birth of Jesus (Roncace) and the one story of his boyhood in Luke 2:40–52 (Briggs), the creation story (Scholz, Roncace), Cain and Abel (Dupertuis), and Ruth (Scholz). The inclusion of animated films and comics (Scholz, Vander Stichele, Dupertuis) adds an important dimension, while the articles by du Toit, Punt, and Lee lend a global perspective. I found the syncretism of the *Taiping Trimetrical Classic* fascinating, and I am curious about the effect on believers of having a heavenly mother and wives for the sons of god. I would welcome more discussions of the ideological use of children's Bible stories in a global context in the future. Reflecting on the collection, I think not so much of disagreements but rather of the overall effect: it stimulated my thinking about the topic. And so, in response to the authors' many pertinent criticisms and valuable insights, in what follows I want to speculate about what form I would like to see children's Bible stories take in order to achieve goals it seems to me the contributors and I share. (Throughout this response, I use the terms "children's Bibles" and "children's Bible stories" to include film versions and comic-book Bibles as well.) I had some questions at the outset:

Who writes children's Bibles and children's Bible stories? Adults, of course. What we find in children's Bible stories is adults' ideas of what children want or need or should have. And as the contributors to this volume dramatically demonstrate, these adults have agendas, acknowledged or not. To complicate matters, we are dealing with a highly ideological source text, one that claims for itself, its chosen people, and its god a special status—a claim that anyone who retells these stories must deal with, one way or another (in the case of the stories discussed here, the claim is taken for granted, but this is not the only option). Authors of children's Bible stories write with an intended audience in mind. Briggs distinguishes different types of retellings based on what their intended (or implied) readers need and what the retellings thus seek to provide: value-driven retellings for moral guidance; dogma-driven to keep the reader on the proper theological path; education-driven, providing background information; and engagement-driven retellings that encourage the child to interact with the story. As Briggs points out, these approaches are not mutually exclusive, and many children's Bibles make use of more than one of them. As it turns out, the contributors (and I) do not like the ideologies of almost all of the retellings discussed here. Most contributors would prefer engagement-driven retellings or, with Briggs, retellings that seek to empower young readers; some are concerned with values; and no one is in favor of dogma-driven retellings ("dogma" is often a label with pejorative connotations; one person's dogma is another person's truth). The contributors would like children's Bible stories that counter theologically conservative retellings with liberal, critical, gender-, race-, class-, and other-inclusive retellings, retellings that capture something of the complexity and ambiguity exhibited by many biblical narratives.

Who publishes children's Bibles and children's Bible stories? Most children's literature is published by trade publishers but this is not the case with children's Bibles or children's Bible stories. England mentions three sorts of Bible retellings for children: traditional religious, literary, and secular humanist. The latter two are seriously underrepresented in this volume and, I assume, at large. Children's Bibles and children's Bible stories are usually published by conservative Christian publishing houses and denomination-affiliated publishers, as are almost all of the examples discussed in the essays in the present collection—a fact that should make us suspicious of their agendas at the outset. Authors are often expected to write to publishers' specifications, and both authors and publishers are interested in sales, even when this is not their primary motivation.

Who buys them? Adults. Until and even after children are able to select books for themselves, the purchasers of these books are adults—very often parents or grandparents, who want children to learn about the Bible and who have specific ideas about the types of books they prefer them to read. Often they are looking for appropriate role models and subtle but suitable lessons for children. They are not likely to buy a book they think would upset or frighten a child or that challenges their own values.

Who reads them? The obvious answer is children. At what age do children select their own books? For many of the children's Bibles discussed here, the children are lap readers, to use du Toit's term. So while I appreciate Koepf's view that children should read the Bible itself (and I find some parts of the Bible more suitable for this than others), I see the value in having retellings aimed at various ages. Adults write, publish, usually buy, and frequently read (out loud to children) these stories. Adults write about children's literature. Thus my title, "What Does a Child Want?" (or, if you will, *Was will das Kind?*, an allusion to Freud's *Was will das Weib?*), is intended to draw attention to children being spoken about but not represented here. What a child wants, however, is a subject everyone can have a view on, since we all remember, albeit selectively, what childhood was like for us.

But who are the children we are talking about? As Koepf and Briggs remind us, "child" and "childhood" are constructs that vary from society to society and over time. Even within the same society, constructions of childhood are affected by variables such as gender, class, ethnicity, and even religion. By and large, the contributors to this volume are working with a construction of childhood as a distinct phase of life and of the child as young, dependent, to a certain extent protected, and, at the same time, capable of dealing with moral complexity and harsh realities of life—one who has the luxury to read or the good fortune to be read to by adults or both. These children should be gently encouraged to be inquisitive, critical readers (perhaps also resistant readers, which they often naturally are).[1] My comments apply to this construction of children as well, for we cannot easily dissociate ourselves from a view so well entrenched in and embraced by our society. A construction created by adults.

---

1. This child is probably also assumed to be an individual with personal rights and not thought of as an economic asset whose primary role is to contribute to the family's income. These and the conceptions above are very different from constructions of childhood in the Bible, as Steinberg shows. It is no accident that children are often peripheral in children's Bibles, since they are peripheral in the Bible.

THE PROBLEM WITH (MOST) CHILDREN'S BIBLE STORIES

What the articles in this volume reveal again and again is that, although many children's Bibles and versions of Bible stories are available, very few are satisfactory. The problem with most children's Bible stories is what one would expect without even reading them: they are patronizing, overly protective (especially where sex and violence are concerned), moralistic, and vastly oversimplified; their preferred techniques for achieving their goals are omission, glossing over, and adjusting their source text. As Bottigheimer so well shows in her pioneering 1996 study, frequently cited by the contributors, they reflect the assumptions, concerns, and values of their producers.

> Children's Bibles express values and standards that are not universal and eternal but particular and ephemeral. Bound by place and time, they adapt an ancient and inspired text to changing manners, morals, ideas, and concerns. For authors, buyers, and readers in nearly every age, children's Bibles have seemed to be texts faithful to the Bible itself. But their authors' common effort to use the Bible to shape a meaningful present has produced Bible stories that mingle sacred text with secular values. (Bottigheimer 1996, 218)

Particularly problematic are the issues of relevance (Bottigheimer; Briggs) and authority, and, while relevance may be a problem writers of other children's stories face, authority is not. Retelling Bible stories for young readers is a real challenge, involving difficult decisions, especially where the god character is concerned (for a brief history of the character of god, see Bottigheimer 1996, 59–69). Problems can arise when authors identify the god of the Bible with their idea of a real god or with what they take to be their readers' assumptions about the relation of the biblical god to modern ideas about god—or when they encourage or simply leave room for this identification. The problem is intensified when the Bible is implied or assumed to be his word (he is so well identified as male—ask any child) or when it is presented as qualitatively different from other literature; for example, by referring to it as an "inspired" or "sacred text" or as "Scripture." Of course readers will have their own expectations about a god and the status of the Bible as well.

The lack of biblical literacy in modern society is frequently bemoaned. It is a commonplace that people buy Bibles but do not read them. Do children's Bibles fare any better? Children should, in my view, be familiar with the Bible because it is a classic (on what makes a "classic," see Clines 2011, 121–23) and because of its pronounced influence on Western culture and literature. Parts of it are, indisputably, great literature,[2] and some of its stories, as Koepf and Pyper stress, help children in working through anxieties, fears, and desires and in negotiating the complex dreaded and desired process of growing up (myths and fairy tales are important for the same reason). I take issue, however, with Roncace, who cites approvingly Lenora Ledwon's view that literature "makes us more moral. It makes us better people." George Steiner puts the opposite argument eloquently:

> To think of literature, of education, of language, as if nothing very important had happened to challenge our very concept of these activities seems to me unrealistic. To read Aeschylus or Shakespeare—let alone to "teach" them—as if the texts, as if the authority of the texts in our own lives, were immune from recent history, is subtle but corrosive illiteracy.… We know now that a man [*sic*] can read Goethe or Rilke in the evening, that he can play Bach and Schubert, and go to his day's work at Auschwitz in the morning. To say that he has read them without understanding or that his ear is gross is cant. In what way does this knowledge bear on literature and society, on the hope, grown almost axiomatic from the time of Plato to that of Matthew Arnold, that culture is a humanizing force, that the energies of spirit are transferable to those of conduct? (1977, ix)

Many adults may have memories of the pleasure of violent or scary biblical stories, stories whose subversive currents, like those of fairy tales, account, in part, for their appeal. I have very clear memories of a book of Greek mythology and tales from the *Iliad* and *Odyssey* that we spent a good deal of time reading and discussing in my sixth-grade class (age eleven). Unfortunately I do not have access to the book (they belonged to the school, not the students), nor do I remember its title, but it represented the model of what I think retellings of classic texts for young readers should be. The stories were fascinating, they were not simplistic or patronizing (though I am sure sex and violence were underplayed), and they were memorable. The golden fleece, Paris awarding the apple to Aphrodite, Achilles dragging Hector's body around the walls of Troy, Odys-

---

2. Some years ago I tried to show how the stories of Saul, Jephthah, the members of Saul's fated house, and David hold a place among the great tragedies of world literature (Exum 1992), and I would argue that the Song of Songs is one of the great love poems of all time (Exum 2005).

seus's men turned into swine, Odysseus outwitting the Cyclops, the perilous course past Scylla and Charybdis, the plight of Pyramus and Thisbe,
Niobe's boast and its consequences, the sufferings of Io, the labors or Her-
cules, and so many others—varied, wonderful tales of adventure, adversity,
courage, cleverness, of fate and the capriciousness of the gods, and a world
that was bewitchingly "other." The author(s) of these stories did not have a
religious agenda, and the gods appeared with all their fantastic powers and
their human foibles. It may be that these stories instilled in me some values
and helped socialize me, but I cannot recall any particular lessons learned.
What they did instill in me was a love of the classics and a knowledge of
Greek mythology that has served me well. Would not retellings that instill
an appreciation of the biblical literature without trying to claim for it a
special status go a long way to encouraging young people to read the Bible
and even study it? Might they possibly inspire their readers to become children's Bible stories writers, illustrators, and filmmakers (cf. Scholz)?

Confessions of a Children's Bible Story Writer

To my knowledge, the only children's Bible stories written by biblical scholars for a trade publishing house are Alice Bach's and my *Moses' Ark* (1989)
and *Miriam's Well* (1991). Working with an experienced author of books for
young readers helped me understand how to tell a story well,[3] and because
Alice was an established children's writer we had a highly respected publisher in Delacorte Press, who matched us with award-winning illustrators
Leo and Diane Dillon. Unlike the daunting and unenviable task of producing a children's Bible, retelling selected stories gave us the freedom to tell
them in a new way, to decide which stories to tell and what parts of them to
focus on. One a Roman Catholic and the other an atheist, we did not have a
religious agenda in mind, but we did have a feminist one. We gave women
voices they did not have in the biblical account, and we told some stories
from a woman's point of view. The illustrators were particularly sensitive to
race as well as gender, well exemplified by the wrap-around cover to *Moses'
Ark*, where five dark-skinned Egyptian women gaze in astonishment at the

---

3. Alice Bach is the author of more than twenty books for young readers, ranging
from a series of picturebooks about twin bears, Ronald and Oliver (1975, 1976, 1977,
1978), to novels for older readers, among which *Waiting for Johnny Miracle* and *He Will
Not Walk with Me* were American Library Association Notable Books, and *Waiting for
Johnny Miracle* and *Molly Make-Believe* were *New York Times* Best Book of the Year.

basket in the bulrushes, and that of *Miriam's Well*, where the women and young girl have dark skin and varied facial features. They could, however, be accused of orientalizing (see Pyper), as in their lavish, stunning illustration of the Queen of Sheba, though that illustration is inspired by the Bible's exotic description.

The articles in the present volume not only stimulated my thinking about what children's Bible stories should look like (more about that below) but also sent me back to stories written over twenty years ago to consider what Alice and I had written and what, with the versatile benefit of hindsight and the critiques of children's Bible stories in the present volume, I would want to do differently. Gunn, Vander Stichele, Scholz, England, and Roncace deal with three of the stories we retold. Rereading our versions in the light of their discussions of children's versions of the Samson story, the flood story, and the creation accounts made me painfully aware of many shortcomings in our retellings (e.g., aligning the young reader with Samson, presenting his death and destruction as for the best, and not mentioning vengeance; underplaying the destruction by focusing on the activity on the ark during the flood) but also of some positive features, like including Noah's wife and sons' wives and not gender-stereotyping the tasks they performed; making patriotism Delilah's motive (and Jael her hero) and using her to reflect on the way women who play important roles do not get recognition;[4] and, for Gen 2–3, beginning with the creation of a "human being" and speaking of a man and a woman only after the woman is created—a feminist perspective missing in Roncace's survey and whose absence in children's Bible films is bemoaned by Scholz.[5]

Although Alice and I were not interested in moralizing, and we tried to capture something of the intricacy of the biblical text, we were, I think

---

4. "I expected my people to recognize my sacrifice, but the Philistines lords took all the credit. They boasted that Dagon our god granted them success. Throughout the city the people cried, 'Our god has given Samson, our enemy, into our hand.' But nowhere did they say, 'Most blessed of women be Delilah, of Philistines women most blessed.'" We also do not have Delilah die in the destruction of the temple (Bach and Exum 1991, 162–63).

5. I agree with Roncace that the two versions of the creation story should not be conflated and should both appear in children's Bibles, but I am not apologetic about not retelling both, since we were retelling only a selection. We chose the lively and dramatic second creation story, but we did mention in our notes that there are two and we pointed out some of the differences. Noteworthy is the absence of Gen 2–3 in the *Taiping Trimetrical Classic* (Lee).

now, too respectful of the text (we, and our publisher, did, after all, want to sell books). I am to blame for our staying so close to the biblical story in *Moses' Ark*; Alice wanted to be more adventuresome. Staying close to the story meant adopting the biblical writer's point of view, which automatically involves othering (Israelite versus foreign, us versus them) and privileging the Israelite god. In *Miriam's Well*, we were freer, as, for example, telling the story of Miriam through the eyes of a young girl and having minor female biblical characters tell their own stories, but we still, on the whole, reflected the biblical writers' points of view. The Dillons made their own choices of what to illustrate, but we were shown the illustrations and given the opportunity to respond. What I most regret is rejecting their illustration to the exodus story, a drawing of women weeping over the body of a young boy in the foreground and a grief-stricken Pharaoh shaking his finger accusingly at Moses and Aaron in the background. At the time we felt that, in creating such sympathy for the Egyptians, the illustration was at odds with our story. Now I think countering the story by showing the Egyptians' point of view would have been a brilliant subversive move.

We included notes at the end of each story, with parents in mind and for older children. Providing notes has the advantage of allowing authors to draw attention to some of the features of the text, the kind of ambiguities and complexities the contributors to this volume are looking for, that cannot easily be accommodated in the story (e.g., the thematic contrast Koepf mentions between great and small in 2 Kgs 5). In our story of Samson, for example, Alice and I pointed out in the notes what we tried to show in the story, the prominence and acuity of Samson's mother. But this left unaddressed the fact that the story nevertheless serves male interests (Exum 1993, 61–93). I wonder, however, how easy that would have been in a story whose primary goal was to capture the imagination of young readers. If space is not an issue, the same biblical story could be told in different versions.[6] After a traditional retelling of the story of Samson and Delilah in *Moses' Ark*, we offered an alternative version in *Miriam's Well*.

Speculating about Alternatives

I would like to see more trade books aimed at a wide, and not just reli-

---

6. Just as children would benefit from watching multiple versions of Bible films (Brenner 2006, 33), they should have the opportunity to read more than one or two children's Bibles or versions of a particular Bible story.

giously motivated, readership. A selection (with a large number of stories, like my sixth-grade mythology book) has advantages over a retelling of the whole Bible, since some texts lend themselves to retelling more easily than others. As the contributors to this collection have indicated, retellings of Bible stories for young readers should respect and represent difference; they should not patronize or marginalize the reader or seek to control the reading process or be afraid to confront young readers with difficult material; and they should seek to convey something of the marvelous complexity and diversity of the Bible.

One appealing way of achieving these goals is by retelling Bible stories from different points of view (for examples in contemporary children's literature, see Yannicopoulou 2010). Pyper relishes *Dinner in the Lions' Den*, a version of the story of Daniel from the lions' point of view, and Koepf writes approvingly of a retelling of 2 Kgs 5:1–15 from the young slave Miriam's point of view. A fine example of what can be accomplished by presenting multiple points of view (despite its overzealous religious agenda and privileging of the god character) is *Wie Feuer und Wind: Das Alte Testament Kindern erzählt*, by Martina Steinkühler (2005b; see also Steinkühler 2005a), whose use of characters as narrators who also report the views of yet other characters enables her to introduce a variety of perspectives on the biblical story (Exum 2010, 247–48 et passim). Including different genres can allow more voices to be heard (Roncace), and Steinkühler does this as well.

I would like to see children's Bible stories written and illustrated for entertainment, not for instruction or to inculcate particular values or religious ideas. One way of doing this is to write stories in which the character god does not play a role (or has only the most minor of roles). Books like Ruth and Esther readily lend themselves to this approach, but it could be tried with others as well: witness Rogers and Fewell's constructive proposals for retelling the story of Jonathan. Yet, appealing as it is, their approach does not really work for me. As far as the biblical story is concerned, the reason that Jonathan cannot be king lies in the god's rejection of his father's house, and, without that divine enmity, the story loses the very element that makes it so powerful (making this one of those difficult texts about acceptance and rejection that children should be trusted to wrestle with).[7] England's examples of marginalizing the role of the god character

---

7. A retelling of the story that both "embrace[s] Jonathan's individuality and com-

in retellings of the flood story also illustrates the pitfalls of writing divine causality out of the story.

A solution would be not to privilege the god character, which would require giving the character a name, such as Yahweh or Iao—a name that, unlike the familiar "God," emphasizes otherness. For example, "While the Philistines were celebrating the victory of their god Dagon, who had saved them from the ravager of their country, Samson prayed for vengeance to his god Yahweh." One could be even bolder, and change the biblical story radically. A delightful example of this approach is Judith Kerr's *How Mrs. Monkey Missed the Ark*, in which "displacements suggest a counterstory, a point of vantage from which to look at the original story, but also untouched by it" (Landy 2007, 373). An example of how gross this approach can be is *VeggieTales: Minnesota Cuke and the Search for Noah's Umbrella*, discussed by Scholz. If retellings depart seriously from the biblical story, one could argue, why bother with the Bible at all? We need only consider how writers and filmmakers have paid tribute to their literary and cinematic heritage, from simple allusions to outright borrowings from their predecessors, to recognize the potential of this approach for encouraging biblical literacy.

Thinking back on how Bach's and my Israel-centric version of the exodus story would have been undermined had we accepted the Dillons' original illustration, I would like to see retellings that deliberately create dissonance between story and illustration in order to show multiple and conflicting viewpoints or to make the reader aware of a story's complexity by foregrounding different features. Consciously using text and illustration to counter each other could be done easily enough by an author-illustrator; otherwise, close collaboration between author and illustrator would be needed, a working relationship that cannot simply be assumed. Fortunately for readers of children's Bible stories, dissonance between a story and its illustrations can happen inadvertently. Disagreement or mis-

---

plexity" (Rogers and Fewell) and recognizes hostile transcendence could emphasize that Jonathan, despite his many qualities, cannot win; it could show how he tries to secure a place for himself and the security of his descendants under David's kingship, but dies at his father's (not David's) side before David's loyalty can be tested. Rogers and Fewell also suggest that the story of Jonathan and David can be used to explore issues of sexual identity, and here I recommend drawing on Heacock's discussion of Jonathan and David's relationship in terms of male friendships (2011).

match between story and illustration is a theme that runs through the present collection.[8]

The emphasis on illustrations in this volume led me to consider what makes Maurice Sendak my favourite children's author and illustrator. Sendak is best known for *Where the Wild Things Are*, but I prefer the other books in the trilogy. In *In the Night Kitchen*, Mickey tumbles out of bed, out of his clothes, and into the night kitchen, where the bakers, Oliver Hardy triplets, mix him in the batter for tomorrow's cake. *Outside Over There*, about the complex feelings of an older child, nine-year-old Ida, whose baby sister is captured by goblins while Ida is not paying attention, is a dark and brooding book that some critics considered not suitable for children. All three books were controversial; as one reviewer put it, each of them "dramatizes fears, rages and appetites that adults would prefer to believe children don't experience" (Clemons 1981, 45). Sendak knew better:

> The qualities that make for excellence in children's literature can be sweepingly summed up in a single word: imagination. And imagination as it relates to the child is, to my mind, synonymous with fantasy. Contrary to most of the propaganda in books for the young, childhood is only partly a time of innocence. It is, in my opinion, a time of seriousness, bewilderment, and a good deal of suffering. It's also possibly the best of all times. Imagination for the child is the miraculous, freewheeling device he [*sic*] uses to course his way through the problems of every day. It's the normal and healthy outlet for corrosive emotions such as impotent frustration and rage; the positive and appropriate channeling of overwhelming and, to the child, inappropriate feelings. It is through fantasy that children achieve catharsis. (cited in Lanes 1980, 66)

As Pyper observes, a book is a commercial success when both adults and children are satisfied. Adults may buy children's books, but children know what they like.

> If a kid doesn't like a book, throw it away.... We should let children choose their own books. What they don't like they will toss aside. What

---

8. I found interesting examples of such a mismatch in children's Bible versions of the David story, where some illustrations of Nathan announcing the death of David and Bathsheba's child were considerably more frightening than the story (Exum 2010, 254).

disturbs them too much they will not look at. And if they look at the wrong book, it isn't going to do them that much damage. We treat children in a very peculiar way, I think. We don't treat them like the strong creatures they really are. (Sendak, cited in Lanes 1980, 106–7)

Sendak's illustrations of selected Grimm's fairy tales in *The Juniper Tree* (Segal, Jarrell, and Sendak 1973) could serve as a model for what could be done with selected Bible stories. In the illustrations Sendak sought to catch "that moment when the tension between story line and emotion is at its greatest, so that the person reading is in for a surprise if he [*sic*] thinks it's just a simple-minded fairy tale" (cited in Lanes 1980, 193). "The Grimm tales are about the pure essence of life—incest, murder, insane mothers, love, sex—what have you," he remarks, and in this they are like the Bible.

> This is the way life is sometimes, these tales say in the most matter-of-fact way. And this is what I believe children appreciate. People rage against the Grimms' tales, forgetting that originally the brothers had assembled them not for children, but for historical and philological reasons.… Well, lo and behold, children began to read them. And the second edition was called *The Household Tales* because children were demanding the stories. The point is that those illustrators and writers who attract me are the ones who do not seem to be at all hung up by the fact that their audiences may be small people. They are telling the truth, just the way it is. (206)

This will all sound familiar to one who has read the present essays. Are these speculations about what form children's Bibles and Bible stories could take realistic? Unfortunately, the market will probably remain dominated by the sorts of conservative, largely Christian, doctrine-driven children's Bibles and children's Bible stories discussed here. Biblical scholars need to do more to change the prevailing public image of the Bible as other compared to other literature, as an object of devotion, and as "a moral, straightforward, and didactic text" (Koepf)—a view, as Koepf points out, often formed at an early age from reading children's Bible stories. Children's Bible stories, then, would seem to be a good place to start.[9]

---

9. Biblical scholars are unlikely to write children's Bible stories, but we can make a difference by taking children's literature seriously and recognizing the study of children's Bible stories as a valuable academic pursuit (Vander Stichele). Including such studies in our teaching could, as Scholz envisages, encourage students to work in this area.

Works Cited

Bach, Alice. 1974. *Mollie Make-Believe*. New York: Harper & Row.

———. 1980. *Waiting for Johnny Miracle*. New York: Harper & Row.

———. 1985. *He Will Not Walk with Me*. New York: Delacorte.

Bach, Alice, and J. Cheryl Exum; Leo and Diane Dillon (ills.). 1989. *Moses' Ark: Stories from the Bible*. New York: Delacorte.

———. 1991. *Miriam's Well: Stories about Women in the Bible*. New York: Delacorte.

Bach, Alice, and Steven Kellogg (ill.). 1975. *The Smartest Bear and His Brother Oliver*. New York: Harper & Row.

———. 1976. *The Most Delicious Camping Trip Ever*. New York: Harper & Row.

———. 1977. *Grouchy Uncle Otto*. New York: Harper & Row.

———. 1978. *Millicent the Magnificent*. New York: Harper & Row.

Bottigheimer, Ruth B. 1996. *The Bible for Children from the Age of Gutenberg to the Present*. New Haven: Yale University Press.

Brenner, Athalya. 2006. "Recreating the Biblical Creation for Western Children: Provisional Reflections on Some Case Studies." Pages 11–34 in *Creation and Creativity: From Genesis to Genetics and Back*. Edited by Caroline Vander Stichele and Alastair G. Hunter. BMW 9/ASBR 1. Sheffield: Sheffield Phoenix.

Clemons, Walter. 1981. "Sendak's Enchanted Land." Review of Maurice Sendak, *Outside Over There*. *Newsweek*, May 25, 45–47.

Clines, David J. A. 2011. "Reading the Song of Songs as a Classic." Pages 116–31 in *A Critical Engagement: Essays on the Hebrew Bible in Honour of J. Cheryl Exum*. Edited by David J. A. Clines and Ellen van Wolde. HBM 38. Sheffield: Sheffield Phoenix.

Exum, J. Cheryl. 1992. *Tragedy and Biblical Narrative: Arrows of the Almighty*. Cambridge: Cambridge University Press.

———. 1993. *Fragmented Women: Feminist (Sub)versions of Biblical Narratives*. Valley Forge, Pa.: Trinity Press International; Sheffield: Sheffield Academic Press.

———. 2005. *Song of Songs: A Commentary*. Louisville: Westminster John Knox.

———. 2010. "A King Fit for a Child: The David Story in Modern Children's Bibles." Pages 241–59 in *The Fate of King David: The Past and Present of a Biblical Icon*. Edited by Tod Linafelt, Claudia V. Camp, and Timothy Beal. LHBOTS 500. New York: T&T Clark.

Heacock, Anthony. 2011. *Jonathan Loved David: Manly Love in the Bible and the Hermeneutics of Sex*. BMW 22. Sheffield: Sheffield Phoenix.

Landy, Francis. 2007. "Noah's Ark and Mrs. Monkey." *BibInt* 15:351–76.

Lanes, Selma G. 1980. *The Art of Maurice Sendak*. New York: Abrams.

Segal, Lore, Randall Jarrell (trans.), and Maurice Sendak (ill.). 1973. *The Juniper Tree and Other Tales from Grimm*. New York: Farrar, Straus & Giroux.

Sendak, Maurice. 1963. *Where the Wild Things Are*. New York: Harper & Row.

———. 1970. *In the Night Kitchen*. New York: Harper & Row.

———. 1981. *Outside Over There*. New York: Harper & Row.

Steinberg, Naomi. Forthcoming, 2013. *The Child in the Hebrew Bible and Contemporary Discourse*. Sheffield: Sheffield Phoenix.

Steiner, George. 1977. *Language and Silence: Essays on Language, Literature, and the Inhuman*. New York: Atheneum.

Steinkühler, Martina. 2005a. *Wie Brot und Wein: Das Neue Testament Kindern erzählt*. Göttingen: Vandenhoeck & Ruprecht.

———. 2005b. *Wie Feuer und Wind: Das Alte Testament Kindern erzählt*. Göttingen: Vandenhoeck & Ruprecht.

Yannicopoulou, Angela. 2010. "Focalization in Children's Picture Books: Who Sees in Words and Pictures?" Pages 65–85 in *Telling Children's Stories: Narrative Theory and Children's Literature*. Edited by Mike Cadden. Lincoln: University of Nebraska Press.

Contributors

Timothy Beal is the Florence Harkness Professor of Religion at Case Western Reserve University and editor-in-chief of *The Oxford Encyclopedia of the Bible and the Arts* (in progress). He has published thirteen books and many scholarly articles on the cultural history of the Bible, religion and popular culture, and relations between critical theory and academic religious studies. He has also published essays on religion and American culture for *The New York Times*, *The Chronicle of Higher Education*, CNN.com, and *The Washington Post* and is a regular contributor to *The Huffington Post*.

Ruth Bottigheimer is research professor in the Department of Comparative Cultural Analysis and Theory at Stony Brook University and studies children's Bibles from sociocultural and historical perspectives. *The Bible for Children from the Age of Gutenberg to the Present* (1996) analyzes key biblical stories as presented to readers from 1170 to the mid-1990s. She has also examined historically significant children's Bibles from the past by Sebastian Castellio (1540s), Nicolas Fontaine (1670 et seq.), and Moses Mordechai Büdinger (1823).

Melody Briggs is a PhD student at the University of Sheffield in England. She holds Masters degrees in both theology and children's literature and has published several journal articles on theological aspects of children's texts. She has previously taught at the University of Durham and is currently researching the hermeneutics of how children read biblical narrative.

Rubén R. Dupertuis is associate professor in the Religion Department at Trinity University in San Antonio. He has written essays on Greek education in the early Roman Empire as well as on the Acts of the Apostles. He is coeditor, with Todd Penner, of a forthcoming volume entitled *Reading Acts in the Second Century* and cochair of the SBL's Ancient Fiction, Early Christian, and Jewish Narrative section.

Emma England is a research fellow at the Amsterdam School for Cultural Analysis at the University of Amsterdam. Her PhD thesis, "The Genesis Flood Story Published for Children: 170 Years of Words and Images," proposes a methodology for analyzing children's Bible retellings that focuses on uncovering ideologies presented in the relationship between words and images. She is interested in the intersections between popular culture and biblical narratives, having published and presented on comics, television, and film.

J. Cheryl Exum is professor emerita of biblical studies at the University of Sheffield and a director of Sheffield Phoenix Press. The author of numerous articles on the Hebrew Bible, her books include *Tragedy and Biblical Narrative: Arrows of the Almighty* (1996); *Fragmented Women: Feminist (Sub)versions of Biblical Narratives* (1993); *Plotted, Shot, and Painted: Cultural Representations of Biblical Women* (1996, 2nd ed., 2012); and *Song of Songs: A Commentary* (2006). She is currently writing a book on the Bible and the arts.

Danna Nolan Fewell is professor of Hebrew Bible at Drew University. Her teaching and research interests focus upon literary, cultural, and ideological approaches to biblical narrative, the Bible in art, children and biblical literature, and the ethics of reading. Her major works featuring children include *The Children of Israel: Reading the Bible for the Sake of Our Children* (2003) and *Icon of Loss: The Haunting Child of Samuel Bak* (2009).

David M. Gunn is professor of religion, emeritus, at Texas Christian University in Fort Worth. He has written extensively in literary and feminist criticism, reception history, and cultural studies of the Hebrew Bible. His most recent book is *Judges through the Centuries* (2004), and he is currently working on a companion volume on 1–2 Samuel in the Blackwell series.

Laurel W. Koepf is assistant professor of Old Testament at Eden Theological Seminary in Saint Louis. Her current research focuses on child-centered biblical hermeneutics, including ancient metaphors of childhood and children's agency as interpreters of text. She has presented her research at the Society of Biblical Literature, American Academy of Religion, and Cultural Studies Association.

Archie C. C. Lee is professor of the Department of Cultural and Religious Studies at the Chinese University of Hong Kong. He has written books and articles in the areas of Old Testament Studies, the Bible in China, cross-textual hermeneutics, Asian biblical interpretation, and postcolonialism. He is the president of the Society of Asian Biblical Studies and, with Athalya Brenner and Gale Yee, one of the editors of a contextual biblical interpretation series, Text@Context by Fortress Press. He has been working on a book for Hawaii University Press on the interpretation of the Bible in China.

Jeremy Punt is professor of New Testament in the Faculty of Theology at Stellenbosch University in South Africa. He has published on hermeneutics and critical theory in New Testament interpretation, including "'All in the Family?' The Social Location of New Testament Households and Christian Claims on 'Traditional Family Values'" in *Acta Patristica et Byzantica* 21 (2010); and "Pauline Agency in Postcolonial Perspective: Subverter of or Agent for Empire?" in *The Colonized Apostle: Paul through Postcolonial Eyes* (2011).

Hugh S. Pyper is professor of biblical interpretation at the University of Sheffield and discipline lead for philosophical and religious studies at the Higher Education Academy in the United Kingdom. He has written widely on the cultural afterlife of the Bible, including its role in children's literary, most recently in his forthcoming book of essays *The Unchained Bible* (T&T Clark).

Cynthia M. Rogers received her Masters of Theological Studies from Drew Theological School, where she was a student of her coauthor, Danna Fewell. A former high school social studies teacher, her present emphasis is nineteenth-century church history. She curated an exhibit on nineteenth-century children's religious literature at the United Methodist Archives and History Center at Drew and is currently researching and writing about the diaries and letters of nineteenth-century Methodist women.

Mark Roncace is associate professor of religion at Wingate University in North Carolina. He is the coeditor of *Teaching the Bible: Practical Strategies for Classroom Instruction* (2005) and *Teaching the Bible through Popular Culture and the Arts* (2007). He is also coeditor of the forthcoming *Global Perspectives on the Bible* (Prentice Hall).

Susanne Scholz is associate professor of Old Testament at Perkins School of Theology in Dallas. Her research focuses on feminist and cultural hermeneutics. Among her publications are *Sacred Witness: Rape in the Hebrew Bible* (2010), *Introducing the Women's Hebrew Bible* (2007), *Biblical Studies Alternatively* (edited; 2003), and *Rape Plots: A Feminist Cultural Study of Genesis 34* (2000).

Jaqueline S. du Toit is professor in the International Institute for Studies in Race, Reconciliation, and Social Justice at the University of the Free State, South Africa. She has written extensively on the interpretation and translation of the Bible for children as it pertains to generational knowledge transfer within and without religious collectives; as well as on the collection and dissemination of bodies of knowledge in ancient and modern times. She coauthored *Canada's Big Biblical Bargain: How McGill University Bought the Dead Sea Scrolls* with Jason Kalman (2010), and her book *Textual Memory: Ancient Archives, Libraries, and the Hebrew Bible* appeared in 2011.

Caroline Vander Stichele is *universitair docent* at the Department of Art, Religion, and Culture of the University of Amsterdam. Her research and publications focus on the rhetoric of gender in early Christian literature and on the cultural reception history of the Bible. Her publications include *Contextualizing Gender in Early Christian Discourse* (with Todd Penner, 2009). She is currently preparing a book on Herodias and coediting a volume on esoteric interpretations of Gen 1–3 with Susanne Scholz.

Index of Biblical Citations

Index of Modern Authors and Artists

CPSIA information can be obtained at www.ICGtesting.com
Printed in the USA
BVOW070117170712

295400BV00001B/2/P